ETHICS AND THE BUSINESS OF BIOMEDICINE

During the last thirty years we have witnessed sweeping changes in healthcare worldwide, including new and expensive biomedical technologies, an increasingly powerful and influential pharmaceutical industry, steadily increasing healthcare costs in industrialized nations, and new threats to medical professionalism. The essays collected in this book concern costs and profits in relation to just healthcare, the often controversial practices of pharmaceutical companies, and corruption in the professional practice of medicine. Leading experts discuss justice in relation to business-friendly strategies in the delivery of healthcare, access to life-saving drugs, the ethics of pharmaceutical company marketing practices, exploitation in drug trials, and undue industry influence over medicine. They offer guidance regarding the ethical delivery of healthcare products and services by profit-seeking organizations operating in a global marketplace, and recommend pragmatic solutions to enhance organizational integrity and curb medical corruption in the interest of patient welfare.

DENIS G. ARNOLD is the Jule and Marguerite Surtman Distinguished Scholar in Business Ethics at Belk College of Business, University of North Carolina, Charlotte. Formerly he was Associate Professor of Philosophy and Director of the Center for Applied and Professional Ethics at the University of Tennessee at Knoxville. He is author of *The Ethics of Global Business* (2009) and co-editor of *Ethical Theory and Business,* 8th Edition (2009) and *Rising Above Sweatshops: Innovative Approaches to Global Labor Challenges* (2003).

ETHICS AND THE BUSINESS
OF BIOMEDICINE

EDITED BY

DENIS G. ARNOLD

University of North Carolina at Charlotte

CAMBRIDGE
UNIVERSITY PRESS

CAMBRIDGE UNIVERSITY PRESS
Cambridge, New York, Melbourne, Madrid, Cape Town, Singapore, São Paulo, Delhi

Cambridge University Press
The Edinburgh Building, Cambridge CB2 8RU, UK

Published in the United States of America by Cambridge University Press, New York

www.cambridge.org
Information on this title: www.cambridge.org/9780521748223

© Cambridge University Press 2009

First published 2009

Printed in the United Kingdom at the University Press, Cambridge

A catalog record for this publication is available from the British Library

Library of Congress Cataloging in Publication data
Ethics and the business of biomedicine / edited by Denis G. Arnold.
p.   cm.
Includes bibliographical references and index.
ISBN 978-0-521-76431-5
1. Medical ethics.   2. Bioethics.   3. Business ethics.   I. Arnold, Denis Gordon.   II. Title.
R724.E821III5   2009
174'.957–dc22
2009008251

ISBN 978-0-521-76431-5 hardback
ISBN 978-0-521-74822-3 paperback

Contents

v

Figures

vii

Contributors

DENIS G. ARNOLD is the Jule and Marguerite Surtman Distinguished Scholar in Business Ethics at the University of North Carolina at Charlotte.

TOM L. BEAUCHAMP is Professor of Philosophy and a Senior Research Scholar at the Kennedy Institute of Ethics at Georgetown University.

DANIEL CALLAHAN is a Co-Founder and Director of International Programs at the Hastings Center, Senior Research Fellow in the Department of Philosophy at Yale University, and Senior Lecturer at Harvard Medical School.

NORMAN DANIELS is Mary B. Saltonstall Professor and Professor of Ethics and Population Health at Harvard University.

RICHARD T. DE GEORGE is University Distinguished Professor of Philosophy, of Russian and East European Studies, and of Business Administration, and Co-Director of the International Center for Ethics in Business at the University of Kansas.

CARL ELLIOTT is Professor in the Center for Bioethics, Professor of Pediatrics, and Professor of Philosophy at the University of Minnesota, Twin Cities.

JASON HUBBARD is a doctoral student in philosophy and an M.B.A. student at the University of Tennessee at Knoxville.

PAUL T. MENZEL is Provost Emeritus and Professor of Philosophy Emeritus at Pacific Lutheran University.

GEORGE KHUSHF is Associate Professor of Philosophy and Humanities Director at the Center for Bioethics at the University of South Carolina.

ANN E. MILLS is Associate Professor at the Center for Biomedical Ethics, Associate Professor of Medical Education, and Co-Director of the Program in Ethics and Policy in Health Care at the University of Virginia.

MARY V. RORTY is a Faculty Associate at the Center for Biomedical Ethics at Stanford University.

PATRICIA H. WERHANE is the Wicklander Chair of Business Ethics and Director of the Institute for Business and Professional Ethics at DePaul University and Peter and Adeline Ruffin Professor of Business Ethics and Senior Fellow at of the Olsson Center for Applied Ethics in the Darden School at the University of Virginia.

DANIEL WIKLER is Mary B. Saltonstall Professor and Professor of Ethics and Population Health at Harvard University.

Acknowledgements

The papers collected in this volume derive from a conference sponsored by the Center for Applied and Professional Ethics and the Department of Philosophy at the University of Tennessee. This conference brought together in Knoxville leading bioethicists and business ethicists to discuss issues such as costs and profits in relation to just healthcare, the influence of industry over the practice of medicine and over bioethics, the obligations of pharmaceutical companies to citizens of developing nations, and related themes. In addition to the contributors to this volume, I am grateful to many conference participants for their intellectual contributions. Special thanks are due to Alfred Beasley, Norman Bowie, George Brenkert, Glenn Graber, John Hardwig, E. Haavi Morreim, Gary Pulsinelli, Charlie Reynolds, Michael Stahl, and Laurie Zoloth.

The conference received the generous support of many academic units at Tennessee including the College of Arts and Sciences, the College of Business, the Office of the Chancellor, the Office of Research, the Law School, and the Baker Center for Public Policy. Special thanks in this regard are due to John Hardwig, Bruce Bursten, and Jan Williams. I am grateful to Ann Beardsley and Susan Williams for their capable administrative support.

Many thanks also to the students in my doctoral seminar on the topic of this volume for their penetrating questions and excellent discussion of these issues. Thanks in particular to Todd Johnson and Tom Harter for their help with the book. Special thanks to Jason Hubbard for his excellent research assistance and cheerful embrace of every assigned task. Hilary Gaskin at Cambridge was an early and enthusiastic supporter of this project. Her patience and dedication to the highest standards of publishing are much appreciated. For their love, support, and patience with this project I am especially grateful to Sara Arnold, M.D., and to Skye.

Introduction

Central to current public debates in North America, the United Kingdom, Europe and elsewhere are issues concerning costs and profits in relation to just healthcare and ethical business practices. These concerns are driven by major shifts in healthcare that took place during the twentieth century. These shifts include the transformation of the professional practice of medicine in the United States from a service orientation to a market orientation; the emergence of powerful pharmaceutical and healthcare corporations with global reach; the development of new, innovative, and expensive biomedical technologies by for-profit enterprises; and steadily increasing healthcare costs in industrialized nations. Furthermore, many of the most important ethical issues regarding the business of biomedicine concern decisions made in healthcare systems rather than in the context of patient–physician relationships. These issues lie at the intersections of two flourishing areas of applied ethics that, at least in recent years, are seldom in conversation: bioethics and business ethics. This volume brings together distinguished scholars from both fields. The shared goal of each of the authors is to evaluate the practices of profit-seeking healthcare organizations, and business-friendly public policies regarding healthcare, and to offer normative guidance regarding the ethical delivery of healthcare products and services by profit seeking organizations operating in a global marketplace.

JUSTICE AND MARKETS IN HEALTHCARE

In industrialized nations increases in healthcare spending continue to outpace inflation. In 2006 national health expenditures (NHE) rose 6.7% in the United States, reaching $2.1 trillion and accounting for 16% of gross domestic product (GDP).[1] Annual rates of increase in the range of 6.5–6.9% have been largely stable[2] since 2002 when the rate of increase peaked at 9.1%.[3] The amount of GDP consumed by healthcare expenditures continues to outpace GDP growth.[4] While the trend is most pronounced in the

I

United States the problem is common to all members of the *Organisation for Economic Co-operation and Development* (OECD). The average, annual, per capita increase in healthcare spending for all OECD countries was 4% in the period from 1995 to 2005.[5] Additionally, average OECD healthcare expenditure as a share of GDP reached 9% in 2005.[6] Both France and the United Kingdom substantially exceeded this rate of growth (by 1% and 0.6% respectively) while Canada saw their expenditure as a share of GDP drop slightly (by 0.1%) during the same period.[7]

In the United States healthcare spending on pharmaceuticals alone has reached $200.7 billion, a nearly 500% increase since 1990. This accounted for 10% of NHE in 2005. Pharmaceutical spending increased at the highest rate of any component of NHE from 1994 to 2003.[8] On average, per capita spending on pharmaceuticals for OECD countries has risen by more than 50% in real terms since 1995. Pharmaceutical spending constituted around 17% of NHE for OECD countries and growth in spending between 1995 and 2005 has averaged 4.6% per year, outpacing the average annual rise in overall healthcare spending of 4% over the same period.[9]

Increases in spending in all sectors of healthcare serve to drive up health insurance premiums. In the United States between 2004 and 2005, 1.3 million additional Americans became uninsured, raising the percentage of non-elderly uninsured Americans to nearly 18%.[10] This brings the total number of non-elderly uninsured Americans to nearly 46.1 million.[11] Rising premiums coupled with the economic downturn in 2001 are seen as the primary reasons for such large increases in the number of uninsured.[12] The economic downturn of 2008 may result in even greater numbers of uninsured. One result of millions of Americans being unable to afford health insurance coverage is that nearly half of all personal bankruptcy filings have partly resulted from an inability to pay medical expenses.[13]

Health insurance premiums are the fastest growing expense for US employers, increasing 87% since 2000. On average employee contributions to health insurance premiums have increased 143% since 2000.[14] Further, increases in pharmaceutical spending have resulted in the establishment of tiered, cost-sharing formulas and increased drug co-payments. In 2005, 74% of workers with employer-sponsored coverage had cost-sharing arrangements with 3 or 4 tiers, 27% higher than workers in 2000. Average co-payments for non-formulary drugs doubled from $17 in 2000 to $35 in 2005 and average co-payments for formulary drugs increased 69% from $13 in 2000 to $22 in 2005.[15] As a result of increased cost sharing out-of-pocket expenses for employees have increased 115% since 2000.[16] While most OECD countries have some form of universal health coverage, significant increases in spending have contributed to the higher national expenditures noted above and constitute additional burdens for those systems. All industrialized countries that provide some form of universal healthcare are struggling to finance their systems in the face of rising costs and aging populations.

In Chapter 1, "Medicine and the Market," Daniel Callahan argues that markets in medicine may be divided into three distinct approaches. One approach is that of ever increasing profit spurred by market innovation. A second approach, one favored by many healthcare economists, views the market in instrumental terms and emphasizes greater efficiency in the delivery of care. A third approach, common in politically conservative literature, views a healthcare marketplace as a necessary and appropriate partner for a thriving democracy. Callahan argues that in thinking about the possible role of the market in healthcare, we can learn from these three approaches. We want, he argues, a healthcare system that preserves and encourages the traditional values of medicine such as individual patient welfare; that is based on the most reliable and well-grounded economic theory and evidence; and that balances individual good with the common good. He argues that European and Canadian healthcare systems better achieve this nexus of values than the United States system because of their commitment to universal coverage and because market forces play a small role in those systems. In contrast, the United States healthcare system is fragmented, lacks a commitment to universal coverage, and market forces play a much more prominent role.

The for-profit business of biomedicine includes pharmaceutical companies, medical equipment manufacturers, healthcare providers, medical facilities, group practices, pharmacies, and insurance companies. In Chapter 2, "Broken Promises: Do Business-Friendly Strategies Frustrate Just Healthcare?," Norman Daniels observes that business-friendly strategies in financing and delivering medical services improve profits for businesses, but he argues that such strategies do not promote just medicine. He examines five market-friendly strategies – he calls them promises – regarding managed care, privatization, and intellectual property that have been promoted as ways to improve the US healthcare system. Daniels argues that each of these promises has been broken in ways that put populations at risk and that these failures provide good reason to subject all such promises to careful ethical and scientific review.

PATIENTS, PROFITS, AND PHARMACEUTICALS

The pharmaceutical industry has been the most profitable industry in the United States for most of the last decade.[17] The industry has seen profits as a percent of revenues between 14.3% and 18.6% for the last ten years compared to a median return of 5.2% for all Fortune 500 companies in 2004, the highest median return in the last 10 years.[18] The industry regards robust profits as the best way to satisfy investors while ensuring the continued development of new and innovative pharmaceuticals. At the same time the industry has received widespread criticism from politicians, bioethicists, clinicians, and consumers. The industry is accused of failing to provide life-saving drugs to the sick and dying in developing nations in order to protect ethically questionable intellectual property rights. It has been accused of exploiting poor, undereducated populations in developing nations in drug trials. And it is alleged to have used the billions of dollars it spends annually on marketing to promote drugs in deceptive and misleading ways.

As diseases ravage developing nations critics have called upon the pharmaceutical industry to expend more resources in efforts to treat diseases that are mainly endemic to the developing world. There are often few treatments for these diseases and what treatments are available are often prohibitively expensive. For example, during an outbreak of malaria in Ethiopia in 2003 the United Nations Children's Fund (UNICEF) was forced to use an outdated combination of chloroquine and sulfadoxine-pyrimethamine (SP) to treat patients. The cocktail was not as effective against newly mutated strains of malaria, with as many as 60% of patients showing resistance to the cocktail. However, the more effective artemisinin was prohibitively expensive at $1 to $2.50 per treatment compared to the $0.20 that the choloroquine/SP cocktail cost.[19] In another case, Melarsoprol, literally the same arsenic found in antifreeze, is used in treatment for sleeping sickness. It kills 5% of those treated and destroys the vein into which it is injected. Despite these side-effects Melarsoprol is used because it is the only viable treatment for the disease. The only realistic alternative treatment, Eflornithine, was so effective at bringing people out of end stage comas it was nicknamed "the Resurrection Drug." However, at $210 per treatment it is nearly four times the cost of Melarsoprol, and access to the drug dried up when Aventis abandoned it upon determining that it was ineffective against cancer, the disease it was originally developed to treat. The fate of Eflornithine highlights another important problem regarding the treatment of diseases in the developing world. How do you get pharmaceutical companies to take an interest in diseases that are largely relegated to the developing world when there is no financial incentive to drive research and development?[20]

One potential solution that has been proposed has been for governments to offer pharmaceutical companies an extension on an existing patent for a drug of their choice in return for the development of treatments for third world diseases. The idea being that continued patent protection of a blockbuster drug will provide the financial incentive necessary to encourage companies to invest in research and development on third world diseases.[21] However, even if effective drugs are developed to treat diseases in developing nations the problem of how to pay for manufacturing and distributing them remains.

In response to this problem Thailand has begun to overrule international patents on several drugs and churn out cheap generic copies. Under a provision of the Agreement on Trade-Related Aspects of Intellectual Property Rights (TRIPS), countries can "compulsorily license" certain drugs, but only under special conditions, which it is not clear that Thailand has met.[22] Similarly, patents are under attack by India's thriving generic drug industry which has won several cases regarding their right to copy patent protected drugs. While Thailand and India's development of generic alternatives to expensive patent protected drugs has demonstrated one way of circumventing the prohibitively high prices of treatments of diseases in the developing world, it is not clear that this will be an effective long-term strategy. With companies feeling the financial impact from the proliferation of cheap generics combined with even less financial incentives for the development of treatments for third world diseases, many have begun to move away from research and development of cures for these diseases.

Nonetheless, some companies have taken positive, unilateral action regarding access to drugs in developing nations. For example, Merck has developed and delivered for free the drug Mectizan, a cure for riverblindness, to hundreds of millions of patients throughout Africa.[23] Novartis has formed the Novartis Institute for Tropical Diseases in conjunction with the Singapore Economic Development Board in order to find new drugs to treat tropical diseases. And the very financial difficulties underlying the development of treatments of diseases in the developing world have led to an innovative decision by GlaxoSmithKline. Hurt by the proliferation of cheap generic alternatives to its AIDS drugs, GlaxoSmithKline chose to sell its AIDS medications at cost to 100 countries and granted 8 local companies licenses to produce generic alternatives. Approximately 90% of their vaccines are now sold at not-for-profit prices to the developing world. By creating 14 different partnerships with the World Health Organization and other non-governmental organizations (NGO's), GlaxoSmithKline has remained profitable while continuing to fund additional research into new AIDS treatments. Additionally, this market model has boosted morale at the company and drawn talented researchers who want their work to improve human welfare.[24]

In Chapter 3, "Are Patents an Efficient and Internationally Fair Means of Funding Research and Development for New Medicines?," Paul Menzel takes up the question of the provision of life-saving drugs to the sick and dying in developing nations. He argues that current global patent law is neither efficient nor fair since it tolerates high expenditures on the development and marketing of non-innovative "me-too" drugs. Moreover, Menzel argues, even with the laudable modification of the Doha Declaration on the TRIPS agreement with respect to patent protection in poor nations, together with the implementation of the most important reforms recommended by critics of current laws, fairness for poor nations will not be achieved without an additional crucial step: an advanced market commitment to purchase medicines for poor nation diseases or a global healthcare research and development fund. These new funding mechanisms, Menzel argues, need not be so comprehensive as to replace patents as partial vehicles for generating and allocating research and development funds.

Many criticisms of the pharmaceutical industry concern the use of undue or illegitimate influence over research subjects, physicians, or patients. The next five chapters are concerned with ethical issues regarding the influence of the pharmaceutical industry. One issue that has arisen in the era of economic globalization concerns the obligations of pharmaceutical companies regarding clinical trials in developing nations. The relatively low cost of conducting trials in developing nations, together with the relative ease of global communication and transportation, has resulted in the developing world becoming a testing ground for new drugs. Conducting trials in nations with minimal regulatory frameworks governing trials has resulted in a concern that the motivation for profit is trumping consideration of basic human rights. For example, recent investigations conducted by the *Washington Post* concluded that, "experiments involving risky drugs proceed with little independent oversight. Impoverished, poorly educated patients are sometimes tested without understanding that they are acting as guinea pigs. And pledges of quality medical care sometimes prove fatally hollow."[25] These concerns are highlighted by the criminal charges and civil rights lawsuit filed by Nigerian authorities against Pfizer in June of 2007. The suit claims that during a 1996 meningitis epidemic Pfizer illegally tested unapproved drugs, in particular the experimental antibiotic Provan, on 200 children without their parents' permission.[26] Nonetheless, in many nations the lure of financial gain from participating in clinical drug trials has created international competition among developing nations as they attempt to entice pharmaceutical companies to conduct drug trials in their countries.[27]

Are pharmaceutical research subjects in developing nations properly understood as exploited? In what ways can pharmaceutical companies be said to exert undue influence over economically disadvantaged individuals who participate in clinical trials? These are the primary questions taken up by Tom Beauchamp in Chapter 4, "The Exploitation of the Economically Disadvantaged In Pharmaceutical Research." As Beauchamp points out, nearly everyone will agree with the abstract rule that we ought not exploit the economically disadvantaged in pharmaceutical research projects, however, it is not so easy to determine what counts as exploitation. And even if we can agree that exploitation is taking place, we still need to determine whether or not such exploitation should always be avoided or whether such exploitation might be acceptable given certain trade-offs. Beauchamp argues that while pharmaceutical research utilizing economically disadvantaged subjects is not inherently exploitative, the issues are more complex and subtle than has been recognized in the literature on the subject.

The influence of pharmaceutical companies on the prescribing practices of physicians continues to trouble many observers. One of the primary means by which the pharmaceutical industry maintains high profit margins is through their immense investment in marketing, nearly $30 billion in 2005 in the United States alone.[28] Of this amount $6.7 billon was spent on direct-to-physician (DTP) marketing. If one includes medical journal advertising and free drug samples, the total amount spent on marketing to American physicians comes to $25.6 billion. Often DTP expenditures are utilized for ethically questionable, but legal activities such as purchasing meals and providing gifts to physicians. Physicians are educated in a culture permeated by the influence of pharmaceutical companies. Medical students attend drug-company-sponsored lectures and seminars. Modestly paid residents are courted by pharmaceutical representatives at expensive restaurants. And medical students, residents, and fellows are keenly aware that some of their faculty are paid handsomely to represent drug companies. Is it any surprise, then, that physicians are quite receptive to "drug reps" after they complete their training? Recognizing the role that medical education plays in shaping the perspectives of physicians regarding drug companies the University of Pennsylvania School of Medicine, Yale School of Medicine, Vanderbilt University Medical Center, and other prominent medical schools, have recently restricted the activities of pharmaceutical company representatives on campus.

Marketing budgets are also used to illegally market drugs. For example, pharmaceutical companies regularly find themselves in legal trouble over the promotion of off-label uses of medications, where drugs are promoted for uses not approved by the FDA. Schering-Plough has settled three times in five years regarding indictments that it has promoted off-label uses of its drugs and lied about drug prices, costing the company a total of $1.3 billion.[29] In 2004 Pfizer pled guilty to charges that it paid doctors to prescribe their epilepsy drug Neurontin for off-label uses, paying $430 million.[30] Pfizer is currently battling lawsuits that claim that it encouraged the prescribing of its cholesterol drug Lipitor to a broader population than allowed under federal rules.[31] In 2006 InterMune settled a suit for $37 million regarding the off-label promotion of Actimmune. Additionally, InterMune recently halted clinical trials designed to approve Actimmune for the very off-label uses InterMune was accused of encouraging after it showed no effectiveness in prolonging the lives of pulmonary fibrosis patients.[32] Cephalon was investigated in 2004 when it came to light that half of prescriptions written for its narcolepsy drug Provigil may have been for off-label uses.[33] Eli Lilly, in their marketing of the antipsychotic medication Zyprexa (Olanzapine), intentionally downplayed health risks and pitched the drug for uses not approved by the Food and Drug Administration. In 2007 Eli Lilly's total payout for Zyprexa-related legal claims came to $1.2 billion to plaintiffs who contracted diabetes or other diseases as a result of taking the drug.[34] Lilly is contemplating a $1 billion dollar settlement with state and federal governments to settle civil and criminal charges that resulted from the false and misleading marketing.[35] In 2008 Merck agreed to pay the US government $671 million to settle, in part, charges that they used money and perks to induce doctors to write more prescriptions for their drugs.[36]

Appealing to a large body of empirical data, Jason Hubbard argues in Chapter 5, "The Dangers of Detailing: How Pharmaceutical Marketing Threatens Healthcare," that many of the techniques that pharmaceutical sales representative's employ actively aim to deceive and manipulate physicians. Hubbard argues that these deceptive and manipulative practices interfere with the capacity of physicians to fulfill their fiduciary duties in prescribing the best treatments for their patients. As a result, he argues DTP marketers act disrespectfully toward physicians and harm patients. Given these problems he calls for a voluntary ban on many of the practices that surround DTP marketing. The industry has recently responded to such criticism with revised guidelines for marketing to physicians that take effect in 2009.[37] However, since the industry lacks transparency with respect to compliance and has not put enforcement mechanisms in place, the new guidelines are unlikely to curb widespread abuse. Hubbard argues that regulatory solutions may be required in order to stop ethically illegitimate marketing to physicians.

The United States is nearly alone among OECD nations in allowing direct-to-consumer (DTC) pharmaceutical manufacturing.[38] However, that may change soon. Currently the pharmaceutical industry is lobbying for DTC advertising to be approved in Europe and Canada. In the United States spending on DTC advertising has quadrupled since it was permitted by an FDA rule change in 1997. Current spending on DTC advertising in the United States is approximately $4.2 billon.[39] Critics of DTC advertising argue that most consumers are not capable of making informed decisions regarding pharmaceuticals and as a result it is dangerous to expose them to such marketing.[40] The pharmaceutical industry claims that DTC advertising merely makes patients more educated consumers regarding diseases and their treatments. And they point out that physicians ultimately control what prescriptions consumers are given. United States Congressman Henry Waxman (D-Calif.) attempted to restrict DTC advertising of pharmaceuticals to drugs that had been on the market for at least three years – enough time to collect useful data on adverse side-effects – by attaching it to a drug safety bill. However, by the time the bill had passed nearly all restrictions on drug advertising had been removed as a result of industry lobbying.[41] More recently, the United States House of Representatives Committee on Energy and Commerce, Subcommittee on Oversights and Investigation held hearings on the subject entitled "Direct-to-Consumer Advertising: Marketing, Education, or Deception?"[42] However, the hearings do not appear likely to result in Congressional action on the issue.

Current FDA oversight of drug advertising appears to be inadequate. Drug makers are only required to submit their advertisement at the time they begin broadcasting and there is often a significant lag between when drug advertisements begin to run and when the FDA actually reviews them. As a result, there have been several cases of drug advertisements being pulled after they have run for significant periods of time. In 2002 GlaxoSmithKline was forced to change an advertisement for their blockbuster antidepressant Paxil in which they stated that the drug was "nonhabit-forming."[43] Pfizer pulled its Viagra advertisement with a man with devilish horns and the phrase "he's back" in 2004 when the FDA determined that the advertisement went too far in indicating what the drug treats when it was supposed to have been a "reminder ad" which allows drug companies to sidestep the requirement that they list side-effects.[44] In addition, Pfizer was cited four times for misleading television and print advertisements for Lipitor and received seven citations for promotions of Celebrex.[45] Similarly, Bayer and GlaxoSmithKline were forced to pull a Levitra advertisement due to the fact that it inadequately stated the drug's side-effects and could not substantiate claims that it was superior to competing drugs.[46] Amgen was forced to pull an advertisement and make efforts to correct misleading information included in their advertisement for the psoriasis drug Enbrel. Schering-Plough has been cited 11 times for its advertisements for Claritin (a record for the most FDA citations), and Merck was cited for minimizing the chance of cardiovascular risk with its drug Vioxx.[47]

Critics of DTC advertising typically call for a ban on such advertising.[48] In response pharmaceutical companies and the advertising industry argue for the right to advertise on constitutional free speech grounds.[49] Denis Arnold considers the ethical status of DTC advertising in Chapter 6, "The Ethics of Direct-to-Consumer Pharmaceutical Advertising." He points out that none of the existing literature on ethical legitimacy of DTC advertising takes seriously the distinction between the three classes of consumer marketing distinguished by the FDA: reminder advertisements, product claim advertisements, and help-seeking advertisements. Arnold explains the distinctions between these three classes of advertisements and asks whether any of these classes of advertising can properly be characterized as educational as the industry contends. He concludes that reminder advertisements and product claim advertisements rely on biased information and peripheral, non-cognitive means of persuasion and as such are manipulative rather than educational. However, he argues that help-seeking advertisements can be made genuinely educational and recommends a solution to the current impasse regarding DTC advertising. His solution preserves the right of the industry to advertise while eliminating the worst industry abuses.

The recent debacle regarding Merck's voluntary withdrawl of Vioxx from the market is perhaps the most prominent of a series of drug recalls that have led to widespread concerns regarding drug safety. These concerns contributed to the passage of a new drug safety bill that gives the FDA modestly expanded powers to protect consumers. The bill allows the FDA to require further study of the safety of medications and to mandate new warnings if deemed necessary. Companies are also required to publicly release the results of all clinical trials that indicate how well their drugs performed, although what precisely this entails has yet to be spelled out. Finally, the FDA gained the capacity to fine drug companies for failure to comply with their new powers and the additional ability to fine drug makers for failure to complete follow-up studies after their drug has been approved.[50] However, many of these reforms are quite modest relative to the range of safety issues with which the public is rightfully concerned.

Safety issues have raised serious concerns over the influence of pharmaceutical companies and transparency regarding drug trials. In March of

2006 GlaxoSmithKline settled a lawsuit over allegations that it hid negative data that indicated its antidepression drug was ineffective with adolescents and led to suicidal thoughts.[51] More well known is the controversy surrounding the safety of Vioxx. Documents at the center of lawsuits over the drug indicate that Merck had early data that indicated an increased risk of heart attacks and strokes and pressured its own medical consultants not to discuss the data.[52] In 2005 Johnson & Johnson came under investigation regarding whether it utilized grants in order to promote pediatric use of its heartburn medication Propulsid.[53] Additionally, a recent study in the *New England Journal of Medicine* concluded that pharmaceutical companies do not publish negative results from clinical trials on antidepressants nearly as often as they publish positive results.[54] In response to mounting criticism some voluntary action has begun to be taken regarding the provision of data. Just days before pulling Vioxx from the market Merck committed to posting all of its drug trials to a web site run by the National Institutes of Health.[55] In 2007, amidst mounting pressure and scrutiny, Eli Lilly agreed to release detailed reports regarding their grants to non-profit groups and educational institutes.[56]

Medical journals and the World Health Organization (WHO) are currently struggling to rein in the problem of industry influence. Recently the *Journal of the American Medical Association* (JAMA) reported that it will toughen its disclosure requirements following a series of embarrassing articles where authors failed to disclose their financial ties with industry.[57] In response to concerns over the disclosure of negative data and failed studies, the WHO has recently created a set of universal rules for disclosing data regarding clinical trials, including 20 data requirements. Such transparency may go a long way towards addressing the controversies raised over the disclosure of data; however, the proposal has sparked sharp opposition by pharmaceutical companies who fear that they will be giving away important information regarding the development of new drugs that competitors may exploit.[58]

Influence of another sort is the subject of Carl Elliott's chapter "Industry-Funded Bioethics and the Limits of Disclosure." While criticisms of pharmaceutical company influence over the clinical judgment of academic medical faculty are well known, Elliott points out in Chapter 7 that the pharmaceutical industry has in recent years increased its influence over academic bioethics. Pharmaceutical companies now fund bioethics centers and pay bioethicists for consulting services. At a minimum this represents a *prima facie* conflict of interest for bioethicists who are, after all, expected to assess the ethical legitimacy of pharmaceutical company practices. This conflict of interest is typically handled in the same way it is handled in medical research, namely through disclosure of financial payments in articles. Elliott argues that disclosure is an insufficient solution because the problem with industry-funded bioethics is not secrecy but undue influence. Further, he argues that since industry funding of bioethics is unnecessary the obvious solution is to sever the financial ties between bioethics and pharmaceutical companies.

It is incontrovertible that over the course of the twentieth century pharmaceutical companies have made substantial contributions to improving human health and welfare. And there is an obvious tension between the regulation of drug safety and the development and distribution of innovative new drugs. Some have argued that current concerns regarding influence and safety threaten to over-regulate the industry, hindering its capacity to develop new innovative therapies.[59] Undoubtedly, the more cautious stance of the FDA following the withdrawal of Vioxx has led to increased requirements for drug-safety warnings and slower approval rates.[60] The number of new drugs being released has fallen dramatically since the 1990s. Additionally, there are concerns over how truly innovative new drugs are, with only a third of the drugs launched over the last few years being the first or second drug in its class. All of this while drug companies continue to pour increasing levels of funding into research and development. Explanations for these trends are numerous and complicated; however, such issues increase the tension between regulation and innovation.[61]

In Chapter 8 Richard De George argues that the pharmaceutical industry in the past 50 years has made tremendous improvements to human health and longevity. He argues that the pharmaceutical industry actually has a stronger ethical position than has previously been realized. First, he argues that insofar as a human right to health can be defended, it is a right primarily to healthcare. This is explicit, for example, in Article 25 of the *Universal Declaration of Human Rights*. It is governments that have the primary responsibility to provide healthcare, and this can be provided via universal healthcare programs such as those of most OECD nations. Second, De George argues that passing responsibility to the private sector, as in the United States, does not relieve government of the responsibility to provide for all those who do not have adequate access to healthcare. It is governments, and not pharmaceutical companies, that have the obligation to make up for market failures and ensure that all citizens have adequate access to safe and effective drugs.

De George is correct in claiming that the right to health specified in the *Universal Declaration of Human Rights* is a right that governments have a duty to enforce. However, critics of healthcare companies often point out that elements of other human rights documents such as Article 12 of the United Nations *Draft Norms on the Responsibilities of Transnational Corporations and Other Business Enterprises with Regard to Human Rights* attribute obligations regarding the right to health to business enterprises. Broader ethical obligations regarding health are attributed to business organizations by various international instruments such as the World Health Organization's *Ethical Criteria for Medicinal Drug Promotion* and *International Code of Marketing of Breast-milk Substitutes*. What's more, many corporations explicitly embrace such obligations in their statement of corporate values. How might organizations that take seriously such obligations regarding the just distribution of healthcare do this? The following chapters address this issue.

ORGANIZATIONAL ETHICS AND MEDICAL PROFESSIONALISM

Healthcare professionals have as a primary duty the provision of quality care to their patients. For profit healthcare companies have, in the eyes of many, a primary duty to their shareholders. Healthcare companies, most of which employ healthcare professionals, also profess to have obligations to healthcare consumers. For example, Johnson & Johnson states in their credo that their first responsibility is to patients and healthcare professionals while stockholders rank fourth after employees and the communities in which they operate. Healthcare companies thus seem to have objectives that will frequently come into conflict. In their contribution to this volume, "The Third Face of Medicine: Ethics, Business and Challenges to Professionalism," Mary Rorty, Patricia Werhane, and Ann Mills seek to resolve this problem in a manner consistent with the professional practice of medicine. They argue in Chapter 9 that medicine has historically been regarded as having two objectives: the promotion of patient welfare and the advancement of medical science. It is in this sense that medicine has been regarded as having two faces like the Roman god Janus. As other chapters in this volume make clear, the advancement of medical science can sometimes come into conflict with patient welfare. One important task of bioethics has been to help ensure that patient welfare is not put at risk by the advancement of science. One important accomplishment in medicine during the twentieth century was the introduction of standards and protocols that help protect patient welfare in relation to scientific exploration. In recent times, however, the practice of medicine has witnessed the emergence of a third main objective: profits. This is the third face of medicine, its business face, and it is one that poses obvious risks to patient welfare. Given their historical focus on the clinical setting bioethicists have been less successful in helping to ensure that the profit motive does not trump considerations of health and welfare.

Rorty, Werhane, and Mills discuss instances from healthcare delivery and research where business decisions have had undesired ethical consequences, and where ethical decisions have had unexpected business consequences. They argue that a narrow perspective that does not consider the organizational and systemic context in which ethical decisions are made can produce results that are contrary to the intentions and desires of organizational leaders. Further, they argue that to rectify this situation we need to draw from the work of business ethicists in order to analyze systems and organizations. They provide specific recommendations for the establishment of systematic organizational ethics programs where the health and welfare of patients is regarded as the primary, but not exclusive, value. Any organization, they argue, that fails to prioritize patients in this way is not a *healthcare* organization at all.

George Khushf mainly agrees with Rorty, Werhane, and Mills. In Chapter 10, "Theoretical Foundations for Organizational Ethics: Developing Norms for a New Kind of Healthcare," he argues that healthcare systems are undergoing a shift from individually oriented, individually practiced medicine to a systems-based, community-oriented form of healthcare, where organizations emerge as agents of healthcare practice. Most OECD nations are much further along in this shift than is the United States. Khushf argues that in general this is a positive development, since a systems-based approach to healthcare can address deficiencies in the traditional biomedical model that could not otherwise be addressed. In particular, there is a need for interprofessional collaboration in order to effectively address the healthcare needs of individuals and populations. He argues that this new organizational ethics will be informed by both clinical and business ethics, but that it must also involve a fundamental transformation and integration of both. A mature healthcare ethics for the twenty-first century, then, will look very different than the healthcare ethics that was dominant in the later half of the twentieth century.

In the 1900s the Carnegie Foundation for the Advancement of Teaching set out to assess the state of American and Canadian medical education. Carnegie Foundation researcher Abraham Flexner visited and evaluated all 155 medical schools then in operation in the United States and Canada and recorded his findings and recommendations in a 1910 report entitled

Medical Education in the United States and Canada.[62] The "Flexner Report," as it is better known, described the wide disparities in the quality of medical education provided by medical schools of the era and called for the standardization and professionalization of medical education. The Flexner Report is widely credited with transforming modern medical education by linking it to university-based science education. As Daniel Wikler points out in the concluding chapter of this book, "A Crisis in Medical Professionalism: Time for Flexner II," the original Flexner Report is largely responsible for the positive reputation of medical schools and the medical profession in general. However, Wikler believes that medical professionalism is currently at risk of losing its good name as a result of the corrupting influence of commercial interests. He argues that the pharmaceutical industry and the medical device industry, as well as other commercial interests, have such pervasive and corrupting influence over physicians that the medical profession is now in crisis.

Many of the practices that concern Wikler have been described in the previous chapters of this book. These include medical journal articles ghost written by industry employees and other undisclosed relationships between physicians and industry, substantial consulting fees paid to physicians willing to help market company products, industry-sponsored lectures at medical schools, and industry-sponsored continuing medical education. He argues that the public is losing confidence that physicians have patient welfare as their foremost concern and that medicine is losing credibility in the United States and elsewhere as a result of the corrupting influence of commercial interests. Wikler argues that on the 100th anniversary of the Flexner Report the time is right for a "Flexner II" commission charged with the task of investigating these alleged corrupt practices. If widespread corruption is found, a Flexner II commission could promote sweeping reforms to support professionalism in ways that justify public trust in physicians and promote public health. Furthermore, such an undertaking could serve as a model for similar healthcare reforms in nations such as China and India which must confront their own unique challenges to medical professionalism as their healthcare systems adapt to market-friendly strategies and practices.[63]

NOTES

1. Aaron Catlin, Cathy Cowan, Micah Hartman, Stephen Heffler, the National Health Expenditure Accounts Team, "National Health Spending in 2006: A Year of Change for Prescription Drugs," *Health Affairs* 27, no. 1 (2008): 14–29, 14.
2. Ibid., 16.
3. Ibid., 14.

4. Ibid., 14.
5. Organisation for Economic Co-operation and Development, *Health at a Glance: OECD Indicators 2007* no. 23 (2007), figure 5.1.2, 87. Available at http://lysander.sourceoecd.org/vl=2729897/cl=24/nw=1/rpsv/~6682/v2007n23/s1/p1l.
6. Ibid., figure 5.2.1, 89. This is up 0.2% from 8.8% in 2003. See Organisation for Economic Co-operation and Development, *Health at a Glance: OECD Indicators 2005* no. 18 (2005), figure 3.7, 71. Available at http://lysander.sourceoecd.org/vl=2707932/cl=15/nw=1/rpsv/ij/oecdthemes/99980142/v2005n18/s1/p1l.
7. Organisation for Economic Co-operation and Development, *Health at a Glance: OECD Indicators 2007*, figure 5.2.1, 89; Organisation for Economic Co-operations and Development, *Health at a Glance: OECD Indicators 2005*, figure 3.7, 71.
8. The Henry J. Kaiser Family Foundation, *Prescription Drug Trends* (2005), 1. Available at www.kff.org/rxdrugs/upload/3057_06.pdf. This trend peaked in 1999, with a rate of increase of 18%, and in 2005 fell slightly below the rates of increase for hospital care and physician services for the first time since 1990 (with rates of increase of 6% for pharmaceuticals, 8% for hospital care, and 7% for physician services). The dramatic curtailment in pharmaceutical spending over the last two years has primarily been due to a "slowdown in Medicaid drug spending, the increased use of generic drugs (driven in part by the proliferation of tiered copayment benefit plans), changes in the types of drugs used, and a decrease in the number of new drugs introduced." Ibid., 1.
9. Organisation for Economic Co-operation and Development, *Health at a Glance: OECD Indicators 2007*, 92. However, indications show that on average OECD countries have experienced a similar drop in the average increase of pharmaceutical spending over the last two years to that of the US. OECD data released in 2005 showed an average increase of 5.6% from 1997–2003 while data released in 2007 showed an average increase of 4.6% from 1995–2005. OECD, 2005, figure 3.16, 75; OECD, 2007, figure 5.4.3, 93.
10. The Henry J. Kaiser Family Foundation, *The Uninsured and their Access to Health Care* (2006), 1. Available at www.kff.org/uninsured/upload/The-Uninsured-and-Their-Access-to-Health-Care-Oct-2004.pdf.
11. Ibid., figure 3, 1.
12. Ibid., 1.
13. National Coalition on Health Care, *Health Insurance Cost* (Washington, DC: 2007). Available at www.nchc.org/facts/cost.shtml.
14. Ibid.
15. Kaiser Family Foundation, *Prescription Drug Trends*.
16. National Coalition on Health Care, *Health Insurance Costs*.
17. Fortune, *Fortune 500 2006: Our Annual Ranking of America's Largest Corporations: Most Profitable Industries: Return on Revenues* (2006), Available at http://money.cnn.com/magazines/fortune/fortune500/performers/industries/return_on_revenues/index.html. The industry recently slipped to a fifth place ranking with a 15.7% return on revenues in 2006.

18. The Henry J. Kaiser Family Foundation, *Trends and Indicators in the Changing Health Care Marketplace,* "Section 1: Trends in Health Spending and Costs, Including Prescription Drugs," Exhibit 1–21, February 2, 2005. Available at www.kff.org/insurance/7031/print-sec1.cfm.
19. Donald G. McNeil Jr., "In Ethiopia's Malaria War, Weapons Are the Issue," *The New York Times,* December 9, 2003.
20. Donald G. McNeil Jr., "Medicine Merchants: A special report; Drug Makers and 3rd World: Study in Neglect," *The New York Times,* May 21, 2000.
21. Roger Bate, "Angels Needed in America," *Forbes,* October 18, 2004, 174.
22. *The Economist,* "A Gathering Storm," June 9, 2007, vol. 383, no. 8541.
23. See Denis G. Arnold, "Merck & Riverblindness," in *Ethical Theory and Business,* 8th edn., ed. Tom L. Beauchamp, Norman E. Bowie, and Denis G. Arnold (Englewood Cliffs, NJ: Pearson-Prentice Hall, 2009), pp. 101–102.
24. Kerry Capell, "GlaxoSmithKline: Getting AIDS Drugs to More Sick People," *BusinessWeek,* January 29, 2007. Available at www.businessweek.com/magazine/content/07_05/b4019007.htm.
25. Joe Stephens, "As Drug Testing Spreads, Profits and Lives Hang in Balance," *Washington Post,* December 17, 2000, A01.
26. Joe Stephens, "Pfizer Faces New Charges Over Nigerian Drug Test," *Washington Post,* June 2, 2007, D01.
27. Jennifer Kahn, "India: A Nation of Guinea Pigs," *Wired,* March 2006, 14, no. 3.
28. Julie M. Donohue, Marisa Cevasco, and Meredith B. Rosenthal, "A Decade of Direct-to-Consumer Advertising of Prescription Drugs," *New England Journal of Medicine* 357 (2007): 673–681, 676.
29. Jeffery Krasner, "Schering-Plough Settles Drug Charges Case for $435 Million," *The Boston Globe,* August 29, 2006.
30. Gardiner Harris, "Pfizer to Pay $430 Million Over Promoting Drug to Doctors," *The New York Times,* May 14, 2004.
31. John R. Wilke and Scott Hensley, "Pfizer is Named in Lawsuit Over Marketing of Lipitor," *The Wall Street Journal,* March 28, 2006, A3.
32. Truman Lewis, "Patients, Doctors Taken in by Off-Label 'Buzz,'" *ConsumerAffairs.com.* Available at www.consumeraffairs.com/news04/2007/03/actimmune.html.
33. Amy Barrett, "This Pep Pill is Pushing its Luck," *BusinessWeek,* November, 1, 2004.
34. Alex Berenson, "Lilly Settles with 18,000 Over Zyprexa," *The New York Times,* January 5, 2007.
35. Alex Berenson, "Lilly Considers $1 Billion Fine to Settle Case," *The New York Times,* January 31, 2008.
36. The Associated Press, "Merck to Settle U.S. Claims for $671 Million," *The New York Times,* February 8, 2008.
37. PhRMA, *Code on Interactions with Health Care Professionals,* Revised July 2008 (Washington, DC: Pharmaceutical Research and Manufacturers of America, 2008).
38. Among OECD nations only the United States and New Zealand permit DTC advertising.

39. Donohue, *et al.* "A Decade of Direct-to-Consumer Advertising of Prescription Drugs," *New England Journal of Medicine*, 676.

40. For a more detailed account of the debate as it currently stands see Hannah Brown, "Sweetening the Pill," *British Medical Journal* 334 (2007): 664–666.

41. Arlene Weintraub, "The Drug Advertising Debate," *BusinessWeek*, July 16, 2007.

42. The hearing was held in May 8, 2008. See http://energycommerce.house.gov/cmte_mtgs/110-oi-hrg.050808.DTC.shtml.

43. Melody Peterson, "The Media Business: Advertising; Judge Orders Drug Company to Alter Ads," *The New York Times*, August 21, 2002.

44. Amy Tsao, "Viagra: A Drug Ad Too Far?" *BusinessWeek*, November 17, 2004.

45. Julie Schmit, "FDA Races to Keep Up with Drug Ads that Go Too Far," *USA Today*, May 30, 2005.

46. Frank Ahrens, "FDA Orders Levitra Ad Off the Air," *Washington Post*, April 16, 2005, E01.

47. Schmit, "FDA Races to Keep Up with Drug Ads that Go Too Far."

48. See, for example, Kurt C. Stange, "Time to Ban Direct-to-Consumer Prescription Drug Marketing," *Annals of Family Medicine* 5 (2007): 101–104.

49. Jim Edwards, "PhRMA Unveils New Guidelines," *Media Week* (August 2, 2005). Available at www.mediaweek.com/mw/search/article_display.jsp?vnu_content_id=1001002068; and Coalition for Health Care Communication "Comments before the U.S. Food and Drug Administration in the Matter of Consumer Directed Promotion" (January 14, 2004), Docket No. 2003N-0344. Available at www.cohealthcom.org/content/current.htm.

50. "Food and Drug Administration Amendments Act of 2007," Public Law 110–85, 110th Congress; Reuters, "Bush signs FDA drug safety bill into law," September 27, 2007. Available at www.reuters.com/article/politicsNews/idUSN2141286320070927.

51. ConsumerAffairs.com, "GlaxoSmithKline Settles Paxil Lawsuit," March 29, 2007. Available at www.consumeraffairs.com/news04/2006/03/paxil_states.html. And Gardiner Harris, "Spitzer Sues a Drug Maker, Saying it Hid Negative Data," *The New York Times*, June 3, 2004.

52. Barbara Martinez, "Merck Documents Shed Light on Vioxx Legal Battles," *The Wall Street Journal*, February 7, 2005, A1.

53. Stephanie Saul, "Senators Ask Drug Giant to Explain Grants to Doctors," *The New York Times*, July 6, 2005.

54. Erick H. Turner, Annette M. Matthews, Eftihia Linardatos, Robert A. Tell, and Robert Rosenthal, "Selective Publication of Antidepressant Trials and Its Influence on Apparent Efficacy," *The New England Journal of Medicine*, 358, no. 3 (January 17, 2008): 252–260.

55. Gardiner Harris, "Merck Says It Will Post the Results of All Drug Trials," *The New York Times*, September 6, 2004.

56. Avery Johnson, "Under Criticism, Drug Maker Lilly Discloses Funding," *The Wall Street Journal*, May 1, 2007, B1.

57. David Armstrong, "JAMA to Toughen Rules on Author Disclosure," *The Wall Street Journal*, July 12, 2006, D2.

58. *The Economist*, "Trials and Transparency," May 20, 2006 vol. 379, no. 8478.
59. *The Economist*, "Safety in Numbers," March 19, 2005, vol. 374, no. 8418.
60. Gardner Harris, "F.D.A. Responds to Criticism With New Caution," *The New York Times*, August 6, 2005.
61. *The Economist*, "Testing Times," June 18, 2005, vol. 375, no. 8431.
62. Abraham Flexner, *Medical Education in the United States and Canada*, Bulletin Number Four (The Flexner Report) (New York: The Carnegie Foundation for the Advancement of Teaching, 1910).
63. Thanks to Jason Hubbard for research assistance and other help in preparing this chapter.

CHAPTER I

Medicine and the market

Daniel Callahan

To enter the jungle of medicine and the market is not only to encounter many choking vines and dense undergrowth, but also to move through a climate alternatively marked by cool, technical winds and hot, ideological cyclones. The topic of medicine and the market touches on some of the oldest and deepest human questions – what, for instance, is the appropriate place of self-interest in human communities, and particularly in the health-care community? It no less forces consideration of a difficult range of technical questions – at what point, for example, does a co-payment for a drug reach a level that it helps control healthcare costs but is harmful to the health of patients on whom it is imposed?[1]

In my experience, the greatest difficulty in talking about medicine and the market is that, for most people, it seems an either/or choice: either love the market or hate it, either see it as the panacea for troubled healthcare systems beset by government bureaucracy, or as a mean-spirited devil designed to destroy the very idea of equitable care. I believe that a government-run or government-regulated healthcare system mandating universal healthcare is the best kind of system – but that there is some room for carefully considered market practices within, or aiming at, such care. Like it or not, moreover, it is almost impossible to imagine any universal health plan politically succeeding in the US unless it is clever enough to work in some market ingredients in a way that helps such a plan, or at least does no harm.

In the European and Canadian healthcare systems we have, so to speak, a long-standing natural experiment with universal care, extending over decades in most places, and a century in a few. That experiment displays a range of outcomes and qualities that by and large are superior to the jerry-rigged American system that mixes the public and private sectors. The European experience also shows that, if used carefully, there are market practices that can serve the ends of universal healthcare. It is not necessarily either/or after all.

My aim here is not to fully make a case for a government-dominated healthcare system. It is, instead, to see if some sense can be made of the medicine-market debate, and to ask how the issues are best framed to lead to a fruitful argument – which I do not believe we have at present.

A place to start is by distinguishing among three different, though often overlapping approaches to, and understandings of, medicine and the market. One of them can be thought of as concerned with the potential, and often real, harm that comes from bringing market values and commercialism into the provision of healthcare.

Healthcare is seen as a source of money and profit (e.g., buying healthcare stocks, opening for-profit clinics). It is the use of medicine and healthcare principally as a vehicle for making money, individual or corporate. Another approach is that taken by many healthcare economists, that of looking to the market as a means of creating incentives, usually financial, to improve the efficient delivery of healthcare or to hold down the costs of such care (e.g., providing financial incentives to physicians to improve the quality of care). The aim is to change behavior by using money as a means to health goals, not its end. Still another approach is that espoused by many political and economic conservatives, that of using the market as a vehicle of individual choice and freedom, an aim that at the same time strengthens democratic institutions (e.g., the use of medical vouchers to allow people to buy whatever kind of healthcare they choose). The market is thus as much a political as an economic vehicle, aiming to maximize freedom.

MEDICAL COMMERCIALISM AND THE MARKET

At the center of a focus on money and commercialism is the tension between the traditional altruistic values of medicine and the centrality of self-interest as a feature of market thinking. Two quotations nicely bring out that tension.

One of them is from Plato, in *The Republic*: "The physician, as such studies only the patient's interest, not his own .... All that he says and does will be with a view to what is good and proper for the subject for whom he practices his art."[2]

The other, better known passage, is from Adam Smith's 1776 book, *Wealth of Nations*: "It is not from the benevolence of the butcher, the brewer, or baker, that we expect our dinner, but from their regard for their own interest .... nobody but a beggar chuses to depend chiefly upon the benevolence of his fellow-citizens."[3]

A long stream of voices over the years have worried about the impact of commercial values on medicine – the loss of Plato's altruism – most recently the editors of the *New England Journal of Medicine* (e.g., Arnold S. Relman,

Marcia Angell, and Jerome P. Kassirer) as well as such distinguished physician educators as Edmund D. Pellegrino.[4] They worry about physician entrepreneurs (opening for-profit clinics, referring to patients as "consumers"), the mercenary interests of drug and device manufacturers and their sway over medical research and practice, direct-to-consumer drug ads, and the way a combination of debt and exceedingly good money lure many medical students into medical specialties.

A New York ophthalmologist who advertises on the local New York CBS radio station that he has performed 30,000 laser eye surgeries is a vivid exemplar of the crassly commercial model in medicine. Nor is it easy to forget the historical resistance of the American Medical Association in the late nineteenth and almost through the end of the twentieth century not only at first to group practice of any kind, but later on to a more persistent and effective opposition to universal healthcare, a.k.a. "socialized medicine." It was the medical establishment's way of maintaining economic control over medicine, protective of physician income, something they feared government would take from them. Even excessive altruism was treated as a threat.[5]

Yet there is some reason to resist too sharp a line between commercialism and altruism. Plato also recognized in *The Republic* that, as one commentator put it, the physician was even then "something of a businessman." As long as physicians sell or barter their services to patients as they have always done, commercialism is present (which can run the gamut from benignity to cupidity).[6] There can be a fine line between a sense of entitlement for hard work and valuable services, and sheer greed. For his part, Adam Smith well understood that the market requires a morally supportive culture, one that works to curb excessive self-interest and to instill the virtues of empathy and concern for the welfare of others. That does not always happen.

Of course the problem of money and commercialism goes well beyond doctors and patients. The American healthcare system as a whole is a combination of for-profit and non-profit hospitals and clinics, insurance companies, the drug and device industry, and companies selling a wide range of ancillary goods and services. The simple fact is that there is money, and good money, to be made in the healthcare industry, and it serves many purposes other than health: profit, jobs, civic prestige, fine stock market investments. When there is a threat that a community hospital might shut down, there is often as much anxiety about the loss of jobs as about dangers to healthcare. There is not much in American life that is not marked by aggressive commercialism, and healthcare is right up there with investment banking as a source of the good (economic) life.

THE MARKET AND EFFICIENCY: INSTRUMENTALISM

As a profession, healthcare economists have an important role in health policy, bringing to bear a discipline most commonly oriented to means not ends, efficiency not equity, and empirical research rather than high theory. Now those are generalizations and, in reality, many healthcare economists do worry about equity.[7] But the discipline itself nudges economists strongly in what I call an instrumental direction. By that I mean a disavowal of professional competence to serve the inner culture of medicine, to determine the proper political and ethical goals of healthcare, and to pass judgment on the personal conduct of physicians. Their questions come to such as these: If one (a nation, a community) has decided on a particular kind of healthcare system, how might it best work – with what balance between government and market – and which modes of organization are likely to be most efficient? How might financial incentives be used to influence physician and patient behavior for goals of cost or quality?

While there has been a market debate in Europe, it has been far less ideology driven and rhetorically charged than in the US. I attribute those traits to a focus by healthcare economists there on which particular market practice and tactics are most likely to make universal healthcare systems to work better, whether to control costs or to enhance quality. What contribution could competition make? How much and what kind of price control will be effective in controlling costs without stifling research and innovation?

European healthcare economists are seemingly more willing than their American counterparts to speak out on the need for equity (not understanding that to be outside of their discipline). A European healthcare economist who called for a dismantling of a government-run system and turning it over to the private sector would be a striking anomaly; but more than a few with that view can be found in the US. On both continents, however, the name of the economic game is the demand for solid empirical evidence to back claims of efficiency, quality, and cost control.

IDEOLOGY AND THE MARKET: CHOICE AND DEMOCRACY

I now come to that group I will call the "politicals." That term characterizes a mixed political and policy group who see the market not just as an instrumental means to achieve efficiency, but even more as a key ingredient of democracy and political freedom. Its economist heroes are Friedrich A. Hayek and Milton Friedman, but it also includes an influential group of neoconservative intellectuals and institutions (e.g., the *Wall Street Journal*, the

American Enterprise Institute, The Cato Institute, the Heritage Foundation), and most importantly of late former President George W. Bush and most Republican politicians.

Their core position (as I read it) is that, in the organization of healthcare, market and personal freedom are more important than equity (though they never speak that bluntly), and that the private sector will produce better healthcare than government. Some would add that, if the market is given a full chance, it could eventually lead to de facto universal coverage. Just as the free market is the economic engine of prosperous and productive societies, raising the standard of living for all, so also can it be the foundation of a good healthcare system. Its main argument is with those who believe that government is the crucial ingredient of a universal healthcare system, and government bashing – inefficiency, bureaucracy – is a standard refrain of its rhetoric. And that rhetoric, unlike the cool style of health economists, can be hot, sometimes even more than the heat of pro-government advocacy.

My surmise is that because for the politicals the market is seen to play a crucial role in a good society (any good society), its penumbra will affect the culture as a whole and its various political parts. If the market is good for societies in general, so the implicit argument goes, it is no less good for its various sub-sectors, including healthcare. For the politicals, the market as a value is, so to speak, politically and morally supercharged.

INTERTWINED VALUES

The three approaches to the market and medicine I have characterized are distinct, but they interact with each other. By and large those worried about the commercialization of medicine and a corruption of its altruistic ideals see market values as the deadly virus. Only a government-run, well-integrated single-payer universal healthcare system can deal with such a virus; and, preferably, a system where the physician is a salaried employee (as in the Kaiser system or the British National Health Service). That would shut out entrepreneurial physicians, an excessive use of well-reimbursed technological procedures of marginal benefit, and a too-potent role for pharmaceutical detail men touting the newest and latest drug. Those in this group make some use of economic data, but on the whole rely on clinical information and experience.

It is unclear to what extent the health economists (of the instrumental kind) affect the thinking of those concerned with medical commercializa-tion as a moral concern or those with a political agenda. Some studies in the

aftermath of the failed 1994 Clinton healthcare plan indicated that economists were divided on universal healthcare and the role of the market.[8] The
distinguished economist Victor Fuchs concluded that, because of their own
internal divisions, economists had little influence in that debate.[9] For their
part, the politicals have their own cadre of economists, using them mainly in
support of their own positions. The politicals appear to have little interest in
the problem of a commercialized medicine. Indeed, because of their pro-
clivity for a privatized medicine they would not be expected to worry much
about it. Neither the instrumentalist economists nor the politicals, it turns
out, pay great attention to the impact of market practices on the culture of
medicine or medical professionalism. That emphasis has come almost
entirely from the physician side.

I have cited these three approaches to the relationship between medicine
and the market to make a simple point: there is more than one way to think
about the market. While there are some overlaps among them, the problem
of the market and medicine can be seen in very different ways. For those
concerned with the culture and professionalism of medicine, there is little in
a market approach that attracts them; it mainly repels them. While they are
prone to support universal healthcare, it is possible that they would accept
some mixed public–private system as long as it supported the traditional
values of medicine.

At the other end of the spectrum, the politicals are the most broadly
ideological. It is not as if they have inductively examined medicine and
healthcare and then determined that a market approach would be best.
They start instead from a belief in the value of the market and then
deductively assume that it will be valuable in healthcare. For them, the
market means a rejection of any but the most minimal governmental role (a
small, not large, safety net), an embracing of a wide range of market
practices, and – most importantly – an embrace of freedom and choice as
the highest moral and political values. There is for them little anxiety about
market failure or a lack of universal coverage. Freedom is a value that trumps
all others. The fact that such a commitment can create its own problems is
no reason to reject it – much as someone committed to democracy would be
little swayed to reject it by evidence of the harms that democracy can bring,
plentiful though they can be.

The instrumentalists are (at least in principle) ideologically neutral and
committed to gathering evidence about the effectiveness of various forms
and systems of healthcare. I have been most influenced by their research, a
philosopher who has come to like numbers and data, not just well-honed
moral arguments.

ESTABLISHING STANDARDS OF JUDGMENT

If it is the case that there are three ways of thinking and talking about the market and medicine, does that mean there can be no unified way of doing so? Not necessarily. A full consideration of medicine and the market should encompass each of the three realms I have described: medical culture and professionalism, empirical evidence and market theory, and ideology and values. Put another way, we should want a healthcare system that (1) preserves and encourages the traditional values of medicine and the highest standards of professionalism, most notably individual patient welfare, (2) that in its economic features is based on the most reliable and well-grounded economic theory and evidence, and (3) that with its ethical and value foundations works to balance individual good and common good within healthcare, and no less to balance the well-being of the healthcare system and all those other collective goods necessary for a decent society (much less commonly considered in healthcare analysis).

VARIETIES OF HEALTHCARE SYSTEMS

There are essentially three forms of healthcare in developed countries:

The American System. The characteristic mark of the American system is its fragmented system of organization, administration, and financing (which many think of as no "system" at all). Its organization encompasses fee-for-service care, for-profit and non-profit group medical practices of many kinds, for-profit and non-profit hospitals and clinics, and government-run hospitals and medical services. Its administration can be found at the state level (and within that level at the county and municipal level) and at the federal level, and within the private sector at the corporate level. Its financing comes from the Federal government, state governments, and the private sector (for employee insurance). Lacking any system of universal care, there is no organized effort to provide decent healthcare for all; and, thus, a large number of uninsured. The combination of these ingredients almost guarantees that the US will spend the most money per capita on healthcare and a larger portion of its GDP on healthcare than any other nation.

The European and Canadian Systems. While there are a wide range of differences among European and Canadian healthcare systems, the common thread running through them is a commitment to universal and equitable care and to the value of solidarity as its foundation. No attempt can be made here to summarize the variety of European systems or the Canadian system. However, a few important categories can be noted.

One of them is the difference between the Bismarckian and the Beveridge systems. The former – called social health insurance (SHI) systems – is traceable to the late nineteenth century and the regime of German Chancellor Otto von Bismarck.[10] It consists in each country of a number of private, and usually competitive, insurance plans but plans closely regulated by the government. The plans are funded by mandatory employer and employee contributions, and buttressed by government payment for the healthcare costs of the elderly and the unemployed. Some degree of additional private insurance is available in such systems. France, the Netherlands, Switzerland, Belgium, Germany and Israel have SHI plans.

The Beveridge systems, by contrast, are supported by direct taxation. As a whole they are directly run by the government, usually by some combination of local and central government management. Private insurance is also available for extra services and avoidance of waiting lists. The tax-based systems include the United Kingdom, Canada, Denmark, Sweden, and Italy.

If all countries, whatever the system, provide or mandate universal care, they exhibit different attitudes toward the market. In our book *Medicine and the Market* we discriminate among three such attitudes: a strong, supportive stance toward the market (the United States), strong resistance to market ideas (Canada and the UK), and a permissive attitude (the Netherlands and Switzerland). In the case of the UK, however, "internal markets" have been employed to improve the efficiency of the National Health Service, even though a general resistance to market ideas has remained strong. In the Netherlands market competition among the insurance providers has been encouraged and managed competition pursued in various parts of the system. It is worth noting that two countries, New Zealand and the Czech Republic, embraced a wide range of market practices in the early 1990s, only to decide that they had been a mistake, reverting back to Bismarckian systems.

Though there is a range of responses to market ideas in Europe – mainly centering on its possibilities for increasing efficiency and controlling costs, and not nearly as ideologically charged as in the US – some market practices can be found everywhere. No healthcare system in the world is purely government run or purely market centered; all display a mix. As an aside, outside the scope of this chapter, I would note that India and China, however, provide no safety nets for hundreds of millions of their citizens and thus one can say that, de facto, they are market-based: if one can not pay up front for care, one can not get it. But that neglect seems more a matter of indifference and poor social organization than an explicit embrace of market theory.

EVALUATING MARKET PRACTICES

It is useful to divide the impact and value of market ideas into two categories, the tactical and the strategic. The tactical comprises a group of discrete market practices of a kind that are ordinarily used to advance market values. The strategic category is meant to evaluate healthcare systems as a whole and the relative strength of market-oriented versus government-oriented systems, each to a greater or lesser extent making use of market practices.

Market Practices

Six market practices are the most commonly employed:

Competition. Competition is at the heart of market theory applied to healthcare: competition among the providers of care leading to greater freedom of patient choice about the cost and quality of care. While there can be and has been competition on quality of care and the provision of various amenities, its most common use in a market context is that of price competition. In that respect, there can be price competition among physicians for patients (not common anywhere), competition among insurers within universal healthcare systems (a feature of European social insurance systems and American healthcare insurers), competition among providers (such as HMOs), competition among hospitals and clinics, and competition among vendors selling everything from drugs and MRIs to hospital bed sheets.

Deductibles and Co-Payments. While not ordinarily thought of by the public as a market practice, cost sharing and co-payments are just that, and their use is endemic in all healthcare systems (particularly co-payments). The latter is in fact the most widely used market practice throughout the world. Their aim is to reduce the costs of healthcare providers, shifting some of them to patients, and to force patients to take cost into account in deciding on medical treatments. American healthcare insurers and HMOs make use of deductibles and co-payments, but so also do European systems, even though they frequently waive them for elderly, poor, and other groups of patients.

Private Health Insurance. There are many things that could be said about private health insurance but I will look at just one. In developing countries it has a special salience: will it suck talent, resources, and political support from government programs – not typically a problem in affluent countries?

Canada does not allow parallel private health insurance for the two major tracks of its universal care program (called Medicare), hospital and physician care. Most European countries do allow such insurance and Canada has in recent years undergone a considerable debate on the matter. The Supreme Court of Ontario declared in 2005 a prohibition of parallel private insurance for hospital and physician care to be unconstitutional for that province, but it is not clear whether or when other provinces will follow. In most universal care countries, private insurance is used for co-payments, better amenities and faster service and, in Canada, private insurance is allowed for pharmaceuticals, not covered under Medicare in any ample way.

For-Profit vs. Non-Profit, Medical Savings Accounts, Physician Incentives. I have grouped these last three market practices together because, as a group, they are found mainly, but not entirely, in the United States. For-profit vs. non-profit clinics and hospitals exist in many developed countries but seem to have been studied mainly in the United States. Physician financial incentives are primarily an American phenomenon, while medical savings accounts were advocated by the Bush administration though they have also been used in South Africa and Singapore – though the former eliminated them in 2005.

THE IMPACT AND VALUE OF MARKET PRACTICES

An examination of each of the six listed practices produces mixed results. The evidence on the effectiveness of *competition* in controlling cost is mixed, working in some places but not in others; its effect on the quality of care is mixed and inconclusive. *Cost sharing* and *co-payments*, but particularly the latter, do reduce healthcare demand, particularly with low-income patients. The European countries usually exempt the poor and the old from co-payments, reducing any potential health threats, but in general there seems no good body of evidence (except in developing countries) that co-payments directly harm health.

Private health insurance is mainly a serious problem in developing countries where it can lure the best physicians out of the public sector, reduce the interest of the affluent (small in number) in the public system, and gradually weaken that system. It has not proved a serious problem in universal care countries, in great part no doubt because it remains a comparatively small part of the overall systems. As for the last three categories – *for-profit/non-profit, medical savings accounts, physician incentives*, they display few striking features for or against their possible benefits, other than one: medical savings accounts will have the most appeal for the affluent, the only group that can easily afford them, while the other market practices probably do little good or little harm.

The general picture that emerges seems to make clear that the most common market practices have neither great value nor do great harm in controlling costs or improving quality. Context can make a difference regarding the effectiveness of market practices. Competition has been used with some minor success in the European healthcare systems but nowhere else in a striking way. Co-payments are the only market practice that are used everywhere. Their ubiquity suggests some consensus on their value, at least for controlling costs.

MARKET STRATEGIES

By market strategy I refer to the place of market practices in healthcare systems as a whole and, in particular, the mix of government and market practices in such systems. The basic question is this: which kind of healthcare systems, market- or government-oriented, provide the best healthcare for their citizens? Some pertinent standards of judgment are costs, health outcomes, patient satisfaction, and quality. The conclusion I draw from my research is that it is almost a "no contest" competition. By just about every meaningful standard, the European universal healthcare systems are superior.

Now it is surely the case that superb medical care can be found in the United States and that those fortunate enough (as I am) to have a good employer-provided healthcare plan are as well-off as anyone in the world. But our healthcare costs are much higher than any other country, a large and growing proportion of people have no health insurance and, by standards of outcome and quality, the US ranks well below most European countries. The Canadian system is not quite as good as the best European systems because of its high costs (second only to the US), its serious waiting list problems, and its poor pharmaceutical coverage. Even so, it is superior to the US.

The United States ranks 1st on per capita healthcare spending; 13th among developed countries in life expectancy; many other countries perform better by some standard quality indicators; more Americans believe their system needs a complete rebuilding than citizens of Australia, Canada, New Zealand, and the United Kingdom; and the US ranks 17th in its citizens' judgment of its healthcare.[11] Universal care countries are commonly derided for by conservative politicals for their waiting lists, but they are a problem mainly in Canada and the UK, with few if any problems in other countries.[12]

The key to the relative success of the European systems is evident enough: considerable government control and regulation. Physician and other health worker salaries are typically negotiated with the government and are lower than in the US. Hospital and clinic charges are no less negotiated, the number of hospital beds controlled, and pharmaceutical prices are usually capped (and, as a result, are considerably lower than in the US). Technological innovations are slower to be accepted, often softly rationed in their use, and their distribution carefully regulated. I have been struck many times by a considerably less driven and enthusiastic drive for improved medical technology in Europe, and less media attention devoted to it.

The fact that no European country allows direct-to-consumer advertising as does the US, nor does Canada, says much about the different national attitudes toward the instrument and drug industries. Healthcare is considered an integral part of European welfare states, and one reason for better health outcomes in Europe is that their welfare systems provide a more solid and capacious safety net, with significantly lower poverty rates – all of which is conducive to good public health. American attitudes toward government-provided healthcare and welfare have historically been, and remain, different: either suspicious of or outrightly hostile to government control and regulation, choice taken to be more important than equity, a love of the market and a rejection of price controls (which is just the beginning of a much longer list of differences).

A note of sobriety is now in order. For all of their past success and continuing good outcomes, the European systems have entered a time of trouble. High unemployment rates, a loss of economic competitiveness, a resistance to still higher taxes, and pressures from a younger generation for more choice and private care, are making market practices more attractive. When European countries find themselves in economic trouble with their healthcare systems, the only escape valve appears to be an increased market role. That was true in the mid-nineties, during another economic downturn, and is true once again. This response is exactly the opposite of that in the United States, where government is more commonly expected to save the economic day. The United States has for years been scratching with its fingernails to move up the mountain to universal care. The Europeans are using their fingernails to hold on to it.

INFINITE TECHNOLOGICAL INNOVATION

The main force pushing up healthcare costs in the United States is either new technologies or the intensified use of older ones. The best estimate is that

40%–50% of cost escalation can be traced to them.[13] No comparable figures are available from Europe but there is every likelihood they would be similar. Technological innovations come from research and, while the National Institutes of Health finances much of the American basic research (and thus of the world in great part), the "translation" of that research into clinical application comes from the private, market sector. While there is no doubt gratification in that sector when health-promoting drugs or devices are developed, it is profit and shareholder satisfaction that are the driving forces.

The progress being pursued at both the research and clinical level is what I call "infinity" research: the pursuit of more progress and more innovation with no finite, much less, final goals in mind: simply MORE. By virtue of the underlying market drive, research and clinical application are utterly relativistic: the medical industry will develop whatever will satisfy customer preferences and be bought by them. The market, as a set of impersonal techniques aimed at influencing behavior, has no interest in equitable distribution of what it develops; that is someone else's problem, ordinarily healthcare systems. The drug companies have only in a lukewarm way pursued the eradication of tropical diseases for one reason only: there are many potential patients but few good commercial prospects.

In considering the market, then, account must be taken of its central place in raising costs, in its unaccountability to few values other than shareholder satisfaction, its bias toward the satisfaction of individual preferences, whatever they may be, and in its attraction to choice as the highest moral value in healthcare. At the basis of European and Canadian healthcare is not a proclaimed individual right to healthcare (though such language is sometime heard), but that of communal solidarity.[14] That notion assumes human interdependence, mutual suffering and threat of illness and death, and the vital role of government in promoting good healthcare.

That cluster of values is, literally, foreign to American culture. By its historical dedication to market theory and practice (not wholly, but heavily), and its individualism, the US has made it politically difficult to enact universal care legislation and has encouraged, through the market, the satisfaction of personal, not community goals. An embrace of the market has no less thwarted any serious attempt to even ask, as a public question, what should count as appropriate, affordable, and economically sustainable medical and health system goals?[15] As a set of impersonal strategies to manage behavior, the market can not, of its nature, ask such questions, much less answer them.

There is a way to soften the harsh light I have thrown on the market. One can return to Adam Smith to recall the high place he gave virtues instilled by markets: self-discipline, restraint, and prudence, among others, and no doubt such virtues are helpful in healthcare. One can also recall the empirical work of the instrumentalist economists, showing that the market can, under the right circumstances, foster useful competition and increase efficiency. Nor of course is choice something wrong in itself. Most people want a choice about their physician, some say in the kind of healthcare they receive; and doctors no less want a considerable degree of choice in the way they medically treat their patients. It is, therefore, hardly out of place to consider possible roles for the market – though it is possible that universal care systems can embody the same values, even if in different ways.

But because of its inability to embody a substantive view of the human good (other than choice and personal preference), or of health, any use of the market must, I believe, be subordinated to universal care systems. It can be used to serve them when possible, but never abandoning the value of solidarity that marks their best practice. Left uncontrolled and unregulated, or allowed to become dominant, the market can be, and often has been, the enemy of solidarity, our human interdependence, and thus indirectly of health as well.

There seems little doubt that, for societies as a whole, the market promotes prosperity, fosters independence and entrepreneurship, and can reinforce democracy. But it is a fallacy to conclude that, because the market in general is a beneficent force for societal good, it is therefore equally valid in organizing and running healthcare *systems*. I call that the "market fallacy." And I emphasize the word "systems" to distinguish the use of individual market practices as part of overall systems rather than their dominating feature. There is no evidence anywhere in the world to draw such a conclusion about their system-wide value.

The market rewards strong, knowledgeable individuals, and tolerates the failure of entrepreneurs and commercial enterprises (and the success of others) as a sign of the potency of competition. But the world of the sick is marked by a loss of strength and independence, by a diminishment of self-management, by a painful dependence upon others. Providing the economic and social goods to well manage that combination of human vulnerabilities has not been a mark of the market anywhere, nor is there any reason to suppose they could or would be.

NOTES

1. Much of the information in this paper draws upon a book I wrote with a colleague: Daniel Callahan and Angela A. Wasunna, *Medicine and the Market: Equity v. Choice* (Baltimore, MD: Johns Hopkins Press, 2006).
2. Plato, *Republic*, 342d, 346a–c.

3. Adam Smith, *An Inquiry into the Nature and Causes of the Wealth of Nations*, ed. R. H. Campbell and A. S. Skinner, 2 vols. (Oxford: Oxford University Press, 1976), pp. i, ii, 27.

4. See, for instance, Arnold S. Relman, "What Markets Are Doing to Medicine," *Atlantic Monthly* 269, no. 3 (1992): 99, 102.

5. Paul Starr, *The Social Transformation of American Medicine* (New York: Basic Books, 1982), passim.

6. Bo Petersson, "Health, Doctors and the Good Life," in *Dimensions of Health and Health Promotion*, ed. Lennart Nordenfeldt and Per-Erik Liss (Amsterdam: Editions Rodop, 2003), p. 13.

7. I have in mind such health economists as Victor Fuchs, Thomas Rice, and Uwe Reinhardt.

8. Roger Feldman and Michael Morrissey, "Health Economics: A Report on the Field," *Journal of Health Politics, Policy and Law* 15, no. 3 (1990): 627–646.

9. Victor Fuchs, "Economics, Values, and Health Care Reform," *Journal of Health Politics, Policy and Law* 15, no. 3 (1996): 1–29.

10. Richard B. Saltman and Hans F. W. Dubois, "The Historical and Social Base of Social Health Insurance Systems," in *Social Health Insurance Systems in Western Europe*, ed. Richard B. Saltman, Richard Busse, and Josep Figueras (Maidenhead: Open University Press, 2004), pp. 21–32.

11. This data is laid out in detail in Daniel Callahan & Angela A. Wasunna, *Medicine and the Market*: 229–233, 237–247.

12. Liz Kowalczyk, "Long Waits for Doctors Targeted," *The Boston Globe*, December 12, 2005.

13. Thomas Bodenheimer, "Rising Health Care Costs. Part 2: Technological Innovation," *Annals of Internal Medicine* 142, no. 11 (2005): 932–937.

14. Ruud ter Meulen, Wil Arts, and Ruud Muffels, eds., *Solidarity in Health and Social Welfare in Europe* (Dordrecht: Kluwer Academic, 2001).

15. The idea of affordability and sustainability are more fully developed in Daniel Callahan, *False Hopes: Overcoming the Obstacles to a Sustainable, Affordable Medicine* (New Brunswick, NJ: Rutgers University Press, 1999).

CHAPTER 2

Broken promises: do business-friendly strategies frustrate just healthcare?

Norman Daniels

2.1 INTRODUCTION

The for-profit business of biomedicine involves not only the production of drugs and medical devices but also the financing and delivery of most medical services in the US and significant and growing proportions of medical delivery in many developing countries. Since the latter provides a significant part of the market for the former, promoting business-friendly strategies in financing and delivering medical services improves the business, that is, the profitability, of producing drugs and medical devices. Does it also promote justice in meeting medical needs?

In Section 2.2, I briefly sketch what I believe are some of the key implications for the financing and delivery of healthcare that follow from a theory of justice for health that I have elaborated over the last three decades. Though the theory supports some widely held views about what equity involves in access to healthcare and in its financing, the theory itself is normatively neutral about important policy questions regarding the mix of public and private schemes for delivering care and financing it. As long as a system can meet the objectives of justice rather than frustrate them, then the theory is open to variations in its organization and financing. If, however, specific business-friendly proposals undercut achievement of those goals, then those proposals must be seen as unjust.

Though important ethical issues, including issues of justice, are raised by the business of producing drugs and medical devices, I shall not discuss them here. Instead, I shall examine briefly (in Section 2.3) several recent market-friendly strategies – I call them market promises – that were promoted as ways to improve health systems here and abroad. The first such promise is the most general: it is the claim that increased competition in the health sector will lower health costs by reducing unit prices. With lower unit prices, a more efficient system could better meet health needs per dollar spent. Were this promise fulfilled without undermining fair access or financing for subgroups in the population, justice would be served. The second promise, that competition among health plans would lower the rate of increase of health costs, was a central feature of both the Clinton proposal for universal coverage in the US and the central strategy of big business after the failure of efforts at universal coverage in the 103rd Congress. A component of that promise was the claim that keeping health costs down would make it easier to provide insurance coverage to Americans. The third promise, embodied in the Bush Administration advocacy for health savings accounts and in the DOJ/FTC report *Improving Health Care: A Dose of Competition*,[1] is that high-deductible health plans will produce wiser purchasing of healthcare and lower health costs. The fourth promise is that competition among drug plans providing coverage in the new Medicare drug benefit will suffice to lower costs and improve access to drugs for the elderly. The fifth promise is not domestic, as are the others, but is an export item to developing countries, namely that the introduction of user fees and the encouragement of a private sector will increase healthcare resources in underfunded systems at the same time they undercut moral hazard. I include the fifth promise because there has been a significant export of broken promises to developing countries.

All these promises about the value of market-friendly solutions are advanced as if they are compatible with the goals of justice. For example, lowering costs may lead to broader or more comprehensive coverage, a clear goal of justice. Justice is not unfriendly to efficiency when it leads to better meeting health needs fairly.

I shall argue that each has already proven to be a broken promise or is soon likely to be. Each frustrates some of the requirements of justice in healthcare delivery or financing. I view the reforms promoted through these promises as social experiments. Like clinical research, they promise benefits to society while also imposing some risks on the populations affected by them. In Section 2.4 I develop the analogy to clinical experimentation and urge that we subject the social experiments that result to more careful ethical and scientific review. Proper monitoring and evaluation of the consequences of acting on these promises should provide an evidence base that will help us resist similar false promises in the future.

2.2 JUST HEALTHCARE DELIVERY

The thrust of my later argument is that various market promises made about our health system and about others have frustrated important goals of justice. To make that argument, I need to say at the outset, albeit very briefly, what I mean here by justice in health and healthcare. More developed arguments for my views can be found elsewhere,[2] most recently in my *Just Health: Meeting Health Needs Fairly*. I do not presuppose agreement with the theory underlying my claims about what justice requires. My argument in Section 2.3 depends on conclusions about equity in healthcare delivery and financing that are widely held and are compatible with a range of accounts of justice and health.

An account of justice for health and healthcare should address (at least) three key questions:[3]

1. Is there a special moral importance to health, and, if so, what is it?
2. When is a health inequality unjust?
3. How can we meet health needs fairly when we cannot meet them all?

My answer to the first question rests on the relationship between health and opportunity. Suppose we think of health as normal functioning, a view central to the practice of those who deliver medical or public health services, as well as to social epidemiologists. Departures from normal functioning limit in varying degrees the opportunities we can effectively take advantage of – or, in Sen's terms, our capability sets.[4] Ill health can shorten life or restrict what we can do while alive, both significant impacts on our opportunities. Any account of justice that establishes social obligations to protect the opportunity range for individuals – whether it is egalitarian, prioritarian, or even a sufficiency view – will thus have a basis for ascribing some special moral importance to promoting normal functioning in a population and distributing it fairly among its members. I use this observation to permit an extension of Rawls's[5] theory of justice as fairness to health and healthcare. Specifically, institutions that promote population health and its fair distribution, including public health and medical systems, should be governed by Rawls's principle assuring fair equality of opportunity. This claim allows us to move beyond Rawls's simplifying idealization, that his social contractors are all fully normal over a normal lifespan. This extension thus provides us with a general theory with implications for justice and health and healthcare.

Even before we provide answers to the other questions, this answer to the question about the moral importance of health and healthcare can support some important claims about the design of healthcare systems. (Throughout, I take "healthcare" to include personal medical and social support measures as well as traditional public health strategies to reduce exposure to health risks.) For example, public health should not only be concerned with the reduction of aggregate population risks but should address inequalities in exposure to health risks, e.g., in the workplace or downstream from sources of water or air pollution. Further, the social obligation to protect opportunity by protecting

and promoting health favors a distribution of services in accordance with
need, not ability to pay. We should, however, distribute the burden of
meeting those needs by ability to pay.

These claims about social obligations to protect the opportunity range
imply, I have argued,[6] a universal coverage system. In short, regardless of
ability to pay, all should have access, based on medical need, to an array of
services that aim to promote normal functioning, as determined by a fair
deliberative process. Since it is a social obligation to provide such access, the
burdens of financing it should be based on ability to pay. But the specific
organization of financing and delivery, for example, regarding the mix of
public and private financing and institutions, remains a more complex
policy issue, and, as I noted earlier, the general theory is neutral among
alternatives as long as they don't frustrate the requirements of justice.[7] If, for
example, the efficiencies generated by private delivery or financing allow
health resources to service more needs and to do so equitably, then there is
nothing in this general view that rules out a private healthcare sector, or a
privately financed, even for-profit employer-based insurance scheme.[8]
What organizational forms are permissible depends on whether the promises of such a private sector are met or broken.

Healthcare – even broadly construed to include traditional public health
measures – is not the sole important determinant of population health levels
or the distribution of health within that population. We know this from the
robust results of social epidemiology, including studies such as the
Whitehall studies,[9] that demonstrate a socioeconomic gradient of health
even among a population with no poverty, basic levels of education, and
universal access to healthcare. How we distribute other important goods in
society – income, wealth, powers, opportunities, basic liberties, including
the political participation, and the social bases of self-respect – affects
population health and its distribution. I infer from this body of social
epidemiological findings that health is a social good more than it is a natural
good, contra Rawls and Nagel.[10]

I also infer that social obligations to protect opportunity through the
promotion of normal functioning mean that health inequalities should be
viewed as unjust if they result from an unjust distribution of the determinants
of health. Specifically, Rawls's principles of justice as fairness happen to
capture the key social determinants of health: if we distributed them according to those principles, socioeconomic status (SES) gradients of health would
be flattened, perhaps as much as we could demand as a matter of justice.[11] Of
course, other conceptions of justice – ones that allow much greater inequalities in society than conformance with Rawls's principles would – may then

create much greater health inequalities. If we expect these health inequalities to be remedied by a just healthcare system, we would be disappointed. Treating people who are inequitably made ill falls short of what justice requires. On the other hand, it is easy for an unjust health system – one lacking universal coverage and equitable financing – to magnify the health inequalities produced by the unjust distribution of the broad determinants of health. Indeed, a system that relies on out-of-pocket or otherwise regressive financing of health services, or that creates unequal levels of benefits for different social groups based on social status, may increase the health inequalities already produced by other social policies and their interaction with inequalities in social status.

The third question, about meeting health needs fairly when not all can be met, also has a bearing on the business of biomedicine. Resource allocation decisions must be made at various levels within a system. Within universal coverage systems, for example, where there is public financing for the system, as in Canada or the United Kingdom, a political "macro" decision determines the overall share of the public budget to be devoted to healthcare (broadly understood). Within that budget, further "meso" decisions must be made at regional, health authority, or hospital levels. Further "micro" decisions may be made about the resources to be devoted to specific, identified patients, though these decisions are heavily constrained by the macro and meso decisions.

All of these decisions are fraught with ethical issues, and reasonable people will disagree about how to resolve their disagreements. For example, a national policy not to cover experimental therapies may be in place, but at the meso level, there may be room left in some budgets for occasional compassionate uses of not fully proven therapies, and specific decisions about them would have to be made at the micro level and supported at the meso level. Reasonable people may disagree about how to weight stewardship of scarce resources against the concern to rescue people from life-threatening illness.

It is because of these ethical controversies and the absence of prior agreement on moral principles fine-grained enough to resolve these disputes that Jim Sabin and I propose relying on a fair, deliberative process that we call "accountability for reasonableness" as a means for securing legitimacy for contested decisions.[12] To be fair and to encourage appropriate deliberation, the process must be fully transparent, abiding by a strong publicity constraint that calls for full disclosure of the rationales underlying limit setting decisions. These rationales must rest on reasons and evidence that all can agree – with appropriate stakeholder involvement, where feasible – are relevant to making limit-setting decisions of this sort. Further, the decisions must be revisable in light of new evidence and arguments, including evidence that specific patients do not fit the presuppositions of the decision. Finally, there must be appropriate regulation that enforces compliance with these conditions. Such a fair process determines over time the benefit package that is included within a health system. We have suggested how it might add legitimacy to decision-making about the coverage of services or the design of pharmaceutical benefits even within for-profit health plans.[13]

Such an approach clearly does not rely on simple market mechanisms, especially ability to pay, to resolve disputes about fair access to needed resources. In this way, it becomes relevant to the topic of the business of biomedicine, though it is not central to the argument of Section 2.3.

Let me summarize the implications of this account of justice and health. These implications are compatible with a range of views about justice and healthcare and I shall judge the market-friendly promises against them and not against any underlying theory. Indeed, these considerations about equity in access and financing are widely held, even standard in discussions of equity in healthcare delivery:

1. Access to healthcare should be based on health needs, not ability to pay. The most direct way to achieve such a goal is a universal coverage insurance system, which can be all public or a mix of public and private schemes.

2. The content of any right to healthcare – the entitlements that individuals actually have – are system relative, depending on the results of determining a benefit package in a fair way. Justice would require a comprehensive benefit package aimed at protecting normal functioning, minimizing tiering or stratification across different groups. (I do not rule out modest tiering for best off groups if there are cross-subsidies from that tier that make the rest of the system better than it could otherwise be.[14])

3. The burden of meeting health needs in a population is a social obligation that must be distributed according to ability to pay in a given society. Specifically, this means that more progressive tax or payment schemes are fairer than less progressive ones, and that, where premiums are involved, community rating is superior to risk-rated premiums. Out-of-pocket payments burden those with the greatest health needs the most, and the justification for them must meet a heavy burden of proof.[15]

These and other objectives of justice in a health system are given more detailed consideration in my work on the Benchmarks of Fairness for

Health System Reform.[16] In effect, the matrix for assessing the fairness of health system reforms could be systematically used to monitor and evaluate a number of the reforms that have been accompanied by the promises I shall turn to in the next section. My proposal to conduct an ethical and scientific review of such promises,[17] using something like this matrix or an improved version of it, is an issue I return to at the end of the review of the promises that follows.

2.3 SOME IMPORTANT MARKET-FRIENDLY PROMISES: ARE THEY BROKEN?

In this section, I consider in varying detail five market-friendly promises. Four are domestic; one is an export. All five share the following feature: they appeal to general economic theory to provide a tactic for addressing the problem of rapidly rising healthcare costs and the goal of making healthcare more affordable through increased efficiency. Each promises benefits to the population but each also involves some clear risks, especially to vulnerable or worse-off groups. What is more, we have plenty of evidence of these risks despite the strong endorsement of these tactics. I shall argue that each promise is partly or largely a broken one because the promised benefits are not achieved, while some of the risks may instead be realized. Each broken promise thus compromises the goals of justice regarding access and fair financing highlighted in Section 2.2.

The promise that competition brings low unit prices

I begin with the most general of the broken promises. In ideally competitive markets, competition lowers unit prices. This is supposed to be a central virtue of truly competitive markets. Of course, the ideal presupposes an absence of monopoly powers on the supply side. Where there are such monopoly powers, or where special protections are provided to powerful forces on the supply side, there may have to be countervailing forces on the demand side, if the resulting market is to mimic the efficiencies of an ideal market. Concentrating power in the hands of some purchasers – creating monopsony power in the hands of public agencies or collaborating health plans, to be specific – may be necessary to counter the market power of drug companies that hold monopoly controls on specific drugs, for example. Promising that "competition" is always the solution to a problem is a false promise wherever power imbalances exist in the market and business-friendly policies protect those with excessive power on the supply side. Such a one-sided appeal to competition may simply make the problem worse by weakening countervailing collaborative efforts among purchasers.

Compared to health systems in developed countries, the US system contains more private sector competition among providers and health plans than any other. If that form of competition were sufficient to produce greater efficiency, then we should see greater efficiency in the US system in the form of much lower unit prices than we see in other systems. Lower unit prices would mean that if more money is spent in a system on healthcare – and country wealth is roughly proportional to levels of spending on health among OECD countries, then we would expect to see more resources delivered to the population. We should be getting more bang for the buck, since – so goes the promise – the bang will be cheaper. If a very wealthy US gets more by spending more on healthcare, that is not itself a problem but only a choice about what to invest its wealth in. If however, we spend more and get less, then that is a broken, business-friendly promise.

Various studies have analyzed OECD spending patterns on health. The United States spends more per capita on healthcare than any other country, exceeding Switzerland's expenditure per capita by 53% in the most recent year (2002) studied.[18] Its expenditures per capita is 140% above the OECD median. Why is spending so much greater?

The key answer is that unit prices are much higher in the United States. This explanation is plausible only after ruling out alternative hypotheses. Among the alternative explanations ruled out by various studies are these:

1. US malpractice costs explain the difference: In fact, malpractice litigation involves only 0.46% of spending.[19]
2. The effect of supply side constraints leads to unacceptable queuing in other countries and this makes costs lower: In fact, queued services are only 4% of US spending.[20]
3. More resources are deployed in the US and these cost more: As we shall see, there is a mixed story about this claim.
4. Population aging accounts for higher US costs: This alternative explanation cannot explain the difference between the US and other OECD countries that have more pronounced societal aging.
5. Administrative complexity raises US costs: This is a significant factor, not an alternative we can rule out. It is one that operates in addition to the increased unit prices – and in any case, competition should drive out such administrative inefficiency, but it does not.

Consider some examples of the unit price differences. The average cost of a US hospital day is $2,434, whereas it is $870 in Canada. Even in the early 1990s, fees for procedures were three times as high as in Canada, and fees for evaluation and management services were 80% higher in the US than Canada.[21] Some of the difference in unit costs is explained by higher US incomes in general (within fields competing for talent with medical personnel) and the higher cost of living. But even after adjusting for GDPpc, US spending is $2,037 higher than the predicted value.

If we spend so much more, do we get more (this bears on the fourth alternative hypothesis, above)? Are more resources made available to Americans than others in OECD countries? The answer is mixed and challenges some common perceptions. For example, though the US disseminated CT and MRI scanners more quickly than other countries, actual supply per capita is greater in some OECD countries, although not in Canada. The rate of use of CT and MRI is higher than elsewhere. The number of hospital beds per capita in the US is in the bottom 25% of OECD countries, but shorter US hospital stays are more intensive in the use of services. The number of US physicians per capita (2.4) is less than the OECD median (3.1) in 2002.[22] The US growth rate in physicians per capita exceeded OECD rates, entirely as a result of immigration of physicians to the US.

Although I am suggesting higher unit prices are the key explanation, there is at least one other very important factor, higher administrative costs. Woolhandler *et al.*[23] estimate that total administrative costs, adding those of insurers, employers, and providers (but excluding patient administrative costs and time costs) were approximately $295 billion in 1999, nearly 24% of US health spending. The figure is astounding compared to administrative cost estimates in other OECD countries, but the explanation for these costs involves several factors: competing plans in a private insurance market spend much of their money excluding people from coverage rather than simply reimbursing for what doctors say is needed, as in other OECD countries. I shall not focus on this issue further other than to emphasize that I could have developed the point into a distinct broken promise about market efficiency.

I return to the main point: How can higher unit prices emerge despite "more competition"? The answer lies in the departures from key assumptions about ideal competition. Monopoly powers, such as those commanded by drug companies holding patents, allow sellers to gain higher prices than ideal competition would allow (the excess of prices above the minimum prices sellers in a competitive market would have to be paid to sell are called "rents"). Various countries reduce rents by creating extra power – monopsony power – among buyers. The extreme of monopsony powers exists in single-payer systems, which can negotiate drug or physician prices for the whole system.

In a multi-payer system, allowing collaboration among private insurers, as in Germany, reduces rents there. Similarly, allowing large public agencies, such as Medicare, or groups of health plans acting collectively, to bargain for better prices would reduce rents, were they allowed to do so.

In short, the best explanation for higher unit prices in the US (in addition to the administrative costs of excluding people from coverage) is the imbalance of monopoly and monopsony powers. What is striking in the US is the business-friendly way in which "competition" is invoked to protect those holding monopoly powers against collective action by buyers. The most famous recent example is prohibiting Medicare to bargain for lower drug prices while pretending that competition among 40 or more health plans will lead to lower drug costs. Another example is advocating the extreme splitting of purchasers into HSAs – where the individual has minimal ability to negotiate for lower prices with any provider – while at the same time calling this strategy a "dose of competition."

The promise that more competition is needed to introduce efficiency, especially in the form of lower unit prices, is thus a broken promise. Policies are pursued that systematically weaken buyer powers to act collectively against the powers of sellers, who are protected by business-friendly strategies. As we consider briefly the specific broken promises that follow, a number include special instances of the promise we have here considered.

The promise that managed competition will control cost increases

At the heart of the Clinton proposal to make "managed competition" among health plans the key element of a universal coverage health scheme lies a special case of the broken promise we just considered. Instead of maximally increasing monopsony powers in the form of a single-payer system, the Clinton proposal involved encouraging competition for quality and price among as many health plans as a particular geographical area could sustain. The theory was that efficiency, and hopefully lower unit prices and lower aggregate costs, would result from health plans working to make utilization and delivery more efficient.

By including all people in an area in these plans, and shifting the focus away from the administrative costs of excluding people from coverage, the Clinton plan would have increased monopsony powers and might have had some impact on cost-containment.

The Clinton plan collapsed, however, largely because large employers believed they could lower their healthcare costs by relying on managed competition without a government-regulated plan. These large purchasers hoped to avoid entanglement with increased government regulation and the threat of even greater concentration of purchasing power in the hands of government. Although these large employers exercised their monopsony powers through this device of competing health plans, the leverage was far less than would have been present in the Clinton plan. Important critics of such managed competition[24] argued that any savings would be a one-time savings, largely from shortening hospital stays, and that after that brief reduction in the rate of increasing health costs, growth rates would increase at the previous rate. The critics believed various drivers of those costs – new technology, population aging – would continue unabated. Yet the promise of controlled costs through more competition among health plans also included the promise that keeping the growth rate of health expenditures down would increase access to care and make expansion of insurance coverage more possible.

The critics, as we know, have proven right. After a brief decline in the rate of cost increases in the mid 1990s, the rate of increase grew until it returned to the projected rate prior to the introduction of managed competition, namely two to three times the rate of inflation. The explanation of the broken promise that there would be lower costs and more access has various elements. The backlash against managed care, orchestrated by the media and by many medical professionals, made it harder to rely on the supply side constraints the plans tried to introduce. The push of cost drivers – new technologies, new drugs, an aging population – remained. But arguably, the fundamental issue was that the competing health plans simply lacked the monopsony powers needed to offset the powers of sellers, and they were saddled with higher administrative costs, as noted earlier. Although they had been promoted as the form of competition that was needed to constrain costs, the strategy served as a diversion from the strategy that works in other OECD countries, where real monopsony powers were sustained.

The promise that consumer-driven health plans (CDHPs) will both lower costs and lead to wiser health purchasing[25]

CDHPs propose to use increased cost sharing as a way to make consumers refrain from healthcare that is not worth its cost to them, in effect making them wiser purchasers. The increased cost sharing in CDHPs comes in the form of a high deductible. Then, enrollees typically face coinsurance similar to that imposed by standard Preferred Provider Organization (PPO) plans. The novel element of CDHP benefit design comes in the form of a spending account – either a health reimbursement account (HRA) that has employer or health plan funding with pretax dollars, or a health savings account (HSA), with various forms of tax incentives.

Proponents of these schemes promise they will curb the moral hazard they allege drives up healthcare utilization when third-party payers largely foot the bill.[26] But if cutting needed care is not the goal, such consumers must know what counts as a good buy. When people shop for a car or a computer, they have good information about cost and quality – through Consumer Reports and its competitors, if no other way. The uncertainty involved in medical decisions and the complexity of health delivery mean similar tools for the medical consumer are simply not available.[27] The kinds of web-based and print access CDHPs give consumers contain only limited information on healthcare costs and procedures and even less in the way of comparative ratings of provider quality and cost, especially regarding physician quality.[28]

Advocates of these schemes know these kinds of consumer supports are both necessary and still missing if the promise of wiser, lower-cost purchasing is to be kept. They emphasize their importance, note their absence, and then persist with the promise the CDHPs can deliver.[29] This adherence to the belief that people will be better consumers despite evidence of the absence of conditions necessary for them to make well-informed choices reflects the ideological faith in markets that is characteristic of Improving Healthcare.

There is an extensive observational literature documenting the negative relationship between patient cost sharing and healthcare utilization.[30] Because of important selection effects most researchers agree, however, that the most reliable elasticity estimates are those that were estimated in the context of quasi-experiments or randomized controlled trials, the largest of which was the RAND Health Insurance Experiment (HIE). The HIE demonstrated that a high-deductible plan would indeed result in cost savings relative to full coverage.[31] The high-deductible plan in the HIE required that families pay 95% of expenses up to an amount that was equivalent to roughly $6,000 in 2004, or a bit more than twice the average family deductible for a typical CDHP.[32] With this relatively large deductible, families spent 25–30% less than families that had free care. While the relationships are clearly not linear, a crude extrapolation from the RAND results suggest that CDHPs would save at most 10–15% relative to a zero-deductible PPO plan with the average co-payment structure currently enjoyed by insured workers. Actual "savings" observed in the market are likely to be lower: comparison plans offer far from "free care" since employers have already introduced deductibles into most PPO and some HMO plans.

The direct empirical evidence of the impact of CDHPs is limited to HRAs. The only peer-reviewed evaluation of an HRA found that after two years, spending on both hospital and physician services increased to a higher level for enrollees in the HRA than those in a competing HMO and PPO offered by the same large employer.[33] The HRA in this case was extremely generous, however, so that the results are unlikely to generalize to plans that expose consumers to a larger gap between the account and the deductible. The findings suggest that there is no magic in how HRAs might save money: cost sharing is the key, if not the only cost control mechanism.

Strong evidence of a savings effect would not, however, be sufficient to show improved efficiency from cost sharing. A reduction in spending would translate into a welfare improvement only if the foregone services are worth less than alternative uses of the savings. While a precise answer to the question of whether increased cost sharing would improve patient welfare is not possible, there is some suggestive evidence, again mostly from past studies of natural and randomized experiments of cost sharing.[34] First, individuals cut back on both effective (as deemed by clinical reviewers) and low-value services in the face of increased out-of-pocket costs.[35] Similar patterns were noted in the evaluation of a change in coinsurance in the Stanford University employee health plan in the 1960s.[36] With respect to outcomes, HIE researchers examining the health effects of the different plans found most enrollees no worse-off, but low-income individuals with pre-existing health problems were significantly negatively impacted by the high-deductible plan.[37] Similarly, a study of medically needy Medicaid enrollees who lost coverage due to a policy change in California found substantial deterioration in health when those individuals were faced with the full price of private care.[38]

To be fair, the design of CDHPs often include some protections against potential under use. Many CDHPs offer more generous coverage for preventive care, and HRAs may also do so for maintenance drugs required by individuals with chronic illness. For most enrollees, there is also telephonic and internet-based support to make better decisions about major treatment options such as when to seek care and how to manage chronic illness.[39] These provisions may reduce the health risks suggested by the RAND HIE – although there is no direct evidence on this point.

The more we rely on individual premiums, especially risk-rated ones and on out-of-pocket payments, like deductibles and co-pays, the more we abandon fair financing. That has been the trend in the US insurance market in the last several decades. This is because in contrast to traditional insurance plans, when employers contribute to savings accounts in CDHPs, they are distributing some portion of the healthcare benefit directly to all enrollees (the account), not just those needing care. These account dollars may exceed annual healthcare spending for healthier workers, while they will quickly be expended by those who are chronically ill. As many have noted, unless savings from CDHPs are realized and redistributed, or other subsidies are given to those who are less healthy, there is an inevitable redistribution in favor of the healthy.[40]

The principle of fair financing may also be violated if CDHPs differentially burden low-income individuals through the way they ration care. While the distributional effects of CDHPs have not yet been studied, there is reasonable evidence that lower-income individuals are more likely than higher-income individuals to cut back on ambulatory care, including preventive services, in the face of increased cost sharing.[41] Thus, while out-of-pocket costs provide incentives to value care more carefully (though better, welfare-enhancing choices will only result if there is good information about costs and quality), they will have larger effects on lower-income people who then may forego relatively high-value care. The effect is that as we depart from fair financing, we also raise financial barriers to fair access with a stronger impact on lower-income groups.

Consider next the redistribution that may result if CDHPs disproportionately attract low-risk individuals, as might be expected from their design. The trend will drive premium costs yet higher for those left in plans with sicker, and likely poorer, populations, increasing the violation of fair financing over time and increasing the chances that people in these alternative plans will become uninsurable. In turn, that would lead to violations of fair access for them. Meanwhile, those attracted into the lower premium plans by incentives that violate fair financing will benefit at the expense of others.

Beyond the costs and benefits to CDHP enrollees and others in the risk pools in which the new plans are offered, there may be external, societal effects of CDHP adoption. On the benefit side, if CDHPs live up to their promise to produce a vanguard of more prudent shoppers who will demand and act upon information on the comparative costs and benefits of treatments and providers, an outcome made unlikely by the absence of good cost and quality information, we might find system wide gains in efficiency and quality. That is, if physicians and hospitals begin competing on the basis of value to consumers, there may be positive spillover effects for enrollees of traditional plans. On the cost side, if CDHPs skim off the healthiest and wealthiest in the small group or individual insurance market, as some of the early data suggest they might, there could be a destabilizing effect that would drive out low-cost HMO or other options that are preferred by higher-risk (and possibly lower-income) individuals.

A further, also speculative societal consequence poses even broader ethical concerns. The attitudes people have toward seeking collective solutions to social problems are in part a product of the institutions that they encounter. People embedded in social insurance schemes tend to sustain attitudes of social solidarity, believing sharing risks is a social obligation. Of course, cultures with social insurance schemes may have had deeper commitment to social solidarity to start with, but the stability of these institutions over the long run in many countries suggests they help shape attitudes as well. American commitment toward solidarity in our Social Security and Medicare schemes – the "third rail" of politics – may be sustained by the benefits produced by the collective sharing of risks. If we intensify risk stratification within private markets for medical insurance, we not only may undermine efforts by workers to seek collective solutions to their problems as employees, and also deflect attention from societal efforts to establish some form of universal coverage, but we may further erode the institutional supports for the mechanisms that generate all kinds of public goods in social systems. This may be the effect, and possibly the intention, behind promoting CDHPs as an element of the "ownership society".[42]

Advocates of CDHPs make a promise the plans are unlikely to keep. We lack the consumer-friendly tools that, even in theory, are necessary if the promise of wiser yet healthy shoppers is to be kept. At the same time the plans impose clear risks – not only to vulnerable consumers who may shop unwisely but to the insurance market itself. This is an unmonitored social experiment, unlike the HIE that preceded it.

The promise that competition among private plans delivering the Medicare drug benefit will control costs and improve access to drugs

There was excellent reason, from the perspective of justice, to add a pharmacy benefit to Medicare. Omitting an out-patient drug benefit in 1965, when Medicare was put into law, was an unfortunate compromise in the overall Medicare benefit package, but as pharmaceuticals emerged as a more and more important component of healthcare over the next 40 years, the omission was glaring. The omission meant that coverage of basic health needs was incomplete. As a result, out-of-pocket payments for those who lacked employer-based drug benefits that carried over into retirement greatly increased.

A Medicare pharmacy benefit should have had the following goals:
a. to provide broad, flexible coverage for a population whose individual needs vary over time as new conditions and co-morbidities emerge;

b. to provide purchasing leverage to reduce pharmaceutical costs to the program in order to make the benefit as sustainable as possible and to keep beneficiary co-pays as low as possible;

c. to reduce out-of-pocket payments for drugs, aiming to make the overall Medicare benefit as equitable in its financing as possible;

d. to offer an easy, efficient transition from the pre-benefit plan to full coverage for the eligible population.

The goals could readily have been met had there been the following:

A. A single drug plan that offered broad coverage contingent on need, and that

B. had the power of the plan to negotiate as a whole with drug companies for the best prices large-scale purchasing could achieve.

Giving Medicare the power to negotiate for drug prices would not only have made the plan more sustainable, but it would have permitted lower co-pays than the current plan. Making Medicare the provider, rather than 40+ plans managing different benefit packages, would have achieved the goal of simple management and simple transition.

Instead, as many now lament, the Bush Administration pushed through a plan that protects drug companies against the increase in monopsony power that is needed to offset the monopoly powers on the supply side. Instead it promised that competition among the many private plans would provide the efficiency needed to lower prices – but the very measure promised prevented countervailing monopsony powers from emerging. As we know, the competing plans meant an avoidably complex system that many seniors are unable to negotiate and that left millions of the poorest elderly so vulnerable – losing coverage they already had – that states had to step in on an emergency basis.

The reliance on market-friendly measures is thus another broken promise. Instead of achieving the goals of justice in a Medicare benefit, the business of biomedicine was promoted in ways that frustrate those goals and the means necessary to achieve them.

The promise that market-friendly reforms, such as user-fees and privatization, will improve sustainability and efficiency in developing country systems

In the 1980s and 1990s, there was a major effort to promote market mechanisms that would be friendlier to the business of biomedicine in both developing countries and in OECD countries in Europe, including the UK. In developed countries, the promise was made that market efficiencies would result from these measures. In addition, these efficiencies would not compromise the strong state efforts at equitable delivery of healthcare. By the 1990s, a general lesson had emerged in much of the developed countries: without a strong state regulatory role, any efficiencies were likely to compromise equity; in addition, the gains were far more modest than what was promised since new transaction costs often accompanied the reforms.

Instead of examining these bio-business-friendly efforts in developed countries, however, I want to comment very briefly on the promises made in the much more vulnerable developing countries. Policies promoted by the IMF and World Bank in the 1980s and early 1990s pushed increased reliance on a private healthcare sector; at the same time, the IMF also emphasized structural reforms that demanded lower funding of the health sector. The latter requirements set the stage for many of the "push" factors – low salary, high work loads, poor career options – that have contributed to the brain drain of health personnel from developing countries to developed ones. In effect, they were business friendly to the labor market needs of wealthy countries. Two promises underlay the proposed reforms: a private sector would add resources and add efficiency to a health system that was underfunded and provide efficient management in the context of a state that was weak and bureaucratic. Both promises disguised clear risks: a private sector might also drain resources from a public one, including personnel. Further, as noted in developing countries, it takes a strong state to regulate a private health sector so that it can assure competency and equity in the delivery of care. I will not review the considerable evidence that these risks often outweighed the gains that were promised. Instead, I note but one specific measure that was promoted widely in developing countries, user fees. These were insisted on by the IMF and World Bank as a way of making public systems more sustainable – resources gained in this way could be used to provide incentives for local providers and would add to the resources available in the system.

Unfortunately, user fees were imposed on many health systems on the advice of international agencies without careful gathering of evidence about their benefits and risks prior to implementation. A number of studies have shown clear negative effects in the form of barriers to access to care, particularly for the poor.[43] Subsequent evidence that exemptions for the poor fail to work effectively and that there are negative impacts on poor and vulnerable populations seems largely to have been ignored. Once implemented, the measures usually stay and continue to be justified by their proponents.[44] There is even evidence that the existence of user fees provides a cover in some settings for increased "under-the-table" payments that add an additional layer of corruption to vulnerable systems. In the current context, the existence of these measures is being used in some settings to argue that anti-retroviral therapies for HIV/AIDS should also be subject to user fees on grounds of improved sustainability and equity across disease conditions.[45] Here, as elsewhere, two wrongs almost certainly do not make a right.

Prior to the introduction of these market-style measures, there was no careful evidence-based review of the effect of user fees on access and sustainability. Ideally, controlled experiments or at least an analysis of pilot trials could have revealed the dangers in a quantifiable way. Unfortunately, this is but one more instance where market-ideology won out over scientific review of policy. As a result promises were made, acted on, and generally broken.

2.4 ETHICAL AND SCIENTIFIC REVIEW OF PROMISES

In this concluding section, I argue that the market-friendly promises we have looked at were made in support of *social experiments* on a population. Unfortunately, these experiments were not subject to the kinds of ethical and scientific review to which we subject clinical research.[46] I want to suggest what such a review should include (I am not, however, advocating IRBs for health system reforms).

The analogy to clinical research may at first seem perverse. Health system reforms – including the market-friendly promises we discussed – are not intended as research aimed at new knowledge. They aim instead to improve population health through better delivery of medical and public health services. Often reform of some sort is not discretionary, as is some clinical research, but obligatory because of serious failings in the system. We might consider some of the run-away costs of our health system as a serious failing we must address, hardly something discretionary.

Nevertheless, reforms – including the broken promises we surveyed – have important similarities to clinical research. They often deploy measures of unknown efficacy – I believe managed competition, consumer-driven health plans, and user fees all constituted experiments using measures of unknown efficacy. The broken promises also imposed risks on a population in addition to the benefits they promised. Managed competition, for example, was accompanied by increased uninsurance, not more insurance coverage. CDHPs risk cutting needed utilization as much as unnecessary utilization – a clear finding in the HIE. User fees led to access barriers for the poorest sectors of the population, even when exemptions were supposed to correct for that effect. Indeed, these negative effects may impose health risks on subgroups in the population much greater than those involved in typical clinical research.

The analogy has other components. Like clinical research, reforms trade on the credibility of science and the medical or public health establishment. Both raise issues about governance, including the control people can exercise over what happens to them in the pursuit of societal goals. Finally, both aim at desirable social goals – new knowledge or improved health delivery; review should not make their pursuit too difficult, especially in light of the urgency of some reforms.

Experiments on human subjects require pro-active ethical and scientific review to ensure that they meet standards set by domestic and international commissions and accords.[47] The review assesses the rationale for the research and the proposed experimental design as well as compliance with principles governing how subjects consent to the experiments and are treated while in them. Leave aside the mechanisms for such review (Institutional Review Boards), since they are probably inappropriate for health system reforms, and focus instead on why some form of review is needed. Research generally imposes risks on relatively small groups of subjects in order to achieve a societal goal, advancing knowledge and technology, without benefiting those subjects directly. It is generally ethically problematic when we deliberately benefit some at the expense of others.

Health system reforms often use unproven measures intended to improve the delivery of medical or public health services to a population. These measures impose risks on population subgroups. For example, decentralization of health systems in developing countries risks undermining the delivery of immunizations or TB treatments by shifting personnel expert in centralized programs to positions where they cannot carry on the work or by substituting local priorities at the expense of important national programs. Successful reforms teach us that certain measures work. Unsuccessful reforms teach us some measures do not work or were not properly implemented. Though knowledge may not be the main goal of reforms, it is a desired consequence that we acquire by imposing risks on our fellow citizens.

If we have good reason to carry out an ethical review of the scientific design of clinical experiments and to insist that people involved in them are not merely "guinea pigs" but appropriately govern their own actions, then we have comparable reason to review pro-actively efforts to transform health systems and to monitor and evaluate their effects so that we can minimize harms they may impose. Labeling health system reforms as "operations" or "managerial prerogatives," not social experiments, ignores the fact that we often lack adequate knowledge about the safety and efficacy of reforms, which is the rationale for conducting clinical trials.

One objection to the analogy between clinical and social experiments is that other mechanisms than pro-active ethical review already assure public accountability for harmful decisions in health sector transformation. Even internationally instigated reforms are matters that the public can hold domestic officials accountable for through democratic processes, or through tort law, where it is developed and enforceable, or even through negative market effects, if private sector reforms prove harmful. Ethical review is an unnecessary extra layer of bureaucratic interference with necessary reforms it is already difficult to initiate.

Where democratic process and tort law are well developed, they work after the fact to hold authorities accountable for harms imposed. Where effective, they offer an incentive to avoid mistaken and dangerous reforms. Unfortunately, they are often not available or effective in the developing countries where externally imposed social experiments are most common. Even where these after-the-fact protections are in place, it is better to equip authorities with a tool, such as a framework for ethical and scientific review, that helps them to avoid problems before they are created.

The ethical and scientific review of clinical research involves three central components. The first is to determine whether there is a plausible scientific rationale, given the scientific literature, for pursuing this line of research in this way. Analogously, in the review of a social experiment, it is important to inquire whether the objectives of the reform have an appropriate ethical and scientific rationale. After establishing that there is an appropriate rationale for the experiment, a second question is whether the design of the experiment is appropriate to the rationale for it. Will it really produce relevant findings? Analogously, once we determine that a social experiment is justified by the problem it purports to address and the rationale it offers for improving the system, we must determine whether the measures it proposes could achieve those ends. Is there good evidence they will do what is promised, if implemented correctly? The third key component of the ethical and scientific evaluation of clinical research is the imposition of appropriate governance conditions on the experiment. These include appropriate gathering of informed consent, but also monitoring and evaluation of the ongoing data to determine whether the experiment remains justifiable. Justification may be lost if the experimental arm is so successful that the control arm is being denied benefits it should have; it is also lost if the experimental arm proves too risky. Social experiments require such monitoring and evaluation as well – so they can be appropriately scaled up or eliminated depending on what kinds of effects they actually produce.

Is there a methodology that might provide some of the content needed to carry out this kind of evaluation of social experiments? I have argued elsewhere[48] that there is. The "benchmarks of fairness" methodology developed over the last decade[49] illustrates a more explicit framework for assessing the goals and outcomes of reform than the simple demand for values clarification. The international version of this framework, agreed upon by collaborating teams from diverse cultures, integrates three central goals of fairness: equity, efficiency, and accountability. Five benchmarks address equity: in the exposure of people to public health risks and distribution of the social determinants of health, financial and non-financial barriers to access to care, inequalities in benefits available to different groups, and burdens of paying for care. Two benchmarks focus on clinical efficiency and quality and administrative efficiency. Two benchmarks concern aspects of accountability and choice in the system. Each benchmark includes criteria that emphasize key components of the goal addressed by the benchmark. For example, the benchmark on non-financial barriers to access includes criteria for the geographical distribution of resources, gender disparities, cultural barriers, and discrimination, and the benchmark on accountability contains criteria calling for public performance reports, transparency in resource allocation decisions, and grievance or appeals procedures in healthcare institutions.

Together, the benchmarks address the complaint that "it is unfair" when the system treats some patients differently from others with similar needs, when some needs are not met because of administrative or other inefficiency, when people have no say in how the system treats them, and when the burdens of meeting health needs is not fairly financed. Fairness involves various claims about what people are owed as a matter of justice.[50] The benchmarks framework integrates these various goals and makes assessment of trade-offs among them. Because of this ethical framework describing the goals of reform, the benchmarks can provide a basis for assessing the rationale for reforms.

The benchmarks also provide a framework for evaluating the degree to which specific measures proposed in a reform are likely to achieve its goals. By seeing which measures in a specific reform purport to address the goals of fairness in a system, and by then gathering existing evidence about their effectiveness in other contexts, or by estimating their effects in the proposed reforms, we may be able to see if reform measures match the goals outlined in the rationale for the reform. To illustrate, consider the CDHPs we looked at earlier: some early efforts at measuring the effects of their deductibles on cost savings might provide evidence about what will really happen when they are more widely adopted. So too is evidence from the HIE relevant. But that early evidence from the HIE gave good reason to think the kinds of deductibles used would not make purchasers wiser buyers of care, contrary to what is being promised, unless there is substantial improvement in information about quality and efficacy of interventions and providers. That piece of reform is largely missing and provides good reason to be skeptical of the proposals.

The benchmarks also provide a monitoring and evaluation tool that gives an evidence base for governance constraints on social experiments. By showing what is going right and what wrong in the implementation of a reform, the Benchmarks provide evidence about how to modify the reform effort and about when it is producing unacceptable risks or burdens on some subgroups. This process is intended to enhance democratic controls over such social experiments, not undermine them.

In a political process, where reforms are implemented by democratically controlled agencies, the analogy to informed consent is democratic oversight of the reform process. Unfortunately, this analogy is problematic wherever democratic control of institutions is weak, whether in developed or developing countries, and wherever powerful external agencies offer large incentives and are not themselves held accountable for the reforms they impose. The remedy, however, is not to mimic clinical research by imposing requirements for some form of informed voluntary consent by the affected public. Rather, the remedy lies in the development of improved mechanisms of accountability for external and domestic agencies and the democratic empowerment of civic society in countries undertaking reform. In addition, the capacity of countries undertaking reform to monitor and evaluate reform efforts must be developed if they are to have evidence needed for the ethical and scientific review.

In short, to carry out ethical and scientific review of social experiments involving health system reforms – to assess market-friendly promises of the sort we have examined very briefly – we need to develop the following. First, we need to develop a framework that plausibly captures and integrates the ethically desirable objectives of reform and that can, with thoughtful local adaptation, be accepted in various settings. Second, such ethical review requires an evidence base that can be used to assess the appropriateness of the measures or means used in system reforms. Not only must there be a research capacity to provide that evidence prior to reforms, but there must be a commitment to ongoing monitoring and evaluation of reforms so there is an ongoing evidence base to reevaluate what is being done. Third, the tools for evaluating reform efforts must include ways of assessing the key elements of governance that are involved in deciding on reforms, implementing them, and taking responsibility for modifying them if they do not go as planned or expected. I have suggested the benchmarks of fairness provide one way to carry out these tasks, but those benchmarks are a work in progress and no doubt much better tools can be developed as we undertake this task.

2.5 CONCLUSION

Five market-friendly promises, I have argued, are broken promises. America's "market-friendly" system has produced high, not low, unit prices. "Managed competition" among managed care organization only temporarily slowed the rise of healthcare costs, and in the decade and a half since Clinton's universal coverage plan failed, those without insurance have increased about 33% to 45 million. The recent promise that CDHPs will both lower costs and lead to wise healthcare purchasing is a promise in the process of being broken – it is doomed by the very theory its advocates cite. The slogan of competition has led to a cumbersome and expensive Medicare drug benefit instead of the more comprehensive and less expensive one that would have resulted from a better balance of monopsony and monopoly powers. Our "exported" program of privatization and user fees has produced many clear problems that offset any benefits. Together, these promises fail to deliver the goods, and they have imposed significant costs and risks on the populations they claim to benefit.

Does this show that the market cannot serve the goals of justice, if properly modified? No, but it is hardly evidence in favor of the view that promoting market-friendly strategies is the most plausible path to improving the fairness of health systems. It does show that the market-friendly strategies actually being pursued do undercut clear demands of justice for equal access to care and for fair financing of it. Does it show that we fail to draw the lessons from our market "experiments" on population health? Yes – perhaps some have too much at stake to want to draw those lessons. Should we be cautious about such market promises, view them as social experiments with demonstrated risks, and subject them to careful ethical and scientific evaluation? Yes, we should, but we do not. I have suggested one approach to doing so that might make the business of medicine more conducive to both our health and to the requirements of justice.

NOTES

1. US Federal Trade Commission and Department of Justice, *Improving Health Care: A Dose of Competition* (Washington, DC: US Government Printing Office, 2004).

2. Norman Daniels, *Just Health Care* (New York: Oxford University Press, 1985); Norman Daniels, Donald Light, and Ronald Caplan. 1996. *Benchmarks of Fairness for Health Care Reform* (New York: Oxford University Press, 1996); N. Daniels, B. Kennedy, and I. Kawachi, *Is Inequality Bad for Our Health?* (Boston, MA: Beacon Press, 2000); A. Buchanan, D. Brock, N. Daniels, and D. Wikler, *From Chance to Choice: Genes and Social Justice* (Cambridge University Press, 2000); N. Daniels, "Justice, Health and Health Care," *American Journal of Bioethics* 1, no. 2 (2001): 3–15; *Just Health: Meeting Health Needs Fairly* (New York: Cambridge University Press, 2008).

3. Daniels, "Justice, Health and Health Care," 3–15.

4. A. Sen, 1992. *Inequality Reexamined* (Cambridge, MA: Harvard University Press, 1992).

5. J. Rawls, *A Theory of Justice* (Cambridge, MA: Harvard University Press, 1971).

6. Daniels, *Just Health Care.*

7. Ibid.

8. N. Daniels, "The Profit Motive and the Moral Assessment of Health Care Institutions," *Business and Professional Ethics Journal* 10, no. 2 (1991): 3–30.

9. R. G. Evans, M. L. Barer, and T. R. Marmor, *Why Are Some People Healthy and Others Not?* (New York: Aldine de Gruyter, 1994); M. Marmot and R. G. Wilkinson, *Social Determinants of Health* (Oxford: Oxford University Press, 1999); I. Kawachi and B. P. Kennedy, *The Health of Nations: Why Inequality is Harmful to Your Health* (New York: New Press, 2002).

10. Rawls, *A Theory of Justice.* T. Nagel, "Justice and Nature," *Oxford Journal of Legal Studies* 17, no. 2 (1997): 303–321.

11. N. Daniels, B. Kennedy, and I. Kawachi, "Why Justice Is Good for Your Health: Social Determinants of Health Inequalities," *Daedalus* 128, no. 4 (1999): 215–251; Daniels, Kennedy, and Kawachi, *Is Inequality Bad for Our Health?*

12. N. Daniels and J. E. Sabin, *Setting Limits Fairly: Can We Learn to Share Medical Resources?* (New York: Oxford University Press, 2002).

13. N. Daniels, R. Teagarden, and J. E. Sabin, "An Ethical Template for Pharmacy Benefits," *Health Affairs* 22, no. 1 (2003): 125–137.

14. N. Daniels, "Rationing Medical Care: A Philosopher's Perspective on Outcomes and Process," *Economics and Philosophy* 14 (1998): 27–50.

15. Daniels, Light, and Caplan, *Benchmarks of Fairness for Health Care Reform.*

16. Daniels, Light, and Caplan, *Benchmarks of Fairness for Health Care Reform*; N. Daniels, J. Bryant, R. A. Castano, *et al.*, "Benchmarks of Fairness for Health Care Reform: A Policy Tool for Developing Countries," *Bulletin of the World Health Organization* 78 (2000): 740–750; N. Daniels, W. Flores, P. Ndumbe, *et al.*, "An Evidence-Based Approach to Benchmarking the Fairness of Health Sector Reform in Developing Countries," *Bulletin of WHO* 83 (2005): 534–540.

17. N. Daniels, "Toward Ethical Review of Health System Transformations," *American Journal of Public Health* 96, no. 3 (2006): 447–451.
18. Gerard F. Anderson, Peter S. Hussey, Bianca K. Frogner, and Hugh R. Waters, "Health Spending in the United States and the Rest of the Industrialized World," *Health Affairs* 24, no. 4 (July/Aug 2005): 903–914.
19. Ibid.
20. Ibid.
21. V. R. Fuchs and J. S. Hahn, "How Does Canada Do It? A Comparison of Expenditures for Physicians' Services in the United States and Canada," *New England Journal of Medicine* 27:323(13) (1990): 884–890.
22. Anderson, *et al.*, "Health Spending in the United States and the Rest of the Industrialized World."
23. S. Woolhandler, T. Campbell, and D. U. Himmelstein, "Costs of Health Care Administration in the United States and Canada," *New England Journal of Medicine* 21:349(8) (2003): 768–775.
24. Henry J. Aaron and William B Schwartz, "Managed Competition: Little Cost Containment Without Budget Limits," *Health Affairs* 12 (Suppl) (1993): 204–215.
25. This section draws on material from M. Rosenthal and N. Daniels, "Beyond Competition: The Normative Implications of Consumer Driven Health Plans," *Journal of Health Politics, Policy, and Law* 31, no. 3 (2006): 671–685 and I use it with Meredith Rosenthal's kind permission.
26. US Federal Trade Commission and Department of Justice, *Improving Health Care.*
27. K. Arrow, "Uncertainty and the Welfare Economics of Medical Care," *American Economic Review* 53 (1963): 941–973.
28. M. Rosenthal, C. Hsuan, and A. Milstein, "A Report Card on the Freshman Class of Consumer-Directed Health Plans," *Health Affairs* 24, no. 6 (2005): 1592–1600.
29. R. E. Herzlinger, "Let's Put Consumers in Charge of Health Care," *Harvard Business Review* 80, no. 7 (2002): 44–50, 52–5, 123; R. S. Galvin, S. Delbanco, A. Milstein, and G. Belden, "Has the Leapfrog Group Had an Impact on the Health Care Market?" *Health Affairs* 24, no. 1 (2005): 228–233; US Federal Trade Commission and Department of Justice, *Improving Health Care.*
30. Peter Zweifel and Willard G. Manning, "Moral Hazard and Consumer Incentives in Health Care," in *Handbook of Health Economics*, ed. A. J. Culyer and J. P. Newhouse (Amsterdam: Elsevier, 2000); Thomas Rice and Kathleen R. Morrison, "Patient Cost Sharing for Medical Services: A Review of the Literature and Implications for Health Care Reform," *Medical Care Review* 51, no. 3 (1994): 235–287.
31. E. B. Keeler and J. E. Rolph, "The Demand for Episodes of Treatment in the Health Insurance Experience," *Journal of Health Economics* 7, no. 4 (1988): 337–367.
32. Joseph P. Newhouse, "Consumer-Directed Health Plans and the RAND Health Insurance Experiment," *Health Affairs* 23 (2004): 107–113.

33. Stephen T. Parente, Roger Feldman, and Jon B. Christianson, "Evaluation of the Effect of a Consumer-Driven Health Plan on Medical Care Expenditures and Utilization," *Health Services Research* 39, no. 4, part 2 (2004): 1189–1210.

34. Zweifel and Manning, "Moral Hazard and Consumer Incentives in Health Care." Rice and Morrison, "Patient Cost Sharing for Medical Services," 235–287.

35. K. N. Lohr, R. H. Brook, C. J. Kamberg, *et al.*, "Use of Medical Care in the Rand Health Insurance Experiment. Diagnosis- and Service-Specific Analyses in a Randomized Controlled Trial," *Medical Care* 24, no. 9 (Suppl.) (1986): S1–87.

36. A. A. Scitovsky and N. M. Snyder, "Effect of Coinsurance on Use of Physician Services," *Social Security Bulletin* 35, no. 6 (1972): 3–19.

37. R. H. Brook, J. E. Ware, Jr., W. H. Rogers, *et al.*, "Does Free Care Improve Adults' Health?" *New England Journal of Medicine* 309, no. 23 (1983): 1426–1434.

38. N. Lurie, N. B. Ward, *et al.*, "Termination of Medi-Cal Benefits: A Follow-up Study One Year Later," *New England Journal of Medicine.* 314, no. 19 (1986):1266–1268.

39. Meredith B. Rosenthal and Arnold Milstein, "Awakening Consumer Stewardship of Health Benefits: Prevalence and Differentiation of New Plan Models," *Health Services Research* 39 (part 2) (2004): 1055–1070.

40. J. C. Robinson, "Reinvention of Health Insurance in the Consumer Era," *Journal of the American Medical Association* 291, no. 15 (2004): 1880–1886; K. Davis, "Consumer-Directed Health Care: Will It Improve Health System Performance?" *Health Services Research* 39, no. 4 (part 2) (2004): 1219–1234.

41. Lohr *et al.*, "Use of Medical Care in the Rand Health Insurance Experiment"; Scitovsky and Snyder, "Effect of Coinsurance on Use of Physician Services"; G. Beck, "The Effects of Co-Payment on the Poor," *Journal of Human Resources* 9 (1974): 129–142.

42. James C. Robinson, "Health Savings Accounts – the Ownership Society in Health Care," *New England Journal of Medicine* 353 (2005): 1199–1202.

43. A. Creese, "User Charges for Health Care: A Review of Recent Experience," *Health Policy and Planning.* 6, no. 4 (1991): 309–319; S. Moses, F. Manji, J. E. Bradley, *et al.*, "Impact of User Fees on Attendance at a Referral Centre for Sexually Transmitted Diseases in Kenya," *The Lancet* 340 (1992): 463–466; C. J. Waddington and K. A. Enyimayew, "A Price to Pay: The Impact of User Charges in Ashanti-Akim District, Ghana," *International Journal of Health Planning and Management*, 5 (1989): 17–47; S. Haddad and P. Fournier, "Quality, Cost and Utilisation of Health Services in Developing Countries. A Longitudinal Study in Zaire," *Social Science and Medicine*, 40, no. 6 (1995): 743–753; Editorial, "Structural Adjustment Too Painful," *The Lancet* 344 (November 19, 1994): 1377–1378. (Also see *The Lancet* November 12, 1356); G. Tipping, "The Social Impact of User Fees for Health Care on Poor Households," Commissioned Report to the Ministry of Health, Hanoi, Vietnam; 2000.

44. J. Akin, N. Birdsall, and D. Ferranti, *Financing Health Services in Developing Countries: An Agenda for Reform,* (Washington, DC: World Bank, 1987); S. Russell and L. Gilson, "User Fee Policies to Promote Health Service Access for the Poor: A Wolf in Sheep's Clothing?" *International Journal of Health Services* 27 (1997): 359–379.

45. N. Daniels, "Fair Process in Patient Selection for Antiretroviral Treatment for HIV/AIDS in WHO's 3 by 5 Program." *The Lancet,* 366 (2005): 169–171.

46. Daniels, "Toward Ethical Review of Health System Transformations."

47. United States National Commission for the Protection of Human Subjects of Biomedical and Behavioral Research, *The Belmont Report: Ethical Principles and Guidelines for the Protection of Human Subjects of Research* April 18, 1979 (Bethesda, MD: United States Government Printing Office, 1979); Nuremburg Code *Trials of War Criminals before the Nuremberg Military Tribunals under Control Council Law No. 10, Vol. 2* (Washington, DC: US Government Printing Office, 1949), pp. 181–182; World Medical Association, "Ethical Principles for Medical Research Involving Human Subjects," adopted by the 18th WMA General Assembly Helsinki, Finland, June 1964 and amended by the 29th WMA General Assembly, Tokyo, Japan, October 1975, 35th WMA General Assembly, Venice, Italy, October 1983, 41st WMA General Assembly, Hong Kong, September 1989, 48th WMA General Assembly, Somerset West, Republic of South Africa, October 1996, and 52nd WMA General Assembly, Edinburgh, Scotland, October 2000. Available at: www.wma.net/e/policy/b3.htm

48. Daniels, "Toward Ethical Review of Health System Transformations."

49. Daniels, Light, and Caplan, *Benchmarks of Fairness for Health Care Reform*; Daniels *et al.*, "Benchmarks of Fairness for Health Care Reform"; Daniels *et al.*, "An Evidence-Based Approach to Benchmarking the Fairness of Health Sector Reform in Developing Countries"; N. Daniels, W. Flores, and J. Gomez-Juaregui, Benchmarking Fairness in Reproductive Health. Consultation on Health Sector Reform, Equity and Reproductive Health, Geneva, Dec 1, 2004. Available at: www.who.int/reproductive-health/tcc/meeting_documents/daniels_et_al.pdf

50. Daniels, *Just Health Care*; Daniels, "Justice, Health and Health Care"; Daniels and Sabin, *Setting Limits Fairly.*

CHAPTER 3

Are patents an efficient and internationally fair means of funding research & development for new medicines?

Paul T. Menzel

3.1 INTRODUCTION

The level and basic structure of research and development funding for new medicines[1] needs to be efficient – the level neither too high (not costworthy[2]) nor too low (inhibiting the development of costworthy medicines), and the distribution of research effective in spurring the development of medicines that are more rather than less health-productive. In addition, the sharing of the burdens of providing R&D funding for new medicines ought to be fair. In particular, the way that funding is obtained should not allow significant "free riding" – for example, if two populations have access to roughly the same wealth and resources from which to contribute and they gain approximately the same worthwhile benefit from a given amount of R&D investment, they ought to pay equally for it.

Time limited patents address both the need for adequate funding of R&D and the need to make all those who use new drugs relatively close to the time of their development pay a fair share of that expense. If, however, they are not paired with some sort of price controls, patents provide drug companies with enormous economic leverage. The reason is a fundamental economic fact: the demand for many drugs is relatively inelastic. That is, up to some limit denoted as simply "unaffordable," rising price is attended by relatively little drop in consumer demand. Price protecting patents can also skew incentives, pulling resources away from developing medicines that have the greatest marginal health benefit toward those which merely provide a good profit – for example, so-called "me-too" (non-innovative) drugs. In an international context, questions about investment incentives become even more daunting than these questions are domestically. Often the very nations with the largest health needs have the least ability to pay, so that even strong patent protections provide pharmaceutical firms with little prospect of profit from any medicines they would develop for diseases

62

affecting mostly poor nations. Moreover, even when the drugs created apply to conditions present in both developed and developing countries, strong patent rights often keep prices unaffordable to poor populations.

This chapter focuses on the use of patents to procure an efficient level and structure of investment in pharmaceutical R&D, paid for in a manner that is fair and neither allows free-riding nor exploits the requirement of fair financial contribution to a point beyond what can be justified. I will first step back and review the fundamental moral arguments for intellectual property rights, noting particular limitations of those arguments both generally and in the particular context of pharmaceutical development. I will then clarify the notion of public goods and the related principle of fairness that justifies the prevention of free-riding, apply that principle to pharmaceutical R&D, and argue that amidst the current shape of R&D investment, it is highly dubious to claim that "reimportation" ("parallel trade") to achieve lower prices constitutes unfair free-riding against US pharmaceutical firms and higher paying consumers. Two different options for changing current patent protection will then be explored: (1) Reforming patents through limitations such as the WTO's Doha Declaration, specific proposals put forth by Jean Olson Lanjouw[3] and Marcia Angell,[4] and a framework for price control such as that used in the UK. (2) At the international level, partially replace patents with a global "R&D-plus" fund, supplemented with "advance market commitments" to purchase any costworthy drugs that may be developed for conditions affecting poor nations. Along the way, I will make certain refinements of our under- standing of efficiency and fair shares required by the complexities of interna- tional context. I will conclude with brief observations on the relative merits of the "reform," "reform and supplement," and "replace" alternatives for funding pharmaceutical R&D.

3.2 BASIC MORAL ARGUMENTS FOR INTELLECTUAL PROPERTY RIGHTS

Patents are often referred to as "intellectual property rights" (IPRs). The "property" language here is commonsensical when we are speaking of patents as *legal protections*, for the legal protection of an invention that constitutes a patent is analogous to the legal protection of non-intellectual property: others, by penalty of law, are barred from using the property without the permission of the owner. "Intellectual property *right*" may also be useful language in conveying the notion that underneath the legal protection is a moral foundation – the *moral* rights of the party who created what is patented. In that respect, however, "property rights" language is also dangerous, inclining the person who holds a patent to think that the grounds for a patent are the same as the moral grounds for other kinds of property. Arguably, however, the grounds for an IPR are different and more conditional.[5]

The Lockean moral argument for strong individual property rights is that a person's labor, both mental and physical, is the most fundamental property a person has. One's physical and mental labor is a short extension (if really an extension at all) of the very body and mind that constitute the person. When mixed with either freely available, non-scarce resources or material obtained in free and fair exchange, the resulting product is morally the property of the one whose labor created it. There is room for controversy aplenty over the degree to which the material with which a person mixes her labor is freely available and not scarce, as well as the degree to which the product is created by her own labor exclusively, as distinct from her labor on top of much labor of others. With pharmaceuticals and many other cases of intellectual property (IP), we can immediately see one major source of ambiguity: all the previous scientific discoveries and medicines on which a new drug is built, whether those be the scientific work of a publicly funded NIH or the work of other drug developers. Admittedly, those ideas are "freely available," but at least in the case of NIH, they are the result of huge investments of public funds usually made with an eye toward the public benefit that will accrue from the advance that a new drug represents.

In addition, all IP has a feature that physical, tangible property rarely if ever has: its use is not naturally "exclusive." That is, IP is infinitely sharable. By contrast, the use of the pot I make out of freely available raw clay is exclusive – when you are using it, I am unable to. By contrast, what strictly needs to be protected when I have created an idea, not a physical object like a pot? Others can use the idea all they want without diminishing my use of it.

IPRs may still have moral defenses, but arguably they are more conditional – or conditional in a different way – than are the defenses of physical property rights. Given the non-exclusive usability of IP, protecting its capacity for profit would appear to be morally more a function of *the societal need to preserve incentives to create IP* than of any inherent character of its origin. Note, though, how easy it then is, at least with the form of IPR we call copyright, for dissident voices to arise. Based on Lockean argument, authors may have a direct moral right to protection of *acknowledgement* (if others use an author's words, they must attribute the words to her), but an author's right to fees for *replication and distribution* are more debatable. Critics of traditional versions of copyright such as Tom Palmer[6] have noted that authors' incentives to create might be well preserved by acknowledgement copyright without replication copyright. An author may gain nearly as much fame – perhaps even more – by the freer circulation of her works that results from having no protection against replication without the author's permission and royalty payments than she will from tight replication copyright.

These suspicions about the degree of protection deserved for IP do not derive just from noticing, within a Lockean individual natural rights framework, the difference between physical and intellectual property. The suspicions are also utilitarian. Palmer's[7] view of copyright noted above is arguably partly utilitarian, and Werhane and Gorman[8] have noticed, for example, the seemingly utilitarian view of inventions held by US founder Thomas Jefferson (1813): "… ideas should freely spread from one to another over the globe, for the moral and mutual instruction of man, and improvement of his condition, seems to have been … benevolently designed by nature …. Inventions, then, cannot, in nature [in natural rights], be a subject of property."

3.3. THE FACTUAL CONTEXT FOR ARGUMENTS ABOUT PHARMACEUTICAL PATENTS

The moral justification of IPRs is undoubtedly complicated. For one thing, for virtually every utilitarian argument against them, in the abstract at least there may seem to be a utilitarian defense. In the case of the strong pharmaceutical patents currently embodied in US law and much of the WTO mediated international economy, a number of facts are relevant to a utilitarian assessment.

Annual R&D spending worldwide by the corporate members of Pharmaceutical Research & Manufacturers of America (PhRMA) exceeds $30b. Their spending for marketing and administration exceeds $60b.[9]

The cost of pharmaceuticals in the US is 3% of GDP, or roughly 20% of the 15% of GDP spent on healthcare. One-tenth of that 3% – $25b, 0.3% of GDP – is spent on pharmaceutical R&D.[10]

Government-funded underlying scientific research through the US NIH, on which a considerable amount of pharmaceutical R&D is built, exceeds $28b annually.[11]

A high proportion of the new drugs developed with the roughly $30b in annual R&D spending by PhRMA are non-innovative drugs (colloquially referred to as "me-too" drugs). Of the 415 new drugs approved by the FDA from 1998 through 2002, only 32% were "new molecular entities" (NMEs – containing new active elements). In 2002 specifically, 17 of 78 were NMEs, and only 7 of those (9% of the total) were regarded by the FDA as improvements over older drugs.[12] Generally, 10–15% of newly approved drugs provide important benefits over existing drugs.[13]

While 90% of the burden of ill health worldwide is born by developing countries, only 10% of R&D worldwide is applied to the health problems that affect them. This is the so-called "10/90 gap."[14]

Patent protection may increase the cost of drugs worldwide by as much as $400b.[15]

The outlines of this factual situation provide the basis for major criticism of the current use of patents.

(1) Very conservatively, let us suppose that the claim that patent protection increases the cost of drugs worldwide by $400b is very high. Suppose it is high by a large factor, say, of four, and that the correct figure is really only $100b. The market leverage provided by patents to pharmaceutical companies, however, would then still greatly exceed what was necessary to profitably recoup $30b in R&D. Apparently, patents do not need to be as protective of market leverage as they are just to provide the incentives needed to develop new medicines. They do to cover large marketing and promotion costs, perhaps, but not just R&D.

(2) The volume of the usually more basic research that is publicly funded through NIH virtually equals the funding of pharmaceutical R&D through PhRMA. Given the size of the public investment and other drug-related academic research, it is safe to say that most new drugs owe their existence to much more than pharmaceutical company R&D.[16]

(3) Current patent protection encourages the development of non-innovative drugs of debatable benefit. In current US Federal Drug Administration (FDA) regulations and US Patent and Trademark Office (USPTO) standards, an applicant does not have to test a candidate drug for efficacy against an existing drug already used for the same target condition, but only test it against a placebo. Thus, new drugs can gain FDA approval and patent protection though they provide little if any new health benefit.[17] How much of the $30b for R&D is used to develop non-innovative medicines with relatively small (if any) treatment benefits is not precisely known, but undoubtedly it is a significant portion of the aggregate $30b. The incentives are not difficult to understand: capturing even ten percent, say, of a large market for treating a widespread condition can constitute a huge profit even if the expense of developing a competing product is large.

This story, however, may have another side in terms of its economics. Granting patents for non-innovative drugs would have the merit, it would seem, of increasing price competition during the period in which all of the existing drugs used for a given kind of treatment are still under patent protection. While the size of the resulting downward effect on patented drug prices is difficult to estimate,[18] noting its possible presence should leave us wary of substantially reducing incentives to develop non-innovative drugs without entertaining price controls. If patents are retained as the basic structure providing incentive for innovation but non-innovative drugs are not allowed into the market as new competitors because they cannot gain FDA approval, the likely effect would apparently be to reduce downward pressure on prices. The only response preserving the downward pressure on prices in this situation would then be price controls. Other things being equal, R&D invested to develop non-innovative drugs is collectively wasteful – beneficial largely only to the firm that develops the drug. But, without price controls, things may not be equal. Oddly, then, in certain circumstances, protecting investment of a portion of R&D in non-innovative drugs may conceivably not be wasteful (or at least not *as* wasteful as it first appears to be).

(4) Patents do little to stimulate development of drugs for poorer nations' populations, and they may even make matters worse by causing higher prices which in turn make drugs unaffordable to all but wealthy developed nations.[19] For new drugs directed at health conditions prevalent largely only in poorer developing countries, patents do not create much of an incentive since, financially, the prospective market is weak. As for the case of drugs to treat conditions that significantly affect both developed and developing nations, unmodified patents protect the prices that usually leave poor nations with only the empty option of unaffordable medicines. Patents have been largely ineffective in pulling in R&D monies for poorer nations' conditions – witness the "10/90 gap" cited above. Patents themselves may not make matters worse, compared to going without the R&D that patents stimulate – poverty, not patents, is arguably still the fundamental explanation of market failure. Nonetheless, if patents do so little to help address poor nations' health problems, we should look for other structures to provide incentives.

(5) Patents may harbor still another major inefficiency. Strong patent protection delivers to pharmaceutical companies large financial resources with which to conduct aggressive marketing and promotion efforts. To the extent that those activities lead to overuse of drugs or the use of drugs that are not the most costworthy, patents create another element of waste.[20]

3.4 PUBLIC GOODS, FREE-RIDING, AND THE STATUS OF PHARMACEUTICAL R&D

Continued pharmaceutical development can be seen as a collective benefit to everyone who might find themselves in need of a drug, which is virtually everyone. How does current patent law then fare as a mechanism for ensuring that few users unfairly free-ride on other users' payments for pharmaceutical R&D? To get us to an answer we first need to clarify the notion of public goods and the related principle of fairness that aims to prevent free-riding.

A good is said to be a "public good" when it can be easily shared and its use by additional consumers cannot be blocked by normal mechanisms of item-for-item sale and purchase. In economists' language, the good's consumption is "non-rival," the cost of sharing the good is zero, and non-paying consumers have open access to the good in a way that cannot naturally be controlled by its producer. Pharmaceutical R&D, without patents, has all of these characteristics. As an intellectual entity, a drug formula can be employed by someone new without interfering with existing use; the sharing and replication of the formula in other people's minds is virtually costless; and without some sort of access control, many people will be able to gain the essential benefits from the original R&D investment without paying a discernible share of its cost.

Public safety, national defense, and the education of a populus to support a modern economy are regarded as some of the clearest examples of public goods. They ground a major part of state's moral legitimacy in using its power coercively, including its power to tax. Once a certain mass of contributors to the operation of these goods is in place, it is difficult if not impossible to exclude from their benefits an individual who chooses not to contribute to their cost. Therefore the state may coercively extract from everyone their fair share of taxes, obedience, or whatever else is necessary to support these goods.

It is very important in terms of political philosophy to note that this power of the state to prevent people from free-riding on public goods is arguably compatible with individual liberty. The key to seeing this is that a crucial ingredient in the properly construed principle of fairness which regulates free-riding is the preference condition that those who are compelled to pay for the public goods would in fact rather pay their fair share of the cost of its production than go without the good. The moral legitimacy of compelling contribution to pharmaceutical R&D in order to gain drugs' benefits must then rest similarly on a fact of user preference – that consumers of the drug, even with its R&D cost built in, still prefer to have the drug available at that price compared to going without the drug at all. Note that this very condition within a principle that justifies the state's coercive power also limits that principle's power: people who would prefer to go without the good entirely rather than pay their proportionate share of its cost of development and production cannot legitimately be coerced to pay – at least not out of fairness in relation to their own preferences.[21]

The larger principle involved here covers both payment for imposing costs on others and payment of a fair share for public goods. It is sometimes referred to as the Anti-Free-Riding Principle:

A person should pay for any costs she imposes on others through voluntary action that she initiates without their informed consent, and a person should be required to pay her share of a collective enterprise that produces benefits from which she cannot be excluded unless she would actually prefer to lose the benefits of the enterprise rather than pay her fair share of its costs.[22]

Applied to pharmaceutical R&D, several things become clear. (1) Because the development of new medicines is certainly to some extent a "public good," the collective power of the state, through taxes or state sanctioned patents, can be legitimately used to extract fair share payments for R&D. (2) The legitimacy of this power depends on the accuracy of the claim that the persons from whom fair share contributions are extracted really would prefer to pay that share than go without the good of developing the new medicines involved. (3) Any compulsory extraction of payment will only be as good as the argument that what is extracted is indeed a "fair share" for that person to pay toward the public good. On the second and third points, things can get very problematic for strong patent rights for pharmaceuticals.

If a large share of R&D is devoted to development of non-innovative drugs for purposes of profitable capture of market share, those who are asked to pay do not reap a degree of health benefit proportionate to the size of the R&D investment. Also, if patents gain for-profit corporations enhanced net revenues, part of which they use to finance very large marketing and promotion efforts of debatable social benefit, objectors can claim that they benefit little, if at all, from *that component* of the higher patent-protected prices they pay. The public good, fair-share argument for patent protection depends straightforwardly on constructing a cogent defense that what is done with the enhanced R&D funding and other greater revenues created by patent protection is indeed costworthy. Otherwise patent protection is being used to make consumers pay a price premium for what is essentially other parties' benefit – pharmaceutical companies and their stockholders.

In reference to the third point noted above, we also have to ask hard questions, especially in an international context. For a poor nation whose citizens could benefit immensely from a drug but who cannot reasonably afford to pay remotely its patent protected price, a morally fair share of R&D is hardly the same thing as a fair share for much wealthier customers.

Imagine, for example, that a given volume of R&D expense needed to bring a set of new drugs to market is one that wealthier consumers are willing to finance through higher prices – they would rather pay that price, sufficient to cover not only production but R&D, than go without the drug being developed. *Why should much poorer users, however, have to pay anything for that R&D if they do not remotely regard the R&D inclusive price as a costworthy bargain given their meager resources and greater competing needs?* And if they do not regard that price as remotely costworthy, what is wrong with allowing *them* access to the drug at a lower generic price that still covers more than the cost or production for the pharmaceutical company, as long as their access to the lower price does not provide wealthier consumers with an escape from their fair share of R&D? Neither the pharmaceutical company nor its wealthy consumers are made worse off by the poorer consumers having generic price access, and the poorer consumers cannot be construed as preferring to pay a share of R&D rather than go without the drug. Neither the drug companies nor wealthy consumers can justifiably complain that poorer consumers are free-riding on public-good R&D.

We can put this discussion into a contemporary context with some concrete facts about who pays what R&D elements in purchasing pharmaceuticals:

In the US, the over $25b spent on pharmaceutical R&D constitutes 10–12% of the $250b in drug costs, or 2% of total healthcare spending and 0.3% of GDP.[23]

On average, pharmaceutical companies commit a larger percentage of sales revenue to R&D in Europe and Canada than they do in the US. Since European and Canadian drug prices are approximately 65% lower than US prices, however, average level of R&D spending there turns out to be roughly equal to that in the US.[24]

Most countries pay around 1% of their GDP for drugs, regardless of how rich or poor they are.[25]

In developed countries the % of GDP spent for pharmaceutical R&D varies from roughly 0.1% in Canada, France, Germany, and Italy to over 0.3% for Sweden and the UK and upwards of 0.5% for Switzerland. The US is in the middle, with 0.24%.[26]

If we exclude the few countries such as Sweden, Switzerland, and the UK that devote a higher percentage of their GDP to pharmaceutical R&D than the US does, the US appears to be spending slightly more than twice the percentage of its GDP on R&D than other countries spend. Whether that constitutes free-riding by others on US R&D depends on several other factors, however. If, for example, two-thirds of US pharmaceutical R&D is spent on non-innovative drugs and only one-third on innovative ones, and if the proportions in other countries are typically the reverse (of their R&D

Table 3.1 *Ratio of pharmaceutical R&D spending to GDP and Ratio of drug prices to US drug prices for Europe, Canada, and the US, year 2000*[44]

	Canada	France	Germ.	Italy	Swed.	Switz.	UK	US
% of GDP	0.08	0.14	0.11	0.06	0.35	0.55	0.32	0.24
% of US price	63.6	55.2	65.3	52.9	63.6	69.2	68.6	100

spending, two-thirds is for innovative drugs), then the US and other countries are making equal contributions to innovative drug development as a percentage of their GDP.[27] If either the proportion of other nations' innovative to non-innovative drug development is even greater than this or the US proportion lower yet, then it is likely that other countries are actually spending a higher percentage of their GDP on productive pharmaceutical R&D than is the US.

These facts can also affect one's assessment of the practice of re-importing drugs into the US (so-called "parallel trade"). Light and Lexchin claim that the figures in Table 3.1 imply that other nations are not generally free-riding on US R&D, especially when those figures are supplemented by the fact that other countries generally devote a higher percentage of their R&D to basic research and a lower percentage to non-innovative drugs. (Without that supplement, however, the data in Table 3.1 would give credence to the charge of free-riding against the re-importation of drugs from Canada in particular, though not from Switzerland or the UK.) The crux of the matter is that *if Canadian consumers are not free-riders at fault for failing to support the US level of R&D that includes heavy investment in non-innovative drugs, then any US consumers who reap the benefit of access to discounted Canadian prices are also not free-riders.* For neither Canadians nor US citizens is it costworthy to invest in the current level of R&D if a high proportion of it is intentionally used to develop non-innovative drugs.[28]

3.6 REFORMING PATENTS: DOHA, LANJOUW, ANGELL, AND PRICE CONTROLS

One of the observations above has been acted on in the international enforcement of patents: poor nations have recently been allowed to skirt patent restrictions and obtain drugs at the "generic" cost of only manufacture and distribution as long as this does not result in back-door importation to wealthy countries' consumers at a similarly low price. Prior to 2001,

the World Trade Organization (WTO) had come to an agreement on
intellectual property known as TRIPS: the Trade-Related Aspects of
Intellectual Property agreement, requiring WTO members to issue 20-
year patents on all areas of technology. Subsequently, the Declaration on
the TRIPS Agreement and Public Health by the WTO in November 2001 –
the so-called Doha Declaration – moderated TRIPS in a way hugely
important for pharmaceutical patents. It declared that the prior TRIPS
agreement "can and should be interpreted and implemented in a manner
supportive of WTO members' right to protect public health and, in
particular, to promote access to medicines for all."[29] This has subsequently
been interpreted as implying that when there is no market in a developing
country for a drug at its patent protected price, that country may arrange for
production and purchase of the drug at generic price. The patent holder is
not thereby made worse off, for there would have been virtually no sales of
and profits from the drug in the exception claiming country anyway.

To clarify incentives to develop drugs for poor nations' health conditions
as well as to handle the same problem addressed by the Doha Declaration,
Jean Olson Lanjouw has proposed a more general solution: clearly separate
various markets as they relate to innovation incentives.[30] Poor countries'
markets usually do not matter to the innovation incentives of for-profit drug
companies in developed countries. Lanjouw's proposal is then elegant and
simple: stipulate to a drug company that in order to gain patent protection
for sales in *other* countries,[31] it must choose *exclusively* between protection
that will apply just to sales in developed, non-poor countries and
protection that will apply only to sales in poor developing countries.
Where incentives are needed to develop drugs for poor countries and
where an actual market can give real force to those incentives, let drug
companies have patents and allow those patents to protect sales in the poor
countries. By contrast, where those R&D incentives are not needed – that
is, where there is a market for the drug in developed countries – use the
Foreign Filing License process to bar companies from claiming patent
protection in developing countries. Lanjouw's proposal and the Doha
Declaration capture one of the most important reasoned judgments about
free-riding on pharmaceutical R&D in an international context: *very rarely,
when poor nations skirt the higher prices caused by global firms' patents, is it
correct to say that they free-ride on developed countries' investments in R&D.*

Marcia Angell, while her dominant concern is the domestic US context,
has made proposals that can also be applied to the international situation.
First (and in Angell's mind, foremost), revise the FDA's standards to require
"that new drugs be compared not just with placebos but with old drugs for

the same conditions."[32] Second (in my order, not hers), establish procedures that make drug prices both "transparent" and as "reasonable and uniform as possible for all purchasers."[33] Third, open "the enormous black box known as 'marketing and administration'" in order to understand and control its effect on pricing.[34] Fourth, close loopholes in current statutory law that have allowed the FDA to let patent holders gain "secondary patents" that stretch out exclusive price protection far beyond the nominal limit of 20 years, and apply the resulting shorter temporal scope of patents to the international context through TRIPS agreements and the Foreign Filing License process.

In relation to the second recommendation, Angell does not make specific suggestions about the structure for "reasonable" pricing. A good illustration of an effective procedural structure for price control is provided by the United Kingdom.[35] British pharmaceuticals are a major domestic and international industry, with the National Health Service by far their largest internal client. Drug prices are controlled to account for production costs, promotion, and R&D. The system generally puts downward pressure on production and promotion costs but not on R&D. A clear lesson of the British system, in fact, is that price controls can be compatible with robust contributions to R&D. In the 1990s contributions in the UK constituted 12% of world wide spending on pharmaceutical R&D. British drug prices were less than half those in the US, but their expenditure on R&D was nearly twice as large a percent of drug sales – 20% in the U.K. as compared to 10–12% in the US. British price controls have apparently not dampened innovation. It should be noted, however, that price controls undoubtedly will dampen R&D investment if they emerge politically from a determination to keep drug prices as low as possible rather than account, as the British attempt to do, for the legitimate elements of efficient production, reasonable promotion, and R&D.[36]

3.6 BEYOND REFORM: "ADVANCED MARKET COMMITMENTS" AND "R&D-PLUS"

One modest way of approaching a comparative assessment of patent-based and non-patent-based systems for procuring funds for R&D is to ask what would still be problematic, from an international perspective, if all the reforms to current patent structure described in the previous section were implemented. Only relatively innovative drugs would receive patent protection, and patents could not be extended by minor modifications. Some form of price control would be adopted both to mimic the absent competitive effect of non-innovative drugs and to reduce expenditures on promotion and marketing. The Doha Declaration would be applied vigorously by the WTO and supplemented by requiring pharmaceutical companies, when they requested that a particular patent to apply to sales outside their country's borders, to choose exclusively between patent protection in either relatively wealthy, developed countries and patent protection in poor, developing nations.

The result of reining in the reach of patent protection in these ways would likely not be to reduce *health-productive* R&D investment, nor would it be to allow those who would then pay lower prices to objectionably free-ride on the R&D investments of others. These two primary moral defenses of existing patent law against the prospect of such reforms thus fail. One huge element, however, would still be missing: a level of investment in developing medicines to prevent or treat illnesses that affect primarily the populations of developing countries, a level that was remotely commensurate with the toll these illnesses take. It is obvious why that element would still be missing – market pressures are simply weak when there is little wealth behind them.

Four examples illustrate the deficiency of the current situation: the very small shares of R&D devoted to malaria, tuberculosis, respiratory infection, and diarrhoeal diseases. Malaria kills one million people per year. Its proportional "global disease burden" share of the world's over $70b health research expenditure would be $1.75b. Tuberculosis kills two million a year; its proportional share would be $3.5b. In fact the annual investment in malaria research was 1/20th of that proportionate share ($85m), and the annual investment in TB research was less than 1/100th of its share ($33m). Respiratory infection kills four million a year, and diarrhoeal diseases 2.2 million, but research on both combined attracts only $100m annually, again roughly 1/100th of their proportionate combined share of $11b.[37] The explanations of the current allocation of global research funding are several: biases in the attendant sights of developed nations' researchers, the self-interested political constituencies of the parties who create the large public funds such as NIH, and the weak market pull of the communities in the world most ravaged by malaria and TB.

The only way to defend such disproportionate distributions of R&D monies is to argue that health and life are no different than the other goods that are typically most efficiently allocated by market mechanisms. That claim may at first seem plausible, but it rests on a further claim that is much less attractive: that the value of lifesaving in a poor country really is lower than the value of lifesaving in a wealthy country. Both because of the key role of disease burdens on the economy and because health and life are arguably the goods in life that principles of global equity speak to most powerfully, one of the areas in which efforts toward global economic and social justice should first gain powerful traction is health and disease.[38] Amidst all the other areas of articulated concern about global economic and social justice, many of which involve responsibility for shaping wise and effective policies on international trade, finance, and debt, why should international discussion and decision-making attention not focus intensively also on the global allocation of health research?[39]

Thus we come face to face with the need to find more just ways of raising and targeting pharmaceutical R&D, among other health related measures. Two specific proposals to do this come into view: "advanced market commitments" (AMCs) to purchase medicines for poor nation diseases, and a global healthcare R&D fund. Proposed AMCs come in different versions with various degrees of departure from patent protection. A global R&D fund, while generally the more ambitious of these two sorts of proposals, can also have versions that vary greatly in their impact on patents, from a virtually full replacement of the current patent incentive system to a modest supplement to patent generated R&D.

AMCs are commitments to R&D enterprises, including pharmaceutical firms, to purchase any costworthy drug that would be developed for a disease largely affecting poor nations. The payoff to the R&D entity includes not just the later purchase of a drug for populations that could not normally afford it, but a significant R&D compensation as well. In return for this commitment, the drug developing entity commits itself (or, if it is a different entity, commits whoever ends up being the subsequent producer of the drug) to sell all doses of the drug to developing nations at a very low, cost-plus price. Beyond these common elements, different versions of AMCs vary greatly in their deference to large pharmaceutical firms and patent protection. The proposal in the 2005 report of the Center for Global Development (CGD), *Making Markets for Vaccines*, for example, would provide the large pay-off only after a drug had been fully developed, the developer would retain proprietary right to new information and discovery produced along the way, and it would retain all IPRs on any drug eventually developed. Donald Light's version of an AMC, by contrast, is much less favorable to large pharmaceutical firms and much more favorable to smaller biotech firms. It uses multiple payouts for credible progress along the way, allowing the entry of small R&D firms into the competition for the agreements involving an AMC. It also requires the release of new information and discovery along the way so as to elicit constructive collaboration from other helpful researchers, and it involves relinquishing the IPRs that could block poor nations from later selling the drug at a cost-of-production price.[40]

The more patent restricting version of AMCs may appear to have the better argument, but one must keep in mind different possible contexts. If the context is one in which strong forms of most of the previously discussed patent reforms are being effectively implemented, then, arguably, the advantages of Light's more restrictive proposal over the CGD's less restrictive one greatly diminish. Either version, however, would probably go a long way from the current situation toward creating real markets for medicines for the diseases otherwise economically orphaned by poor nations' inability to pay.

AMCs would require some mechanism of international financing to give substance to their R&D compensation and prospective purchase components. Here they connect with proposals for some sort of global health R&D fund, which I refer to as "R&D-plus."[41] Modest versions would supplement existing R&D contributions with a special global need allocation fund to finance R&D on economically orphaned diseases. R&D-plus arrangements might also involve minimum total R&D contribution standards for every country according to its level of per capita GDP. There might, for example, be three tiers: over $10,000 per capita GDP, $1500–10,000, and under $1500.[42] If a country's total public and private spending on health related R&D fell below a stipulated percentage of GDP, it would have to contribute the difference to the global fund, above and beyond any small basic contribution that was already required of all developed countries to get the fund off the ground.

The more ambitious version of an R&D-plus arrangement would virtually replace the patent system with a global fund.[43] Required country contributions would be by percentage of either GDP or total drug sales, and wealthy countries could still "buy up" with additional R&D investments of its own. Allocations from the fund could be prospectively by a disease's proportion of the global disease burden and retrospectively upon success in proportion to the health-benefit contribution of the medicines developed. Obviously such an ambitious version of R&D-plus would involve an organizational structure for allocation requiring individual countries to cede a great deal of their current influence on R&D spending to an international body. In that respect, its realistic chances of adoption in the remotely near future are probably tiny. A modest version, however, is not only feasible but perhaps even highly likely, for it is hard to imagine any significant R&D effort aimed at poor nations' diseases succeeding without it.

3.7 CONCLUSION

Primarily because it allows high expenditures both on developing non-innovative drugs and on aggressive marketing and promotion, current global patent law – especially US law – cannot claim to be either efficient or internationally fair. Clear attention to the nature of intellectual property, to the notion of public goods, and to the principle of fairness that condemns free-riding does not help much to defend current patent law but, to the contrary, strongly bolsters the moral case for extensive reform. Moreover, even with the Doha Declaration's laudable modification of patent protection in poor nations and implementing the most important reforms recommended by Landouw and Angell, fairness for poor nations will not be achieved without another crucial step: some form of advanced market commitment or a global healthcare research and development fund. The requisite versions of those new structures, however, do not have to be so extensive as to replace patents as partial vehicles for generating and allocating R&D funds.

NOTES

1. Hereafter usually "pharmaceutical R&D" (or just "R&D"). I realize that some new medicines might not be correctly referred to as "pharmaceuticals."
2. I use the term "costworthy" of an expenditure in a traditional sense of economic efficiency: when the marginal benefit of an expenditure is equal to or greater than the marginal benefit of expending equivalent resources on an alternative. Often for purposes of simplicity in health policy contexts, the marginal benefits of different alternatives that are compared are all *health* benefits – the analysis is then called "cost-effectiveness." The richer notion of comparison with benefits of all kinds constitutes "cost–benefit" analysis.
3. Jean O. Lanjouw and William Jack, "Trading Up: How Much Should Poor Countries Pay to Support Pharmaceutical Innovation?" *CGD Brief* 4, no. 3 (2004), available at www.cgdev.org/content/publications/detail/2842/ (accessed June 14, 2006).
4. Marcia Angell, *The Truth About the Drug Companies: How They Deceive Us and What to Do About It* (New York: Random House, 2004).
5. For one of the most comprehensive discussions of the intricacies of current controversy about IPRs in biotechnology, including their extension to biologically natural materials, see Baruch A. Brody, "Intellectual Property and Biotechnology: The U.S. Internal Experience – Part I" and "... Part II," *Kennedy Institute of Ethics Journal* 16 no. 1 (2006): 1–38 and 16, no. 2 (2006): 105–128.
6. Tom G. Palmer, "Intellectual Property: A Non-Posnerian Law and Economics Approach," *Hamline Law Review* 12, no. 2 (1989): 261–303 and Tom G. Palmer,

"Are Patents and Copyrights Morally Justified? The Philosophy of Property Rights and Ideal Objects," *Harvard Journal of Law & Public Policy* 13, no. 3 (1990): 817–865.

7. Ibid.

8. Patricia H. Werhane and Michael E. Gorman, "Intellectual Property Rights, Access to Life-Enhancing Drugs, and Corporate Moral Responsibilities," in *Ethics and the Pharmaceutical Industry*, ed. Michael A. Santoro and Thomas M. Gorrie (New York: Cambridge University Press, 2005), pp. 260–281.

9. Angell, "The Truth About the Drug Companies," p. 48. By one frequently cited estimate, each new drug costs $800m to develop. Merrill Goozner, *The $800 Million Pill: The Truth Behind the Cost of New Drugs* (Berkeley, CA: University of California Press, 2004) p. 3 and ftn 16 and Angell, *The Truth About the Drug Companies: How They Deceive Us and What To Do About It*, p. 37. Other reputable estimation methods that attend carefully to *after-tax* costs and other disputable elements involved in the $800b figure, however, put the average new drug's R&D cost around $100m. See Goozner, *The $800 Million Pill*, p. 246 and Angell, *The Truth About the Drug Companies*, p. 40, ftn 5, and p. 271.

10. James Love, "CPTech Comments on U.S. Department of Commerce Study of International Drug Pricing," Consumer Project on Technology, July 1, 2004, available at www.cptech.org/ip/health/rndtf/drugpricestudy.html (accessed June 14, 2006) and Angell, *The Truth About the Drug Companies*, p. 3.

11. Love, "CPTech Comments."

12. Angell, *The Truth About the Drug Companies*, p. 16 and 75.

13. Donald W. Light and Joel Lexchin, "Foreign Free Riders and the High Price of U.S. Medicines," *British Medical Journal* 331 (2005): 958–960. Very recent examples are provided by Alex Berenson, "Lipitor or Generic? Billion-Dollar Battle Looms," *New York Times*, October 5, 2005, A1 and B4 and Benedict Carey, "Study Finds Little Advance in New Schizophrenia Drugs," *New York Times*, September 20, 2005, D1 and D16. In any case, it is important to distinguish "NME" from "innovative drug": some NMEs are not innovative, and in some rare cases an innovative new drug is not a NME.

14. Global Forum for Health Research, *The 10/90 Report of Health Research 2003–2004* (Geneva: Global Forum for Health Research, 2004) and Commission on Health Research for Development, *Health Research: Essential Link to Equity in Development* (New York: Oxford University Press, 1990).

15. Love, "CPTech Comments."

16. For specific descriptions, see Goozner, *The $800 Million Pill*, Chapter 4, "A Public-Private Partnership," and US General Accounting Office, *Technology Transfer: NIH-Private Sector Partnership in the Development of Taxol*, Report GAO-03-829, (Washington DC: US General Accounting Office, June 2003) On the international setting of basic research that leads to the discovery of important new drugs, see Donald W. Light, "Basic Research Funds to Discover Important New Drugs: Reframing the 10/90 Report on Research for Neglected Diseases," in *Monitoring Financial Flows for Health Research 2005: Behind the*

Global Numbers, ed. M. A. Burke and A. de Francisco (Geneva: The Global Forum for Health Research, 2006), pp. 29–46.

17. A large degree of confusion can accompany this matter of what kind of control group is required in the clinical trials to establish efficacy. Representatives of pharmaceutical companies often claim that they test their new products against existing best practice in treatment of the target condition, not just against placebos, and in fact they often do. For basic FDA approval, however, a clinical trial testing the new candidate against the most effective currently approved drug is not *required*. Five types of control groups are considered acceptable: placebo, dose comparison, no treatment, active treatment (tantamount to "existing best practice"), and historical. Russel Katz, "FDA: Evidentiary Standards for Drug Development and Approval," *NeuroRx: The Journal of the American Society for Experimental NeuroTherapeutics* 1 no. 3 (2004): 307–316, 308. To be sure, a company's case for obtaining expedited review by the FDA can be greatly enhanced by the presence of a best active treatment control group, and market leverage with physicians can similarly be enhanced. Moreover, to claim explicitly *in advertising* that its drug is more effective than a competitor's – or even just as effective – a pharmaceutical company must cite studies demonstrating superiority or equivalence, Katz, "FDA: Evidentiary Standards," 313. Nonetheless, a basic designation of "effective" can be achieved with only a placebo comparison. Spokespersons for the FDA, in fact, vigorously opposed revisions of the Declaration of Helsinki that would require comparison with best existing therapies, arguing for the milder standard of placebo comparison because new candidate drugs ought to be approved not just when they are more effective than best existing therapies but when they have milder side effects. Tom Hollon, "FDA Uneasy About Placebo Revision," *Nature Medicine* 7, no. 1 (2001): 7.

    Patents, of course, are a separate designation from FDA approval for marketing a drug. An invention can be patented if it is "useful, novel, and nonobvious." In addition to a drug's chemical composition, its physical form (such as liquid or capsule), and its method of manufacture, patents can be granted for the method of use, i.e., to treat a particular condition. In respect to this last, "method of use" basis for granting a patent, effectiveness studies are relevant and placebo controls become one way to establish plausible use. Generally, with all these options, the USPTO's standards for granting a patent are less stringent than the FDA's for marketing approval. Moreover, while drug patents are for 20 years, pharmaceutical companies have a variety of ways to stretch out a drug's effective life of patent protection considerably longer, including applying for an additional patent on the same drug for a different characteristic (a new treatment use, e.g., despite the same chemical composition). In all these respects, see Angell, *The Truth About the Drug Companies*, pp. 175–82. For prescription drug patent standards specifically, see US Federal Trade Commission, *Generic Drug Entry Prior to Patent Expiration: An FTC Study* (Washington, DC: US Government Printing Office, July 2002). For other material on patent standards, see the USPTO's website www.uspto.gov. USPTO, www.uspto.gov (accessed June 23, 2008).

18. I have found no estimates in the literature of the size of this effect. Some indirect evidence even calls into question whether the competition introduced by FDA approval of non-innovative drugs has any price-reducing effect: classes of drugs with many patent-protected competitors often are among those carrying the highest prices; Families USA, "Enough to Make You Sick: Prescription Drug Prices for the Elderly," June 2001, available at www. familiesusa.org/assets/pdfs/Enough-to-Make-You-Sick.pdf (accessed June 14, 2006) and Families USA, "Sticker Shock: Rising Prescription Drug Prices for Seniors," June 2004, available at www.familiesusa.org/assets/pdfs/ Sticker_Shock5942.pdf (accessed June 14, 2006). One plausible explanation is the power of direct-to-physician marketing based on inflated allegations of relative treatment benefit. Only the presence of robust generics clearly depresses prices. On direct-to-physician advertising, see Wazana (2000). For observations on this matter of competitive price effect I am indebted to Jason Hubbard, graduate student, Department of Philosophy, University of Tennessee-Knoxville, May 2006.

19. Gathei, James T, "Third World Perspectives on Global Pharmaceutical Access," in *Ethics and the Pharmaceutical Industry*, ed. Michael A. Santoro and Thomas M. Gorrie (New York: Oxford University Press, 2005), pp. 336–351.

20. As to what that extent actually is, I make no claims and have located no data.

21. A host of complications can bedevil this argument, including questions about whether it justifies coercion of the individual rather than merely a moral judgment that the individual should pay her fair share. See Paul T. Menzel, *Strong Medicine: The Ethical Rationing of Health Care* (New York: Oxford University Press, 1990), subsection on "Presumed Prior Consent" and the principle of fairness, pp. 29–34 and Paul T. Menzel, "Justice and the Basic Structure of Health Care Systems," in *Medicine and Social Justice: Essays on the Distribution of Health Care*, ed. R. Rhodes, M. Battin, and A. Silvers (New York: Oxford University Press, 2002), pp. 24–37.

22. Within this larger AFRP, the second component addressing compulsory pay-ment of a fair share of the cost of a public good is widely known in the philosophical literature as the "Principle of Fairness" or the "Duty of Fair Play." See H. L. A. Hart, "Are There Any Natural Rights?" *Philosophical Review* 64 (1955): 175–191, 185; Robert Nozick, *Anarchy, State, and Utopia* (New York: Basic Books, 1974), pp. 93–95; John A. Simmons, "The Principle of Fair Play," *Philosophy and Public Affairs* 8 (1979): 307–337; Richard Arneson, "The Principle of Fairness and Free-Rider Problems," *Ethics* 92 (1982): 616–633; George Klosko, "Presumptive Benefit, Fairness, and Political Obligation," *Philosophy and Public Affairs* 16 (1987): 241–259; and the excellent survey of the philosophical literature by John Morelli, "The Fairness Principle," *Philosophy and Law Newsletter* (American Philosophical Association) Spring (1985): 2–4. Note that the "fair share" and "willing to pay" elements in my statement of the principle already include the exemption that would often be claimed for people unable to pay. In their case, either the fair share of payment is virtually nothing, or, with their meager resources, they

would not have been willing to pay to get the benefits; they thus have no duty to pay just because we cannot now exclude them from the benefits. On the general point about not obligating people unable to pay, see David Schmidtz, *The Limits of Government: An Essay on the Public Goods Argument* (Boulder, CO: Westview Press, 1991).

23. Love, "CPTech Comments" and Angell, "The Truth About the Drug Companies," p. 3. One sees conflicting figures on this. PhRMA reports that its companies invest on average 18–19% of domestic sales into research. The US National Science Foundation's data show only 12.4% of gross domestic sales spent on R&D – 10.5% in house and 1.9% contracted out. Light and Lexchin, "Foreign Free Riders."

24. Light and Lexchin, "Foreign Free Riders" see Table 3.1 below.

25. Love, "CPTech Comments."

26. Light and Lexchin, "Foreign Free Riders" see Table 3.1 below.

27. Two-thirds of the US 0.24% spent on me-too drugs leaves 0.08% of GDP spent on innovative medicines. One-third of Germany's 0.11% spent on me-too drugs leaves 0.0733% of GDP also spent on innovative drugs.

28. For an alternate defense of re-importation, see James Love and Sean Flynn, "Legal and Policy Issues Concerning Parallel Trade (aka Re-Importation) of Pharmaceutical Drugs in the United States," March 31, 2004, available at www.cptech.org/ip/fsd/love03312004.pdf (accessed June 14, 2006).

29. World Trade Organization (WTO), "Declaration on the TRIPS Agreement and Public Health" commonly known as the Doha Declaration, November 14, 2001, summary available at www.cid.harvard.edu/cidtrade/issues/ipr.html (accessed June 14, 2006) and Tim Hubbard and James Love, "A New Trade Framework for Global Healthcare R&D," *PloS Biology* 2, no. 2 (2004): 0147–0150, available at biology.plosjournals.org/archive/1545–7885/2/2/pdf/10.1371_journal.pbio.0020052-L.pdf (accessed June 23, 2008).

30. Jean Olson Lanjouw, "Beyond TRIPS: A New Global Patent Regime," *CGD Brief* 1, no. 3 (2002), available at www.iprsonline.org/ictsd/docs/cgdbrief003.pdf (accessed June 14, 2006).

31. Such protection is achieved by US pharmaceutical firms through the Foreign Filing License process. Most countries have a similar process.

32. Angell, *The Truth About the Drug Companies*, p. 240.

33. Ibid, p. 255.

34. Ibid, p. 254.

35. Baruch A. Brody, *Ethical Issues in Drug Testing, Approval, and Pricing* (New York: Oxford University Press, 1995), pp. 234–242.

36. For a basic description of Canadian and EU price control policies that are often quite different than those in the UK, see Daniel Callahan and Angela A. Wasunna, *Medicine and the Market: Equity v. Choice* (Baltimore, MD: Johns Hopkins University Press, 2006) pp. 176–83. One of the different forms is "reference pricing" – used by Germany, the Netherlands, and New Zealand, among others – in which reimbursement levels, but not the manufacturer's price, are controlled. Drugs are grouped by similar treatment effect on given

health problems, and a reference price is established as the maximum for which any drug in a similar treatment-effect cluster will be reimbursed. On-patent drugs are usually grouped with off-patent compounds, though that characteristic is not a necessary component of reference pricing per se; Patricia M. Danzon and Jonathan D. Ketcham, "Reference Pricing of Pharmaceuticals for Medicare: Evidence from Germany, the Netherlands, and New Zealand," *Frontiers in Health Policy Research* (National Bureau of Economic Research) 7 (2004): 1–54 and Reinhard Busse; Jonas Schreyogg; and Klaus-Dirk Henke, "Regulation of Pharmaceutical Markets in Germany: Improving Efficiency and Controlling Expenditures," *International Journal of Health Planning and Management* 20, no. 4 (2005): 329–349. Danzon and Ketcham believe that reference pricing used comprehensively in the US would dampen research incentives, but they do not attempt to distinguish between innovative and non-innovative drugs.

37. James H. Flory and Philip Kitcher, "Global Health and the Scientific Research Agenda," *Philosophy and Public Affairs* 32, no. 1 (2004): 36–65, 39.
38. Thomas W. Pogge, "Human Rights and Global Health," *Metaphilosophy* 36 (2005): 182–209.
39. Lanjouw and Jack come at the explanation of this in a somewhat different way. One of the important elements of an equitable burden is "marginal social cost" (MSC). The MSC of raising a given dollar for investment in healthcare or healthcare research is much higher in a very poor country, for it reduces the well-being of persons there much more than raising that dollar elsewhere. Lanjouw and Jack infer from this both that charging remotely equal prices for drugs in rich and poor nations is profoundly inequitable, and that poor nations cannot equitably be asked to contribute virtually anything to pharmaceutical R&D. Lanjouw and Jack, "Trading Up."
40. Donald W. Light and Joel Lexchin, "Foreign Free Riders and the High Price of U.S. Medicines," *British Medical Journal* 331 (2005): 958–60.
41. The term is borrowed from Love and Hubbard. The proposal for which they coin this label is specific and relatively expansive, not the generic category for which I use the term. The origin of the term is the "TRIPS-Plus" label used for regional and bilateral supplements to the WTO-wide TRIPS agreements. James Love and Tim Hubbard, "Make Drugs Affordable: Replace TRIPs-Plus by R&D-Plus," 2004, available at www.cptech.org/ip/health/rndtf/bridges042004.pdf (accessed June 14, 2006).
42. These tiers are modifications of a proposal made in terms of 1995 $. Lanjouw and Jack, "Trading Up."
43. Hubbard and Love, "A New Trade Framework."
44. Light and Lexchin, "Foreign Free Riders."

CHAPTER 4

The exploitation of the economically disadvantaged in pharmaceutical research

Tom L. Beauchamp

Many media reports, books, articles, and government documents serve up searing criticisms of the power and influence of the pharmaceutical industry. The industry as a whole stands accused of a sea of injustices and corruptions, including aggressive and deceptive marketing schemes, exploitative uses of research subjects, a corrupting influence on universities, a shameful use of lobbying, suppression of vital data, bias and amateurism in the presentation of data, conflicts of interest that bias research investigators, and corruption of the clinical judgment of medical students and practicing physicians.[1]

Each of these charges derives from concern about some form of *influence* exerted by pharmaceutical companies. I cannot here consider the full array of alleged forms of influence. I telescope to one area: the recruitment and enrollment in clinical research of vulnerable human subjects, in particular the economically disadvantaged. I focus on the charge that subjects in clinical trials are exploited by manipulative and unfair payment schemes. I treat three problems. The first is the problem of whether the economically disadvantaged constitute a vulnerable group. I argue that classification as a "group" is a misleading characterization that may cause paternalistic over-protection. The second problem is whether the vulnerable poor are exploited by payments that constitute either an undue influence or an undue industry profit. I argue that such assessments should be made situationally, not categorically. The third problem is whether the poor give "compromised" or non-voluntary consents. I argue that this third problem, like the second, is nuanced, but practically manageable, and therefore that pharmaceutical research involving the poor and vulnerable can be carried out in an ethically responsible manner. Whether the research is so conducted is another matter – an empirical problem beyond the scope of my argument.

Some writers seem to argue that these problems are pseudo-problems in the US because the research oversight system for clinical research in the US protects subjects against excessive risk and exploitation, while demanding good science and clinical promise. If the system fails, this argument goes, then the system should be repaired, thereby resolving concerns about exploitation.[2] This approach is understandable and tempting, but I think overly sanguine. There is no evidence that research oversight systems have a firm grasp on problems of exploitation of the economically disadvantaged, let alone that these problems can safely be dismissed. Moreover, I intend my argument to apply globally, in all contexts of pharmaceutical research, irrespective of a country's system of oversight or lack thereof. Accordingly, I do not assume anything about the adequacy of oversight systems.

VULNERABILITY AND ECONOMIC DISADVANTAGE

Some commentators have maintained that we should not use humans as research subjects under any circumstances; others have said that human research subjects should be volunteers only, not persons induced by rewards to participate. I will assume that neither view is defensible and that (under specifiable conditions) it is permissible to involve humans as research subjects and to pay them for their time and inconvenience. However, I do not presume anything about the involvement of persons who are particularly vulnerable to abuse or exploitation, or anything about levels of acceptable risk. Special protections may be needed for some subjects, and sometimes it may be inappropriate to use such subjects at all; there may also be a need for strict controls on the level of risk allowed.

I will here consider only economically disadvantaged, decisionally competent persons. Several issues arise: Are these subjects vulnerable to morally objectionable enticement into pharmaceutical research? If so, what renders them vulnerable? Do they lack a mental capacity of resistibility to influence? Is the worry that their inability to gain access to healthcare forces them to accept research? Is it that offers of money or healthcare are made that are too good to be refused? Is there something about the level of risk of harm that renders subjects vulnerable? Answers to these questions are understandably controversial.

Vulnerabilities and Vulnerable Groups

Everyone agrees that ethical research requires impartial review to safeguard the rights and welfare of all subjects and that some research involving vulnerable subjects needs special scrutiny. Less clear is which populations, if any, should be classified as vulnerable to inappropriate influences.

Discussion of issues about the vulnerability of research subjects – commonly referred to as "vulnerable groups" – have primarily focused on embryos, fetuses, prisoners, children, psychiatric patients, the developmentally disabled, those with dementia, and the like. Until recently relatively little attention had been paid to populations of persons who possess the *capacity* to consent, but whose consent to participation in research might nonetheless be compromised, invalid, or unjust. Prisoners have been the paradigm class, but the economically distressed are an equally good example.

My concern is with persons who are impoverished, may lack significant access to healthcare, may be homeless, may be malnourished, and yet do have mental capacity to "volunteer" in safety and toxicity (phase I) drug studies sponsored by or managed by pharmaceutical companies. They possess a basic competence to reason, deliberate, decide, and consent. Data suggest that somewhere between 50% and 100% of subjects who are healthy volunteers self-report that financial need or financial reward is the primary motive for volunteering.[3] Persons of this description are certainly involved in some pharmaceutical research in North America, though the extent of their use is not well understood.[4] It is also known that the poor are used in other parts of the world, sometimes in so-called developing countries, but the scope of their use there is even less well studied and reported. I will not here distinguish between the economic conditions in diverse countries in which research is conducted, but I will distinguish between conditions in which it is reasonable to expect that basic healthcare is available to subjects outside of contact with research teams and circumstances in which basic healthcare is fundamentally unavailable to research subjects.

It is often assumed that the economically disadvantaged are more vulnerable to exploitation by pharmaceutical companies than those subjects with stable economic resources.[5] This claim is intuitively attractive, but no data specific to pharmaceutical research support it, and some data in non-pharmaceutical research cast doubt on it.[6] Nonetheless, I will assume its plausibility. What cannot be assumed is that there is a clear connection between economically disadvantaged groups and vulnerability or between vulnerability and exploitation by pharmaceutical companies.

The class of the economically disadvantaged who are vulnerable has sometimes been treated in the literature as narrow, at other times as broad. Those so classified may or may not include individuals living on the streets, low-income persons who are the sole financial support of a large family, persons desperately lacking access to healthcare and physicians, persons whose income falls below a certain threshold level, etc. These individuals could have been in their current situation for many years, but they could also be temporarily unemployed, enduring a family disruption, working through bankruptcy, or fighting a short-term illness.

The notion of a "vulnerable group" has today lost much of its historical significance in bioethics and health policy (first established in the 1970s), because so many groups have been declared vulnerable – from the infirm elderly, to the undereducated, to those with inadequate resources, to whole countries whose members lack rights or are subject to exploitation. The language of "vulnerable groups" suggests that all members of a vulnerable group – all prisoners, all poor people, all pregnant women, etc. – are by category vulnerable, and perhaps also incompetent to make their own decisions. The problem is that for many groups a label covering all members of the group serves to overprotect, stereotype, and even disqualify members capable of making their own decisions.[7] "Vulnerable" is an inappropriate label for any class of persons when some members of the class are not vulnerable. For example, pregnant women as a class are not vulnerable, though some pregnant women are. Accordingly, I will not speak of the economically disadvantaged – "the poor" – as a categorically vulnerable group, though they have often been so categorized.[8]

However, I will speak of *vulnerabilities*. As necessary, I will focus on the forms, conditions, and properties of vulnerability. Ideally, research ethics will supply a schema of forms and conditions of vulnerability, rather than a list of vulnerable groups. These forms and conditions would be comprised of the properties and circumstances that render a person vulnerable as a research subject (e.g., incompetence to consent, misunderstanding the objectives of research, increased risk, and socioeconomic deprivation that breaks down one's resistance to influence attempts).[9]

The Concept of Vulnerability

"Vulnerability" is poorly defined and analyzed in literature on the subject. Many point to incapacities to give an informed consent, whereas others point to unequal relationships of power and resources, such as those between the economically disadvantaged and research sponsors or investigators. The notion of vulnerability in research requires some form of influence either by a second party or by some condition that renders the person susceptible to a harm, loss, or indignity.[10] "Harm" and "loss" are here to be understood in terms of a thwarting, defeating, or setting back of some party's interests.[11] "Harm" is sometimes constructed broadly to include actions that cause discomfort, offense, indignity, or annoyance. Narrower accounts view harms as setbacks to bodily and mental health. Whether a broad or a narrow construal is preferable is not a matter I need to decide. Everyone agrees that significant bodily harms and comparable setbacks to significant non-bodily interests are paradigm instances of harm, and I will restrict myself to these arenas.

The economically disadvantaged are vulnerable in several ways to influences that introduce a significant risk of harm. Their situation leaves them lacking in critical resources and forms of social power, especially access to economic resources and government programs that might be brought to bear on their behalf. They may not be able to resist or refuse acceptance of the risk involved, requiring trade-offs among their interests.[12] What, then, should be done to protect the interests of those who might be abused or exploited in pharmaceutical research?

CATEGORICAL EXCLUSION OF THE ECONOMICALLY DISADVANTAGED

A tempting strategy is to exclude economically disadvantaged persons categorically, even if they are not categorically vulnerable and even if they meet all conditions for participation in clinical trials. This remedy would eliminate the problem of their unjust exploitation in pharmaceutical research, but it would also deprive subjects of the freedom to choose and would often be economically harmful to them.

Nothing about economically disadvantaged persons justifies such an exclusion as a group, from participation in pharmaceutical research, just as it does not follow from their status as disadvantaged that they should be excluded from participation in any legal activity. There is an increased risk of taking advantage of the economically distressed, but to exclude them altogether would be an inexcusable form of discrimination. Exclusionary protections of competent, disadvantaged persons may only serve to further marginalize, deprive, stigmatize, or discriminate against them. Many economically disadvantaged persons believe that participation in research is a worthy and personally satisfying social contribution as well as a means to the reduction of their economic plight. To them research provides an opportunity to earn money in exchange for short-term and unskilled effort, whereas exclusion from participation is an unjust deprivation of liberty and an offensive form of paternalism.

Consider the weakly analogous case of what has long been the paradigm of competent persons who are categorically excluded from phase I clinical trials – namely, prisoners. The right to volunteer as a research subject has been denied to prisoners in US federal policy on grounds of the potential for manipulation or coercion in penal institutions. Were this same potential to exist for economically disadvantaged persons, the same categorical exclusion might be appropriate. However, this problem needs to be examined in each context to see if persons who are capable of an informed consent are not able to consent freely in that circumstance.

Assume, for the moment, both that we can obtain consents that are adequately informed and voluntary and that the research is welcomed by subjects as a source of income (and possibly also as a source of contact with healthcare authorities). Under these conditions, a subject's situation of economic disadvantage is irrelevant. These subjects will be more advantaged by research participation than would other potential subjects, because the money earned will be more significant to them. To exclude voluntary subjects from participation would doubly disadvantage them, depriving them of money in their already economically disadvantaged circumstance.

PAYMENT AS INDUCEMENT: PROBLEMS OF UNDUE INFLUENCE AND UNDUE PROFIT

Payments and rewards such as free healthcare offered to potential pharmaceutical research subjects present issues about the acceptability of inducements in exchange for services. Problems of voluntariness are again prominent.

Voluntariness and Types of Influence

A person acts voluntarily if he or she wills an action without being under the controlling influence of another person or condition. Of course not all influences are *controlling*, and not all controlling influences are *unwarranted*. What, then, are we to say about payments to potential subjects? Are they controlling? Are they warranted?

Three categories of influence need to be distinguished: persuasion, manipulation, and coercion.[13] In *persuasion* a person believes in something through the merit of reasons another person advances. This is the paradigm of an influence that is *not* controlling and that is warranted. *Manipulation*, by contrast, involves getting people to do what the manipulator wants through a means other than coercion or persuasion. In recruitment for clinical studies, the most likely forms of manipulation are (1) informational manipulation that non-persuasively alters a person's understanding and (2) offers of rewards. Critics of pharmaceutical company recruiting practices have accused companies of informational manipulation through withholding critical information and through misleading exaggeration. Other critics have said that offers of money and healthcare are excessively attractive.

Finally, *coercion* occurs if and only if one person intentionally uses a credible and severe threat of harm or force to control another.[14] Some threats will coerce virtually all persons, whereas others will coerce only a few persons. Coercion itself is probably rare in the setting of clinical research, but a sense of being left without any real choice other than acceptance of an offer that one would prefer to decline may not be uncommon. I turn now to that problem.

Constraining Situations

Subjects do sometimes report feeling heavily pressured to enroll in clinical trials, even though their enrollment is classified as voluntary.[15] These individuals may be in desperate need of some form of medication or research may be a source of income. Attractive offers such as free medication, in-clinic housing, and money can leave a person with a sense of having no meaningful choice but to accept research participation. Influences that many individuals easily resist are felt by these potential subjects as constraining.

In these constraining situations – sometimes misleadingly called *coercive* situations – there is no coercion, strictly speaking, because no one has *intentionally* issued a threat in order to gain compliance. A person feels controlled by the constraints of a situation such as severe illness or lack of food and shelter, rather than by the design or threat of another person. Sometimes people unintentionally make other persons feel "threatened" by their actions, and sometimes illness, powerlessness, and lack of resources are perceived as threats of harm that a person feels compelled to prevent. No doubt these situations are significant constraints on choice, though not ones that involve threats.

The prospect of another night on the streets or another day without food could constrain a person to accept an offer of shelter and payment, just as such conditions could constrain a person to accept a job cleaning up hazardous chemicals or sewers that the person would otherwise not accept. The psychological effect on persons forced to choose may be similar, and a person can appropriately say in both cases, "I had no choice; it was unthinkable to refuse the offer."

Payment, Undue Influence, and Undue Profit

In constraining situations, monetary payments and related offers such as shelter or food give rise to questions of *undue influence*, on the one hand,

and *undue profit*, on the other. The "Common Rule" in the United States requires investigators to "minimize the possibility of" coercion and undue inducement, but it does not define, analyze, or explain these notions.[16] Issues of exploitation, undue inducement, and undue profit are inadequately handled in the bioethics literature as well.

Monetary payments seem unproblematic if the payments are welcome offers that persons do not want to refuse and the risks are at the level of everyday activities. Becoming a research subject, under these conditions, seems no different than taking a job offer or agreeing to a contract that, without payment, one would not accept. Indeed, the offer of research involvement *is* an offer of a job or contract in which mutual benefit can and should occur (here setting aside all questions of sanitary conditions, impartial committee review and approval, and the like).[17] But inducements become increasingly problematic (1) as risks are increased, (2) as more attractive inducements are introduced, and (3) as the subjects' economic disadvantage is increased. These are the conditions that should be considered in assessing whether exploitation occurs.[18]

The heart of the problem of exploitation is that subjects are situationally disadvantaged and without viable alternatives, feel forced or compelled to accept attractive offers that they otherwise would not accept, and assume increased risk in their lives. As these conditions are mitigated, the problem of exploitation diminishes and may vanish; and as these conditions are increased, the problem of exploitation looms larger and larger.

As this formulation suggests, the condition of an irresistibly attractive offer is a necessary condition of "undue inducement," but this condition is not by itself sufficient to make an inducement *undue*. There must also be a risk of harm of sufficient seriousness that the person's welfare interest is negatively affected by assuming it, and it must be a risk the person would not ordinarily assume.[19] I will not try to pinpoint a precise threshold level of risk, but it would have to be above the level of such common job risks as those of unskilled construction work. Inducements are not undue, then, unless they are both above the level of standard risk (hence "excessive" in risk) and irresistibly attractive (hence "excessive" in payment) in light of a constraining situation. Although these offers are not coercive, because no *threat* of excessive risk or of taking money away from the person is involved, the offer can, of course, be manipulative. Indeed, since irresistibly attractive payment is involved, these offers almost certainly should be categorized as manipulative.

Undue inducements should be distinguished from *undue profits*, which occur from a distributive injustice of too small a payment, rather than an irresistibly attractive, large payment. In the undue profit situation, the subject gets an unfair payment and the sponsor gets more than is justified. Often, I think, this is what critics of pharmaceutical research believe happens: The subjects are in a weak to non-existent bargaining situation, constrained by their poverty, and are given a pitifully small amount of money and unjust share of the benefits, while companies reap unseemly profits from the research. If this is the worry, the basic question is how to determine a non-exploitative, fair wage.

How, then, should these two moral problems of exploitation – undue inducement (unduly large and irresistible payments) and undue profit (unduly small and unfair payments) – be handled? One possible answer is that if this research involves exceptional (and therefore excessive) risk (that is, risk having more than a minor increment above minimal risk), it should be prohibited categorically for healthy subjects, even if a good oversight system is in place. This answer is appealing, but we would still need to determine what constitutes excessive risk, irresistibly attractive payment, unjust underpayment, and constraining situations – all difficult problems that seem largely ignored in literature on the subject.

As if these problems are not difficult enough, there is a deeper moral dilemma than the analysis thus far suggests. To avoid undue influence, payment schedules must be kept reasonably low, approximating an unskilled labor wage – or possibly even lower. Even at this low level, payment might still be sufficiently large to constitute an undue inducement for some subjects. As payments are lowered down a continuum of wages to avoid undue influence (avoiding making an excessively attractive offer), it is predictable that research subjects (in some circumstances) will increasingly be recruited largely or perhaps entirely from the ranks of the economically disadvantaged. Somewhere on this continuum the amount of money paid will be so little that it is exploitative by virtue of undue profits yielded by taking advantage of a person's misfortune. If the payment scales were reversed and run up the continuum – that is, increased to avoid undue profit – they would at some point become high enough to attract persons from the middle class; at or around this point, the offers would be declared exceptionally (excessively) attractive, and therefore would stand as undue inducements for impoverished persons.[20] This problem becomes an ever more profound problem of potential injustice as the pool of research subjects is comprised more or less exclusively of the economically disadvantaged. (See, further, the section on Background Justice below.)

The argument thus far yields the conclusion that exploitation occurs either when there is undue profit (offering too little for services) or when there is undue influence (offering too much for services). The most straight-forward way to avoid such exploitation is a golden mean that strikes a balance between a rate of payment high enough that it does not exploit subjects by underpayment and one low enough that it does not exploit by undue inducement. If this is right, there is no a priori way to set a proper level of payment – for example, at the level of unskilled labor – because that level might not satisfy the golden mean standard. Payment at the level of unskilled labor rates might themselves be exploitative, either by creating an undue influence or generating an undue profit. The general objective should be that the research sponsor pay a fair wage at the golden mean for moderate risk studies and not increase the wage in order to entice subjects to studies with a higher level of risk.[21] If this mean is unattainable, then any such research will be, by definition, exploitative: either an undue profit by underpayment or an undue influence by overpayment.[22]

If this analysis is correct, there may be situations in which payments that are too high (creating undue inducements) are, *at the same time*, payments that are too low (creating undue profits). To the desperate, $0.25/hr or $10/hr might be irresistibly attractive, while distributively unfair. Critics of the pharmaceutical industry often seem to me to suggest that something like this problem is common in the research context and that pharmaceutical companies routinely take advantage of these situations. If this is the charge, critics of the pharmaceutical industry could turn out to be right. As far as I know, such questions have never been carefully studied, and I have not tried to decide these questions. From what I know, at least some contexts of research conducted in North America do not seem to involve either undue inducement or undue profit, but my argument here does not require such an assumption about North America or any other part of the world. My argument only tries to locate the moral problems and to consider possible paths to resolution.

A conclusion that it is tempting to draw at this point is that pharmaceutical companies are morally obligated to avoid any situation in which the dilemma I have traced over payments cannot be satisfactorily resolved by recourse to the golden mean. That is, companies would be morally prohibited from sponsoring research in circumstances that make it exploitative by paying too much or too little. Critics of the industry would presumably be happy with this outcome; and, I believe, well-off pharmaceutical companies would also be happy with it, because it would tell them where not to locate their research in order to avoid criticism. They would then locate, or relocate, elsewhere.

I am not convinced, however, that this conclusion is the right one to draw. Some moderate risk research seems non-exploitative in adequately supervised circumstances even if an offer is irresistibly generous and choices are constrained – and perhaps even if the company could afford to pay the subjects more. However, supporting this conclusion would take more argument than I have provided, and I will not pursue it further. I make only one comment to frame the issue: An important reason for caution about prohibiting research or about encouraging pharmaceutical companies to pull out of poor communities is that payments for studies are a vital source of needed funds for the economically disadvantaged and a vital way to build an infrastructure and jobs in these communities. One of the few readily available sources of money for some economically distressed persons are jobs such as day labor that expose them to more risk and generate less money than the payments generated by participation in phase I clinical trials.[23] To deny these persons the right to participate in clinical research on grounds of the potential exploitation discussed above can be paternalistic and demeaning, as well as economically distressing.

Moreover, many pharmaceutical companies have the resources to make life better for subjects not only by paying them a decent wage, but by improving their lives in other respects. For example, in some countries research centers could afford to include in their budgets a range of health-care benefits (including ancillary medical care not elsewhere available), financial planning, and personal counseling. These centers could make a tangible contribution to the education and social welfare of disadvantaged persons, not merely a contribution to their financial welfare. These programs too must be viewed as offers of benefits (no different from monetary offers) and therefore as potentially creating problems of undue influence (no different from monetary offers). At the same time, it would be unfeeling to disregard the contribution that such programs could make to the lives of the economically disadvantaged.

A maneuver that I do think should be prohibited, as a matter of policy, is a sliding scale that would raise or lower payments based on an attempted assessment of risk of injury, pain, or discomfort. This maneuver would simply magnify concerns about exploitation. To reward taking risks by offering increased payment would too easily induce the most disadvantaged to take the highest risks; and to take the view that the higher the risk, the *less* one should pay in order to avoid the problem of undue inducement would be to discriminate by penalizing persons for their economic disadvantage. These are morally unacceptable outcomes that should be avoidable by not conducting research with increased risk in any location in which this problem might arise.

COMPROMISED CONSENT

Compromised consent presents another concern about the vulnerability of research subjects, one modestly different from worries about undue influence and undue profit. The typical concerns about consent in pharmaceutical research center either on whether the *consent* is adequately informed or on whether subjects have the *ability* to give an informed consent to research participation. I am not concerned here with the ability to consent, as I am discussing only subjects who do have this ability. I am rather concerned with the process used in the research context to obtain consent and the ways in which consent can be compromised.[24]

The most frequently mentioned problems of consent in pharmaceutical research are undisclosed data, unknown risks, and inadequate discussion with trial participants about risks and inconveniences.[25] Some practices of obtaining consent are clearly shams, where consent is invalid even if a written consent document exists. Consider a paradigm case of this problem: On November 2, 2005, Bloomberg News reported that SFBC International, Inc, a global clinical research and drug development services company, had recruited a number of economically disadvantaged participants for drug testing contracts by making inadequate disclosures regarding the risk of the research. SFBC was reported to have manipulated participants through increases of compensation during the course of the research and to be using illegal, non-English-speaking immigrants fearful of exportation, some being used in numerous trials. The amount of compensation was reported in some cases to be very high (an undue influence), and in other cases very low (an undue profit).[26] If these reports are even half correct, SFBC engaged in a blatant series of violations of nondisclosure, in the manipulation of consent, and possibly even in coercion. This case is without moral subtleties, and all would recognize it as an egregious wrong.

However, there are many subtle and difficult problems of consent, including ways in which information is presented initially and then throughout the trial.[27] Without appropriate monitoring of consent, even an *initially* informed and valid consent can become uninformed and invalid. The appropriate framework for obtaining and updating consent in pharmaceutical research, I suggest, is not a single event of oral or written consent, but a supervised, multi-staged arrangement of disclosure, dialogue, and permission-giving that takes place after adequate oversight of a protocol.

One stage in the informational process should occur at the interview stage when a potential subject responds to an advertisement announcing an upcoming study. Potential subjects should learn basic facts such as whether the study is an in-patient or out-patient study, the study's duration, forms of testing, disqualifying medical conditions, requirements such as age and smoking status, and how eating and drinking are controlled during the study. The goals should be to inform people of what they will experience and to prevent people from coming to the clinic or research center who will be excluded from the studies.

A second stage in the informed consent process should be comprised of discussions that occur during in-house screening and laboratory testing. If laboratory values and other inclusion criteria are met, potential subjects should be scheduled for an interview and physical examination. If potential subjects come back, the nature and content of the consent form should be explained. At this stage, potential subjects should be told about the drug being tested, the route of administration, diseases for which the drug is being developed, amount of blood sampling, unusual risks, etc. They should be asked whether they have understood why they are being screened, and there should be an established way of testing for adequate understanding.

A third stage should be comprised of a session devoted to the formalities of informed consent: disclosure, discussion to increase understanding, and the like. These sessions should be limited to individual or small group sessions, with informed professionals in the room. The goal should be a comprehensible explanation of the study and the authorization form. Potential volunteers should come to know enough to elect to participate in the study or decide not to participate.

Answering questions, eliciting the concerns and interests of the subject, and establishing a climate that encourages questions are necessary conditions of the consent process, which is essential to justified human-subjects research. To fail to conform research to the conditions in the three stages mentioned in this section is to obtain what I am calling a compromised consent. Research that does not meet these conditions seems to me an inexcusable disregard of the rights of subjects, no matter who conducts it or where it occurs.

CONSIDERATIONS OF BACKGROUND JUSTICE

Several issues I have been considering should also be set against a richer background of concerns about social justice. Many considerations of justice suggest that society should take a greater interest in the economically disadvantaged than it often does not because they have become or might become research subjects, but because of their status as exploitable members of society who are poorly served by social services.

One problem of pharmaceutical research is the potential injustice that occurs when a benefit is generated for the well-off through a contribution to research made largely by disadvantaged members of society. Research, as currently conducted, places a minority of persons at risk in order that others, or sometimes only the well-off, benefit. However, how the burdens of research involvement (if they are *burdens*, itself still an underanalyzed idea) should be distributed in a population has never been established in any authoritative code, document, policy, or moral theory. The notion of "equity," commonly used in current discussions, is often poorly analyzed and poorly implemented. Today, it remains unclear, and controversial, when a research endeavor becomes a morally objectionable or marginal form of co-opting the economically disadvantaged for the benefit of the privileged.

Suppose, however, that a corporation were to *target* the economically disadvantaged in its recruitment of subjects and were to use these subjects *exclusively* in its research. This activity raises some seldom discussed questions about disproportionate uses of the economically disadvantaged. It may be appropriate to have selection criteria that demand that the research enterprise not specifically target the economically disadvantaged and that the percentages of economically disadvantaged subjects in research protocols be restricted, while ensuring that research subjects are drawn from suitably diverse populations. This standard does not imply that it is always unfair to recruit (even heavily) from an economically disadvantaged population, only that recruitment introduces problems of distributive justice not covered by the issues considered above. If this is right, then pharmaceutical companies should have policies requiring that they carefully monitor the numbers and percentages of persons who are economically disadvantaged.

One issue is whether there is an upper level of acceptable participation by members of the economically disadvantaged in a protocol or research center. Setting a quota would disqualify some potential subjects, which has the potential of being unfair to them. If no categorical problem exists over the involvement of economically disadvantaged adults as subjects, as I suggested earlier, then why should we worry about numbers, quotas, or percentages? The relevant conditions would seem to be that each individual in a trial, whether economically disadvantaged or not, is physically qualified, does not have a disqualifying condition, gives an informed consent, and the like. If a given individual qualifies, there seems no reason to set a numerical limit on the number of studies in which he or she can participate.

This approach should be taken seriously, but I am not convinced that it adequately addresses the background considerations of justice that should be attended to. Requiring diversity in a subject pool potentially protects against several conditions that might otherwise too easily be tolerated in the research process – for example, that drug studies would be conducted in dreary and depersonalizing environments, that the same subjects would be used repeatedly in studies, and that a dependency on money would set in, making subjects dependent on drug studies for their livelihood. Related problems concern whether it is problematic for individuals to be repeatedly involved by volunteering for multiple studies, a problem that would be exacerbated as financial inducements are increased.[28]

CONCLUSION

Everyone agrees with the abstract rule that we should not exploit the economically disadvantaged in a pharmaceutical research project. I have argued, however, that it is not so easy to determine what counts as exploitation, the conditions under which it occurs, who is vulnerable to exploitation, how to avoid it, and whether certain trade-offs or compromises are acceptable. The recommendations I have made about the conduct of studies involving the economically disadvantaged have centered on vulnerabilities and exploitation. I have argued that while pharmaceutical research need not be exploitative or unjustified when conducted with the economically disadvantaged – indeed it would be unfair to *exclude* economically disadvantaged persons categorically – these problems are more nuanced and difficult than they have generally been treated in literature on the subject. We also know relatively little about the conditions under which inducements are accepted and about whether those who accept those inducements view them as unwelcome exploitations or as welcome opportunities.[29] We need to get clearer – conceptually, morally, and empirically – about the populations involved in research and about the difference between the unethical and the mutually beneficial when inducements are offered to those in these populations. We confront a considerable task.

NOTES

1. Marcia Angell, *The Truth About the Drug Companies: How They Deceive Us and What to Do About It* (New York: Random House, Paperback 2005); House of Commons Health Committee, *The Influence of the Pharmaceutical Industry*, Fourth Report of Session 2004–05 (London: Stationery Office, March 22, 2005), esp. pp. 43ff; T. S. Faunce and G. F. Tomossy, "The UK House of Commons Report on the Influence of the Pharmaceutical Industry: Lessons for Equitable Access to Medicines in Australia," *Monash Bioethics Review* 23,

No. 4: 38–42; Department of Health and Human Services, Office of the Inspector General, *Prescription Drug Promotion Involving Payments and Gifts: Physicians' Perspectives* OEI-01–90–00481 (Washington: DHHS, 1991) and also DHHS, "Pharmaceutical Company Gifts and Payments to Providers," in *Work Plan for Fiscal Plan 2002* (Washington, DC: DHHS, 2001); Jerome P. Kassirer, *On the Take: How Medicine's Complicity with Big Business Can Endanger Your Health* (Oxford/New York: Oxford University Press, 2005); Dana Katz, Arthur L. Caplan, and Jon F. Merz, "All Gifts Large and Small," *American Journal of Bioethics* 3 (2003): 39–46; Merrill Goozner, *The $800 Million Pill: The Truth Behind the Cost of New Drugs* (Berkeley, CA: University of California Press, 2004); Jerry Avorn, *Powerful Medicines: The Benefits, Risks, and Costs of Prescription Drugs* (New York: Vintage Books, 2005); Jerry Avorn, M. Chen, and R. Hartley, "Scientific versus Commercial Sources of Influence on the Prescribing Behavior of Physicians," *American Journal of Medicine* 73 (1982): 4–8; Fran Hawthorne, *Inside the FDA: The Business and Politics Behind the Drugs We Take and the Food We Eat* (Hoboken, NJ: John Wiley & Sons, 2005); Jacky Law, Big Pharma: How Modern Medicine is Damaging Your Health and What You Can Do About It (New York: Carroll & Graf, 2006); Jennifer Washburn, *University Inc.: The Corporate Corruption of Higher Education* (New York: Basic Books, 2005); A. Wazana, "Physicians and the Pharmaceutical Industry: Is a Gift Ever Just a Gift?" *Journal of the American Medical Association* 283 (2000): 373–380; Arnold S. Relman, "Separating Continuing Medical Education from Pharmaceutical Marketing," *Journal of the American Medical Association* 285 (2001): 2009–2012.

2. Ezekiel Emanuel, "Ending Concerns about Undue Inducement," *Journal of Law, Medicine, & Ethics* 32 (2004): 100–105.

3. Carl Tishler and Suzanne Bartholomae, "The Recruitment of Normal Healthy Volunteers," *Journal of Clinical Pharmacology* 42 (2002): 365–375.

4. Tom L. Beauchamp, Bruce Jennings, Eleanor Kinney, and Robert Levine, "Pharmaceutical Research Involving the Homeless," *Journal of Medicine and Philosophy* (2002), 547–564; M. H. Kottow, "The Vulnerable and the Susceptible," *Bioethics* 17 (2003): 460–471; Toby L. Schonfeld, Joseph S. Brown, Meaghann Weniger, and Bruce Gordon, "Research Involving the Homeless," *IRB* 25 (September/October 2003): 17–20; C. E. van Gelderen, T. J. Savelkoul, W. van Dokkum, J. Meulenbelt, "Motives and Perceptions of Healthy Volunteers Who Participate in Experiments," *European Journal of Clinical Pharmacology* 45 (1993): 15–21.

5. Glenn McGee, "Subject to Payment?" *Journal of the American Medical Association* 278 (July 16, 1997): 199–200; Leonardo D. de Castro, "Exploitation in the Use of Human Subject for Medical Experimentation: A Re-Examination of Basic Issues," *Bioethics* 9 (1995): 259–268; Laurie Cohen, "To Screen New Drugs for Safety, Lilly Pays Homeless Alcoholics," *Wall Street Journal*, November 14, 1996, A1, A10.

6. Scott Halpern, Jason Karlawish, David Casarett, Jesse Berlin, and David A. Asch, "Empirical Assessment of Whether Moderate Payments are Undue or

Unjust Inducements for Participation in Clinical Trials," *Archives of Internal Medicine* 164 (2004): 801–803.

7. These problems, including the vast range of groups and populations declared to be vulnerable in the bioethics and public policy literature, are assembled and discussed in Carol Levine, Ruth Faden, Christine Grady, Dale Hammerschmidt, Lisa Eckenwiler, Jeremy Sugarman (for the Consortium to Examine Clinical Research Ethics), "The Limitations of 'Vulnerabililty' as a Protection for Human Research Participants," *American Journal of Bioethics* 4 (2004): 44–49; Debra A.DeBruin, "Reflections on Vulnerability," *Bioethics Examiner* 5 (2001): 1, 4, 7. For examples of treatments of these issues that assume broadly stated – and numerous classes – of vulnerable groups, see Council for International Organization of Medical Societies, *International Ethical Guidelines for Biomedical Research Involving Human Subjects*, www.cioms.ch/frame/guidelines; Ruth Macklin, "Bioethics, Vulnerability, and Protection," *Bioethics* 17 (2003): 472–486; and Laura B. Sutton, *et al.*, "Recruiting Vulnerable Populations for Research: Revisiting the Ethical Issues," *Journal of Professional Nursing* 19 (2003): 106–112.

8. See Ruth Macklin, "'Due' and 'Undue' Inducements: On Paying Money to Research Subjects," *IRB* 3 (1981): 1–6; Tishler and Bartholomae, "The Recruitment of Normal Healthy Volunteers."

9. See Debra A. DeBruin, "Looking Beyond the Limitations of 'Vulnerability': Reforming Safeguards in Research," *The American Journal of Bioethics* 4 (2004): 76–78; National Bioethics Advisory Commission, *Ethical and Policy Issues in Research Involving Human Participants*, vol. 1 (Bethesda, MD: Government Printing Office, 2001); Kenneth Kipnis, "Vulnerability in Research Subjects: A Bioethical Taxonomy," National Bioethics Advisory Commission, *Ethical and Policy Issues in Research Involving Human Participants*, vol. 2 (Bethesda, MD: Government Printing Office, 2002), pp. G1–13.

10. Gail E. Henderson, Arlene M. Davis, and Nancy M. P. King, "Vulnerability to Influence: A Two-Way Street," *American Journal of Bioethics* 4 (2004): 50–53.

11. Joel Feinberg, *Harm to Others*, vol. 1 of *The Moral Limits of the Criminal Law* (New York: Oxford University Press, 1984), pp. 32–36.

12. Cf. Anita Silvers, "Historical Vulnerabililty and Special Scrutiny: Precautions against Discrimination in Medical Research," *American Journal of Bioethics* 4 (2004): 56–57.

13. Ruth R. Faden and Tom L. Beauchamp, *A History and Theory of Informed Consent* (New York: Oxford University Press, 1986), Chapter 10; R. B. Cialdini, *Influence: The Psychology of Persuasion* (New York: Quill William Morrow, 1993); Patricia Greenspan, "The Problem with Manipulation," *American Philosophical Quarterly* 40 (2003): 155–164.

14. See Robert Nozick, "Coercion," in *Philosophy, Science and Method: Essays in Honor of Ernest Nagel*, ed. Sidney Morgenbesser, Patrick Suppes, and Morton White (New York: St. Martin's Press, 1969), pp. 440–472; and Bernard Gert, "Coercion and Freedom," in *Coercion: Nomos XIV*, ed. J. Roland Pennock and John W. Chapman (Chicago, IL: Aldine, Atherton Inc., 1972), pp. 36–37.

15. See Sarah E. Hewlett, "Is Consent to Participate in Research Voluntary," *Arthritis Care and Research* 9 (1996): 400–404; Hewlett, "Consent to Clinical Research – Adequately Voluntary of Substantially Influenced?" *Journal of Medical Ethics* 22 (1996): 232–236; Robert M. Nelson and Jon F. Merz, "Voluntariness of Consent for Research: An Empirical and Conceptual Review," *Medical Care* 40 (2002) Suppl., V69–80; and Nancy E. Kass, *et al.*, "Trust: The Fragile Foundation of Contemporary Biomedical Research," *Hastings Center Report* 25 (September/October 1996): 25–29.

16. Common Rule for the Protection of Human Subjects, US Code of Federal Regulations, 45 CFR 46.116 (as revised October 1, 2003); and Emanuel, "Ending Concerns about Undue Inducement," 101.

17. The justification of monetary inducement in terms of mutual benefit is defended by Martin Wilkinson and Andrew Moore, "Inducement in Research," *Bioethics* 11 (1997), 373–389; and Wilkinson and Moore, "Inducements Revisited," *Bioethics* 13 (1999): 114–130. See also Christine Grady, "Money for Research Participation: Does It Jeopardize Informed Consent?" *American Journal of Bioethics* 1 (2001): 40–44.

18. In some cases, the offers may blind prospective subjects to risks and inconveniences, but such blindness is a concern about adequately informed consent.

19. Procedures performed in the conduct of research protocols do present real risks of injury, and a threshold level of appropriate or acceptable risk must be established. Some have suggested a threshold standard of "minimal risk," which is defined in federal regulations: "Minimal risk means that the probability and magnitude of harm or discomfort anticipated in the research are not greater in and of themselves, than those ordinarily encountered in daily life or during the performance of routine physical or psychological examinations or tests." 45 CFR 46.102i (as revised October 1, 2005). For many adult populations, a more realistic threshold standard is a "minor increase above minimal risk." Published evidence and commentary indicate that most phase I and phase IV studies of drugs present such minor increases over minimal risk. For studies of risks and safety in pharmaceutical research, see: M. Sibille *et al.*, "Adverse Events in Phase one Studies: A Study in 430 Healthy Volunteers," *European Journal of Clinical Pharmacology* 42 (1992): 389–393; P. L. Morselli, "Are Phase I Studies without Drug Level Determination Acceptable?" *Fundamental and Clinical Pharmacology* 4 Suppl. 2 (1990): 125s–133s; M. Orme, *et al.*, "Healthy Volunteer Studies in Great Britain: The Results of a Survey into 12 Months Activity in this Field," *British Journal of Clinical Pharmacology* 27 (February 1989): 125–133; H. Boström, "On the Compensation for Injured Research Subjects in Sweden," in President's Commission for the Study of Ethical Problems in Medicine and Biomedical and Behavioral Research, *Compensating for Research Injuries: The Ethical and Legal Implications of Programs to Redress Injured Subjects* (US Government Printing Office, Stock No. 040-000-00455-6, Washington, 1982; the Appendix to this Report is Stock No. 040-000-00456-4), Appendix, pp. 309–322; P. V. Cardon; F. W. Dommel; and R. R. Trumble, "Injuries to

Research Subjects: A Survey of Investigators," *New England Journal of Medicine* 295 (1976): 650–654; C. J. D. Zarafonetis, P. A. Riley, Jr., P. W. Willis, III, *et al.*, "Clinically Significant Adverse Effects in a Phase I Testing Program," *Clinical Pharmacology and Therapeutics* 24 (1978): 127–132; J. D. Arnold, "Incidence of Injury During Clinical Pharmacology Research and Indemnification of Injured Research Subjects at the Quincy Research Center," in President's Commission for the Study of Ethical Problems in Medicine and Biomedical and Behavioral Research, *Compensating for Research Injuries: The Ethical and Legal Implications of Programs to Redress Injured Subjects* (US Government Printing Office, Stock No. 040-000-00455-6, Washington, 1982; the Appendix to this Report is Stock No. 040-000-00456-4), Appendix pp. 275–302.

20. See Neal Dickert and Christine Grady, "What's the Price of a Research Subject?: Approaches to Payment for Research Participation," *New England Journal of Medicine* 341 (1999): 198–203; David Resnick, "Research Participation and Financial Inducements," *American Journal of Bioethics* 1 (2001): 54–56; Wilkinson and Moore, "Inducement in Research," 373–389; Macklin, "'Due', and 'Undue' Inducements: On Paying Money to Research Subjects," 1–6; Lisa H. Newton, "Inducement, Due and Otherwise," *IRB: A Review of Human Subjects Research* 4 (March 1982): 4–6; Ruth Macklin, "Response: Beyond Paternalism," *IRB: A Review of Human Subjects Research* 4 (March 1982): 6–7.

21. Compare the rather different conditions proposed by de Castro, "Exploitation in the Use of Human Subject for Medical Experimentation: A Re-Examination of Basic Issues," 264, and by Beauchamp, Jennings, Kinney, and Levine, "Pharmaceutical Research Involving the Homeless." See also Schonfeld, Brown, Weniger, Gordon, "Research Involving the Homeless: Arguments against Payment-in-Kind," 17–20.

22. One issue that will constantly have to be monitored is how to keep the offer from being irresistible. This elicits the question "irresistible by what standard?" An offer that is irresistible to one person may be resistible to another, or what one greets as a welcome offer, the other may greet as unwelcome; and this is so even if the offers are identical. How an offer is perceived and whether it will be accepted depend on the subjective responses of the persons who receive the offer. On this analysis, *undue influence* in the acceptance of increased risk occurs only if the person receiving the offer finds it irresistible.

23. See Nik Theodore, Edwin Melendez, Ana Luz Gonzalez, "On the Corner: Day Labor in the United States," www.sscnet.ucla.edu/issr/csup/uploaded/files/Natl/DayLabor-On/the/Corner1.pdf

24. I am also not concerned with situations in which there is a signed and adequately informed consent, and yet the consent is invalid. For example, the protocol may be scientifically inadequate, there may have been an unjust selection of subjects, risks and inconveniences may not warrant the research, etc. I am not concerned with such invalidating conditions. I am also not here concerned with problems of consent deriving from the problems of undue

inducement (controlling influences and constraining situations) examined above. Constraining situations may compromise the voluntariness of consent, but we need not revisit that problem here.

25. House of Commons Health Committee, *The Influence of the Pharmaceutical Industry*, pp. 49ff.

26. Kerry Dooley Young and David Evans, with reporting by Michael Smith in Rio De Janiero, "SFBC's Top Two Officials Quit Amid U.S. Senate Probe," *Bloomberg News*, January 3, 2006. The original report of problems was by the same reporters, Bloomberg News, November 2, 2005, "Poor Latin Immigrants Say Miami Test Center 'Is Like a Jail'." Bloomberg has issued numerous later reports in the case and continues to do so.

27. See Christopher K. Daugherty, Donald M. Banik, Linda Janish, and Mark J. Ratain, "Quantitative Analysis of Ethical Issues in Phase I Trials," *IRB* 22 (May/June 2000): 6–14, esp. 12–13.

28. Paul McNeill, "Paying People to Participate in Research: Why Not?" *Bioethics* 11 (1997): 390–396; Beauchamp, Jennings, Levine, and McKinney, "Pharmaceutical Research Involving the Homeless"; Michael A. Grodin and Leonard H. Glantz, eds. *Children as Research Subjects: Science, Ethics, and Law* (New York: Oxford University Press; 1994): 193–214; National Commission for the Protection of Human Subjects of Biomedical and Behavioral Research, *The Belmont Report: Ethical Guidelines for the Protection of Human Subjects* (Washington, DC: DHEW Publication (OS) 78–0012, 1978).

29. See David Casarett, Jason Karlawish, and David A. Asch, "Paying Hypertension Research Subjects: Fair Compensation or Undue Inducement," *Journal of General Internal Medicine* 17 (2002): 651–653; and Scott Halpern, Jason Karlawish, David Casarett, Jesse Berlin, and David A. Asch, "Empirical Assessment of Whether Moderate Payments are Undue or Unjust Inducements for Participation in Clinical Trials," 801–803.

CHAPTER 5

The dangers of detailing: how pharmaceutical marketing threatens healthcare

Jason E. Hubbard

We benefit immensely from pharmaceuticals. The best of them allow us to live longer, healthier lives. Yet the industry is plagued by sustained criticism regarding its marketing practices. For the past decade the pharmaceutical industry has been the most profitable industry in the US, only recently slipping to fifth.[1] At the same time US healthcare costs have been rising faster than at any point in history, driving up insurance premiums and undermining the economic welfare of American families and employers.[2] High drug prices are seen as a contributing factor in the spiraling cost of healthcare. Prohibitively high prices on life-saving treatments for diseases such as cancer and AIDS have led many to accuse pharmaceutical companies of profiteering.[3] The aggressive marketing techniques that drive the industry's profitability have led many to accuse the industry of engaging in manipulative, deceptive, and exploitative practices.[4] The specific practice of direct-to-physician (DTP) marketing, commonly referred to as "detailing," is the focus of this chapter.

DTP marketing practices target both physicians and their support staff and include advertising in medical journals, small gifts such as calculators, camera bags, and stationary, purchasing meals for entire office staffs, dinners for physicians at expensive restaurants, all expense paid trips to continuing medical education (CME) conferences which are themselves sponsored by pharmaceutical companies and serve to highlight their newest and greatest products, paying physicians to serve as drug company consultants, advisory board members, and public speakers, along with a multitude of other controversial practices.[5] While there have been efforts to limit and discourage many of the most worrisome marketing strategies there is still concern that they continue to undermine the practice of medicine.

Difficulties inherent in the practice of medicine put pressure on physicians to rely on outside sources for information and expertise regarding pharmaceuticals. As a result, many physicians look to interactions with the pharmaceutical industry as a valuable resource for information on drugs and

therapies. This sets up a special relationship between physicians and industry, in particular between physicians and pharmaceutical sales representatives (PSRs) as they engage in DTP marketing of drugs. However, as it will
be argued below, the pharmaceutical industry has exploited these relationships with physicians, utilizing deceptive and manipulative techniques in
order to encourage increased prescriptions. These deceptive and manipulative techniques violate the respect physicians are due as moral agents,
undermine the fiduciary duties of physicians to their patients, and pose a
serious threat to patient care. As such, DTP marketing is unethical and
there is a duty for individual pharmaceutical companies, as well as the
Pharmaceutical Research and Manufacturers of America (PhRMA)[6] and
its sister organizations abroad such as the Association of the British
Pharmaceutical Industry (ABPI), to voluntarily ban DTP marketing.
Despite the hope that a voluntary ban may be sufficient to address the
issues raised here, financial incentives make this an unlikely scenario. If this
is the case it will be the responsibility of governments and regulatory
agencies to step forward and institute a mandatory ban on most forms of
DTP marketing.

5.1 DECEPTION, BIAS, AND AUTONOMY

Before examining the details of DTP marketing it will be useful to discuss
the objections raised against such practices and the moral underpinnings
that ground them. Critics of DTP marketing charge that it is inherently
deceptive, where deception is characterized by intentionally providing false
or misleading information to an agent with the goal of influencing or
shaping their opinion or decision.[7] What is objectionable about deception
is closely tied to autonomy and the idea of respecting persons.[8] When an
agent is deceived selective information is provided to them with the aim of
influencing an agent's decision or course of action. In order for an agent to
effectively make autonomous decisions they must have access to reliable
information. Without access to pertinent information the ability of an agent
to act as a self-legislator is undermined. While they may still set their own
ends, the pursuit of those ends may be frustrated or misguided if they do not
possess the necessary information. Thus, by providing deceptive information to an agent a deceiver may encourage an agent to pursue their ends in a
manner that meets the goals or aims of the deceiver. In the language of Kant,
the agent is not treated as an end and instead is regarded merely as a means
for the fulfillment of the ends of the deceiver.[9] The agent, in other words, is
not respected as an autonomous agent.

Physicians generally pursue the end of fulfilling their fiduciary duties to their patients by making the best prescribing decisions available. As originally articulated as a concept of law, fiduciary responsibility is defined by stating that, "the agreement to act on behalf of the principal causes the agent to be a fiduciary, that is, a person having a duty, created by his undertaking, to act primarily for the benefit of another in matters connected with his undertaking."[10] When applied to the practice of medicine, fiduciary responsibilities require that "the principal focus of medical practice should be the patient's interest. The physician's conduct in the clinical realm should consistently reflect this."[11]

Echoing these fiduciary responsibilities is a well-established and long-standing ethic which places patient care as a physician's primary responsibility. In their *Code of Medical Ethics*, the AMA characterizes the patient–physician relationship by stating that, "the relationship between patient and physician is based on trust and gives rise to physicians' ethical obligations to place patients' welfare above their own self-interest and above obligations to other groups, and to advocate for their patients' welfare."[12] This strong ethic is necessary because of the generally vulnerable position of the patient.[13] Patients seek the physician as expert and must trust that expert to offer the best treatment and care possible. Without proper training, there is no way for the patient to know whether their physician is providing the best treatment for them. Since the relationship between patient and physician is clearly governed by duties of fiduciary responsibility, the patient is warranted in assuming that the decisions made by their physician are made in their best interests. By fulfilling their fiduciary duties to their patients, physicians act as responsible moral agents. As such, the pursuit of the end of fulfilling their fiduciary duties deserves respect. Therefore, any act that unacceptably interferes with the physician's capacity to act as a moral agent in the pursuit of fulfilling their fiduciary duties shows an unacceptable lack of respect for physicians as moral agents.

Within this context, if the physician has inaccurate information about the effectiveness of a treatment or the advantages/disadvantages between two competing treatments, the physician may make a prescribing decision that is not in the best interests of her patient. Thus, while the physician has made a rational decision based on the ends she has set for herself, her effectiveness in achieving that end has been undermined by the inaccuracy of the information she has based the decision on. However, physicians never have perfect access to information and their goals may often be frustrated by this fact. What makes deception morally objectionable is that the information the physician relies on in making her decision has been purposefully distorted in the aim of increased prescribing of a particular drug. Since one of the elements necessary for the physician to effectively operate as a moral agent has been denied her, the purposeful distortion of information shows an inherent lack of respect for the physician as a moral agent. Thus, deception violates the negative duty of noninterference derived from respect for persons.[14]

The industry characterizes and defends DTP marketing as primarily an educative endeavor. In their "Code of Interactions with Health care Professionals," PhRMA states that, "Informational presentations and discussions by industry representatives and others speaking on behalf of a company provide valuable scientific and educational benefits."[15] They go on to claim that, "Interactions should be focused on informing healthcare professionals about products, providing scientific and educational information, and supporting medical research and education."[16] Similarly, the ABPI states that, "Information, claims, and comparisons must be accurate, balanced, fair, objective and unambiguous and must be based on an up-to-date evaluation of all the evidence and reflect that evidence clearly. They must not mislead either directly or by implication, by distortion, exaggeration or undue emphasis."[17]

Despite claims to the contrary made by the industry, it is commonly accepted that interactions with PSRs are not the reliable, educative exchanges they are touted as. Numerous articles from the UK, Canada, and the US discuss the problems inherent in utilizing information provided by PSRs, all recognizing that information provided is not likely to be balanced or fair.[18] This perception of what is actually provided in exchanges with PSRs has led to many articles aimed at providing guidance to physicians in an attempt to help them separate the useful information from that which is biased and unreliable.[19] Nearly universal acknowledgement within the medical community that information provided by PSRs is not balanced and reliable provides strong circumstantial evidence that the true priority of PSRs is the selling of a product, not educating physicians.

Beyond a predominance of opinion within the profession and the literature several studies have attempted to objectively determine the accuracy and reliability of information provided by PSRs. Elina Hemminki conducted two Finnish studies in which she analyzed information provided by PSRs.[20] Both studies found indications of strong bias and often times dangerous omissions of side-effects and contraindications.[21] A third US study was conducted in 1995 by Ziegler et al.,[22] with 11% of the statements analyzed considered inaccurate and finding similar indications of bias.[23] Raising even more concern is the fact that the presentations analyzed in the

Ziegler *et al.* study were given to a group, including at least one faculty physician, and the PSRs knew they were being recorded. As a result, it seems likely that the findings of the US study may underestimate the bias and inaccuracy of exchanges that take place in a more private setting.

The relevance of the Hemminki studies may be disputed both because of their age and the fact that they took place exclusively in Finland. Yet, despite the fact that the studies were conducted in Finland the pharmaceutical companies represented were multinational corporations with operations in most industrialized nations. It seems reasonable that these corporations would hold their PSRs to the same standards in each country they operate in. Certainly, codes of conduct concerning interactions with healthcare professionals are meant to apply universally to all employees of these multinational corporations, with the only exception being when local laws are more restrictive than the policies outlined in the codes. As for concerns over the age of the studies, these objections may be mitigated by the fact that each successively more recent study seems to substantiate the conclusions of the earlier studies. Finally, the fact that the Ziegler et al. study was conducted in the United States with similar findings to the two earlier Finnish studies helps to assuage concerns that the findings are unique to Finland.

There is also reason to be concerned that PSRs may not be sufficiently educated to provide the reliable information that it seems reasonable to expect them to provide. Carl Elliott has highlighted this issue in discussing what is apparently a common sentiment of PSRs. Elliot quotes one PSR as saying that "Reps are the last to know [about potential problems with their drugs]."[24] Concerns over the knowledge possessed by PSRs are mirrored in another study conducted by Hemminki in which she tested PSRs' knowledge of clinical trials and tetrogenicity, with a mean average of correct answers on the test of 62%.[25] Hemminki also found that there was a tendency to emphasize capabilities as a salesperson over technical knowledge and education in advertisements for job openings for PSR positions.

Not only does evidence suggest that the information provided by PSRs is unreliable, but there is also a great deal of evidence that clearly links DTP marketing to prescribing practices that threaten the care of patients. Studies suggest that prescribing decisions are often based on the influencing factors of PSRs instead of being based on concern for which therapy options may best serve the patient.[26] These findings substantiate the concerns raised above about the deceptive nature of interactions between pharmaceutical reps and physicians. If information was reliable and unbiased it is reasonable to assume that such pervasive, negative effects would not be so overwhelmingly associated with interactions between physicians and PSRs. It is also clear that the practice of DTP marketing negatively impacts quality of care through improper prescribing, excessive prescribing, and the early adoption of newer, less proven, and possibly more dangerous medications.[27]

Within this context Newcomer notes that, "researchers studying elderly patients found that 38 percent of those who received antidepressants, 19 percent who received oral hypoglycemics, 18 percent who received sedatives, and 13 percent who received nonsteroidal anti-inflammatory drugs (NSAIDs) were given a potentially inappropriate drug."[28] As DTP marketing has clearly been shown to negatively affect prescribing it bears much of the responsibility for such findings. Further, DTP marketing is highly effective at encouraging physicians to quickly adopt new, more expensive medications. Enthusiastic adoption of new pharmaceuticals raises serious safety concerns. Since harmful side-effects are often not identified until a drug has been on the market for several years, a policy of cautious, gradual adoption instead of rapid prescribing of new pharmaceuticals seems to be the best strategy from the perspective of patient care.[29]

An example that illustrates this problem is the heavy prescribing of Cox-2 arthritis medications. These are drugs that were heavily promoted both to physicians and directly to consumers in the US. However, "studies show that the medicines are not more effective for pain relief than their predecessors were."[30] Their only advantage over standard aspirin for the relief of pain is their presumed decrease in the occurrence of stomach ulcers. Yet, "UnitedHealth Group pharmacy data show[s] that Cox-2 drugs now account for 40 percent of all prescription costs in this class, but only 14 percent of patients receiving the drugs have arthritis."[31] The concern over such rapid adoption of a new therapy is highlighted by the heavily covered case of the withdrawal of Vioxx, a Cox-2 drug, from the market by Merck in 2004 after it was linked to increases in heart attack and stroke. If the data from UnitedHealth Group is any indication, many of those who were placed at risk or suffered adverse side-effects from Vioxx did so when they had no medical need for the drug or an existing therapy would have proven just as effective.

While exchanges between physicians and PSRs are difficult to assess there is a preponderance of circumstantial evidence that indicates that what is provided is far from the fair, balanced, educative exchange that the industry defends it as being. Further, the handful of empirical studies that do exist that have attempted to assess the reliability of information provided by PSRs provide corroborating evidence in support of the conclusion that exchanges with PSRs are unreliable and biased. Finally, there is a substantial body of evidence that strongly correlates worrisome changes in prescribing behavior with interactions with PSRs. As a result, it seems clear that while claiming to provide reliable educative material to physicians, PSRs in fact provide unreliable and biased information. Further, physicians who are exposed to this unreliable information show a substantial increase in improper prescribing decisions regarding their patients.

The deceptive tactics utilized in exchanges with physicians directly interferes with their ability to fulfill their fiduciary duties in making the best prescribing decisions for their patients. Through exposure to deceptive and biased information physicians will often times make prescribing decisions based on this tainted information. As a result, they will not make the best prescribing decisions for their patients, in violation of their fiduciary duties. Since deceptive and biased marketing interferes with physicians' ability to pursue the end of providing the best care for their patients, such tactics do not show physicians the respect they deserve as moral agents. As a result, the deceptive techniques employed are immoral and there is a moral imperative to cease such exchanges.

5.2 PHYSICIANS AS CONTEXTUALLY VULNERABLE

Is not all marketing to some degree deceptive? Market exchanges are competitive in nature and market clients[32] bear a responsibility to educate themselves about the products and services they purchase.[33] The responsibility that market clients bear means that generally marketing may not have to be entirely honest and transparent. Market clients understand that claims made by marketers should not be taken at face value and resources exist for clients to educate themselves and the responsibility to do so is implicit in market exchanges. As a result, under proper market conditions persuasive marketing may not constitute a violation of the principle of respect for persons. Since the client knows her responsibilities in the exchange and has the opportunity to correct the influence of marketers by educating herself about a purchase, such techniques do not constitute an unacceptable influence and does not violate an agent's ability to operate as a rational moral agent. In fact, by providing information about new products and highlighting features or advantages of certain products a savvy market client may in fact benefit from exposure to marketing. While one might agree with that assessment of most marketing, it is not my goal here to comment on marketing in general and its relationship to autonomy. Instead my claim is that many physicians are particularly vulnerable to influence by PSRs and that the relationship between physicians and PSRs is a special circumstance that imposes distinct obligations and restrictions on their exchanges.

While not generally considered a vulnerable population, physicians are vulnerable within the context of the marketing of pharmaceuticals.[34] Complicated or technical products place market clients in a particularly vulnerable position as they are generally at an informational disadvantage. As such, they may not be capable of effectively assessing information provided. In such circumstances a market client who would generally not be considered vulnerable may find it difficult to protect their interests and may be particularly vulnerable to the influence of marketers. In the case of pharmaceuticals physicians are properly understood as market clients because they are responsible for prescribing decisions. Due to the dangerous and technical nature of pharmaceuticals patients are not considered competent to make decisions regarding medications. As a result, due to their training and expertise physicians make prescribing decisions for the patients they represent, effectively operating as a proxy market client.

While subject to stringent standards of education and training, physicians are also forced to manage busy schedules and must juggle a multitude of obligations. As the cost of care continues to rise and cost containment measures are implemented in order to stall out of control spending, physicians often feel this impact. As a result, physicians are forced to find ways to cope with ever increasing patient loads. As the demands on physicians' time continues to increase, physicians find themselves with less time to spend with individual patients and on other aspects crucial to their work, including educating themselves on new healthcare products and treatments.[35] Beyond increasing demands on their time physicians must contend with growing numbers of drugs, therapies, and treatments. As a result, physicians must endeavor to educate themselves on an ever changing body of information regarding a multitude of different diseases and their treatments, of which pharmaceuticals are a key component.[36]

The problem is compounded by the fact that some physicians generally have a rather limited knowledge of pharmacology, in particular general practitioners.[37] In fact, often the only working knowledge of pharmacology that general practitioners possess beyond that learned in basic medical school courses comes from professional articles, continuing medical education (CME) sessions, and encounters with PSRs. Further, in some schools clinical pharmacology has been phased out in favor of more modern studies such as molecular biology and in some instances (including Harvard Medical School) entire pharmacology departments have been shut down with its function folded into other departments.[38] Thus, despite the fact that physicians are highly educated, for certain groups of physicians there is often a significant deficiency in their knowledge of pharmacology.

Additionally, new pharmaceuticals are generally the most aggressively marketed. As such, the physician may have little or no exposure to, or working knowledge of the mechanics or characteristics of the new product. This raises concern over whether the physician may have enough information to ask the right questions and effectively fill in gaps left by inaccurate or biased information. Further, a PSR characteristically markets only one specific product, or at most a select handful of products. Thus, the expectation that the PSR is capable of reviewing and educating themselves on all of the pertinent information about a product is not unreasonable. However, due to their schedules and the multitude of products and therapies that they must educate themselves about, the expectation that a physician has the time and capacity to independently research and become an expert on each product she utilizes is often unrealistic.

There is also disturbing evidence that much of the empirical information that physicians have access to may be biased and unreliable. Increasing numbers of pharmaceutical companies[39] are coming under scrutiny and facing criticism for withholding or hiding lab data indicating dangers or problems associated with particular drugs.[40] Similarly, many academic journals have been criticized for publishing biased articles and several have begun instituting more stringent standards regarding the disclosure of ties with industry, often requiring studies funded by industry to undergo additional reviews by an independent third party.[41]

Additionally, two recent studies have found evidence that comparative drug trials sponsored by pharmaceutical companies often utilize special techniques in order to tweak the results of the study in the favor of the sponsoring company's product.[42] An American study by Daniel Safer identified thirteen distinct mechanisms[43] that were utilized to tailor studies to benefit the sponsoring company's drug while a Swedish study by Hans Melander, *et al.*, found three.[44] The result is that "an estimated 89 to 98% of comparative drug treatment studies funded by pharmaceutical companies yield results that are favorable to their company's product."[45]

So while physicians are increasingly forced to rely on opinions and information provided by others to help inform and guide their decisions they have access to quite limited resources to assess them by. As pharmaceuticals are inherently dangerous, prescribing decisions that are made based on the influence of marketing by PSRs carry a significant risk of harm. The risk of harm to patients is obvious; however, by eroding the trust that is foundational to the patient–physician relationship the damage done by prescribing treatments that are not in the best interests of patients is significant for physicians as well.

The risk of harm involved in marketing to vulnerable groups entails that marketers must adjust their marketing strategies and techniques in order to avoid unfairly taking advantage of the vulnerabilities of market clients.[46] In order to fairly market to physicians PSRs must provide accurate and unbiased information. To provide biased or inaccurate information would take unfair advantage of the vulnerability that stems from the informational asymmetry that exists between physicians and PSRs. As discussed above, deceptive or biased marketing may not be problematic in certain circumstances because market clients are aware of the need to educate themselves about the claims made by marketers and have the ability to do so. However, in the case of pharmaceuticals the complexity of the product and the limited ability of some physicians to assess claims made about the product precludes them, as market clients, from operating in this manner. This is especially so when one considers that much of the information that physicians can turn to in an attempt to educate themselves about a product may itself be unreliable and biased. Since many physicians may not be sufficiently capable of critically assessing the information provided in marketing exchanges with PSRs they are not capable of protecting their interests, nor the interests of the patients they represent. Physicians who are not capable of assessing the claims made by PSRs will often be deceived by inaccurate or biased information. As a result, they will make prescribing decisions based on tainted information instead of accurate and reliable information.

When one considers the principle of respect for persons, it is clear why it is an ethical duty for PSRs to provide information that is accurate and unbiased. By providing inaccurate or biased information PSRs deceive physicians and undermine their capacity to provide the best care to their patients. As argued above, since physicians properly act as moral agents when they pursue the fulfillment of their fiduciary duties they are due respect. In order to respect physicians as they endeavor to provide the best care to their patients PSRs must refrain from interfering with the pursuit of that end. Since deceptive and biased marketing interferes with physicians' capacity to provide the best care for their patients this does not show physicians the respect they are due. Thus, in the case of marketing of pharmaceuticals the provision of inaccurate or biased information does pose an unacceptable violation of the principle of respect for persons.

5.3 MANIPULATION AND GIFT GIVING

Beyond charges of deception regarding the practices surrounding DTP marketing, many have criticized the industry for utilizing measures that are inherently manipulative. While distinct concepts, manipulation is objectionable on similar grounds to that of deception. Manipulation consists of the purposeful utilization of generally unconscious or subconscious influences on our character or natural predispositions to achieve the aim or goal of the manipulator.[47] While we strive to make rational decisions, people are notoriously susceptible to non-rational influences. Often these influences may come to interfere with our ability to make a properly rational decision. While such influences constantly bombard and affect agents, it is the intentional nature of manipulation that is objectionable. When a manipulator plays on a physiological or psychological feature of one's makeup or personality with the aim of influencing an agent, that agent's ability to make a rational decision regarding the determination and pursuit of their ends is undermined. Instead of making a decision based on their rational assessment of what end to pursue and the proper means by which to pursue it, the agent will instead make a decision based on those influences. By intentionally playing on those characteristics a manipulator undermines the ability of that agent to make a rational decision. Since the rational nature of an agent is what allows her to operate as a lawgiver to herself in the realm of ends this shows an inherent lack of respect for that agent. The agent is treated as a means to the end of the manipulator as manipulative techniques are utilized to drive an agent towards the desired end. As such, due to the actions of the manipulator the agent is not truly free to set and pursue her own ends, but instead chooses an end and the means to pursue it largely based on the influences of the manipulator. Within the context of DTP marketing, if meals purchased and gifts provided by pharmaceutical companies can be shown to play on certain characteristics of physicians and influence their goal of making the best prescribing decision in the interests of their patients then this shows an inherent lack of respect for physicians as moral agents.

Stories abound detailing the extravagant gifts given to physicians by pharmaceutical companies.[48] Physicians are taken to meals at plush restaurants, treated to hard to get tickets to sold out events, provided all expense paid vacations at exotic locations, and even given gift cards and cash in exchange for attending sessions.[49] As accounts of these often time outlandish gifts gained attention in the United States, Congress began to consider legislation to govern interactions between industry and healthcare professionals. In response PhRMA, individual pharmaceutical companies, and the American Medical Association (AMA) voluntarily adopted guidelines that severely restricted the practice of gift giving.[50] Under those guidelines gifts are restricted to "items primarily for the benefit of patients" with a value of less than $100 and "items of minimal value … primarily associated with a healthcare professional's practice (such as pens, notepads, and similar "reminder" items with company or product logos)."[51] Additionally tickets to recreational events have been banned and restrictions have been placed on meals.[52]

However, in response to sustained criticism regarding the continued giving of gifts PhRMA has passed new guidelines that went into effect in January of 2009. These guidelines still allow for the purchasing of meals for physicians and their staff but restrict such meals to those which may be provided in the physician's office or the hospital. Additionally, the new guidelines have banned the giving of small promotional gifts such as note-pads and pens.[53] While PhRMA still contends that such exchanges are not manipulative in nature and that their primary motivation is to remove the "perception" of impropriety, it will be shown that these practices are in fact inherently manipulative. Whether PhRMA's motivations are self-serving or a true recognition of the issues raised in this chapter, PhRMA deserves a degree of praise for this proactive step in addressing these concerns.

On the other side of the Atlantic similar measures to PhRMA's 2002 guidelines have been taken in the UK. In 2005 the British House of Commons released a report on the influence of the pharmaceutical indus-try,[54] which was quickly followed by an additional report delivered to Parliament.[55] The two combined reports served to highlight concerns over an industry with increasingly pervasive influence within the UK. The result has been the release of a new ABPI code of practice.[56] The ABPI guidelines are similar to those currently endorsed by PhRMA and the AMA, with the primary difference being that gifts are restricted to no more than £6.

However, despite these attempts at self-regulation there is evidence that PSRs are violating their own guidelines and that physicians are still accept-ing gifts and meals that these guidelines ban.[57] As a result, in some instances even the most outlandish gifts continue to be provided despite the new guidelines. Further, many critics are highly skeptical about the effectiveness of PhRMA's newly published marketing code of ethics.[58] Each of these critics points out that PhRMA's guidelines are merely suggestions and carry no punishments for firms that disobey them. A troubling indication that these reforms are primarily intended as a public relations effort and not truly intended to discourage the practices the new guidelines address is PhRMA's intensive lobbying efforts against legislation in Massachusetts intended to legally ban all gifts to physicians, including fines of up to $5,000 for violations.[59] PhRMA's vehement opposition to this legislation stands in stark contrast to their efforts to discourage these very same practices within their new voluntary guidelines. Additionally, the ability of these voluntary guidelines to discourage the practices in question is further undermined by a statement released by the Prescription Project, a Boston-based national coalition of groups that monitors pharmaceutical marketing, which notes that "promotional spending by the pharmaceutical industry has increased since PhRMA adopted its first guidelines on gifts in 2002."[60] It seems reasonable to believe that if these guidelines were truly effective at curbing the worrisome practices in question, a decrease in promotional spending would be seen instead of an increase. However, as full analysis of these findings has yet to be undertaken and a myriad of additional elements may play a role such conclusions are circumstantial at best. Still there is strong reason to be skeptical as to both the motivations of PhRMA and the likely effectiveness of these guidelines. As a result, even with the passage of PhRMA's new guidelines the analysis of these practices that follows will still be important in determining the potential need for more stringent policies which include penalties for non-compliance.

The concern with very large gifts such as all expense paid vacations and cash gifts is that they resemble bribery. Physicians are given expensive and extravagant gifts in exchange for prescribing the drug being promoted. Clearly cases where physicians are given kickbacks in exchange for increased prescription rates are an instance of bribery. However, in the case of very large gifts the size and value of the gift clearly implies that the reciprocity of the relationship is understood by both parties. As a result, even if the expectation is not explicit and the gift is given merely in the expectation that the physician will increase prescribing, such cases are reasonably characterized as instances of bribery.

By accepting a bribe physicians make prescribing decisions in reciproca-tion for the gift received in violation of their fiduciary duties to their patients. Additionally, by offering a bribe a PSR encourages a physician to violate her fiduciary duties. As such, the PSR becomes complicit in the violation of those obligations. Additionally, the offering of a bribe consti-tutes an unacceptable inducement, and by attempting to undermine the end of fulfilling her fiduciary duties, does not show appropriate respect for the physician as moral agent. Thus, the giving of expensive and extravagant gifts is unacceptable and there are good reasons to ban them.

What about the small gifts currently allowed in the United States and Britain? There is an enormous body of social science data that examines the impact of gift giving. Evidence suggests that when a gift of any size is presented it creates a sense of indebtedness in the recipient.[61] Some even claim that reciprocal behavior is an adaptive mechanism that has helped advance human society.[62] Additionally, the degree that the recipient feels an obligation to reciprocate does not seem to be related to the size of the gift.[63] Even more, there is evidence that suggests that we are more receptive to information when it is received while eating.[64] Finally, pharmaceutical companies employ highly educated and intelligent marketers and it seems safe to assume that they would not invest the substantial resources in terms of time, money, and manpower in the providing of gifts to physicians if they were not aware of the impact that such practices have. Thus, there is a significant body of evidence that indicates that the practice of gift giving by pharmaceutical companies capitalizes on deep seated social and psychological tendencies to try and reciprocate. Since the only way that physicians can generally reciprocate is by increased prescribing of the drug marketed by the PSR this explains why gift giving often leads to increased prescribing. This occurs at a subconscious level with few physicians believing that accepting small gifts could influence their behavior.[65] As a result, PSRs give small gifts with the aim of capitalizing on the physician's instinct to reciprocate. Natural predispositions are utilized in a subconscious manner in order to alter the physician's behavior.

Studies have also shown a strong correlation between the accepting of gifts and higher incidences of problematic prescribing behavior. Physicians who accept gifts are shown to have increased incidences of improper prescribing, excessive prescribing, and the early adoption of newer, more expensive, less proven, and possibly more dangerous medications.[66] As noted above, such alterations in prescribing behavior pose a serious threat of harm to patients. Further, by not prescribing the best medication or the proper amount of the medication, physicians violate their fiduciary duties to their patients. To the degree that accepting gifts correlates to these alterations in prescribing behavior the practice of gift giving does pose a serious threat to patient care and the fulfillment of the fiduciary duties of physicians. Physicians who regularly accept gifts, and continue to reciprocate via their prescription activity are complicit in the practice and clearly violate their fiduciary duties. Those who continue to believe that such practices have no impact on their prescribing behavior must recognize the predominance of empirical data that indicates that this is not the case. However, since the practice of gift giving plays on unconscious tendencies to reciprocate and so effectively alters prescribing behavior it clearly constitutes a case of manipulation. As a result, by capitalizing on the influences inherent in gift giving the practices represent an unacceptable interference with physicians' capacity to fulfill their fiduciary duties. By interfering with their capacity to fulfill their duties as a moral agent they are not shown the respect they deserve.

5.4 REGULATION AND INNOVATION

Through the provision of inaccurate and biased information and the giving of gifts PSRs deceive and manipulate physicians. As prescribing behavior is altered through these practices patients are harmed and physicians fail to fulfill their fiduciary duties to their patients. Patients and physicians are not given the respect they are due as moral agents and are utilized as mere means to enhance the profitability of the pharmaceutical industry and of individual PSRs. However, despite a clear moral imperative for PhRMA, the ABPI, the AMA and similar groups to voluntarily abandon the practices of DTP marketing, there is strong reason to doubt their ability to effectively curtail such exchanges. Previous discussions serve to starkly illustrate the corrupting influences of profit. DTP marketing is the primary mechanism through which the industry maintains the substantial profits they have come to enjoy for so long. It is naïve to expect them to readily discard their most effective tool for generating those profits. Even more, as noted above, there is evidence that companies are already abandoning the modest reforms that have been only recently enacted. This has led Kassirer to claim that, "already, less than a year after the PhRMA guidelines were issued, there is evidence that the companies are violating their own guidelines on meals, and despite the new AMA guidelines, physicians are still accepting their invitations."[67]

Further, limitations on the types and size of gifts to physicians and strong curtailment of PSRs ability to "wine and dine" physicians has resulted in greater efforts being expended in the less well regulated area of continuing medical education (CME). Physicians are increasingly utilized as so-called "thought" or "opinion leaders." These physicians speak on behalf of pharmaceutical companies about certain drugs and usually receive substantial honorariums in return.[68] The rise of such practices can be traced to the institution of more restrictive codes of conduct by PhRMA and the AMA. Worrisome practices such as these have led Kassirer to conclude that, "gifts and subsidies are so important to the marketing efforts of industry that the companies will undoubtedly find creative ways to continue the largesse."[69]

Physicians are complicit in the failure of reform as well. Despite a strong professional ethic, physicians are no less susceptible to the corrupting influence of money than others. More importantly, studies show that for the most part physicians feel they are immune to the influencing effects of gifts.[70] As long as physicians are unwilling to recognize the dramatic affects that are correlated with interactions with industry, they are unlikely to voluntarily abandon such practices. If physicians and the industry are not capable of effective self-regulation then the only alternative may be regulation.

However, there are two primary lines of criticism regarding a ban on DTP marketing. The first centers on the claim that physicians will lose access to one of their primary sources of information on new drugs and therapies. As noted above, physicians struggle to keep themselves educated regarding new treatments and therapies. At the same time PSRs are highly accessible and provide information that is easily digestible. As such, they constitute a major resource for many physicians to remain educated about new pharmaceuticals. Therefore, the argument goes that if physicians truly have so little time to educate themselves about new pharmaceuticals and interactions with PSRs are a primary resource for information on new drugs then their working knowledge of new drugs will be harmed by bans on many DTP marketing practices.

While there is good reason to doubt the value of information provided by PSRs, the problems of increasing pressures on physicians' time and the question of where physicians should turn to find reliable information about pharmaceuticals remains. However, a reliable alternative to industry sponsored detailing already exists. "Academic detailing" utilizes the same face-to-face methods used in traditional detailing, providing information in a similarly easily digestible format.[71] However, as opposed to traditional detailing, academic detailing is independently funded by research institutes. Since academic detailing is insulated from the influence of industry indications have shown that it has been immensely successful at removing inaccuracy and bias from research and information provided to physicians.[72] As a result, physicians already have an alternative that carries most of the benefits of traditional detailing (information provided quickly in an easily accessible format) while protecting them from the biased and unreliable information provided in traditional detailing.

The second concern centers on the issue of innovation. There is a common defense that is rolled out every time the high profits of the industry are cited as a reason for regulation of drug pricing. The argument is that high profits are required to encourage investment in pharmaceutical companies, which is in return required for investment in R&D. Since the success rate of developing new drugs is so low and investment in the industry so risky, high profits are required in order to make the risk worthwhile for investors. As a result, in order for the industry to continue to develop innovative new drugs, high profits must be maintained.[73] Therefore, any reforms that place the status quo at risk threaten to stifle innovation. It follows that since DTP marketing is so successful at generating high profits for the industry, any measures taken to regulate its practice may result in a decrease in the development of innovative new drugs. Thus, what is at play is a consequentialist claim that while DTP marketing may be deceptive and harmful, it is a necessary evil for the continued production of innovative new drugs. However, the argument that regulation will stifle innovation simply does not hold.

The first objection to this line of argument comes from Marcia Angell. In her book, *The Truth About Drug Companies*, Angell provides strong evidence that indicates that a substantial percentage of new drugs being produced by the pharmaceutical industry are so-called "me-too" drugs.[74] These drugs are generally only very slight modifications on existing molecular formulas and provide little or no advantage over existing treatments and therapies.[75] Since these drugs often offer no significant advantage over existing treatments and are often substantially more expensive than older alternatives, in particular generics that have come off patent protection, drug companies rely on the highly effective techniques involved in DTP marketing in order to create a market for these drugs. Thus, if Angell is correct in her assessment of the industry and the preponderance of me-too drugs then what is truly at work is a feedback cycle where DTP marketing is used primarily to facilitate the prescribing of unnecessary me-too drugs with profits merely funneled back into the development of new me-too's. Therefore, by banning many DTP marketing practices what should result is a move from the dominant concentration on me-too drugs back to truly innovative R&D. Since pharmaceutical companies cannot rely on DTP marketing to create a market for me-too drugs they will be forced to rely on the merits of their drugs to market themselves, which will inevitably drive innovation.

Secondly, it seems that most of the research on truly innovative drugs does not come from the pharmaceutical industry itself. According to Angell, "at least a third of drugs marketed by the major drug companies are now licensed from universities or small biotech companies, and these tend to be the most innovative ones."[76] Further, it is likely that most of the research portion of R&D comes from NIH (the National Institute of Health) grants in the United States. While this is a claim that has been frequently cited as justification for government regulation of pharmaceutical pricing, the industry counters by citing a study conducted by the NIH to determine the extent to which federal funding of research had led to the development of blockbuster drugs.[77] The study found that of the top 47 drugs on the market in 2001, only four could be definitively linked to NIH funding of research. While this has been widely touted by the industry as proof that most of the truly innovative research stems from internal R&D by pharmaceutical companies instead of through public funding of the NIH, in reality the study merely points out that the NIH had not been vigilant in its tracking of the development of new pharmaceuticals that resulted from federal funding. As Angell points out, "what the facts really show is that the NIH, in violation of the Bayh-Dole Act, failed to keep proper records of patenting and licensing arrangements."[78] However, even if there is only a limited correlation between NIH funding and the development of innovative blockbuster drugs, this does not mean that NIH-funded research has no bearing on innovation. It is important to note that, "even though the NIH spends nearly as much money on research as does the industry, it concentrates on basic research. Only about 10 percent of clinical trials are sponsored by the NIH, usually in academic medical centers."[79] Since the NIH spends such significant sums on basic research it means that NIH-funded research is the primary source of research into the underlying mechanisms of disease, which is necessary for the successful development of new treatments.[80] Thus, in one form or another, much of the cost for initial research into new, innovative drugs is born by public funding through the NIH, leaving the pharmaceutical industry merely responsible for the development side of the equation. While development carries the brunt of the cost of bringing a new drug to market, it seems that most of the truly innovative work takes place outside of the industry, calling into question the degree to which decreased profits may stifle innovation.

In the end, a brief glance at the allocation of revenues by the top seven pharmaceutical companies shows that the claim that any loss of revenue will negatively affect innovation is patently false. Let us not forget that pharmaceutical companies are immensely successful. This is not an industry struggling to maintain viability. As has been widely cited, the industry has been the most profitable industry in America for most of the last decade.[81] Further, a 2005 report by Families USA points out that 32% of company revenues were allocated to marketing, advertising, and administration by the top seven pharmaceutical companies, whereas only 14% of revenues were allocated to R&D. Even further, these companies reported 18% of revenue as profits.[82] When one considers that the median return for all Fortune 500 companies in 2004 was only 5.2% these profits are incredible. Even more, 2004 was the highest median return in the last 10 years.[83] Even if investment in pharmaceuticals is risky the claim that the industry requires a return on profit more than three times that of the average of all Fortune 500 companies is implausible. Thus, while a ban on DTP marketing will likely have an impact on the profitability of companies the claim that profits at such exorbitant levels are required for continued investment is not credible. If allocation into R&D does suffer, this will be a decision made by executives who have concluded that continued profits at the current levels are more important than the development of innovative pharmaceuticals. However, even if this is their initial reaction, it seems clear that it would only be a temporary outcome of regulation. With the denial of the industry's ability to continue to profit from the proliferation of me-too drugs through their reliance on DTP marketing, the only way for these companies to remain viable will be for them to return to a primary focus on creating innovative new drugs. Therefore, counter to claims made by the industry, it is likely that development of innovative new medications will increase in the long run. In the end, we wind up with a more streamlined, efficient industry with a much desired shift of focus back to innovation instead of the current impetus to take the easy route and rely on DTP marketing to create an artificial market for me-too drugs.

NOTES

1. Fortune 500, "Our Annual Ranking of America's Largest Corporations: Most Profitable Industries: Return on Revenues," 2006, http://money.cnn.com/magazines/fortune/fortune500/performers/industries/return_on_revenues/index.html (accessed March 22, 2007).

2. Christine Borger, *et al..*, "Health Spending Projections Through 2015: Changes on the Horizon," *Health Affairs Web Exclusive* W61, February 22, 2006.

3. The most well known example of claimed profiteering was the marketing of AZT. When AZT was released in 1987 it was the only AIDS treatment available. Burroughs Wellcome charged approximately $8,000 for a year's treatment at the time, well outside the means of many AIDS patients. Public outcry quickly followed with activists taking to the streets and five individuals being arrested after they chained themselves to a balcony inside the New York Stock Exchange. Russell Mokhiber, "The 10 Worst Corporations of 1989," *The Multinational Monitor* 10, no. 12 (1989), http://multinationalmonitor.org/hyper/issues/1989/12/mokhiber.html (accessed October 14, 2007); Philip J. Hilts, "AIDS Drug Maker Cuts Price by 20%," *The New York Times*, September 19, 1989, http://query.nytimes.com/gst/fullpage.html?res=950DE6D9163EF93AA2575AC0A96F948260&sec=&spon=&pagewanted=print (accessed October 14, 2007); Jay Branegan, "An Uproar Over AIDS Drugs," *Time*, April 6, 1987, www.time.com/time/magazine/article/0,9171,963926,00.html (accessed October 14, 2007).

4. Just to name a few recent articles: Stephanie Saul, "Drug Makers Pay for Lunch as They Pitch," *The New York Times*, July 28, 2006, www.nytimes.com/2006/07/28/business/28lunch.html (accessed October 14, 2007); Scott Haig, "Attack of the Pharma Babes," *Time*, January 2, 2007, www.time.com/time/health/article/0,8599,1573327,00.html (accessed October 14, 2007); Jeffrey Macdonald, "Fighting the Freebies," *Time*, November 6, 2005, www.time.com/time/magazine/article/0,9171,1126716,00.html (accessed October 14, 2007).

5. Thomas Abrams, "The Regulation of Prescription Drug Promotion," in *Ethics and the Pharmaceutical Industry*, ed. Michael A. Santoro and Thomas M. Gorrie

(New York: Cambridge University Press, 2005), pp. 153–169; Richard L. Allman M.D., "The Relationships Between Physicians and the Pharmaceutical Industry: Ethical Problems with the Every-Day Conflict of Interest," *Healthcare Ethics Committee Forum* 15, no. 2 (2003): 155–170; Marcia Angell M.D., *The Truth About the Drug Companies: How They Deceive Us and What To Do About It* (New York: Random House, 2004); Jason Dana and George Lowenstein, "A Social Science Perspective on Gifts to Physicians From Industry," *Journal of the American Medical Association* 290, no. 2 (2003): 252–255; Carl Elliot, "The Drug Pushers," *The Atlantic Monthly*, (April 2006): 2–13; Jerome W. Freeman M.D., and Brian Kaatz PharmD, "The Physician and the Pharmaceutical Detail Man: An Ethical Analysis," *The Journal of Medical Humanities and Bioethics* 8, no. 1 (1987): 34–39; David Griffith, "Reasons for Not Seeing Drug Representatives," *British Medical Journal* 319, no. 10 (1999): 69–70; Delon Human, "Conflicts of Interest in Science and Medicine: The Physician's Perspective," *Science and Engineering Ethics* 8, no. 3 (2002): 273–276; Dana Katz, *et al.*., "All Gifts Large and Small: Toward an Understanding of the Ethics of Pharmaceutical Industry Gift-Giving," *The American Journal of Bioethics* 3, no. 3 (2003): 39–46; Joel Lexchin, "Doctors and Detailers: Therapeutic Education or Pharmaceutical Promotion?" *International Journal of Health Services* 19, no. 4 (1989): 663–679; Arnold S. Relman M.D., "Defending Professional Independence: ACCME's Proposed New Guidelines for Commercial Support of CME," *Journal of the American Medical Association* 289, no. 18 (2003): 2418–2420; Lars Reuter, "The Ethics of Advertising Strategies in the Pharmaceutical Industry," *Ethics & Medicine; A Christian Perspective on Issues in Bioethics* 19, no. 3 (2003): 171–175; Marc A. Rodwin, *Medicine, Money, and Morals: Physicians' Conflicts of Interest* (New York: Oxford University Press, 1993); Alexander C. Tsai, "Policies to Regulate Gifts to Physicians From Industry," *Journal of the American Medical Association* 290, no. 13 (2003): 1776; Ashley Wazana M.D., "Physicians and the Pharmaceutical Industry: Is a Gift Ever Just a Gift?" *Journal of the American Medical Association* 283, no. 3 (2000): 373–380; Michael Ziegler, *et al.*., "The Accuracy of Drug Information From Pharmaceutical Sales Representatives," *Journal of the American Medical Association* 273, no. 16 (1995): 1296–1298.

6. America's trade association of pharmaceutical companies who set many of the guidelines that govern the industry.

7. Michael Kligman and Charles M. Culver, "Interpersonal Manipulation," *Journal of Medicine and Philosophy* 17 (1992): 173–197.

8. In the second formulation of the categorical imperative Kant states, "Act so that you treat humanity, whether in your own person or in that of another, always as an end and never as a means only" (Kant 2002, p. 421). For Kant our dignity is grounded in our ability to act as self-legislators and impose the moral law upon ourselves. By setting and pursuing our ends we give our lives meaning. This capacity arises from our rationality. Thus, as rational agents capable of self-governance we are to be regarded with respect. Yet in order to operate as moral agents we must be capable of rationally engaging in the world and setting our

own ends. Thus, respect for persons must include respect for those capacities necessary for us to function as self-legislators. In the negative sense we must not purposefully interfere with others' abilities to rationally set and pursue their own ends as moral agents. On the positive side we may derive duties to foster and encourage the development of the capacities that are necessary for the fulfillment of our role as a moral legislator. Immanuel Kant, *Groundwork for the Metaphysics of Morals*, trans. Arnulf Zweig, (Oxford: Oxford University Press, 2002); Denis G. Arnold and Norman E. Bowie, "Sweatshops and Respect for Persons," *Business Ethics Quarterly* 8, no. 2 (2003): 221–242; Norman E. Bowie, *Business Ethics: A Kantian Perspective* (Malden: Blackwell Publishers, 1999); Thomas E. Hill Jr., *Dignity and Practical Reason in Kant's Moral Theory* (Ithaca: Cornell University Press, 1992).

 9. Barbara Herman, "Leaving Deontology Behind," in *The Practice of Moral Judgment* (Cambridge, MA: Harvard University Press, 1993), pp. 208–243.
10. American Law Institute: *Restatement (Second) of the Law-Agency* § 13, 1957, 58.
11. Freeman, "The Physician and the Pharmaceutical Detail Man," 34.
12. AMA, "The Patient Physician Relationship," In *AMA Code of Medical Ethics*, 2006–7, E-10.015.
13. John F. Peppin argues against fiduciary responsibilities being sufficient to restrict marketing of pharmaceuticals. He contends that, as stated, the fiduciary responsibility should underlie all human interaction and as such, has no special bearing on drug marketing. However, what Peppin misses is the problematic disparity of power and information that permeates interactions in professions such as medicine and law. The patient seeks out the physician to aid in the pursuit of health. The physician is consulted because of their training and expertise in the exercise of medicine, which the patient cannot hope to achieve on their own. Because of the disparity of technical knowledge, the patient is naturally in a position of vulnerability. It is because of this inherent vulnerability that the exercise of professions such as law and medicine must be governed by respect for the principal who seeks out their services. So while I do not argue that some form of a fiduciary responsibility should underlie all relationships where an element of trust is present, it is the inherent vulnerability of principals endemic to these professions that makes the principle stronger and more binding. Since the vulnerability of the principal makes it problematic for them to guard against abuses of trust, active measures must be taken to protect them from such abuse. John F. Peppin, "An Engelhardtian Analysis of Interactions Between Pharmaceutical Representatives and Physicians," *The Journal of Medicine and Philosophy* 22 (1997): 623–641; John F. Peppin, "Pharmaceutical Sales Representatives and Physicians: Ethical Considerations of a Relationship," *The Journal of Medicine and Philosophy* 21 (1996): 83–99.
14. Deception violates personal autonomy. However, the case must be made that violations of personal autonomy constitute morally unacceptable violations of Kantian autonomy. Since physicians act as autonomous moral agents when they endeavor to fulfill their fiduciary duties to their patients, physicians are due respect in the Kantian sense. Since deception may often prevent physicians

from fulfilling their fiduciary duties this shows an inherent lack of respect for physicians as moral agents. Thus, by violating personal autonomy in this manner a deceiver violates the respect physicians are due as moral agents in the Kantian sense. For a discussion of the slippage that often occurs in discussions of personal autonomy and the moral demands associated with it see Tom L. Beauchamp, "Who Deserves Autonomy, and Whose Autonomy Deserves Respect," in *Personal Autonomy*, ed. James Stacey Taylor, (Cambridge: Cambridge University Press, 2005), pp. 310–30.

15. PhRMA, "Code of Interactions with Health care Professionals," www.phrma. org/files/PhRMA%20Code.pdf, 2004, 9 (accessed March 22, 2007).
16. Ibid., 7.
17. ABPI, *Code of Practice for the Pharmaceutical Industry*, 2006, www.pmcpa.org. uk, 16 (accessed June 12, 2007).
18. Griffith, "Reasons for Not Seeing Drug Representatives"; Lexchin, "Doctors and Detailers"; Joel Lexchin, "What Information do Physicians Receive from Pharmaceutical Representatives?" *Canadian Family Physician* 43 (1997): 941–945; Helen Prosser, and Tom Walley, "Understanding why GPs see Pharmaceutical Representatives: A qualitative Interview Study," *British Journal of General Practice* 53 (2003): 305–311; David Strang, et al.., "National Survey on the Attitudes of Canadian Physicians Towards Drug-Detailing by Pharmaceutical Representatives," *Annals of the Royal College of Physicians and Surgeons of Canada* 29, no. 8 (1996): 474–478.
19. William T. Carpenter, "How the Doctor can Counter Commercial Bias in the Dissemination of Pharmacotherapeutic Knowledge," *The Journal of Nervous and Mental Disease* 190, no 9 (2002): 593–596; Allen F. Shaughnessy, et al.., "Separating the Wheat from the Chaff: Identifying Fallacies in Pharmaceutical Promotion," *Journal of General Internal Medicine* 9, no 10 (1994): 563–568; Allen F. Shaughnessy, et al., "Teaching Information Mastery: Evaluating Information Provided by Pharmaceutical Representatives," *Family Medicine* 28, no 3 (1996): 166–167; Elizabeth Wager, "How to Dance with Porcupines: Rules and Guidelines on Doctors' Relations with Drug Companies," *British Medical Journal* 326 (2003): 1196–1198.
20. Elina Hemminki, "Commercial Information on Drugs: Confusing the Physician?" *Journal of Drug Issues* 18 (1988): 245–257; Elina Hemminki, "Content Analysis of Drug-Detailing by Pharmaceutical Representatives," *Medical Education* 11 (1977): 210–215.
21. In her first study Hemminki found that in almost half of the presentations given PSRs did not mention side-effects and contraindications, even though they were listed in the *Remedia Fennica*. Other drugs for the same condition were often mentioned, however, in 78% of the cases the drug was preferred to the alternative drug, and 19% of the time the alternative was said to be equally good in principle but the presented drug was better because of some special feature. In her second study Hemminki found that side-effects were not mentioned in contradiction to the drug catalogue 67% of the time, up from 44% in the 1977 study. Contraindications were omitted 65% of the time, up

from 46% in 1977. And once again competing treatments were often mentioned with 82% of the comparisons favoring the PSRs drug. In 18% of the comparisons the drugs were presented equally but the PSRs drug was never the drug of second choice. Hemminki, "Commercial Information on Drugs;" Hemminki, "Content Analysis of Drug-Detailing."

22. Ziegler, "The Accuracy of Drug Information."

23. The study found that out of a sample of 106 statements made by 12 pharmaceutical reps in 13 presentations, 12, or 11% of the statements, were inaccurate. The study also found that 49% of statements made about the promoted drug were favorable, 31% were neutral, and only 19% were unfavorable. Additionally, all of the statements made about a competitor's drug were unfavorable and the PSRs "usually do not mention adverse effects or better alternative agents" (Ibid., 1297).

24. Elliot, "The Drug Pushers."

25. Elina Hemminki and Terttu Pesonen, "The Function of Drug Company Representatives," *Scandinavian Journal of Social Medicine* 5 (1977): 105–114, 108.

26. Dana, "A Social Science Perspective on Gifts"; Katz, "All Gifts Large and Small"; Wazana, "Physicians and the Pharmaceutical Industry."

27. G. M. Anderson, *et al.*, "Auditing Prescription Practice using Explicit Criteria and Computerized Drug Benefit Claims Data," *Journal of Evaluation in Clinical Practice* 3 (1998): 283–294; T. S. Lesar, *et al.*, "Medication-Prescribing Errors in a Teaching Hospital: A Nine-Year Experience," *Archives of International Medicine* 28 (1997): 1569–1576.

28. Lee N. Newcomer, "Medicare Pharmacy Coverage: Ensuring Safety Before Funding," *Health Affairs* March/April, (2000): 59–62, 60.

29. Some may argue that the rapid prescribing of pharmaceuticals is beneficial since many side-effects are often rare and will not be identified until a substantial number of patients are prescribed to the medication. However, I find such an argument troubling. While certainly rare side-effects may be discovered more quickly by aggressively adopting new medications, how many additional patients may suffer those side-effects due to the aggressive adoption of the medication? Instead, by employing a policy of gradual adoption one would hope that the number of patients who suffer that side effect would be minimized since as soon as a sufficient number have been identified proper action may be taken. This means that there is a potentially smaller pool of affected patients at the time of discovery than would be the case with a more aggressive policy.

30. Newcomer, "Medicare Pharmacy Coverage," 60.

31. Ibid., 60.

32. Market clients are individuals who "willingly and knowingly engage in market relations," "know they should shop around and are able to do so," "are competent to determine difference in quality and best price," "have knowledge of the products and their characteristics," and "have the resources to enter into market relations." George G. Brenkert, "Marketing and the Vulnerable," *Business Ethics Quarterly*, Special Issue 1 (1998): 7–20, 11–2.

33. Newcomer, "Medicare Pharmacy Coverage."
34. George Brenkert provides an excellent discussion of the special obligations that exist when marketing to vulnerable populations. While his discussion centers on groups that are generally considered vulnerable (the elderly, children, etc.) the case can be made that certain contexts constitute instances of marketing to the vulnerable, even when that group is not generally considered vulnerable. Brenkert, "Marketing and the Vulnerable."
35. It is interesting to note that it is the increasingly difficult position of physicians and the growing demands on their time that pharmaceutical companies use in order to justify practices such as taking physicians to lunch or dinner. The logic goes that they have to eat and since they are so busy you might as well use that time wisely in order to educate them about a new product.
36. For an in depth account of the difficulties inherent in physicians' attempts to stay educated about pharmaceuticals see, Jerry Avorn, "Information," in *Powerful Medicines: The Benefits, Risks, and Costs of Prescription Drugs* (New York: Alfred A Knopf, 2004), pp. 269–348.
37. Certain specialties such as oncology and anesthesiology have much more stringent education requirements regarding pharmacology and constitute a less vulnerable group than general practitioners.
38. Avorn, *Powerful Medicines*, p. 272.
39. In recognition of this issue, and partially due to increased scrutiny brought about by recent recalls such as Vioxx, Merck has committed to disclosing the results of all drug trials and several trade groups have committed themselves to releasing more data about drug trials. Gardner Harris, "Merck Says It Will Post the Results of All Drug Trials," *The New York Times*, September 6, 2004, www.nytimes.com/2004/09/06/business/06merck.html?ei=5070&en=8f807c6 ff60a90fe&ex=1185595200&adxnnl=1&adxnnlx=1185491395-ysPrJ1t/Qv2xOoq XEL4IdQ (accessed July 26, 2007); Barry Meier, "Drug Industry Plans Release of More Data About Studies," *The New York Times*, January 7, 2005, www. nytimes.com/2005/01/07/business/07trials.html?ex=1185595200&en=5b441a7c 5de3b388&ei=5070 (accessed July 26, 2007).
40. Amy Barrett, "Pull the Veil From Drug-Study Secrets," *BusinessWeek*, September 9, 2004, www.businessweek.com/bwdaily/dnflash/sep2004/ nf2004099_4610_db042.htm?chan=search (accessed July 27, 2007); Amy Barrett, Kerry Capell, and Susann Rutledge, "When Medicine and Money Don't Mix," *BusinessWeek*, June 28, 2004, www.businessweek.com/magazine/ content/04_26/b3889080_mz018.htm?chan=search (accessed July 27, 2007); Barbara Martinez, "Merck Documents Shed Light on Vioxx Legal Battles – Records Show Safety Panel Had Early Data Indicating Higher Heart-Problems Risk," *The Wall Street Journal*, February 7, 2005, A1; Barry Meier, "Contracts Keep Drug Research Out of Reach," *The New York Times*, November 29, 2004, www.nytimes.com/2004/11/29/business/29research. html?ex=1185595200&en=8664feafa056e0c0&ei=5070 (accessed July 27, 2007); Amy Tsao, "Spitzer's New Target: Big Pharma," *BusinessWeek*, June

3, 2004, www.businessweek.com/bwdaily/dnflash/jun2004/nf2004063_6698_
db016.htm?chan=search (accessed July 27, 2007); The Economist, "Trials and
transparency," 379, no. 8478, May 20, 2006, 82–3; The Economist, "The
Sounds of Silence," 372, no. 8391, May 19, 2006, 75–6.

41. David Armstrong, "JAMA to Toughen Rules on Author Disclosure," *The Wall
Street Journal*, July 12, 2006, D2; Scott Gottleib, "Journalistic Malpractice," *The
Wall Street Journal*, May 29, 2007, A15; Arlene Weintraub, "How the Journals
are Cracking Down," *BusinessWeek*, October 23, 2006, www.businessweek.com/
magazine/content/06_43/b4006083.htm?chan=search (accessed July 26, 2007).

42. Hans Melander, *et al.*, "Evidence B(i)ased Medicine – Selective Reporting of
Studies Sponsored by Pharmaceutical Industry: Review of Studies in New
Drug Applications," *British Medical Journal* 326 (2003): 1171–1173; Daniel J.
Safer, "Design and Reporting Modifications in Industry-Sponsored
Comparative Psychopharmacology Trials," *The Journal of Nervous and
Mental Disease* 190, no. 9, (2002): 583–592.

43. The mechanisms Safer identified were: using doses outside the usual range for
competitive advantage, substantially altering the dose schedule of the comparison drug for competitive advantage, using self-serving measurement scales and
making misleading conclusions from measurement findings, selecting the
major findings and endpoints post hoc, masking unfavorable side-effects,
repeatedly publishing the same or similar positive studies to increase the
impact, selectively highlighting findings favorable to the sponsor, editorializing
for the sponsor in the abstract, publishing the obvious to emphasize a point,
touting nonsignificant but favorable differences and negating dropout difference statistically, selecting subjects and altering the duration of trials to achieve
a favorable outcome, withholding unfavorable results, and masking sponsorship. Safer, "Design and Reporting Modifications."

44. The mechanisms identified by Hans, *et al.* were: duplicate publication,
selective publication, and selective reporting. Melander, "Evidence B(i)ased
Medicine."

45. Safer, "Design and Reporting Modifications," 583.

46. Brenkert, "Marketing and the Vulnerable," 14.

47. Kligman, "Interpersonal Manipulation."

48. While free samples are a prominent form of gift giving this is not what I have in
mind when I refer to the practice of gift giving and are not included in my
objections to the practice.

49. Abrams, "The Regulation of Prescription Drug Promotion"; Allman, "The
Relationships Between Physicians and the Pharmaceutical Industry"; Angell,
The Truth About the Drug Companies; Dana, "A Social Science Perspective on
Gifts to Physicians from Industry"; Elliot, "The Drug Pushers"; Freeman,
"The Physician and the Pharmaceutical Detail Man"; Griffith, "Reasons for
Not Seeing Drug Representatives"; Human, "Conflicts of Interest in Science
and Medicine"; Katz, "All Gifts Large and Small"; Lexchin, "Doctors and
Detailers"; Relman, "Defending Professional Independence"; Reuter, "The
Ethics of Advertising Strategies"; Rodwin, *Medicine, Money, and Morals*; Tsai,

"Policies to Regulate Gifts to Physicians"; Wazana, "Physicians and the Pharmaceutical Industry"; Ziegler, "The Accuracy of Drug Information."

50. AMA, "Gifts to Physicians from Industry," in *AMA Code of Medical Ethics*, 2006–7 E-8.061.

51. PhRMA, "Code of Interactions," 19.

52. The restrictions on meals have been quite minimal. The new restrictions merely require that meals must include an educational presentation and must be conducted in a venue that is judged as "modest" by local standards. Additionally, the inclusion of spouses and guests has been banned as have "dine and dash" programs where physicians briefly attend a session while takeout food for the whole family is prepared. Ibid., 9.

53. PhRMA, *Code on Interactions with Health Care Professionals*, updated code January 2009, available at www.phrma.org/files/PhRMA%20Marketing%20Code%202008.pdf (accessed July 13, 2008).

54. House of Commons Health Committee, "The Influence of the Pharmaceutical Industry," 2005, www.parliament.the-stationery-office.co.uk/pa/cm200405/cmselect/cmhealth/42/42.pdf (accessed June 12, 2007).

55. Secretary of State for Health, "Government Response to the Health Committee's Report on the Influence of the Pharmaceutical Industry," 2005, www.official-documents.gov.uk/document/cm66/6655/6655.pdf (accessed June 12, 2007).

56. ABPI, "Code of Practice."

57. Jerome P. Kassirer M.D., *On the Take: How Medicine's Complicity with Big Business can Endanger your Health* (New York: Oxford University Press, 2005).

58. Kay Lazar, "Drug industry tightens rules on gift-giving," *The Boston Globe*, July 11, 2008, available at www.prescriptionproject.org/assets/pdfs/Lazar_Globe_Massgiftban_7-11-2008.pdf (accessed July 13, 2008); Gardner Harris, "Drug Industry to Announce Revised Code on Marketing," *The New York Times*, July 10, 2008, available at www.nytimes.com/2008/07/10/business/10code.html?_r=2&oref=slogin&oref=slogin (accessed July 13, 2008); Avery Johnson, "Drug Group Sets Marketing Code," *The Wall Street Journal*, July 11, 2008, B7.

59. Lazar, "Drug Industry Tightens Rules on Gift-Giving."

60. Ibid.

61. Alvin W. Gouldner, "The Norm of Reciprocity: A Preliminary Statement," *American Sociological Review* 25 (1960): 161–178; Claude Levi-Strauss, *The Elementary Structures of Kinship* (Boston: Beacon Press, 1969); Marcel Mauss, *The Gift* (London: Routledge & Kegan Paul, 1954).

62. Richard E. Leakey, and Roger Lewin, *People of the Lake* (New York: Anchor Press, 1978).

63. Robert B. Cialdini, *Influence: The Psychology of Persuasion* (New York: Quill William Morrow, 1993); Hershey H. Friedman and Paul J. Herskovitz, "The Effect of a Gift-Upon-Entry on Sales: Reciprocity in a Retailing Context," *Mid-American Journal of Business* 5 (1990): 49–50.

64. Irving L. Janis, Donald Kay, and Paul Kirshner, "Facilitating Effects of Eating-While-Reading on Responsiveness to Persuasive Communications," *Journal of Personality and Social Psychology* 1 (1965): 181–186.

65. Dana "A Social Science Perspective on Gifts to Physicians"; Wazana, "Physicians and the Pharmaceutical Industry."

66. Dana, "A Social Science Perspective on Gifts to Physicians"; Katz, "All Gifts Large and Small"; Wazana, "Physicians and the Pharmaceutical Industry."

67. Kassirer, *On the Take*, p. 10.

68. Angell, *The Truth About the Drug Companies*; Elliot, "The Drug Pushers"; Kassirer, *On the Take.*

69. Kassirer, *On the Take*, p. 9–10.

70. Dana, "A Social Science Perspective on Gifts to Physicians"; Wazana, "Physicians and the Pharmaceutical Industry."

71. Meredith B. Rosenthal and Julie M. Donohue, "Direct-to-Consumer Advertising of Prescription Drugs," in *Ethics and the Pharmaceutical Industry*, ed. Michael A. Santoro and Thomas M. Gorrie, (New York: Cambridge University Press, 2005), p. 181.

72. Jerry Avorn and Stephen B. Soumerai, "Improving Drug-Therapy Decisions through Educational Outreach: A Randomized Controlled Trial of Academically Based Detailing," *The New England Journal of Medicine* 308 (1983): 1457–1463; Stephen B. Soumerai and Jerry Avorn, "Predictors of Physician Prescribing Change in an Educational Experiment to Improve Medication Use," *Medical Care* 25, no. 3 (1987): 210–221; Stephen B. Soumerai and Jerry Avorn, "Principles of Educational Outreach ('Academic Detailing') to Improve Clinical Decision Making," *Journal of the American Medical Association* 263, no. 4 (1990): 549–556.

73. This line of reasoning is best articulated by Ian Maitland. While his argument does not directly address DTP marketing or me-too drugs, it is easy to extend it to encompass these issues; Ian Maitland, "Priceless Goods: How Should Life-Saving Drugs be Priced?" *Business Ethics Quarterly* 12, no. 4 (2002): 451–480.

74. Angell, *The Truth About the Drug Companies.*

75. Evidence for this conclusion lies in the FDA's classification of new drugs. In 2004, 31 (27%) of the 113 newly approved drugs were new molecular entities (NMEs). Only 25 (22%) of the 113 were classified as having a "significant improvement compared to marketed products in the treatment, diagnosis, or prevention of a disease," with only 17 of the NMEs falling under that category. Even if these figures underestimate the benefit of these new drugs, the fact that so few are NMEs and so few are classified as significant improvements over existing alternatives are truly disturbing statistics. US Food and Drug Administration, "CDER NDAs Approved in Calendar Years 1990–2004 by Therapeutic Potential and Chemical Type," 2005, www.fda.gov/cder/rdmt/pstable.htm (accessed October 17, 2007).

76. Ibid., 8.

77. Department of Health and Human Services National Institutes of Health, "NIH Response to the Conference Report Request for a Plan to Ensure Taxpayers' Interests are Protected: A Plan to Ensure Taxpayers' Interests are Protected," July, 2001, www.nih.gov/news/070101wyden.htm (accessed March 22, 2007).

78. Angell, *The Truth About the Drug Companies*, p. 71.
79. Ibid., p. 30.
80. Ibid., p. 22.
81. *Fortune 500*, "Our Annual Ranking of America's Largest Corporations: Most Profitable Industries: Return on Revenues," 2006, http://money.cnn.com/magazines/fortune/fortune500/performers/industries/return_on_revenues/index.html (accessed March 22, 2007).
82. Families USA, "Health Care for People or Drug Industry Profits," 2005, www.familiesusa.org/assets/pdfs/The-Choice.pdf (accessed March 22, 2007).
83. Kaiser Family Foundation, "Trends and Indicators in the Changing Health Care Marketplace," 2006, www.kff.org/insurance/7031/ti2004-1-21.cfm (accessed August 12, 2007).

CHAPTER 6

The ethics of direct-to-consumer pharmaceutical advertising

Denis G. Arnold

American consumers are nearly alone among the citizens of industrialized nations in being directly targeted by prescription drug advertising that tout the benefits of specific drugs.[1] This may change in the near future as the pharmaceutical industry is currently lobbying the European Union to allow the practice. In 1997 the US Food and Drug Administration (FDA) altered its policy on direct-to-consumer (DTC) advertising in such a way as to make it possible for the widespread use of television commercials for prescription pharmaceutical advertising. Since that time spending on direct-to-consumer advertising has increased substantially. However, the practice of advertising directly to consumers has come under sustained criticism. Critics of DTC advertising argue that the practice undermines physician–patient relationships and drives up the cost of prescription drugs. In response, drug manufacturers and their trade group the Pharmaceutical Research and Manufacturers of America (PhRMA) argue that DTC advertisements empower consumers and have no impact on the cost of drugs. Furthermore, the pharmaceutical industry is currently engaged in a lobbying campaign in the European Union to allow individual companies to market their drugs to European consumers.[2] In this chapter it is argued that branded DTC advertising is unethical because it illegitimately manipulates consumers, increases risks to patients, and drives up overall healthcare costs. However, it is also argued that genuinely non-branded DTC advertising by the pharmaceutical industry is ethically permissible and can play a beneficial role in the healthcare marketplace for both patients and the pharmaceutical industry.

THE RISE OF DTC ADVERTISING

In the US the FDA is charged with administering federal regulations regarding pharmaceutical sales and marketing. Both the amount and expense of DTC advertising has increased substantially over the past

20 years. Between 1983 and 1985 the FDA had in place a temporary, voluntary moratorium on DTC advertising while it studied the issue. In 1985 the FDA concluded that consumers were sufficiently protected by existing regulations, especially the requirement to state adverse affects of the drug in all advertisements, and so lifted its voluntary moratorium on DTC advertising.[3] In the late 1980s and 1990s advertisements targeting consumers, similar to those targeting physicians, appeared with increasing frequency in magazines. Prior to 1997 full product DTC advertisements were restricted to print media such as magazines. This is because the "adequate provision" of information component of existing regulations required manufacturers to provide a summary of the adverse information about a drug that is contained in the FDA approved product labeling. Since it was impractical to do this in television and radio advertisements, such advertisements were restricted to print media. However, in August 1997 the FDA issued new draft guidelines for meeting the adequate provision requirements. The guidelines, finalized in 1999, specify that broadcast advertisements met the legal requirements regarding the adequate provision of information if they included the following:

1. Reference to a toll-free phone number where viewers could obtain all adverse information about the drug contained in approved product labeling.
2. Reference to a web site where viewers could obtain all adverse information about the drug contained in approved product labeling.
3. Reference to a currently running print ad where viewers could obtain all adverse information about the drug contained in approved product labeling.
4. Reference to a healthcare professional as an additional resource regarding adverse information about the drug contained in approved product labeling.[4]

Since 1997 there has been a steady annual increase in the number of advertisements submitted for after-market assessment to the FDA's 40-person Division of Marketing, Advertising, and Communications. In 1999 the figure was 32,100, by 2003 the figure had increased to 40,000 and by 2004 had reached 52,800. While they often have the largest audience, broadcast advertisements make up a small percentage of these advertisements. For example, in 2003 the figure was 474 and in 2004 the figure was 586. Since 1997 approximately 125 drugs have been marketed via broadcast advertisements. The advertisements have targeted a range of symptoms and disorders. Examples include depression, anxiety, osteoporosis, attention deficit disorder, erectile disfunction, heartburn, obesity, diabetes, arthritis, high cholesterol, insomnia, and acne.[5] Unsurprisingly, spending on DTC advertising has also been increasing. In 2006 $4.74 billion was spent in the US on DTC advertising, up over six times the $760 million spent in 1997.[6] DTC advertising is the fastest growing segment of pharmaceutical marketing in the US. One recent study points out that in 1996 pharmaceutical industry spending on professional promotion, or direct-to-physician (DTP) marketing, was 4.4 times that of DTC marketing. In 2005 spending on DTP marketing was only 1.7 times more than spending on DTC marketing.[7] At the same time, the pharmaceutical industry is lobbying the European Union to lift its strict ban on marketing to patients regarding drugs.[8]

The FDA distinguishes between three varieties of DTC advertising. First, "product claim" advertisements refer to drugs by name and include its use or claims about its effectiveness. Such advertisements are supposed to provide a "fair balance" of information about the product. Second, " reminder" advertisements include the product name but are not allowed to make usage claims. Historically targeted at physicians, such advertisements are intended to remind the target audience of the availability of the product and build brand recognition. For this reason they are exempted from having to include warnings regarding adverse effects. The FDA reports that, increasingly, such advertisements are "testing the limits of what might be considered a product claim" and that they serve "no useful purpose in the DTC arena."[9] Third, " help-seeking" advertisements discuss diseases or disorders and recommend that consumers consult their physicians to obtain more information. Because these advertisements do not tout particular products, they are not regulated by the FDA. Since 1997 the FDA has issued 146 citations for DTC advertising and statutory and regulatory violations.[10] The most common violations include "minimization or omission of risk information, overstatement of effectiveness or safety, misleading comparative claims, and promotion for uses that are not in the product labeling."[11]

THE DEBATE OVER DTC ADVERTISING

The pharmaceutical industry argues that DTC advertisements play a valuable role in educating consumers. For example, PhRMA literature states that "DTC advertising's overarching purpose is to inform and educate consumers about treatable conditions, the symptoms that may help them identify diseases, and available therapies."[12] Hank McKinnell, Chairman of the Board and Chief Executive Officer of Pfizer Inc. from 2001–2006, argues that DTC advertising should not be understood as advertising at all, but rather as education. He writes,

DTC advertising can be a powerful public good – making people familiar with various therapies and promoting the primacy of the doctor-patient relationship. Good DTC communication should encourage people to talk with their physicians about their medical conditions. DTC advertising should help demystify sensitive medical problems and encourage people to seek treatment even for conditions stigmatized by society. For all these reasons, I prefer to describe our efforts as DTC education.[13]

While preliminary research has been undertaken regarding both consumer and physician attitudes toward DTC advertising, most researchers believe that the impact of such advertising is not well understood. For example, one recent study concluded as follows, "We still know very little about the effects of DTC advertising, especially its impact on consumer behavior (as opposed to attitudes and knowledge) and, ultimately, on consumer health."[14]

Critics of DTC advertising raise numerous objections to the practice. First, it is claimed that DTC advertising undermines patient–physician relationships.[15] One way it is alleged to do so is by persuading consumers to believe that they need a particular drug to be normal, just as other marketing campaigns persuade consumers that men need to give women diamonds in order to have normal, intimate relationships. Many of these consumers, in turn, place pressure on physicians to prescribe specific medications, even when such medications are not the physicians' preferred method of treatment. And in many cases physicians acquiesce to such pressure. One physician described the experience as follows. "As my patients' ideas about the best approach to their medical care became increasingly influenced by the drug advertisements, I would try to help them understand how this process serves the drug companies' interests, not their health. Often I was successful, but once it became clear that a patient was unwilling or unable to reconsider, I often gave in (unless there was a real danger …)."[16] Busy physicians who want their patients to leave happy may not have the time to talk through alternative treatment options such as lifestyle changes or generic alternatives, especially in the face of a patient determined to have the advertised brand. Second, DTC advertising is alleged to encourage the over-medication of consumers since the overall message of such advertisements is that drugs, and not lifestyle changes, are the best solution for such comparatively normal experiences as anxiety, sleeplessness, and mild depression.[17] Third, DTC advertising is alleged to needlessly increase the cost of pharmaceuticals. Critics argue that DTC advertising is unnecessary, since it is the proper role of physicians and not patients *qua* consumers to determine whether or not a specific drug regimen is ultimately warranted. This unnecessary expense is passed on to consumers via higher drug prices and to employers, governments, and individual purchasers via higher insurance premiums.[18]

The pharmaceutical industry is well aware of these criticisms and has deployed considerable resources to counter them. As we have seen, industry representatives argue that DTC advertisements are to be praised insofar as they play an important role in educating consumers regarding healthcare options. Far from encouraging inappropriate pressure on physicians, the industry argues that DTC advertisements encourage patients to partner with physicians in making healthcare decisions. As one Pfizer policy analyst argues

Given sufficient and accurate information about options – information greatly enhanced by DTC advertising – a consumer knows better than anyone else whether he or she would prefer a product with fewer unpleasant side effects even at slightly higher risk of some serious event. Consumers who are not professionally trained in health care are not so foolish as to discard the expert advice of medical professionals. Valuing and using technical experts is not the same, however, as electing to abdicate decision making to them. Rather, the ideal – and the emerging model – is a full partnership between patient and health care professional.[19]

According to this view, DTC advertising enhances patient autonomy and thus improves healthcare. In response to the second major criticism of DTC, namely, that it increases the costs of pharmaceuticals, PhRMA points out that DTC advertising represents a small portion of the total cost of drugs and that little evidence supports the claim that DTC advertising has a direct, causal connection to increased drug prices.[20] Finally, in response to the claim that DTC advertising encourages the overuse of prescription drugs, PhRMA cites a recent study that found underuse of medications where medications were appropriate treatment.[21] In November 2005 PhRMA issued fifteen "Guiding Principles" for DTC advertising (Appendix 1). These principles were widely interpreted as an effort by the industry to respond to criticism and prevent further regulation of DTC advertising.[22] According to PhRMA, the guidelines are intended to ensure that DTC advertisements educate patients and consumers.

There is a typical and seldom recognized feature of the arguments of both critics and defenders of DTC advertising. In both cases, there is normally a failure to distinguish between "product claim" and "reminder" advertisements on the one hand, and "help-seeking" advertisements on the other hand. The distinctions between these classes of advertisements are important, since in the former case the advertisements mention specific drugs while in the latter case they do not. What we shall call "branded" advertisements carry with them specific mention of brand name drugs such as Vioxx, Paxil, or Effexor, whereas non-branded advertisements do not carry with them the names of specific drugs although they may include the name of the pharmaceutical company that sponsors the non-branded advertisement. This distinction is of vital importance for any analysis of the ethics of DTC advertising since the arguments for and against DTC advertising do not necessarily apply equally to each category of advertisement. For example, the criticism that DTC advertisements place pressure on physicians to prescribe specific medication does not apply to non-branded DTC advertisements. So too, a defense of DTC advertisements that appeals to the undertreatment of certain conditions where medication is appropriate fails to undermine criticism of the use of branded advertisements that target, e.g., routine anxiety or ennui.

Reminder Advertisements

According to the US Food and Drug Administration, reminder advertisements include the name of the drug product but do not include indications or any recommendation regarding the use of the product.[23] There are no legal restrictions on where such advertisements can be placed or how much money can be spent on them. Examples of reminder advertisements include Schering-Plough's early Claritin "blue skies" campaign; GlaxoSmithKline and Bayer's placement of advertisements for Levitra on the final table of the World Series of Poker, on the stairs and escalators of Alltel Stadium in Jacksonville, Florida for Super Bowl thirty-nine, and in 15-second television commercials; and Pfizer's sponsorship of Mark Martin's Nascar number six Ford Viagra car and its 15-second and 30-second "wild thing" television commercials. From the perspective of pharmaceutical company marketing executives, the advantage of reminder advertisements directed at consumers is that they are not subject to the same legal restrictions as product claim advertisements. The primary marketing purpose of these advertisements is to build brand awareness. However, because the advertisements contain little more than the product's name and an association of the product with a particular image, representation, or sport, it is implausible to characterize the advertisements as educating consumers.

To its credit, PhRMA partly acknowledges this point in its "Guiding Principles." Principle number ten states that "DTC television advertising that identifies a product by name should clearly state the health conditions for which the medicine is approved and the major risks associated with the medicine being advertised." This voluntary restriction on broadcast reminder advertisements should be welcomed. Nonetheless, the principle is too narrowly defined allowing, as it does, print and other forms of reminder advertisements (such as those described above by GlaxoSmithKline, Bayer, and Pfizer to advertise their erectile disfunction drugs). Non-broadcast advertisements do not differ from broadcast advertisements in any substantive way that would justify permitting them to continue being used to build brand identity. In other words, if there are ethically sound reasons for banning broadcast reminder advertisements then, barring an argument to the contrary, there are ethically sound reasons for banning all reminder advertisements. PhRMA should articulate a plausible justification for permitting non-broadcast reminder advertisements or ban such advertisements as well. Given that all reminder advertisements are commonly understood within the advertising industry to build brand awareness of a product, rather than to educate consumers regarding the range of appropriate therapies for specific medical conditions, it is difficult to imagine how such advertisements could be ethically justified.

It is also the case that not all signatories of the Guiding Principles are adhering to the ban on broadcast reminder advertisements. Sepracor has publicly committed to adhering to the principles but continued running broadcast reminder advertisements for Lunesta. And Pfizer initiated a new broadcast reminder advertisement for Viagra in Canada well after it committed to adhere to PhRMA's Guiding Principles. At present, PhRMA invites public comment on compliance with the Guiding Principles (submitted by fax and conventional mail only). This material is collected and distributed to individual companies who in turn are encouraged to respond to individual commentators. PhRMA does not make the comments, or the companies, or the company responses public.[24] If PhRMA is to be taken seriously as an organization whose purpose is, in part, to self-regulate the pharmaceutical industry it needs to track the compliance with its guidelines and codes by signatory companies, report its findings to the public, and disavow the marketing practices of those signatory companies that violate its guidelines. If companies such a Sepracor can publicly commit to adhering to PhRMA's DTC advertising guidelines, while at the same time running broadcast advertisements that violate the guidelines, both the guidelines and PhRMA will rightly be regarded as lacking credibility.

Product Claim Advertisements

Let us now examine the ethical legitimacy of "product claim" advertisements. Let us do so by considering the impact of such advertisements relative to two contested matters. First, the impact of such advertisements on healthcare costs. Second, the role of such advertisements in promoting consumer education regarding medical conditions and their treatments.

The pharmaceutical industry consistently denies that DTC advertising raises the price of prescription pharmaceuticals. In defense of this position they argue that there is no evidence to support the claim that rapidly increasing numbers of DTC advertisements are causally related to rising drug prices. That this would be the case is not surprising, since such a causal connection would be difficult to document. Nonetheless, the billions of dollars spent annually in the US on DTC advertising must be accounted for somehow. There are a limited number of sources for such money. The three most obvious and sustainable of these include cuts in other areas of corporate spending such as research and development or wages and benefits, lower return on equity to shareholders, or increased revenues from drug sales. It is not unreasonable to think that a significant portion of the cost of DTC advertising is passed on to consumers via higher drug prices. However, even if it could be made clear that DTC advertising causes the price of prescription drugs to rise, this would not by itself constitute an objection to DTC advertising. Additional arguments would be needed. For example, it would need to be argued that pharmaceutical companies, rather than governments, have an ethical obligation to ensure that prices for innovative, new drugs do not exceed certain limits. While such a claim may be plausibly developed, grounded perhaps in a recognition of efficacious and life-improving drugs as social goods, that is not a position that will be argued for in the space of this chapter. Alternatively, it could be argued that some DTC advertising uses manipulative marketing techniques to increase spending on pharmaceuticals. If increased spending can be tied to the intentional manipulation of consumers, then there would be good reason for arguing that the increased costs are illegitimate. This is the strategy that will be utilized in the remainder of this section.

DTC advertising may have adverse effects on the cost of healthcare by simply increasing unnecessary spending on pharmaceuticals. Many of the drugs pitched by pharmaceutical companies in DTC advertisements are no better than much less expensive drugs already available. Consider, for example, the antihistamine Claritin manufactured by Schering-Plough. This drug was one of the first to be marketed to consumers after the change in FDA rules regarding DTC advertising. Despite the existence of equally good or better, but much less expensive, allergy medications, DTC advertisement driven patient spending on Claritin rose to $2.6 billion in 2000. Numerous prescription drugs with equally unremarkable profiles in comparison to their much less expensive competitors have been marketed via DTC advertising. Among the most well known of these are the cox-2 inhibitors Vioxx (manufactured and marketed by Merck) and Celebrex (manufactured and marketed by Pfizer), and the nonsteroidal anti-inflammatory Relafen (manufactured and marketed by SmithKline Beecham).

Product claim advertisements for such drugs often lead patients to believe that only the advertised drug will do. One physician characterized his interactions with his patients, in the wake of the Claritin campaign, in the following terms,

> It certainly convinced many of my patients that they needed not just any allergy medicine, but Claritin and only Claritin. They resisted the idea that there were equally good and perhaps better ways to relieve their allergy symptoms than a new (and therefore less well tested) drug. Moreover, they were unconcerned about Claritin's cost (more than $2.10 per day): most had prescription drug coverage as part of their health insurance.[25]

This anecdotal evidence is supported by a recent study that concluded that "Patients' requests for medicines are a powerful driver of prescribing decisions."[26] The aggregate impact of millions of patients exerting similar influence over physicians is a substantial and scientifically unwarranted increase in the cost of healthcare. Editors at the *Canadian Association of Medicine Journal* concluded that if DTC advertising were to be introduced in Canada, prescription drug costs to the government would increase on an annual basis by Cdn$1.2 billion.[27] While some of that spending would be on drugs that patients need and which are the best available for the price, much of the spending would be on expensive "me-too" drugs, or on drugs that medicalize normal human experience. Consumer driven spending on such drugs has amounted to additional billions of dollars being spent on healthcare in the US. These increased costs are primarily born by public and private health insurance companies, employers and subscribers via higher premiums, and taxpayers. There is, of course, shared responsibility for these increased costs. The US government permits the use of such advertisements, patients pressure physicians to provide them with branded drugs, physicians often acquiesce to such pressure, and insurance companies may not adequately dissuade patients from choosing expensive drugs. Nonetheless, because pharmaceutical companies develop and aggressively market these drugs in a manipulative manner, they bear a disproportionate level of responsibility for these increased healthcare costs.

Expenditures on such drugs are objectionable primarily when those expenditures are the result of manipulative advertising campaigns for

brand name products. Manipulation has both a metaphorical and nonmetaphorical usage.[28] It is in the nonmetaphorical sense that we say that one
manipulates a complicated object or system such as a magnetic resonance
imaging machine. Such manipulation typically involves a sophisticated
understanding of the object to be manipulated. Interpersonal manipulation
is similar in that it typically involves a complex understanding of the agents
involved, or of relevant feature of human psychology in general, as well as an
instrumental treatment of those agents. Manipulation of this sort, as contrasted with rational persuasion, is characterized by the skillful control of
circumstances and information in a manner intended to alter the judgment or
behavior of a person in a manner consistent with the preferences of the
person, group, or organization responsible for the manipulative activity. In
such cases one does not merely seek to provide straightforward reasons for an
agent to act in a particular way, one seeks to engineer that outcome via
peripheral means and regardless of the victim's judgment.[29] The carefully
crafted manner in which influence is brought to bear on victims of manipulation often involves deceptive practices that are themselves objectionable.[30]

Manipulation is *prima facie* wrong because it treats the subjects of
manipulation as mere tools, as objects lacking the rational capacity to
choose for themselves how they shall act.[31] The Kantian origins of this
concept of respect for persons are well known.[32] In this view, all persons
possess dignity, or intrinsic value, and that this dignity must be respected.[33]
The obligation that we respect others requires that we not use people as a
means only, but instead that we treat other people as capable of autonomous, principled action. The pharmaceutical industry explicitly denies that
it uses manipulative or even persuasive, mass market advertising to sell drugs
to consumers. As we have seen, the pharmaceutical industry argues repeatedly and consistently that it is in the business of educating consumers about
healthcare choices.

Product claim advertisements are properly characterized as manipulative
for several reasons. First, it is clear that many product claim advertisements
make use of peripheral techniques that appeal to emotion and unreflective
dispositions rather than a central route of rational persuasion. Social scientists who work with the elaboration likelihood model of persuasion refer to
an elaboration continuum with the central, analytic route having high
cognitive elaboration and the peripheral route having low or no cognitive
elaboration.[34] When product claim advertisements make use of image such
as cartoon moth lulling restless sleepers into a sound slumber (Lunesta),
men with horns sprouting from their temples (Viagra), and friendly
Hollywood stars such as Sally Field giving medical advice (Boniva), they

are making use of low elaboration models of persuasion. In other words, they are working to persuade consumers to seek these drugs using the standard low elaboration techniques of persuasive advertising.

Given the pervasiveness of peripheral advertising techniques in the US, and the apparent widespread acceptance of such techniques, it is worth considering why the pharmaceutical industry does not openly defend its right to advertise to consumers in this way. The reason, of course, is that there is also widespread acceptance of the view that pharmaceuticals are different in important ways from soap, automobiles, clothing, jewelry, and even over-the-counter drugs. Prescription pharmaceuticals are different in kind from consumer goods. Indeed, they can usefully be characterized as a hazardous substance along with hazardous materials such as arsenic, toluene, and plutonium insofar as they (a) are potentially harmful to human health and (b) are products that require specialized scientific or technical knowledge in order to be used safely. It is this quality of pharmaceuticals that is the statutory basis for the criteria used to distinguish prescription pharmaceuticals from over-the-counter pharmaceuticals in US law. The 1951 Durham-Humphrey Amendment to the Food, Drug, and Cosmetic Act specifies that drugs that can only be used safely under the supervision of a physician require a prescription.[35] Prescription pharmaceuticals differ from other consumer goods in that they have been determined by scientific experts to require the supervision of a physician for their effective and safe use. Physicians themselves need to be familiar with the physician package insert (PI) provided by the drug manufacturers in compliance with FDA guidelines, which indicate usage and proper dosage, detail known side-effects, and specify drug interactions, among other important details. These inserts are written in technical language intended to be understood by physicians, and are not typically intelligible to non-physicians. Without knowledge of these technical details, as well as the clinical and scientific knowledge necessary to interpret these details, consumers are not in a position to determine whether or not such drugs are appropriate for their personal use, and if so whether other available drugs are more appropriate for medical or economic reasons. There is then a compelling public safety argument against branded DTC advertising.

The second reason for characterizing DTC advertising as manipulative is that it is implausible, on any reasonable definition of education, to characterize non-cognitive persuasion as education. Since these advertisements are defended as educational, and given that they do not meet minimum standards of education, it is reasonable to characterize this defense of DTC advertising an attempt to manipulate consumers into believing a proposition that is not true. Pharmaceutical companies must characterize their branded DTC advertising as purely educational because there is no plausible case to be made in defense of the use of peripheral marketing techniques to increase sales of prescription drugs.

In reply, defenders of DTC advertising argue that DTC advertisements enhance consumer autonomy and empower patients to communicate with physicians regarding their healthcare needs. This claim is unpersuasive in the case of branded advertisements for several reasons. First, the advertisements themselves do not provide sufficient information to assess the efficacy of the drug in relation to the consumer's current health. Second, the information that is presented is almost always biased in favor of the drug being pitched. Third, the vast majority of consumer's lack the sophisticated knowledge of medicine necessary to assess the claims being made to determine whether or not the claims have validity.

While it is important to distinguish individual advertising campaigns from one another and to assess their accuracy on an individual basis, there is significant evidence that branded DTC campaigns constitute intentionally manipulative and misleading efforts to persuade consumers to purchase branded drugs rather than genuine educational campaigns.[36] Indeed, a major FDA survey found that most physicians believe that DTC advertisements provide unbalanced information regarding the risks and benefits of the drugs they are selling.[37] According to the FDA,

Seventy percent (70%) of primary care physicians said that DTC advertising confuses their patients either "a great deal" (28%) or "somewhat" (42%) about the relative risks and benefits of prescription drugs, whereas about 60 percent of specialists rated the confusion as either "a great deal" (24%) or "somewhat" (36%). Seventy-five percent (75%) of physicians of both categories indicated that DTC advertising causes patients to believe either "a great deal" (32%) or "somewhat" (43%) that drugs work better than they actually do.[38]

This should not be surprising, for a full accounting of the risks and benefits of a drug cannot be depicted in broadcast advertisements and are difficult to communicate in print advertisements. Recall that the FDA approved product claim broadcast advertisements so long as such advertisements refer consumers to print advertisements where "adequate provision" of the adverse risks of such drugs are explained in detail. The difficulty here is that the print advertisements do not meet the adequate provision requirement. To provide consumers with the requisite information such advertisements would need to be intelligible to a significant majority of the adult population in the US. A study by the American Association of Retired Persons found that one-third of 1,310 adults failed to notice the fine print, and of those who did notice it one-third read the fine print.[39] The study did not assess comprehension of the fine print by the approximately one-fifth of adults surveyed who actually read that fine print. However, a Kaiser Family Foundation survey of 1,872 adults found that 70% of those shown advertisements reported that they had learned little or nothing about the condition requiring treatment.[40] Finally, the authors of a recent study found that of 69 print advertisements that were studied all required a college or graduate level education in order to be understood.[41] Just 27% of the adult population in the US is college educated.[42] These surveys confirm what common sense would suggest, namely, that most DTC advertising is unsuccessful at educating consumers about diseases, the appropriate use of the advertised drugs, and their risks. DTC advertising seems instead to play the role described in a pharmaceutical trade magazine, namely, to "ensur[e] that patients walk out of the doctor's office with a prescription for a particular brand, rather than for a competitor's product or for some other form of therapy."[43]

DTC advertising that was genuinely educational would provide consumers with objective and impartial information about the drug being advertised. As a minimum, this would include a description of the disease or ailment that the drug is approved to treat, an accurate and balanced account of the drug's risks and benefits in relation to other available medications, available non-drug therapies, and a cost comparison for the consumer *qua* patient in relation to other available medications. Branded "product claim" advertisements typically cannot fulfill these educational goals because the purpose of such advertisements is not to provide patients *qua* consumers with the information they need to have informed conversations with their physicians regarding possible treatment regimens. Rather, the goal of such advertisements is to have patients communicate a preference for a particular brand to the physician, with the well-founded assumption that the physician will comply at least some of the time. Branded advertisements that purport to be educational, but actually pitch specific products are manipulative insofar as they use patients as tools to secure prescriptions from doctors for the advertised drugs. It is, of course, within the power of physicians to deny these requests when they are not in the best interest of their patients. However, pharmaceutical companies rely on the fact that many physicians may themselves be persuaded by demanding patients in conjunction with pharmaceutical marketing representatives (see Chapter 5). The claim that physicians are themselves capable of being manipulated into prescribing particular drugs should not be surprising to anyone familiar with the ways in which pharmaceutical companies spend $22 billion annually on marketing to physicians.[44]

Help-Seeking Advertisements

Despite these objections to "product claim" advertisements, it would be wrong to conclude that all DTC advertising is unethical. Non-branded, "help-seeking" advertisements have the potential to play genuinely educational roles while at the same time enhancing the revenues of pharmaceutical companies in ethically legitimate ways. This could be accomplished with careful, non-branded advertisements that do two things. First, describe an ailment or disease, such as diabetes, hypertension, or osteoporosis. Second, invite consumers interested in learning more about symptoms and treatments of the disease to consult a web page or call a toll free number to obtain a brochure. The information obtained from these sources would be the same and would contain the following information:

1. a detailed description of the disease or ailment
2. available non-drug therapies
3. a description of available medications, including an accurate and balanced account of the risks and benefits
4. a cost comparison of medications in relation to other available medications.

Consumers who had access to such information would be genuinely empowered to have informed conversations with their physicians regarding the problem for which they are seeking help and available treatment options. Companies with pharmaceuticals that are competitive on the basis of therapeutic and economic value would have a clear incentive for producing such non-branded DTC advertisements.

Some company executives may suspect that competitors may not produce genuinely objective informational brochures, if it is in their self-interest not to do so. There is merit to this concern, but there is also a ready solution to the problem. The responsibility for overseeing the design of non-branded DTC brochures should be turned over to a new Center for Pharmaceutical Education at the National Institutes of Health. The new NIH Center would have responsibility for overseeing the design and distribution of the brochures and the web pages. The center would be funded by the companies running the help-seeking advertisements. However, the companies would not be entitled to directly influence the information provided by NIH. Instead, the information would be provided by NIH researchers and would be grounded in the scientific literature. Such a strategy is consistent with concern for the well-being of patients, as well as fair and honest competition among pharmaceutical companies in the healthcare marketplace.

APPENDIX I PHRMA GUIDING PRINCIPLES

1. These Principles are premised on the recognition that DTC advertising of prescription medicines can benefit the public health by increasing awareness about diseases, educating patients about treatment options, motivating patients to contact their physicians and engage in a dialogue about health concerns, increasing the likelihood that patients will receive appropriate care for conditions that are frequently under-diagnosed and under-treated, and encouraging compliance with prescription drug treatment regimens.

2. In accordance with FDA regulations, all DTC information should be accurate and not misleading, should make claims only when supported by substantial evidence, should reflect balance between risks and benefits, and should be consistent with FDA approved labeling.

3. DTC television and print advertising which is designed to market a prescription drug should also be designed to responsibly educate the consumer about that medicine and, where appropriate, the condition for which it may be prescribed.

4. DTC television and print advertising of prescription drugs should clearly indicate that the medicine is a prescription drug to distinguish such advertising from other advertising for non-prescription products.

5. DTC television and print advertising should foster responsible communications between patients and healthcare professionals to help patients achieve better health and a more complete appreciation of both the health benefits and the known risks associated with the medicine being advertised.

6. In order to foster responsible communication between patients and healthcare professionals, companies should spend an appropriate amount of time to educate health professionals about a new medicine or a new therapeutic indication before commencing the first DTC advertising campaign. In determining what constitutes an appropriate time, companies should take into account the relative importance of informing patients of the availability of a new medicine, the complexity of the risk–benefit profile of that new medicine and healthcare professionals' knowledge of the condition being treated. Companies should continue to educate healthcare professionals as additional valid information about a new medicine is obtained from all reliable sources.

7. Working with the FDA, companies should continue to responsibly alter or discontinue a DTC advertising campaign should new and reliable information indicate a serious previously unknown safety risk.

8. Companies should submit all new DTC television advertisements to the FDA before releasing these advertisements for broadcast.
9. DTC television and print advertising should include information about the availability of other options such as diet and lifestyle changes where appropriate for the advertised condition.
10. DTC television advertising that identifies a product by name should clearly state the health conditions for which the medicine is approved and the major risks associated with the medicine being advertised.
11. DTC television and print advertising should be designed to achieve a balanced presentation of both the benefits and the risks associated with the advertised prescription medicine. Specifically, risks and safety information in DTC television advertising should be presented in clear, understandable language, without distraction from the content, and in a manner that supports the responsible dialogue between patients and healthcare professionals.
12. All DTC advertising should respect the seriousness of the health conditions and the medicine being advertised.
13. In terms of content and placement, DTC television and print advertisements should be targeted to avoid audiences that are not age appropriate for the messages involved.
14. Companies are encouraged to promote health and disease awareness as part of their DTC advertising.
15. Companies are encouraged to include information in all DTC advertising, where feasible, about help for the uninsured and underinsured.[45]

NOTES

1. Among industrialized nations, only New Zealand also allows DTC advertising.
2. Les Toop and Dee Mangin, "Industry Funded Patient Information and the Slippery Slope to New Zealand," *British Medical Journal* 335 (October 2007): 694–695.
3. Rachel E. Behrman, Deputy Director, Food and Drug Administration, "The Impact of Direct-to-Consumer Advertising on Seniors' Health and Health Care Costs," Testimony before the Special Committee on Aging, United States Senate, September 22, 2005, 3. Available at www.hhs.gov/asl/testify/t050929.html.
4. Food and Drug Administration, US Department of Health and Human Services, "Guidance for Industry: Consumer-Directed Broadcast Advertisements," (August 1999), pp. 2–3.
5. Behrman, "The Impact of Direct-to-Consumer Advertising on Seniors' Health and Health Care Costs," 12–15.
6. Matthew Arnold, "DTC: The First Ten Years," *Medical, Marketing & Media* (April 2007): 39. These figures are slightly different than those cited by Julie E.

Donohue and her collaborators who put the 1996 figure at $985 million. See Julie M. Donohue, Marisa Cevasco, and Meredith B. Rosenthal, "A Decade of Direct-to-Consumer Advertising of Prescription Drugs," *New England Journal of Medicine* 357 (2007): 673–81.

7. Donohue, *et al.*, "A Decade of Direct-to-Consumer Advertising of Prescription Drugs," 676.

8. Andrew Jack, "Call to Widen Drug Information in Europe," *Financial Times*, September 28, 2006; and Toop and Mangin, "Industry Funded Patient Information and the Slippery Slope to New Zealand."

9. Behrman, "The Impact of Direct-to-Consumer Advertising on Seniors' Health and Health Care Costs," 3.

10. Ibid., 6.

11. Thomas Abrams, "The Regulation of Prescription Drug Promotion," in Michael A. Santoro and Thomas M. Gorrie, *Ethics and the Pharmaceutical Industry* (New York: Cambridge University Press 2005): p. 162.

12. PhRMA, "Pharmaceutical Marketing & Promotion Q&A: Tough Questions, Straight Answers," 10. Available at <www.phrma.org/files/Tough_Questions. pdf>.

13. Hank McKinnell, *A Call to Action: Taking Back Health Care for Future Generations* (New York: McGraw Hill, 2005): p. 181.

14. John E. Calfee, "Public Policy Issues in Direct-to-consumer Advertising of Prescription Drugs," (July 8, 2002): 46. Available at www.fda.gov/ohrms/ dockets/dailys/02/Sep02/092302/02N-0209_emc-000183-01.pdf.

15. See, for example, Barbara Mintzes, "Direct to Consumer Advertising is Medicalising Normal Human Experience," *British Medical Journal* 324, April 13, 2002: 908; John Abramson, *Overdosed America: The Broken Promise of American Medicine* (New York: HarperCollins, 2005), Chapter 10; and Jerry Avron, *Powerful Medicines: The Benefits, Risks, and Costs of Prescription Drugs* (New York: Random House, 2007): p. 289.

16. Abramson, *Overdosed America*, p. 155.

17. See, for example, Matthew F. Hollon, "Direct-to-Consumer Advertising: A Haphazard Approach to Health Promotion," *Journal of the American Medical Association* 293, 16 (April 2005): 2030–2033, 2031 and "Direct-to-Consumer Marketing of Prescription Drugs: Creating Consumer Demand." *Journal of the American Medical Association* 281, 4 (January 1999): 382–384; Richard L. Kravitz, *et al.*, "Influence of Patients' Requests for Direct-to-Consumer Advertised Antidepressants: A Randomized Controlled Trial," *Journal of the American Medical Association* 293, 16 (April 2005): 1995–2002.

18. See, for example, Abramson, *Overdosed America*, pp. 158–159; and Avorn, *Powerful Medicines*, pp. 288–290.

19. Alison Keith, "Information Matters: The Consumer as the Integrated Health Care System" in *Prescription Drug Advertising: Empowering Consumers Through Information.* Published by Pfizer as part of the series *Economic Realities in Health Care Policy*, 2, 1 (East Brunswick, NJ: Pfizer, 2001). Available at: www.pfizer.com/about/public_policy/resources.jsp.

20. PhRMA, "Pharmaceutical Marketing & Promotion Q&A," 6.
21. Ibid., 8.
22. Stephanie Saul, "Drug Makers to Police Consumer Campaigns," *New York Times*, August 3, 2005.
23. US Food and Drug Administration, Division of Drug Marketing, Advertising, and Communications, "Prescription Drug Advertising and Promotional Labeling," *Center for Drug Evaluation and Research Handbook*, p. 8. Created April 16, 1998; revised November 7, 2006. Available at www.fda.gov/cder/ddmac/FAQS.HTM#reminder.
24. PhRMA Office of Accountability, "Report of Second Survey of Signatory Companies," (2006). Available at: www.phrma.org/office_of_accountability/.
25. John Abramson, *Overdosed America*, p. 152.
26. Barbara Mintzes, *et al.*, "Influence of Direct to Consumer Pharmaceutical Advertising and Patients' Requests on Prescribing Decisions: Two Site Cross Sectional Survey," *British Medical Journal*, February 2, 2002, 279.
27. "Ads and Prescription Pads," *Canadian Medical Association Journal*, 169, 5 (September 2, 2003): 381.
28. Joel Rudinow makes this point in "Manipulation," *Ethics* 88 (1978): 338–347, 339. The overall account of manipulation provided here follows my argument in Denis G. Arnold, "Coercion and Moral Responsibility," *American Philosophical Quarterly*, 38: 1 (January 2001): 53–67.
29. Michael Kligman and Charles Culver, "An Analysis of Interpersonal Manipulation," *The Journal of Medicine and Philosophy* 17 (1992), 186–187.
30. As Joel Rudinow convincingly argues, manipulation does not always involve deception. See Rudinow, "Manipulation," 340.
31. It is important to distinguish between personal autonomy and moral autonomy. Here I am primarily concerned with personal autonomy, or the capacity for self-governance, rather than moral autonomy or the capacity to act in a manner consistent with moral law. Kant defends a moral account of autonomy, but contemporary Kantians frequently defend non-substantive accounts of personal autonomy. For discussion, see Tom L. Beauchamp, "Who Deserves Autonomy, and Whose Autonomy Deserves Respect," in *Personal Autonomy*, ed. James Stacey Taylor, (Cambridge: Cambridge University Press, 2005), pp. 310–330.
32. For discussion of a contemporary Kantian view of respect for persons see Joseph Raz, *Value, Respect, and Attachment* (Cambridge: Cambridge University Press, 2001), esp. Chapter 4.
33. For detailed discussion of the concept of dignity as it is used here see Thomas E. Hill, Jr. *Dignity and Practical Reason* (Ithaca, NY: Cornell University Press, 1992), esp. pp. 202–203.
34. For an overview of this literature see R. E. Petty and D. T. Wegener, "The Elaboration Likelihood Model: Current Status and Controversy," in *Dual Process Theories in Social Psychology*, ed. S. Chaiken and Y. Trope (London: Guilford, 1999).

35. For discussion see Eric P. Brass, "Changing the Status of Drugs from Prescription to Over-the-Counter Availability," *The New England Journal of Medicine* 345, 11 (2001): 810–816.
36. This point is made by the editors of the *Canadian Medical Association Journal* in "Ads and Prescription Pads."
37. Kathryn J. Aikin, John L. Swasy, and Amie C. Braman, "Patient and Physician Attitudes and Behaviors Associated With DTC Promotion of Prescription Drugs: Summary of FDA Survey Research Results, Final Report," November 19, 2004. Available at www.fda.gov/cder/ddmac/researchka.htm.
38. Ibid, 73.
39. "Free Rein for Drug Ads? A Slowdown in FDA Review Has Left Consumers More Vulnerable to Misleading Messages," *Consumer Reports*, February 2002. Available at www.consumerreports.org:80/cro/health-fitness/drugs-supplements/drug-ads-203/overview/index.htm.
40. Ibid.
41. Kimberly A. Kaphingst, *et al.*, "Literacy Demands of Product Information Intended to Supplement Television Direct-to-Consumer Prescription Drug Advertisements," *Patient Education and Counseling* 55 (2004): 293–300.
42. Nicole Stoops, US Census Bureau, *Educational Attainment in the United States: 2003.* (Washington, DC: June 2004). Available at www.census.gov/prod/2004pubs/p20-550.pdf.
43. "Free rein for drug ads?"
44. Donohue, *et al.*, "A Decade of Direct-to-Consumer Advertising of Prescription Drugs," 676.
45. The Pharmaceutical Research and Manufacturers of America, "PhRMA Guiding Principles: Direct to Consumer Advertisements About Prescription Medicines." Available at www.phrma.org/publications/policy_papers/phrma_dtc_guiding_principles/.

CHAPTER 7

Industry-funded bioethics and
the limits of disclosure

Carl Elliott

Over the past several years, a range of different enterprises in bioethics have
become financially tied to the pharmaceutical and biotechnology industries.
Bioethicists have started moonlighting as advisors and consultants to industry; bioethics centers have begun looking to industry for operating support
and grants; even the ethical oversight of biomedical research has transformed itself into a for-profit, commercial enterprise funded largely by the
pharmaceutical industry. As these various industry-funded bioethics activities have emerged, they have generated an ethical question of their own. Do
pharmaceutical industry ties represent a conflict of interest for bioethicists?[1]

To many outside observers, it is clear that they do.[1] Bioethicists often
review industry-sponsored clinical trials on Institutional Review Boards;
they help make policy relevant to industry practices for governmental and
professional bodies; they write articles about the ethics of industry practices
for scholarly journals and the popular press. And of course, they teach
classes on the ethics of industry practices to university students, medical
residents and practicing physicians.

Although a variety of approaches to handling financial conflicts of
interest have emerged in different areas of public life, the solution that
bioethicists have generally relied on for their own potential conflicts is
disclosure.[2] This solution parallels the standard practice in science and
medicine. If bioethicists make it a policy to disclose their financial conflicts
in their articles, it is argued, readers can take this knowledge into consideration when they evaluate what they read.

As a practical matter, it is difficult to imagine how disclosure would work.
To whom should the disclosures be made? It is one thing to say that ethicists
should disclose their corporate ties in their peer-reviewed articles, but quite
another to ask them to disclose to every person who might be affected by
them. Should university teachers be required to list their financial ties on
course descriptions? During lectures? Is a bioethicist obligated to make a
disclosure to every journalist who calls for a comment? Should their

financial ties be disclosed to audiences during television appearances? Should they disclose to the research subjects enrolled in the studies evaluated by the IRBs on which they serve? How exactly would they do that?

I will argue that disclosure is insufficient as a remedy for the problems of industry funding, and that it is unlikely to be effective. The problem with industry-funded bioethics is not so much secrecy as influence, and the best remedy is simply to cut the financial ties between bioethics and industry. I will present five separate but related problems with disclosure as a solution for conflict of interest, and I will finish by calling into question the actual *need* for industry-funded bioethics. But first we need to ask: what is the extent of the problem?

THE VARIETIES OF INDUSTRY FUNDING

The most straightforward sources of industry funding come in the form of donations to bioethics centers (or to health law and medical humanities centers), usually as gifts or general operating support.[3] For example, the Hastings Center, an independent think-tank in Garrison, New York, and one of the oldest bioethics institutions in the world, has for many years accepted funding from a range of corporate sources, including biotechnology and pharmaceutical corporations such as Roche, Affymetrix, Millenium Pharmaceuticals and the Biotechnology Trade Organization. The University of Pennsylvania Center for Bioethics has been supported by an even wider range of companies, including Pfizer, Wyeth and Astra Zeneca.[4] The Merck Company Foundation has founded and supported ethics centers in the United Arab Emirates, Turkey, South Africa and Colombia.[5] The University of North Florida has a bioethics center sponsored by Blue Cross Blue Shield, a health insurer.[6] Pfizer sponsors a self-standing "medical humanities" initiative with a variety of different grant-making functions, and has supported programs at NYU medical school, among others.[7]

Other universities have industry-funded chairs or lectureships, such as the Pfizer lectureship in medical humanities at the University College and Royal Free Medical School in London, or the Sanofi-Aventis Chair in Bioethics and Drug Development at the ESSEC Business School in Paris.[8] The University of Toronto Joint Centre for Bioethics was directed by the occupant of the Sun-Life Financial Chair in Bioethics, while several other universities have offered visiting professorships sponsored by industry, such as the Merck visiting lectureship in health law at Seton Hall University, or the SmithKline Beecham visiting lectureship at Arizona State University.[9]

A related avenue for industry support comes in the form of grants for specific projects. Occasionally this money goes to educational efforts, such as the initiative sponsored by the American Medical Association's Council for Ethical and Judicial Affairs aimed at educating doctors about accepting gifts from industry. That initiative was supported by a $670,000 gift from a variety of pharmaceutical companies.[10] More often, however, directed funding supports bioethics research. Several years ago, for example, the Stanford Center for Bioethics accepted nearly a million dollars for a research project from SmithKline Beecham (now GlaxoSmithKline.) The current University of Pennsylvania website lists research projects funded by Dow, Dupont, Monsanto and Pfizer. The editor of the *American Journal of Bioethics* recently co-authored an article on genetics that acknowledged support from deCode Genetics, while a group at the University of Toronto Joint Centre for Bioethics has published a number of papers on biotechnology and the developing world funded by matching grants from GlaxoSmithKline, Pfizer and Merck.[11]

Somewhat more difficult to document is the extent to which individual bioethicists are employed as private consultants or advisors to industry. Industry press releases and university annual reports indicate that the practice could be fairly widespread. Recent press releases and university reports suggest that bioethicists are consulting for companies such as Johnson and Johnson, Pfizer, Dupont, Wyeth, Affymetrix, Roche Genetics, Genomics Collaborative, Sequenom, Novartis, Eli Lilly, GlaxoSmithKline, and PhRMA, the pharmaceutical trade group. Some biotechnology companies, such as Geron and Advanced Cell Technologies, have hired bioethics advisory boards. When the American Society for Bioethics and Humanities commissioned a panel to examine private consultation to industry in 2002, its published report indicated that eight of the ten panel members had financial ties to industry of the sort that it was examining.[12]

A handful of bioethics journal editors have also consulted for industry. The editor of the research ethics journal *IRB* later acknowledged consultation fees from Eli Lilly that would have been earned during the time when he was editing the journal.[13] The editor of *Accountability in Research* chaired an ethics advisory board for GlaxoSmithKline.[14] The editor of the *American Journal of Bioethics* served on an ethics advisory board for Advanced Cell Technologies.[15] Occasionally pharmaceutical companies have supported bioethics conferences, some of which have been translated into journal issues. For example, the proceedings of conferences at the University of Chicago funded by Merck, Pfizer and PhRMA, the pharmaceutical trade group, have been published in *Perspectives in Biology and Medicine* and *The Yale Journal of Health Policy, Law and Ethics*.[16]

For many years pharmaceutical companies have paid physicians, usually academic physicians, to give lectures on topics relevant to the company's products. These lecturers are known in the industry as "thought leaders" or "Key Opinion Leaders." More recently, companies have begun sponsoring lectures by bioethicists. Occasionally these lectures are to company executives. The editor of the *American Journal of Bioethics*, for example, has disclosed payment for a lecture to executives at Johnson and Johnson.[17] Occasionally these lectures are delivered to meetings of industry trade associations.[18] Paid lectures to industry groups are probably less common than paid consultations and advisory board memberships, but the lecture fees can be very high. According to the fee schedules for some speakers' bureaus, a well-known bioethicist can command speaking fees of up to $25,000 per lecture.[19]

Finally – and perhaps most importantly – is an emerging, for-profit intersection between bioethics and the protection of research subjects.[20] In most countries, subjects who volunteer for medical research are protected by ethics committees, which review research protocols to ensure that they are ethically sound. In the United States, these committees are known as Institutional Review Boards (IRBs). IRBs originated in the 1970s after various scandals involving medical research. The idea behind IRBs was that a research protocol ought to be reviewed by a committee independent of the researchers conducting the study, whose scientific enthusiasm might lead them to cut corners or downplay the safety of research subjects, thus placing them at inappropriate risk. Most academic IRBs are composed of researchers and healthcare personnel working in the same university or hospital where the investigator of the study works. They also usually include members from the lay community, as well as at least one member trained in ethics, such as a bioethicist or a member of the clergy.

When IRBs were first established, however, medical research was conducted mainly by individual investigators working in academic settings who were funded by the federal government. These investigators usually had little or no financial stake in their studies. Today, medical research is an enormously profitable, multinational corporate enterprise. The primary financial engine of clinical medical research is no longer universities but the pharmaceutical industry. As recently as ten or fifteen years ago the pharmaceutical industry usually contracted with academic researchers to test new drugs. Today, however, the pharmaceutical industry employs Contract Research Organizations (CROs) to arrange for clinical studies to be conducted in physicians' offices, industry laboratories and private testing sites. According to a recent article in the *New England Journal of Medicine*, 63%

of clinical trials took place in academic settings in 1994. By 2004, that figure had dropped to 26%.[21]

Alongside this movement of clinical trials from academic settings to for-profit sites has come a movement of ethics review from academic settings to for-profit IRBs. For-profit IRBs (sometimes called commercial IRBs, private IRBs or Non-Institutional Review Boards) are independent, profit-making entities that provide ethics review to pharmaceutical companies or CROs in exchange for a fee. For-profit IRBs review most of the studies done in private testing sites or physicians' offices. Some for-profit IRBs are quite small and meet infrequently, while others are large, comprehensive and very profitable.

Yet for-profit IRBs have a built-in conflict of interest. Their purpose is to protect research subjects from the risks of research studies, yet their financial livelihood depends on money from the corporate entities conducting the studies. For-profit IRBs market themselves to industry not on the strictness of their ethics review, but on their speed and efficiency. If a for-profit IRB rejects a study as unethical, the company sponsoring the study can simply send it somewhere else.

THE SOCIAL CAUSES OF INDUSTRY-FUNDED BIOETHICS

The striking thing about industry-funded bioethics is not so much its scope or extent but the fact that it is relatively new – and apparently on the rise. As recently as ten or fifteen years ago it was rare to see any association between bioethics and the pharmaceutical or biotechnology industries; now, if still not exactly commonplace, industry-funded bioethics is common enough so that it does not raise any eyebrows anymore. What has happened to bring about this change?

First, many bioethics centers and programs are now being set up in medical schools, hospitals and academic health centers. Increasingly, faculty members in medical settings are expected to generate their salaries and research funding through a combination of patient care (for which they can bill third-party payers) and external research grants. When bioethicists are employed in these settings (as opposed to, say, departments of philosophy or religious studies, or law schools) they are often subject to the same expectations. Given a limited number of government and philanthropic funding sources, it is not surprising that they should turn to the pharmaceutical industry.

Second, the public profile and influence of bioethicists has grown significantly over the past two decades. Because bioethicists hold positions in a range of government agencies and professional bodies, they are perceived to have political and professional power. The perception of power has made industry more interested in funding bioethicists (or, at least, in using them). Bioethicists, in turn, have been willing to accept industry consultancies and research funding, because these things are now seen as a mark of status in universities.

Third, the pharmaceutical industry became extraordinarily profitable during the 1990s, and thus it generated more income for marketing and public relations. The biotechnology industry also began to thrive, but saw many of its projects (such as cloning and embryonic stem cell research) attracting ethical scrutiny. Pharmaceutical research began moving out of universities and into the private sector. Rather than contracting with academic researchers to test new drugs, the pharmaceutical industry found it cheaper and more efficient to conduct studies in physicians' offices, industry laboratories, and private testing sites. With private-sector clinical research and a profitable pharmaceutical and biotechnology industry has come more opportunities for privately funded ethics – ethics advisory boards, ethics consultants, corporate compliance officers, and for-profit IRBs.

Each of the different forms of industry-funded bioethics raises different problems, and if managed separately, each would require a different solution. (Unless, of course, the ties with industry were simply eliminated.) What I want to argue here, however, is that whatever the extent and shape of those problems, and whatever their root causes, mere disclosure will not be enough to fix them.

PROBLEM I: NON-COMPLIANCE

The first problem with disclosure is purely practical: people do not disclose their industry ties, even when they are asked. Anyone who has begun digging into the question of which bioethicists are working for which corporations will have discovered that industry-funded bioethicists rarely disclose their corporate ties in their publications or on their CVs, even when asked. In this they are no different from physicians. As Leslie Ingraham, director of Continuing Medical Education at the University of New England College of Medicine told *Medical Meetings* magazine, "The funny thing about speakers is how many are not honest on their disclosure form."[22]

Although nobody has done a formal study of bioethicists, Sheldon
Krimsky at Tufts University has published a series of studies about disclosure
in scientific and medical journals (many of which are collected and discussed
in his book, *Science in the Private Interest*).[23] One of those studies found that
only 0.5% of over 60,000 published articles in the scientific literature
included any disclosure of competing financial interests. Krimsky pointed
out that in reality, it had been generally estimated that about a quarter of
those researchers actually had industry ties. These articles were published in
high-impact journals that had clear guidelines on conflict of interest; most
scientific journals did not even *ask* authors to disclose potential conflicts. In
2002, only 2 of 53 bioethics journals had conflict of interest policies in place.[24]

In fact, many journal editors do not even believe that disclosure is necessary. In a 1997 editorial titled "Avoid Financial Correctness," the editors of
Nature dismissed disclosure as a waste of time, writing, "This journal will
persist in its stubborn belief that the research as we publish it is indeed
research, not business."[25] Several years later the *Nature* non-disclosure policy
came under attack. The *New York Times* reported that Charles Nemeroff, an
Emory University psychiatrist writing in *Nature Neuroscience* (one of several
Nature journals) had praised three experimental psychiatric treatments from
which he stood to profit, including a transdermal lithium patch for which he
held the patent. According to the *Washington Monthly*, Nemeroff stood to
gain as much as $1 million in stock from a company that manufactured one of
the products he praised.

In response to his critics, Nemeroff rightly claimed that *Nature* had never
asked him to disclose his financial ties. And the *Nature* editors reluctantly
changed the journal's conflict of interest policy. *Nature* journals now
require authors either to disclose their financial ties or to say that they
decline to disclose them. But the views of the *Nature* editors on disclosure
remain fundamentally unchanged, as do those of many scientists.[26] Many
scientists simply feel that research should speak for itself, regardless of the
financial ties of its authors, and that asking them to reveal their potential
financial conflicts is an insult.

Some bioethicists apparently share this view, including some editors of
bioethics journals. The editors of *Theoretical Medicine and Bioethics*, for
example, have argued against financial disclosure in bioethics, suggesting
that disclosure encourages readers to judge an article by its funding rather
than by its merits.[27] Similarly, a policy on bioethics consultation developed
by the American Society of Bioethics and Humanities did not recommend
disclosure; when that policy was published in *The Hastings Center Report*, its
authors declined to disclose their own financial ties to industry.[28]

This resentment towards disclosure as a remedy is not so much wrong as incomplete. Disclosure cannot fix the underlying problem of industry funding, which is influence. What we worry about with industry funding is that its recipients, consciously or not, will be influenced in a way that conflicts with their proper roles and duties as researchers, regulators, teachers or scholars. What disclosure can do is raise an alarm. Of course, that alarm might be misinterpreted or wrongly used – and this, I suspect, is what these journal editors are worried about. But just as it would be a mistake to think that setting off an alarm is a solution to the problem, it would also be a mistake to get rid of the alarm without fixing the problems to which it is alerting us.

PROBLEM 2: REBOUND EFFECTS

The second problem, related to the first, is that disclosure may actually *normalize* the conflicts for which they are intended as a remedy. Part of the reason why people fail to disclose their conflicts as a matter of routine is that they are slightly ashamed of them. They worry if they reveal their corporate ties, their colleagues, students and readers may treat their arguments and opinions with skepticism. (Empirical evidence suggests the opposite, but more on that later.) Of course, it is the fact that others might well be justified in treating their arguments with skepticism that suggests the need for corporate ties to be disclosed, yet if disclosure becomes a matter of routine, so also might the corporate ties themselves. That is, if there is no shame to prevent ethicists from taking industry money (and no policies either), then more ethicists might well feel justified in taking it.

Social psychologists such as Robert Cialdini call this "the principle of social proof."[29] When we are unsure of what to do in a given situation, we look to other people to see what is correct. Then we do what they do. This is why barristas at coffee shops salt the tip jar. If you see bills in there, you are more likely to put a bill in there yourself. Disclosure of conflicts may work in a similar way: the more common the perception, the more common the reality. As more and more bioethicists begin to believe that it is common for people in the field to work for industry, the chances increase that they will come to do it themselves.

This kind of normalization parallels the problems that come with commodification. Often we will resist introducing a good into the sphere of the market at least partly because to do so seems to degrade that good.[30] This helps explain why most of us resist the idea of selling sex, kidneys or babies; pricing and selling a good transforms it in ways that make many of us uncomfortable. Degradation is not the only reason to worry about commodification, of course. Exploitation and coercion are worries too. But the notion of degradation helps explain why we occasionally go to some length to insulate a good from the market in order to keep it from feeling completely like a commodity. Adoption agencies are one example. Adoption fees may sometimes make the practice of adoption feel uncomfortably like a market in babies, but we surround the practice with other bureaucratic structures in order to prevent it from feeling (or becoming) completely like one.

The problem is the slipperiness of this sense of degradation, and how quickly what once seemed degrading eventually begins to seem normal. At first it might seem strange, even morally disturbing, to see, say, a doctor's office in a shopping mall, or a medical school named after a corporate CEO, or a university chair named after an insurance company. Slowly, though, it begins to seem normal, and that sense of uneasiness goes away. A decade or two ago it seemed worrying that a university athletic event would be renamed for a corporation. Today Americans watch the Fedex Orange Bowl, the Tostitos Fiesta Bowl even the Chik-Fil-A Bowl without so much as a blink. During the NCCA basketball tournament, Mike Kryzewski, the coach of the Duke University basketball team, delivers sales pitches for Chevrolet and American Express during commercial breaks. For a college coach to be selling credit cards no longer seems degrading or even strange, as long as the commercials are in good taste. It seems like an ordinary business practice.

Something similar may happen in bioethics. Five years ago the influx of pharmaceutical industry money into ethics seemed disconcerting. Now bioethicists are getting used to the idea. Many American bioethicists do not cringe anymore when they see the Sanofi-Aventis Chair in Bioethics and Drug Development, or the Pfizer Program in Medical Humanities. They seem normal now. If anything, that sense of normality might be hastended by disclosure. The more common pharmaceutical funding of bioethics seems, the more common it might become.

PROBLEM 3: PUBLIC RELATIONS

Many types of pharmaceutical marketing have become such a part of ordinary medical life that no one sees them as unusual, such as sales visits from drug representatives and advertising in medical journals. But the most interesting marketing practices are those that do not initially look like marketing. These marketing practices are less like advertising than like public relations. As Edward Bernays, the father of American public relations, once put it, the key to effective public relations is to take the credibility of a trusted authority and use that authority for one's own purposes.

Traditionally, the pharmaceutical industry has relied on the authority of physicians, especially academic physicians. For decades now the pharmaceutical industry has recruited academic physicians as consultants and speakers, partly as a way of gaining credibility for their products in the medical community. More recently, with the rise of the Internet and the devolution of authority from physicians to patients, the industry has begun funding patient support groups and advocacy groups. It is against this backdrop that industry has begun funding bioethics. But do the pharmaceutical and biotechnology industries really want ethical advice? Do they want to promote ethical discussion, or do they want PR?

Patient advocacy groups have been asking themselves the same question. Pharmaceutical companies that donate money to patient groups often portray the donation as a charitable gift. Yet the donations themselves usually come from the marketing division of the company, not the charitable arm. The donations are often planned as part of a larger marketing scheme, and the amount of money donated rises and falls with promotional spending.[31] As *The Philadelphia Inquirer* recently reported, Merck and Pfizer donated a combined $1.65 million to the Arthritis Foundation in 2000 when they were launching Vioxx and Celebrex, respectively. Merck made its foundation gifts a part of its overall sales strategy, according to a 2001 memo disclosed in product-liability litigation. But as marketing of the Cox-2 inhibitors dropped off, so did charitable giving. By 2004, after Vioxx and other Cox-2 inhibitors had been linked to an increased risk of heart disease and sales had dropped, the donations by Merck and Pfizer to the Arthritis Foundation dipped below $375,000.

Should this matter? Some patient advocates think not. Perhaps this is simply a case where the needs of a corporation happen to overlap with those of a group strapped for money. When asked about the Merck donation plan by the *Inquirer*, the president of the Arthritis Foundation replied, "We envision that as an educational program. Their marketing folks envision it as marketing." Perhaps the same could be said for industry-funded bioethics. Is it a problem for bioethics if the industry sees it as a device for public relations?

The most-known case of bioethics as public relations, originally reported in *The Wall Street Journal*, was developed by Eli Lilly for its sepsis drug, Xigris.[32] When Lilly introduced Xigris several years ago, the company had high hopes for it. Xigris was supposed to be their next blockbuster drug, after Prozac. But Xigris had not really sold well, and one reason for its poor sales was that the drug was so expensive. Standard therapy for sepsis is about $50 per day; when Xigris was introduced, it cost about $6,800 per treatment. Physicians were reluctant to prescribe an expensive drug whose advantage over standard therapy looked marginal at best.

Lilly had a marketing problem, and to deal with the problem they hired a PR firm called Belsito and Company. Belsito's solution? A PR campaign called "The Ethics, the Urgency and the Potential." The message of the campaign was that it would be unethical *not* to use Xigris. To reinforce the point, Lilly funded a $1.8 million dollar bioethics project called the Values, Ethics and Rationing in Critical Care Task Force (VERICC). It was composed mainly of bioethicists and critical care specialists, and the idea was to look at healthcare rationing from an ethical perspective. Or so its members said. The architect of that campaign, Marybeth Belsito, told *PR Week* magazine that in creating the ethics task force, "You had a group of 20 leaders acknowledging publicly, in the media, that Lilly did something great … Lilly just created a group of champions."[33]

When the VERICC task force was reported on television, the news stories about it often led with reports about the dangers of withholding effective treatment because of its cost. A Fox News report began with the anchor saying, "Your doctor may be withholding life-saving treatment." Another one reported, "Robert Lieberman is lucky to be alive … He was on a ventilator near death when he got a new biotech drug called Xigris that probably saved his life."[34]

This particular worry – that ethicists are being used as PR – presents problems for disclosure as a remedy. If companies are recruiting ethicists as public relations tools – if, in fact, the ethics advisory boards, the industry-sponsored academic chairs, and the industry-funded task forces are actually meant to advertise the corporate responsibility of the company – then what purpose is disclosure actually serving? For ethicists to keep their corporate ties hidden seems wrong, but disclosing them probably serves as good PR for the company. If anything, many companies would like to advertise their ethicists as widely as possible, in order to generate a halo of corporate responsibility.

PROBLEM 4: PUBLIC TRUST

Historically, the past half-century is often described as a period in which the public, for various reasons, lost trust in a range of institutions – the government, the press, the professions, even the priesthood. As an institution, bioethics does not have a large reservoir of public trust to draw upon, especially in comparison to medicine. It is a new field; most people, if they know it at all, know it largely from television and maybe a university class or two. If bioethics becomes linked to the pharmaceutical industry in the public mind, how is it likely to affect public trust in bioethics as an institution?

The difficulty with conflict of interest as a way of framing the problem of industry funding is that it directs our attention only to individuals. An individual author has a conflict of interest, or an individual researcher, or an individual doctor; and as a consequence, we worry about how that individual's financial ties might affect his or her judgment. But by directing our attention to individuals, this way of framing the issues makes it sound as if these financial ties are a purely individual problem – that an individual has a conflict and we need to manage it.

But the larger conceptual problem is the effect of such financial ties on social institutions. A better term for this might be "corruption." Corruption gets at the notion that some sources of funding, if they are illegitimate, or even perceived as illegitimate, will undermine public trust in the institution. For the public to trust the courts it must not believe that judges are being paid off under the table; for the public to trust the news media it must not believe that journalists are being paid by the subjects of their coverage; for patients to trust the FDA they must not believe that FDA employees or advisors are being paid by the companies whose products they are evaluating. The same point could be made for bioethics. If the public is to trust bioethics as fair arbiters in ethical matters, it must not believe that bioethicists are being paid by corporations with an interest in influencing them.

The rationale usually given for disclosure, of course, is transparency. But if transparency allows the public to see financial ties between bioethics and the pharmaceutical industry that it regards as illegitimate, then the effect may well be to undermine public trust in bioethics. Disclosure may link bioethics to the pharmaceutical industry in the public mind. Given the way that the reputation of the pharmaceutical industry has plummeted in recent years, this is unlikely to be a positive development for bioethics.

PROBLEM 5: DISCLOSURE WORSENS BIAS

One reason that is often given for disclosure as a remedy for conflict of interest is the idea that transparency will eliminate, or at least minimize, the potential for bias. As long as people understand that the person they are listening to has certain financial incentives, they can take those incentives into consideration in deciding whether or not the person is biased. But empirical studies in psychology suggest that disclosure does just the reverse: it actually *increases* the potential for bias. The most interesting work on the topic has come from a group at Carnegie Mellon University. Their work suggests that, far from remedying the bias created by conflicts of interest, disclosure may actually make the bias worse.[35]

The Carnegie Mellon group devised an experiment in which there were two groups of people, one called "estimators" and the other called "advisors." The estimators were instructed to stand off at a distance from large jars filled with coins and estimate how much money the jars had in them. The estimators were given a financial incentive to guess correctly. The closer the estimator came to guessing the right amount, the more money that particular estimator would get.

The other group, the advisors, had a different job and a different set of incentives. Their job was to stand much closer to the jars, look at the coins a lot more carefully, and then give written advice to the estimators. Unlike the estimators, though, they were paid according to how high their estimators guessed. Their financial incentive was not based on how close to the truth their estimators got, but on how high their estimators' guesses were. They had a financial incentive to give misleading advice.

Some of the results were predictable. When the estimators listened to the advisors, for example, they made higher guesses. This is exactly what one would expect: after all, the advisors were getting paid to get the estimators to guess high.

But another result was more surprising. When the advisors *disclosed* to the estimators that they were getting paid to have them guess high, the disclosure did not improve the estimators' guesses. That is, even though estimators knew that the advisors were being paid to advise them to guess high, they continued to guess high. The fact that they heard a disclosure didn't make them any more skeptical of the advice they were getting.

A third finding was even more interesting. Once the advisors disclosed their conflicts, their advice got worse. They began to give advice that was even more biased than before. It was as if the advisors had decided, "All bets are off now. I've disclosed my conflicts so now I'm free to say whatever I like." The Carnegie Mellon group summed this finding up nicely when they said: coming clean means playing dirty.

The Carnegie Mellon research suggests that if the purpose of disclosure is to minimize the bias created by financial interests, then it may well be backfiring. But it also suggests that the effects of financial interests are more complex than we realize. As the Carnegie Mellon researchers point out, conflicts of interest are often not a problem of overt corruption or bribery. The people with conflicts are not intentionally misrepresenting the advice they give so that they will benefit financially. Rather, the bias in their advice is usually unintentional and unconscious.[36]

This can be seen in medicine, where gifts and honoraria to doctors from the pharmaceutical industry are widespread. Doctors often defend taking the gifts by arguing that the gifts do not affect their judgment. Of course, they don't dispute the argument that influence is the purpose of the industry gifts. What they dispute, often with passion and vehemence, is that the gifts actually work. If the gifts are bribes, many doctors argue, they must be singularly ineffective bribes, because they have no discernible effect. Often doctors can't even remember which company bought their dinner, or who exactly paid for the concert they attended. And if they can't even remember who gave them the gift, how could the gift have an effect?

But it does. One of the best studies of industry influence was conducted over a decade ago in Cleveland.[37] The authors of the study looked at industry-funded trips. Trips are probably the most widely criticized type of industry gift, simply because the trips cost so much. And while it is true that most trips feature lectures and seminars, which are also arranged by the drug industry (this is why the trips are billed as "conferences" or "advisory board meetings") they are usually held at golf, beach or ski resorts. In the early 1990s two researchers at the Cleveland Clinic, James Orlowski and Leon Wateska, came up with a way of measuring the effects that these trips had on doctors.

In the late 1980s, drug manufacturers had treated members of the Department of Internal Medicine at the Cleveland Clinic to a number of free trips to various vacation spots. Orlowski and Wateska wanted to see if these trips had made any difference in the number of prescriptions written in their hospital. They picked two different drugs, an antibiotic and a heart drug, whose manufacturers had each sponsored free trips for the department. (Orlowski and Watesaka chose drugs which could only be administered intravenously and so could be easily tracked through records at the hospital pharmacy.) Then they charted the prescriptions written at their hospital for each drug. First they looked at the use of the drugs during the

22 months before the department members were treated to an industry-funded trip, and then they looked at the 17 months after the trip.

The change was astonishing. For the antibiotic, prescriptions during the period right after the trip spiked to *ten times* what they were before the trip. Shortly thereafter prescriptions leveled off, but still they leveled off to a rate that was over three times the rate before the trip. For the heart drug, the jump was more modest, but it was still impressive; prescriptions increased to a rate 2½ times that of the rate before the trip. In fact, prescriptions increased even before department members actually took the trip. Their first spike came immediately after the invitations were offered.

But perhaps even more revealing than these huge spikes in prescriptions was the doctors' confidence that the trips would not affect their clinical judgment. 19 of the 20 doctors who took trips predicted that the trip was unlikely to influence their prescribing. This confidence is consistent with other studies of doctors. In one small study, in fact, researchers found that the more gifts that medical residents accepted, the more confident they were that the gifts did not affect their judgment.[38]

The belief of doctors that they are incorruptible appears to be sincerely held. Yet this deeply held belief in one's own incorruptibility does not always extend to others in the same position. Even doctors who think that they are personally impervious to industry gifts are willing to concede that gifts might influence *other* doctors.[39] One study found that medical students who thought it was inappropriate for politicians to accept industry gifts still thought that it was fine for doctors to accept them.[40]

Psychologists call this phenomenon the "self-serving bias" – the tendency to conflate fairness with self-interest. The classic study of self-serving bias was published in 1956 under the title, "They Saw a Game." In that study researchers asked students at Dartmouth and Princeton to watch a film of a Dartmouth–Princeton football game and count the infractions committed by each team. Predictably, students from each college counted up the infractions in a way that was favorable to their own team. Princeton students saw more Dartmouth infractions than Dartmouth students saw, and Dartmouth students saw more Princeton infractions than Princeton students saw. Apparently, what we see as fair, proper and righteous usually corresponds to what happens to benefit us.

That we confuse fairness and self-interest is not surprising, of course. What is surprising is how tenaciously we cling to the belief in our own righteousness even when that belief has been exposed as irrational, biased or false. In the face of clear evidence to the contrary, we continue to insist that we have been wronged; that we actually did more work than the records show; that anyone with eyes could see that we were cheated by the referee. The same self-serving bias may help explain why we cling to disclosure as a solution to conflict of interest. We do not really believe that it is a problem; but since others think it is a problem, we choose a solution that allows us to keep the money.

CONCLUSIONS

Why have bioethicists, who have spent no small amount of time teaching and writing about conflicts of interest, been so reluctant to take their own conflicts of interest seriously? Perhaps many bioethicists believe that money does not influence them. But unless ethicists are a lot different from doctors, or any number of other professions who have been studied, it almost certainly does. Of course, with ethicists influence would be much harder to detect. Each ethicist has a different moral view, and each is always free to change his or her mind. Unlike, say, the case of doctors, whose prescribing patterns can be tracked and measured, it is hard to imagine a way of detecting whether an ethicist's views have changed as a result of financial incentives. (In fact, in the case of consultants or advisory board members, a pharmaceutical company does not need to change an ethicist's mind. All they need to do is to cherry-pick the ethicists who are likely to give them the ethical advice they want.)

Other bioethicists argue that there is no such thing as clean money in a medical center. In the end, they suggest, so much money in any given medical center comes from tainted corporate sources – the pharmaceutical industry, medical device manufacturers, corporate grants, hospital chains, insurance companies – that any effort to insulate bioethics would be futile. Yet this argument misrepresents that nature of the problem. If you follow any money back far enough you are likely to find some dirt at the end of the trail. But the reason we institute conflict of interest rules is because some money is more likely to produce influence than other money is. If I give $100 to a policeman, it could be considered a bribe. But if I pay $100 in taxes to fund the police department, I am doing my civic duty. In the same way, the fact that a pharmaceutical company is among the financial supporters of the academic medical center where I work does not produce the same sorts of worries that would emerge if the pharmaceutical company were sending me a regular consultancy fee.

The reason why bioethicists have fallen back on disclosure as a remedy for conflict of interest is easier to guess: it allows them to accept the money. In this sense, disclosure has something for everyone. The pharmaceutical industry can keep giving money to ethicists, and ethicists can keep taking it, and each side can rest easy that the conflict has been "managed."

Yet what is most striking about the move towards industry-funded bioethics, and even the adoption of disclosure as the favored remedy, is how unnecessary it is. There is no pressing *need* for industry to fund bioethics. Bioethics centers could be funded like philosophy departments; research could be regulated by externally funded bodies; bioethicists could stop giving lectures funded by the drug industry; the bioethics consulting business could simply disappear. It is not at all clear that American society has improved with the corporate-driven bioethics that has emerged over the past decade or so. In fact, it may well have gotten worse.

The assumption behind the expansion of bioethics into the corporate domain is that the more bioethics we have, the better off we will all be. Industry-funded bioethics centers will produce more bioethics research, and corporations will behave more ethically if they get sound ethical advice from consultants. Yet it is not obvious that more industry-funded bioethics consultation and research is actually a positive development. There is no evidence that pharmaceutical companies are behaving more ethically; and if litigation is any indication, there is considerable evidence that their behavior has gotten worse. At the same time, bioethics has gradually moved from an academic discipline, with an emphasis on teaching and scholarship, to a fixture in institutional bureaucracies, with an emphasis on policy-making and consultation. This move has generally gone unnoticed. Perhaps the issue that needs more examination is not what bioethics has done for industry, but what industry is doing to bioethics.

NOTES

1. Nell Boyce, "Code of conduct for bioethics branded 'soft' on corporate ties," *Nature* 417, no. 6892 (2002): 885; Nell Boyce, "A View from the Fourth Estate," *Hastings Center Report* 32. no. 3 (May/June 2002): 16–17; Sheryl Gay Stolberg, "Bioethicists Find Themselves The Ones Being Scrutinized," *New York Times*, August 2, 2001, A1.
2. Stuart J. Youngner and Robert Arnold, "Who Will Watch the Watchers?" *Hastings Center Report* 32, no. 3 (2002): 21–22.
3. The funding sources that I cite have generally been made available in annual reports, press releases, web announcements or other such documents, which are available from me on request. Some of them were reported in my fact-checked article in *The American Prospect*, Pharma Buys a Conscience, September 2001.
4. Current sources of funding can be found at: www.bioethics.upenn.edu/resources/. Past sources are not posted on the web but some are available on request from me.

5. www.merck.com/cr/docs/Merck_Corporate_Responsibility_Report_2005.pdf; accessed June 8, 2006.
6. www.unf.edu/dept/ceppp/; accessed June 8, 2006.
7. www.positiveprofiles.com/; accessed June 8, 2006.
8. http://mh.bmjjournals.com/cgi/content/extract/27/2/69; accessed June 8, 2006 www.essec-aventis.com/us/index.html; accessed June 8, 2006.
9. www.utoronto.ca/jcb/about/singer.htm; accessed June 8, 2006; http://law.shu.edu/healthlaw_programs/merck_visiting_scholar_program.html; accessed June 8, 2006; www.law.asu.edu/?id=8315; accessed June 8, 2006.
10. Susan Okie, "AMA Criticized for Letting Drug Firms Pay for Ethics Campaign," *Washington Post* August 30, 2001.
11. Jon F. Merz, Glenn E. McGee, and Pamela Sankar, "'Iceland Inc.'?: On the Ethics of Commercial Population Genomics," *Social Science & Medicine* 58, no. 6 (2004): 1201–1209; P. A. Singer and A. S. Daar, "Harnessing Genomics and Biotechnology to Improve Global Health Equity," *Science* 294, no. 5540 (October 5, 2001): 87–89.
12. "Bioethics Consultation in the Private Sector," *Hastings Center Report* 32, no. 3, (May/June 2002): 14–20.
13. Tom L. Beauchamp, Bruce Jennings, Eleanor D. Kinney, and Robert J. Levine, "Pharmaceutical Research Involving the Homeless," *Journal of Medicine & Philosophy* 27, no. 5 (October 2002): 547–564.
14. www.umaryland.edu/bmb/faculty/shamoo.html; accessed June 8, 2006
15. http://bioethics.org/institute/faculty/profiles.php?first=glenn&last=mcgee; accessed June 8, 2006.
16. *Perspectives in Biology and Medicine*, 48 (Winter 2005 Supplement); "Symposium – Pharmaceutical Innovation and Cost: An American Dilemma," *Yale Journal of Health Policy, Law and Ethics* 5, no. 2 (Summer 2005).
17. Disclosure available from author.
18. www.tweisel.com/twpds?_fwdtourl_=/ShowDocument?DocType=news&DocId=562; accessed June 8, 2006; www.thestemcellmeeting.com/bio/Advisory_Board; accessed June 8, 2006.
19. www.washingtonspeakers.com/speakers/Speaker.cfm?SpeakerID=3105; accessed June 8, 2006.
20. Trudo Lemmens and Benjamin Freedman, "Ethics Review for Sale? Conflict of Interest and Commercial Research Review Boards," *Milbank Quarterly* 78, no. 4 (2000): 547–584.
21. M. Steinbrook, M, "Gag Clauses in Clinical Trial Agreements," *New England Journal of Medicine* 352 (2005): 2160–2162.
22. *Medical Meetings*, September/October 2002, 6.
23. Sheldon Krimsky, *Science in the Private Interest* (Lanham, MD: Rowman and Littlefield, 2004).
24. www.cspinet.org/new/bioethics_061102.html; accessed June 8, 2006.
25. *Nature* 385, no. 6616 (February 6, 1997): 469.
26. Shannon Brownlee, "Doctors without Borders," *Washington Monthly*, April 2004.

27. L. A. Jansen and D. P. Sulmasy, "Bioethics, Conflicts of Interest and the Limits of Transparency," *Hastings Center Report* 33, no. 4 (July/August 2003): 40–3.
28. "Bioethics Consultation in the Private Sector," *Hastings Center Report*, 32, no. 3 (May/June 2002): 14–20.
29. Robert Cialdini, *Influence: The Psychology of Persuasion* (New York: Collins, 1998).
30. Michael Sandel, "What Money Can't Buy: The Moral Limits of Markets," The Tanner Lectures in Human Values; www.tannerlectures.utah.edu/lectures/sandel00.pdf, accessed June 8, 2006.
31. Thomas Ginsberg, "Donations Tie Drug Firms and Non-Profits," *Philadelphia Inquirer*, May 29, 2006.
32. Antonio Regalado, "To Sell Pricey Drug, Eli Lilly Fuels a Debate over Rationing," *Wall Street Journal*, September 18, 2003, A1.
33. *PR Week*, December 6, 2004.
34. Video clips available from author.
35. D. Cain, G. Loewenstein, and D. Moore, "The Dirt on Coming Clean," *Journal of Legal Studies* 34, no.1 (2005): 1–25.
36. Jason Dana and George Loewenstein, "A Social Science Perspective on Gifts to Physicians from Industry," *Journal of the American Medical Association* 290 (2003): 252–55.
37. James P. Orlowski and Leon Wateska, "The Effects of Pharmaceutical Firm Enticements on Physician Prescribing Patterns: There's No Such Thing as a Free Lunch," *Chest* 102, no. 1 (1992): 270–273.
38. Brian Hodges, "Interactions with the Pharmaceutical Industry," *Canadian Medical Association Journal* 153 (1995): 553–559.
39. J. Hopper, M. Speece, and J. Musial, "Effects of an Educational Intervention on Residents' Knowledge and Attitudes Toward Interactions with Pharmaceutical Representatives," *Journal of General Internal Medicine* 12 (1997): 639–642.
40. P. Palmisano and J. Edelstein, "Teaching Drug Promotion Abuses to Health Profession Students, *Journal of Medical Education* 55 (1980): 453–455.

CHAPTER 8

Two cheers for the pharmaceutical industry

Richard T. De George

8.1 CONTRIBUTIONS OF THE PHARMACEUTICAL INDUSTRY

The pharmaceutical industry in the past sixty years has made tremendous strides in developing life-saving, life-prolonging and life-enhancing drugs. From 1965 to 1996, the development of antibiotic drugs reduced mortality rates from rheumatic fever and rheumatic heart disease by 93%; ACE inhibitors, Beta-Blockers and Nitrates reduced mortality rates by 74%; anti-inflammatories and bronchodialators decreased mortality rates from emphysema by 57%; and antihypertensives and diuretics decreased mortality rates by 21%.[1] Life expectancy at birth in the United States increased from 68.2 in 1950[2] to 77.7 in 2005.[3]

Not only has the industry increased longevity and come up with cures for many diseases, but in the process it has also helped reduce the cost of healthcare. In an era of ever-increasing medical costs, drugs have helped shorten the time of hospital stays and have made it possible to treat without hospitalization many illnesses that previously required them. According to Pfizer, not only is the cost of pharmaceutical drugs a relatively low percentage of the total cost of healthcare,[4] but another of its studies claims that a $1.00 expenditure in pharmaceutical drugs is associated with a $3.65 reduction in healthcare expenditures.[5] New drugs have also added to the economy by decreasing the number of days missed by employees.

Despite these impressive and substantial successes, the industry has come under growing and intense criticism.[6] The common complaints center on exorbitant prices, excessive profits, patent "gaming," and questionable practices. The typical response of the pharmaceutical industry to critics is that unless pharmaceutical companies are allowed to operate as they do, the industry will have little or no incentive to spend the hundreds of millions of dollars it takes to develop new drugs. The industry thus defends the status quo, and warns that any change could be disastrous. The critics dismiss such claims and insist on the right to healthcare, which they interpret to mean healthcare for all at prices that all can afford.[7]

The very success of the pharmaceutical industry has raised perhaps unrealistic and unrealizable expectations on the part of the public for a constant stream of effective, safe, and affordable drugs. This expectation has in some measure been fostered by the industry in its ads, and especially in its defense of its profits. The AIDS epidemic focused public attention on the large numbers of people facing death from AIDS at the same time that alleviating drugs had been developed. Although the drugs have been developed, they are too expensive for many people, especially those in the poor countries of sub-Saharan Africa. Hence the claim that greedy companies are allowing people to die when they could save them by making drugs available gratis or at prices the needy could afford.

Even if all the criticism made of the pharmaceutical industry were correct and all the charges substantiated, we would still have to admit that the advances made by the industry in the past sixty years have been remarkable. Were no new drugs discovered from today on, we would look back on this past period as the high point of advances in civilization's fight against illness. Moreover, we should keep our criticism and charges in perspective. The complaints are not against all companies or all the products of any company. Most of the controversy focuses on price, accessibility, and profits during the seven to ten year period of market exclusivity for a drug.[8] Thereafter, if the drug is useful, generic versions of it appear. The market mechanism then works through competition to drive the price down. A drug which possibly was priced beyond the buying power of poor individuals becomes available to them. So even if it were unjust that the rich have access to drugs which the poor cannot afford for that protected seven to ten year period, the drug thereafter goes off-patent, enters the public domain, and becomes available to all forever thereafter. Unlike many other injustices, if the allocation is unjust, it is for the limited period. This is not intended to be an argument that justifies injustice, but an attempt to place the controversy in perspective, since those who are a party to the dispute focus on the period of protection and often forget the long-term benefits to all that follow when the protection expires. If it were the case that without that period of protection there would be no new drugs developed, one would have to ask whether morality demands that society forgo new drugs.

Pharmaceutical companies receive most criticism with respect to the United States and less developed countries. I shall argue that in both cases, although the pharmaceutical companies are not above reproach and are in specific instances guilty of unethical behavior, they are not as much at fault as critics claim. In particular, in both the United States and in the less developed countries the primary failure is the failure of governments. In the United States the contributor to the current situation is the US government's failure to follow a consistent policy with respect to the market. In the less developed countries it is the failure of national governments to provide basic services. Government is supposed to make up for market failures. Instead the pharmaceutical companies are often held responsible to make up for government failures.

The moral aim is to maximize the welfare and so the health of all people. If this can be achieved by a better system than the one by which the giant strides in the development of new drugs in the past half-century have been made, then it is society's moral obligation to develop that system. But unless one is found, the safest and so the morally preferable solution would be to fix the defects in the present system rather than to replace it.

8.2 HUMAN RIGHTS AND THE ALLOCATION OF RESPONSIBILITY

Of the healthcare industries, the pharmaceutical industry is the only global one. Typically, hospitals and doctors are located in a certain country and that is where they provide their services. That is where their patients are, and they are not responsible for patients in other countries.

The pharmaceutical companies, by contrast, operate in many countries and thus operate in the United States within a system of free enterprise; in Europe, Japan, Australia, and other countries under a system of medicine or insurance provided by the government; and in the less developed countries under a variety of systems, most of which are financially and many of which are politically burdened. The responsibilities of pharmaceutical companies varies in each of the settings, which makes the industry and individual companies open to a large number of demands and expectations by a variety of different constituencies.

The tension between the pharmaceutical industry and its critics (including many people who make up the general public) comes from an apparent conflict of two rights. On the one hand is the right of for-profit corporations to make a profit within the bounds set by law and ethics. The agreement with society has been that corporations are allowed to earn profits, even great profits, providing they provide goods and services of reasonable quality at a reasonable price (kept so by competition), and that they provide jobs for members of the society. In this respect there are no special rules for corporations in the healthcare industries. On the other hand are the human rights of all people to life, and so to healthcare, which seem to impose obligations on those able to provide such care. These are obligations not placed on other corporations. The automotive industry is not expected to give cars away to the needy or to provide them to the needy at greatly reduced prices. Nor are most of the other industries, whether they provide goods or services.

The two stated rights are not the only considerations, however, and their reconciliation can only properly take place when we view the problem from a more holistic point of view that includes the economic, the political, and the social system in which the clash of rights arises. There are not only two actors to consider, namely the healthcare industries (and for our purposes the pharmaceutical companies in particular) on the one hand and the general population on the other; the government is the third central actor on the stage and plays a vital role. From this holistic perspective, the pharmaceutical industry actually has a stronger ethical position than it has thus far realized or articulated. It has adopted the strategy of substituting for ethical language social responsibility language, which is being used by critics to press for demands to which the industry is not ethically obliged to accede.

The human right to *health* (and derivatively the human right to healthcare) as stated in the Declaration of Human Rights is a right primarily (although not exclusively) against government. The right can and has been defended from a variety of philosophical perspectives, and can be seen as derived from the right to life. I shall not present another justification for it, and shall assume it as defensible. If it is not defensible, then the argument raised by many critics seems to have little force. But that still leaves open the thorny issues of interpretation. In the UN statement the right to health involves the obligation on the part of the government to provide clean water, sanitation, etc., as well as the obligation to provide protection, to the extent it can, against pandemics, such as bird flu. In the United States, government at many levels, for the most part, recognizes this. In the area of health, government is the primary provider, for instance, of potable water. It owns and runs the reservoirs, the water treatment facilities, the sewage lines. It charges what is usually considered a minimal rate for the water it makes available, much of the additional cost being covered by the general tax base. Similarly, the government helps ensure a livable environment, either by directly providing sanitation or by requiring industries to restrict pollution. The government has the obligation to keep pollution from becoming life-threatening, to drain swamps that lead to malaria, and so on. These are all parts of providing for the common good. In less developed countries providing safe drinking water and sanitation and ensuring pollution control would go further from the same expenditure of funds than would the provision of more healthcare.

The line between the negative and the positive right to health is, in this area as in so many others, far from sharp. Obviously one has the negative right to health in the sense that no one should directly interfere with another's pursuit of his or her health. It is the obligation of government to provide safe drinking water, but this is an obligation to do something, rather than to refrain from interference with the liberty of the rights-holder. Enterprises are precluded from pouring untreated toxic waste into rivers used for drinking water by people downstream because of the harm such wastes do to the health of those people. The government in turn has the positive obligation to make sure that such enterprises do not act in such a way as to adversely affect the health of people. In a similar way enterprises must protect the health of their employees to the extent that they may not expose them to toxic materials without adequate protection, provide healthy working conditions, and so on, with the government having the responsibility to set standards and to see that they are met.

The right to health together with the general right not to be harmed imposes on individuals the obligation not to transmit communicable diseases to others, for example, AIDS through sexual contact. The right to health also imposes on individuals the obligation to care for their own health and observe the standards of care, cleanliness, etc., that promote their health, at least to a minimal extent. Although smoking is known to adversely affect health, in a free society those who wish to risk the adverse affects are allowed to do so on the somewhat dubious ground that the negative consequences are suffered primarily by the agent. The individual is frequently in the best position to preserve his or her own health, but health is not only an individual good but also a social good. As a social good, the main obligation falls to the government, since individual actors are unable to produce the needed conditions through individual action.

Consider the threat of avian flu. The reaction of people in the United States has been to look to government to in some way protect them, and government has accepted that as part of its obligation. Why is government responsible for trying to prevent a pandemic? The answer again would be that this is part of their providing for the common good, a nation's health being a social good. In this case government will do so both by controlling the spread of the disease among fowl to the extent possible and by making sure that an appropriate flu vaccine is available.

A comparable analysis can be made of healthcare. The right to *healthcare* can be derived from the right to health. But here the order of discussion can be reversed. Given the right to health, one is allowed negatively to pursue the means one needs in order to preserve one's health and to restore it as best one can when one's health is adversely affected. Hence if the wealthy wish to spend a great deal of what they have on their healthcare, they are allowed to do so. This means that the degree of healthcare for individuals may, in a free society, vary according to one's means and according to how one wishes to allocate one's individual resources. This is to understand the right to health-care as a negative right. Neither government nor others should preclude an individual's pursuing his or her good in the area of health, providing no harm is done thereby to others. The consequence is unequal healthcare. Some have more money and are willing to pay more than others. This principle seems to be recognized by a recent Canadian Supreme Court ruling that the provincial governments could not ban private medical insurance and private clinics by those who wish the advantages these provide in addition to the services provided by the state's healthcare system.[9] This consequence is unpalatable to some. They claim that every-one's life is equally important, and that everyone therefore deserves the same level of healthcare, regardless of whether they are rich or poor. They there-fore argue in favor of restricting the negative or freedom right to pursue one's own care to the level that one wishes and can afford, beyond what is provided or available to all.

Whatever position one takes on that issue, however, one can still argue that one's right to healthcare imposes on some others, and government especially, not only the negative injunction not to interfere, but the positive injunction to provide at least a basic level of healthcare. Healthcare, here, as health above, is seen not only as a private good but also as a social good. The reason it is a social good is that it is the means of achieving the social good of health for members of the society. If healthcare is only a private good then the obligation of others to provide it seems to be secondary to the individ-uals providing it for themselves.

The question then becomes: who is obliged to provide healthcare and to what level are they obliged to do so?

The positive right to *healthcare* imposes an obligation primarily on government. In societies that have socialized medicine, the government directly provides healthcare to its citizens. In the United States, the US government through the NIH and NSF and other government agencies sponsors and funds research into health-related activities, as well as funding basic research that makes possible new developments in medicine and healthcare. But healthcare is provided primarily by non-governmental agents, many of which are for-profit entities, whether they be pharmaceutical drug companies, for-profit hospitals or for-profit medical providers or HMOs. Passing responsibility to the private sector, however, does not relieve government of the responsibility to provide for all those who do not have adequate access to healthcare through the private sector. Government has the obligation to make up for market failures, e.g., in making sure that all are provided health insurance, in making sure that vaccines, new antibiotics, and orphan drugs that are not cost-beneficial for companies to produce are produced, and in making sure that all have adequate access to basic needed drugs.[10]

The right to healthcare everywhere is primarily a right to *basic* healthcare, and nowhere to the best and most expensive care available. The question then becomes what one means by "basic." Every society has some means of providing healthcare, whether it be folk medicine or modern medicine. "Basic" includes access to hospitals, clinics, doctors and nurses or other care givers, and those life-saving drugs that are available. Many poor countries that spend only $2.00 per year per person on healthcare fall below this basic level of care and have some call on others for help. Basic care varies from society to society and in the poorest countries may not rise above a minimal level. Richer and more developed societies typically consider basic care to be at a higher level than poorer and less developed societies. A society with socialized medicine might decide that it has sufficient resources and wishes to expend them to provide well beyond basic healthcare to all its citizens. That level will vary from society to society, and different societies with equal right choose to allocate resources differently. As long as each society provides all its citizens with basic healthcare, they may provide as much beyond that as they choose. This is comparable to the liberty principle of the individual.

To the extent that healthcare is a social enterprise, the obligation is for the state to treat all its citizens justly, where this means treating equals equally and unequals unequally. Hence the state need not spend the same amount of money on each individual. Some illnesses and treatments are more expensive than others. Yet under the principle of equality, all with the same illness, other things also being equal, should have available the same treatment. One's financial condition, just as one's gender or race, does not determine the care one gets under the state-provided system.

In all cases the widely accepted dictum, that no one is obliged to do what it is impossible for them to do, applies. Taken within a social context, governments cannot provide healthcare beyond the means they have available for that social good, which comes up against other social goods – including providing for healthy conditions, as well as such other goods as education, roads, security, and so on. Yet when it comes to basic healthcare one can nonetheless argue that if a given society is too poor to provide basic healthcare, then the obligation falls more broadly on the international community, whether that be nations, international NGOs, multinational corporations, or, from a cosmopolitan point of view, on individuals able to help.

In countries with socialized medicine, the government decides on the level of care it can provide, including the drugs it will purchase and distribute and those it will not. In the United States, the function of deciding on the level of care is decided in part by government under programs such as Medicare and Medicaid, in part by insurance companies that provide medical and drug insurance, by doctors and hospitals, and by patients. If a new drug is developed that is extremely expensive and is only marginally better than another available drug, one's right to healthcare does not extend to access to the former. If it is extremely expensive and the only treatment available, similarly one's right to healthcare does not automatically extend to that drug. There is no right to continued life at any price. The view that people are entitled to live as long as possible, no matter what their condition and no matter what the cost, is a view that may be popular, but it is difficult to defend. Clearly there are limits to what any society can spend on healthcare, including pharmaceuticals. Under a free enterprise system, if a society decides through its purchasing agents that it cannot afford a certain drug, that sends a message to the drug companies that producing drugs that are that expensive is not profitable. The result may well be the development of fewer drugs of that type. This is a price that society may be forced to pay. American society has had no general public discussion of such decisions.

The British National Health Service was sued by a woman suffering from early-state breast cancer because the Service refused to grant her use of Herceptin, which costs from $36,000 to $47,000 per patient per year. A court ruled in favor of the Health Service's right to withhold the treatment "solely on the grounds of cost."[11] New biotech drugs are among the most expensive being produced. Genentech has announced its new cancer drug Avastin will cost $100,000 per year per patient. Depending on one's insurance coverage, the co-pay for patients will be between $10,000 and $20,000 a year. The average extension of life for patients with colon cancer using this drug is eleven months.[12] Is the cost worth the benefit? Cerezyme, used in the treatment of Type 1 Gaucher disease, costs $200,000 for the average patient. One cancer drug, Erbitux costs $114,000 annually and the average patient survives by only a few weeks or months.[13] Insurance plans typically cover such high costs when the drug is reasonably cost-effective and when the number of patients requiring the drugs is small compared to the number of people covered. If the number needing such expensive drugs grows large, hard choices will have to be made by insurance companies, those who pay for the insurance, doctors who will have to weigh costs versus benefits, and patients, who have to pay a portion of the costs. Already some insurance plans that pay only up to 50% of the cost of a drug are passing on to patients costs of up to $600,000.[14] Clearly that is more than most patients can afford.

The point is that there are limits to what any society can afford, and the need to consider those limits seriously seems to be fast approaching. Under the US system Medicare will have to make hard choices about what drugs are to be approved for use, as will insurance companies. The decisions will in turn send messages to the drug companies about whether new expensive drugs will be purchased in sufficient quantity to commercially justify their development. It is more likely that if allowed to operate, the market will signal unsustainable levels of spending on medical care, including pharmaceuticals, better and earlier than any government bureaucracy.

8.3 SHORTCOMINGS OF US POLICY

The United States is one of the few developed countries that does not have a system in which either medical care or medical insurance is socialized. Yet that does not mean that the government does not recognize healthcare as either a right or as a social good, nor that it denies it has an obligation to see to it that all its citizens have access to at least basic healthcare. It has opted for the private sector to provide both most healthcare and much of the healthcare insurance. The government's obligation in such a system is to ensure that the market provides adequate healthcare to all to the extent that it can, with the government making up for market failures.

Within the US free enterprise system government provides for other social goods, such as education, while also allowing private educational institutions for those who prefer them. Even with respect to security it does not prohibit private security, at least to the extent that it does not interfere with public security. The same is true in healthcare.

Yet a basic difficulty with US policy is its inconsistency in its approach to balancing the private and governmental responsibilities in the realm of healthcare. Part of a just solution would be to allow the market to operate and oblige the government to make up for market failures. Three areas are especially pertinent: 1. the failure of the government to let the market work with respect to pricing; 2. the failure of the government to let the market work correctly with respect to advertising; and 3. the failure of the government to cover market failures.

1. The failure to let the market work with respect to prices

An ethically consistent and coherent US policy would help clarify the proper role of both government and the pharmaceutical industry. Most importantly, such a policy would allow Medicare to negotiate drug prices with the drug companies, just as private insurers do under the free market system. The present system of private insurers is chaotic and is not the market at work since the government provides subsidies to the insurance companies to insure seniors covered by Medicare. To prevent Medicare from negotiation by law is to undermine the free-market system to the benefit of the drug companies. Allowing Medicare to negotiate what it will pay is not a form of price control by the government. It is simply allowing the market to work. One result would be the lowering of the cost of medicines to many, especially the elderly, and with that perhaps a lowering of the profits of drug companies. That is part of what market economy involves. This will put pressure on the companies to be more efficient in their drug development so as to lower their costs.

In the United States the cost of drugs is borne primarily through Medicare, Medicaid, and insurance companies, with businesses paying part of the insurance premiums and the individual paying the remainder and any co-payment required by the insurance provider. The system to a large extent insulates the end-user, the patient, from caring about the cost of a drug that will be paid by a third party. The patients focus only on the amount they will pay, and doctors often tend to assume that the cost of medicines will be covered by insurance and is not their concern. The price mechanism thus fails to work as it does in most other areas. That various pharmaceutical companies have exploited this failure to their advantage, is undoubtedly true. But the remedy is not simply to encourage the drug companies to rein in their greed or to charge less for their drugs or to regulate themselves in some other way. The remedy is for government to let the market work and to allow those who purchase drugs to bargain for the best price. In a fair market the end-user, namely the patient, would have informed choice and would put pressure on insurance companies to keep premiums down. Insurance companies should refuse to pay high prices for drugs that are no more effective than their generic counterparts, and should pay for drugs that can prevent or reduce the need for hospitalization or expensive medical procedures. The same should be true of other preventive care uses to avoid situations in which insurers refuse to pay $150 for patients to see podiatrists to treat ailments that, without such treatment as they could provide, means having to pay $30,000 for a foot amputation.[15] The market here simply does not work rationally.

2. The failure to let the market work with respect to advertising

At present the drug companies in the United States engage in direct consumer advertising. This practice may be faulted in three ways. First, prescription drugs are a controlled substance. They are not over-the-counter drugs, which can be freely purchased by the consumer. They can only legitimately be obtained with a doctor's prescription. The general principle that what can be legally sold may be legally advertised does not apply in this case. It is illegal, for instance, to advertise cigarettes to those too young to purchase them. Here government policy is consistent. It is not consistent with respect to prescription drugs, since on the one hand it prohibits their free access while on the other it permits their free advertising.

Second, patents give drug companies a period of exclusivity or a legal monopoly. Where government grants a monopoly on a social good, it imposes the necessary restrictions. In this case one arguably appropriate restriction is to prohibit direct advertising to consumers, as used to be the case. That this is the usual case in market societies is shown by the fact that the US is presently one of only two countries (the other is New Zealand) in which such advertising is permitted. If one result of such advertising is rising costs of drugs such as to prevent access by many, the government can justifiably restrict such advertising. The onus of showing that no harm is done by this practice is arguably on the side of the government.

Third, in a free market a fair exchange is one that takes place between free (uncoerced) agents, with access to the appropriate information, and from which both parties benefit. With respect to drugs the transaction is unfair to the extent that the user does not have access to the pertinent information. This is in part because comparisons are not available and in part because consumers lack the medical knowledge to make informed comparisons. Lack of technical knowledge may be tolerated in a purchaser's comparing two computers and not knowing what all the comparative specifications mean. But their lives or health do not depend on that knowledge or on making the appropriate purchase.

The drug companies justify direct consumer advertising as giving the consumer information. Yet the information the consumer gets is only partial. Consumers typically do not know what the competing drugs are, how much more beneficial one drug is in comparison with another, or whether the additional benefit is proportional to the additional price. In other areas of the economy, individuals can compare prices and decide what trade-offs of benefits to price they wish to make. Not many can afford top of the line Mercedes or Lexus, and make do with less expensive but perfectly adequate Fords or GM products or other less expensive cars. The market clearly does not work this way with respect to pharmaceutical drugs. This can be seen as a market failure, for full information is not available to the consumer.

Over-the-counter drugs can be advertised to the public because they then become comparable to any other commodity. Since prescription drugs, by contrast, can only be made available with a doctor's prescription, it is the doctor who has the responsibility to be informed about the drugs appropriate for different treatments, about the relative effectiveness of competing drugs, and about the cost–benefit ratio of available drugs. This information is not available to the general consumer who is bombarded by TV ads to "ask your doctor" about the drug being advertised, whose virtues are praised. A much-advertised drug may be only modestly or perhaps not at all more effective than an alternative available. But since it will do the job, since the patient asks for it, and since the patient's insurance company will pay for all or most of it, the path of least resistance is for the doctor to prescribe it. This is not the market at work, but an instance of manipulation by advertising.

One remedy is to prohibit, as used to be the case before 1997, direct marketing of drugs to consumers on TV, and even better to prohibit the direct marketing of all prescription drugs to consumers. Doctors presumably have the requisite knowledge about the comparative benefits of drugs and should be expected to use this in their prescriptions. Alternatively, the insurance companies and Medicare can make judgments about the comparative value of drugs, and of how much more they will pay for drugs depending on the greater effectiveness, ease of use, or other factors. Australia uses such a practice, paying, for instance, 10% more for a drug that is 10% more effective than its competitor.

Another remedy in addition to or instead of prohibiting direct marketing of prescription drugs to the general public, is to render the transaction fair by making all pertinent information available to the public. The comparison of drugs, their efficacy and price, is done by many countries with socialized medicine. Norman Daniels, J. Russell Teagarden and James Sabin have proposed an "ethical template" for providing appropriate information to health benefit planners as well as ordinary users about the available drugs.[16] The template would compare treatment vs. enhancement, the effectiveness of different drugs, the comparative cost and benefits of drugs for treating a specific condition, and so on. Along similar lines, Alan Garber, head of the Center for Health Policy at Stanford, advocates establishing an independent federal agency for assessing the value of drugs, modeled on the United Kingdom's National Institute for Health and Clinical Excellence.[17]

Making comparative information about drugs easily available would go a long way not only in helping society set fair limits but also in making the market operate more efficiently and fairly by providing all parties with access to appropriate information.

3. The failure to cover market failures

The market fails with respect to those who, for any number of reasons, do not have insurance and cannot afford needed drugs. It also fails with respect to those who suffer from diseases that do not affect large numbers of people, since the market is too small to justify the expenditure of hundreds of millions of dollars by drug companies which they cannot recoup because of the small number of potential sales. The obligation of government in both areas is to make up for such market failures.

The cases where people are uninsured or grossly underinsured are well known and have received much public attention. Nonetheless, the needs of many such people remain unmet. Some states have programs that cover children who would otherwise be without proper care. Although some drug assistance programs fill part of the needs of the uninsured, the problem is too serious to be handled by charity. It is a clear instance of a market failure and the burden for correcting it properly falls on government. As noted above, Massachusetts has taken a major step in trying to address the problem using market mechanisms and a governmental safety net.

The other area of market failure is the area of orphan drugs. Here the US government has taken positive steps and has provided a model which others have copied and improved upon.

Orphan drugs for diseases afflicting 200,000 people or less in the United States are covered by special legislation. The government encourages the production of these drugs by granting the producing company seven years of marketing exclusivity from the date of FDA approval, whether or not the drug is patented; it makes available accelerated FDA review; and it provides tax credits for research and development, and in some cases research grants or foundation support. Other countries have developed somewhat similar legislation with respect to orphan drugs.

The example of orphan drugs can, moreover, be fruitfully applied in other areas where the market fails to provide enough incentive for needed drugs. Two areas that fall into this category are vaccines and new antibiotics.[18] In the case of vaccines where the risk of suit might be high, the government could indemnify the company against suits, or serve as an insurer of last resort. The government with respect both to vaccines and to new antibiotics (where typically older antibiotics are used until a doctor runs up against a patient who has developed resistance to the older drugs) might subsidize research, it might provide tax incentives, and it might contract for a sufficiently large quantity at a price sufficient to make it worthwhile for a drug company to pursue development. The point is that it should be proactive in making up for the market failure by providing market-type incentives.

8.4 THE OBLIGATIONS OF DRUG COMPANIES

Thus far I have argued that the major responsibility for healthcare falls on government. What of the pharmaceutical industry? As part of the healthcare complex, does it not also have moral obligations? I shall suggest that the answer is a qualified yes; but that its obligations are less than many critics claim. To begin with, of course, pharmaceutical companies have all the obligations concerning health and safety that all corporations have. In addition they arguably have additional special obligations because they are in the health field. In particular I shall look at the production obligation, the access obligation, and the obligation of rescue.

Production Obligation

The production obligation is the obligation to produce life-saving, and to a lesser extent life-enhancing, drugs. The pharmaceutical industry is the only one capable of doing this. The industry in this respect includes both the major drug companies and the manufacturers of generic drugs. For the most part the major drug companies are the ones who develop new drugs in the first instance, although sometimes much of the research that takes place is done as well in government labs and at universities, often funded by government money.

While it is in the self-interest of drug companies to develop break-through drugs that can be sold to large numbers of people at a good profit, it is not in their self-interest to develop drugs for those who cannot pay for them, for example, drugs for tropical diseases suffered only or primarily by people in poor countries in Africa, or by small numbers of people. Hence the importance of governments' role in providing incentives and in making the development of these latter drugs financially attractive. In this regard, we have already mentioned the US Orphan Drug Act. But much more needs to be done.

The obligation in general for the production of drugs falls on those who own the rights to the drug. It would not be in the self-interest of the company not to produce a successful drug it had developed. It would also be unethical for it both not to do so and fail to make it available for others to do so. Using a patent to preclude the production of a developed drug would be an abuse of patent rights, and in such a situation governments can legitimately require mandatory licensing to a company willing to produce it. The justification for this action is based on the claim that health is a social good, appropriately promoted and protected by government. With respect to the development and production of needed drugs for diseases suffered primarily by those in poorer countries, the obligation for development falls on those able to do so. But it does not fall directly on any particular company, if many are able in theory to do so. Rather the obligation falls first on governments, second on the industry, and third on the companies.

The obligation of the pharmaceutical industry can only be met by the companies that make up that industry. But if no company chooses to develop drugs for specific illnesses, even given government financial incentives, then it is up to the industry to decide how the work is to be apportioned. There is a fine line between the leaders of an industry or an industry association recognizing their joint obligation and working out a means of addressing the problems that distributes the burden fairly on the one hand, and that avoids collusion for the benefit of the participating companies on the other. There is presently neither a mechanism for governments to fairly collect and allocate resources for this purpose nor for the industry to do so, although there are international health organizations and associations of pharmaceutical manufacturers.

Various ways of encouraging drug companies to develop drugs for illnesses for which there is no profitable market are possible; but government's role in providing incentives, whether through tax reductions, guaranteed purchase of a certain number of drugs at a certain price, a guarantee of exclusivity such as that offered by the Orphan Drug Act, or through some other means, is essential. I shall develop this point later, and here simply note that the obligation is not one that the pharmaceutical industry has to bear by itself. The pharmaceutical industry retains all the rights to profit that other industries enjoy.

The Access Obligation

The right to access to needed drugs places an obligation on some parties to ensure that access to needed drugs is available to all within the limits set by available resources. We have already seen that it does not consist of the right to access to any drug, no matter how expensive. Different nations have different ways of fulfilling the access obligation. Under the system of free enterprise, the access obligation works together with the production obligation. Pharmaceutical companies have the obligation to see that the drugs they develop become available to the general public. They have the obligation not to prevent access, although they have little incentive to do so, since their profitability comes from sales of their products. The primary bearer of the responsibility for providing access to basic needed drugs, however, is not the pharmaceutical industry but government. The part of the access obligation that falls on the pharmaceutical companies is to provide needed drugs in sufficient quantity to handle the demand.

The claimed obligation of pharmaceutical companies to provide access to the drugs they produce by giving them away to those who cannot afford them, or by pricing their drugs at levels all can afford, seems based on a claimed obligation to rescue, so it is to that obligation that we turn. The obligation to rescue should not be confused with tiered pricing (which I shall discuss later).

The Obligation to Rescue

Does the obligation to rescue impose special obligations on pharmaceutical companies? The obligation to rescue falls on those who can aid another in serious need or who can rescue them from serious harm, such as death, to the extent that they can do so without undue cost to themselves. The obligation is construed by some so that the cost to oneself may be considerable, though it does not require that one reduce oneself to the condition of the person rescued; others interpret the obligation as being less demanding.[19] On either interpretation, the pharmaceutical companies seem to be in a much better position than others to provide needed medicines, since they have and produce them. To this argument is added another, namely that the right to life trumps the right to property.

Thus, there are three parts to the usual argument as applied to pharmaceutical companies. The first is based on the obligation to aid those in need. The second is based on the claim that the right to life trumps the right to property. The third is based on efficiency, namely that the pharmaceutical companies have the required drugs at hand and therefore are the most efficient providers.

(a) The obligation to help those in need, as developed by Peter Singer, starts from the intuition that if a child who falls into a pond and is drowning and someone passing by is the only one nearby capable of saving the child, that person has the obligation to do so, even at some cost to him or herself. He then generalizes that intuition into a principle which can be defended from both a utilitarian (as he does) and a deontological perspective. But in its general form it still most clearly applies to individuals in individual cases. As one gets further from the clear case, the applicability becomes more questionable. Singer draws the conclusion that we should all do a great deal more to help the poor than the vast majority of us do and that the obligation applies regardless of distance. That is very different from the intuition with which we started of an individual's responsibility to help the child in the given instance. The obligation, moreover, as generalized, applies to all. If one then extends this to corporations, it would apply to all corporations. The obligation to aid here also includes all the aid that all people need and so the obligation to relieve starvation, malnutrition, lack of shelter and other results of poverty, as well as helping provide needed sanitation, clean water, and medical care, including medicines. Simply stating the obligation to aid and jumping to the obligations of pharmaceutical companies is a leap that requires a good deal of justification.

(b) In *Les Miserables*, Jean Valjean, unable to find work and with a starving family, steals a loaf of bread from a baker's cooling rack. He is caught and severely punished. The story moves the reader to reflect not only on the injustice done to Valjean but on the injustice of the whole system. One of the intuitions on which the story trades is the intuition that the right to life trumps the right to property – an intuition that has found philo-sophical justification in the writings of Thomas Aquinas, John Locke, and many since their time.

Consider changing the story slightly. Jean Valjean, still penniless and without work, now steals from the pharmacist a drug his wife needs, perhaps insulin, for her diabetes. He is not caught and the following week again steals the needed insulin. Surely if the theft was justifiable the first time, it is justifiable the second time. It would appear that it would be justifiable as long as the conditions remain the same. The pharmacist will notice that each Monday some insulin is gone, and when he finds out that Valjean is taking it because his wife needs it to survive, he may feel he has the obligation to permit the action without reporting it, on the basis that those who are able to help another in dire need with small cost to themselves are morally required to do so. If he were sufficiently ethical and took the obligation to rescue seriously, he would even give him the insulin so that Valjean did not have to steal it. That the pharmacist would have to do this indefinitely far into the future as long as Valjean's condition does not change is, however, somewhat less intuitive than Valjean's taking the insulin once.

Now others in situations comparable to Valjean follow his example, and with exactly the same justification also take insulin. How much does the pharmacist have to give away? Surely at some point he will no longer be required to continue providing insulin free; and if the point at which refusal is justified is costly enough, he may well close up shop and turn to some other trade where he can make and keep his profit rather than having to give a good part of it away. He should go into selling something that is not necessary for life – luxury items rather than necessities.

Stealing the drugs from pharmaceutical companies would be equally justifiable, but far more difficult. Since the right to life trumps property rights, if the one in dire need may steal the drug, he should also be allowed to steal from others, say, from the jewelry store, the money he needs to buy the drug. There is no apparent reason why the right to life over property applies specifically to the pharmacy but not equally to all others who are not in dire need. And here most people's intuitions probably falter.

On the one hand, the needy have the right to life, which trumps the right to property of the pharmacist. On the other hand the pharmacist has the right to run a profitable business. That he sells pharmaceutical drugs rather than Rolex watches does not seem to change his right to make a profit. The former seems to have greater obligations than the latter with respect to those in need of drugs only because he has them. Yet they are both business people, and the fact that they sell different commodities seems irrelevant from a business perspective or from a consideration of life versus property.

That people have the right to life, to health, and to healthcare is clear. Yet there seems no reason why a specific baker or pharmacist has to bear the burden of supplying bread or drugs to the needy. Nor, by analogy, is it clear why the pharmaceutical industry has special obligations, different from other industries, in virtue of the products it makes, to rescue. I suggest that the problem is that the cases are viewed in abstraction from the larger picture of which they are a part.

What the case shows is that there is something wrong with a system that forces people to steal bread or drugs, or money to buy them, in order to live. The moral of the story is neither that theft is justifiable nor that pharmaceutical companies have the obligation to give drugs to the needy, but that the system needs changing.

(c) This leaves the efficiency argument. The pharmaceutical companies have the drugs, for example, to treat AIDS. Therefore they have the obligation to provide those whom they can save with the drugs. This claim, however, seems too broad, since this would mean they have the obligation to provide the drug to all with AIDS, rich or poor, in sub-Saharan Africa or in the United States. Surely no one claims that. Those who are able to afford the drugs should pay for them. Otherwise the drug companies would go bankrupt and could produce no drugs. So the claim must be that more affluent individuals and all corporations (including pharmaceutical corporations) should provide the needy in this case (and all others) with the money they need to buy the drugs (and food, shelter, etc.) they need.

Why does the obligation fall primarily or exclusively on the pharmaceutical companies? The argument from efficiency says that they are the best placed to supply the drug. But saying this is to say that they have the obligation to make the drugs available by producing and delivering them. Individuals and corporations can contribute money to buy medicines as readily as pharmaceutical companies can contribute medicines. They may have the obligation to price the medicines at a price close to or only slightly above that required to cover production and distribution costs. Doing so might arguably fulfill this part of the general obligation to rescue, leaving the rest of the obligation on individuals, other corporations, governments, NGOs, and so on. To argue that since all the rest fail to fulfill their obligations, the full obligation falls at the present time on the pharmaceutical companies, and appropriately falls on them for the foreseeable future, is to require too much. The claim ignores all the structures already in place for providing aid by governments, NGOs, individuals, and corporations, as well as the action that can and should be taken to do more. The pharmaceutical industry should not be asked to bear the shortcomings of government, individuals, and other corporations.

Moreover, the demand that pharmaceutical companies give away AIDS drugs falls only on those companies that produce them. A case may be made that any MNC that operates in and so benefits from operations in a less developed country is obliged to provide more to that country than those MNCs that do not operate there. To the extent that argument is made out, however, it applies to all companies, not just to pharmaceutical companies.

The upshot of the three arguments that defend the obligation to rescue is that the obligation applies most appropriately for individuals when the opportunity for rescue presents itself to an individual in a particular case – you pass by a lake just as a child falls in and you are in the appropriate place to save the child from drowning. But when the situation involves the needs of millions of people, obviously the obligation can only be met collectively by the joint effort of millions of people, and by the coordination mechanism provided by governments and other agencies. With respect to access to drugs, I suggest that this is the situation. The obligation does not fall primarily or only on the drug companies because they produce the drugs, but on all companies, and more broadly on all those able to take part in the rescue, and primarily on governments. This is not to say the drug companies are expected to do nothing. But it is to say that they should be expected to do only their fair share, with others doing their fair share as well.

Several drug companies have assistance programs under which they give their drugs in the United States to those of minimal means who have no drug coverage and in some less developed countries to those with AIDS or other diseases. Typically the companies consider these programs to be instances of fulfilling their social responsibility – which they see as voluntary – rather than as fulfilling the right of those people who need the drug. Social responsibility in this context is more properly seen as an instance of charity rather than as fulfilling even an imperfect duty, unless one raises charity to the level of an imperfect duty.

Within our current system this is praiseworthy. The companies correctly claim that the programs are voluntary and that therefore they do not have to specify the criteria they use for choosing which drugs to give away or to whom to give them.

The practice in the United States tends to help the companies justify the prices they charge others in the United States, and it helps cover over the failure of the government to provide access for all. Big Pharma correctly claims that it does not have the obligation to provide access to all. That obligation falls on government.

However, by adopting the language of social responsibility – rather than that of philanthropy, for instance – the industry has actually done itself a disservice. The industry, as other industries, adopted the language to deflect public criticism. But the language has become so widely adopted that the industry has lost control of what it means. As a result NGOs and many individuals and industry critics are using it to demand that the pharmaceutical companies do more and more in the way of giving away drugs and have put on the shoulders of the industry obligations that properly belong to governments.

Although drug companies engage in give-away programs in Africa, especially with respect to AIDS drugs, there is little or no pressure on generic manufacturers to act similarly. The drug originators are able to answer the demand to a large extent by earning sufficient profits, particularly in the United States, to offset such programs. Americans might be willing to bear that cost if it were made clear and transparent. They are less willing to see European countries, Canada, Japan, and other developed countries fail to bear what seem to Americans to be their just portion of the burden.

Just as those whose lives are in peril are equally justified in stealing from other businesses as from pharmacies, so other businesses share in the obligation to help the needy with respect to prescription drugs. The fair solution is for society, perhaps through taxation, to ensure that all have access to the drugs.

8.5 PATENTS, PRICES, PROFITS, AND MISPLACED CRITICISM

Patents, prices, and profits by themselves are not the major impediments to access. Nor are they the only or obvious reason for lack of access by the poor. The primary culprit in both the US and less developed countries is government and government policies. Placing the blame for lack of access on patents, prices and profits shifts the blame onto the pharmaceutical companies. Although they may be guilty of abuses of the system, they are not responsible for the system.

Patents

Although drug patents have come under heavy attack from a variety of quarters, it is the abuse by some pharmaceutical companies of the patent system rather than the system itself that deserves criticism and change. Both the ethical and legal arguments in favor of the patent system in general are well enough known to need little rehearsing here. Unless companies are guaranteed the opportunity provided by patents to recoup their investment and make a profit, they will have no incentive to produce new drugs. The patent protection for drugs, given the long period required for testing and approval tends to be ten years. At the expiration of the patent, generic versions of the drug can, and for popular drugs do, enter the market. The result of the competition is the lowering of the price of the drug.

Does everyone have a right to every drug that is developed, no matter how expensive? I have argued that no one has that right, and that societies have to decide how much they wish and can afford to spend on the newest and most expensive drugs. The same thing is true of drugs that are no longer covered by patent. If a drug, as some of the newest drugs seem to be, is very expensive to produce, even at the margin, that drug remains very expensive even after the patent expires. Patents alone do not determine price.

Price

What constitutes a fair price for drugs? The general answer of what constitutes a fair price is what the market under conditions of fair competition determines it to be.[20] What needs discussion is whether the price of drugs, which are covered by patent and so are granted a monopoly, are subject to conditions of fair competition. This does not seem to be a problem in developed countries in which the government is the only buyer and can negotiate the price on equal terms with the only seller, the drug manufacturer. I have argued that the problem arises in the United States because the government has through legislation interfered with the workings of a fair market by precluding Medicare, the largest purchaser of many drugs, from negotiating with the drug manufacturers. The result is a disparity in the price of drugs in the United States and in other developed countries. That the same drug produced in the same plant should be much cheaper in Canada, for instance, than in the United States, appears to many to be evidence of price-gouging and unfair pricing by the drug industry. Brand name drug prices are, according to one report, on average between 31% to 48% cheaper in Canada, France, Germany, Italy, and the UK than in the United States.[21] That fact alone, however, does not prove the pricing in the US is unfair or exploitative. It rather raises the question of why the government does not let the market mechanism function as it should.

The answer, of course, is that Congress prohibited Medicare from bargaining, largely as a result of the strong lobbying campaign mounted by the pharmaceutical industry. Companies have a moral obligation not to lobby for unjust legislation. If the bill that was passed is unjust, then it should be repealed. If lobbying is unfair for some reason, then appropriate restraints should be placed on all companies. The claim that the pharmaceutical industry was morally obliged not to lobby for its self-interest in this instance, however, requires an argument, and that argument is not only not self-evident but so far as I know is unmade. Moreover, it is odd to blame the resulting legislation on the pharmaceutical industry rather than on Congress, or to require the industry rather than Congress to make up for the unpalatable results. Unless the US wishes to restructure or prevent lobbying by all, everyone or every group is allowed to lobby for its self-interest. It is the obligation of the members of Congress to pass legislation that benefits the common good. If it passes poor legislation, it is no excuse to claim (and of course legislators never do) that the blame goes to the lobbyists or to those who made large campaign contributions.

Finally, price discrepancy across markets, or tiered pricing, is compatible with both justice and a free market. The obligation to rescue should be distinguished from tiered pricing. Tiered pricing is the practice of charging different countries or groups different prices for the same product. Thus, many products, including pharmaceutical products, are priced lower in less developed countries than in the United States. The reason is that if the price were the same as in the US, there would be few, if any buyers, because the income level and the cost of living are so much lower than in the US. If a drug manufacturer makes sufficient profit from its US market to cover the cost of developing its drugs as well as production and distribution costs, then it can sell its product in less developed countries at a level to cover the actual production costs at the margin, plus distribution costs, at literally no cost to itself. If it can in addition charge a small amount for profit, that is pure gain, and it would be in its self-interest to do so. The prices in Europe and the profit margins there are higher than in less developed countries. As I have already argued, price discrepancy is not in itself unjust. The US could get lower prices by letting the market work.

Profits

The profits of pharmaceutical companies have come under fire together with the complaints about the high cost of drugs. The height of the criticism came in the years surrounding the recent turn of the century, when the pharmaceutical companies for almost a decade made headlines for the highest profits of any industry. The industry responded that the profits were justified because of the high risk under which the companies worked. The fate of Merck with its Vioxx suits might be taken as a case in point (although some fault Merck for covering up the seriousness of some of the side-effects of the drug). The argument against the companies, however, was never very clear. Some industry had to have the highest rate of profit. If it had been the computer industry, or the automotive industry, would the criticism have been the same? In 2005 the pharmaceutical industry fell to number five in profitability.[22] Simply being the most profitable does not show that the prices were unjustifiably high, although it does indicate that they might have been somewhat lower and the industry would still have done well. That argument, however, does not show the companies behaved unethically. Now that the profits of pharmaceutical companies have dropped, the argument based on the industry's being the most profitable one is no longer pertinent. Yet this says nothing about the ethics of the pricing by companies or the justifiability of their present or past profits.

Similarly the arguments about the pharmaceutical companies spending more on marketing (both to doctors and advertising to consumers) and on lobbying, in comparison to the amount spent of R&D, is also to some extent misconceived. There is no ethically mandatory ratio of the one to the other or any ethical requirement that the R&D expenses be greater (as some companies claim they are). The question is whether the companies are developing new drugs, at least to the extent that they have the obligation to do so.

Moreover, pharmaceutical companies are for the most part transnational. Although the home office may be in a given country, many are incorporated in many countries and, as is true of many industries, the research, development, production and sales are spread around the globe. Even if most of the profits come from sales in the United States, that by itself says nothing about the ethical justifiability of the profits.

The point that the industry tends to make is that if profits decline, drug development will decline. Their claim gains some support from the fact that for the period from 1962 to 1996 the percentage of gross margins and R&D outlays track each other.[23]

Whether as profits decline there will be fewer drugs developed remains to be seen. Some within the industry believe that reduced profits will force the companies to be more efficient and to use their resources to better advantage in the creation of new drugs. But if the trade-off is in fact that lower profits and/or lower prices lead to the development of fewer drugs, then that is a decision that society or societies collectively are free to make. The difficulty is that the general public, because of the impressive development of new drugs, has come to see a continuous stream of new and better drugs to cure or alleviate more and more diseases and ailments as an entitlement where no such entitlement exists. People tend to want effective, safe, and cheap drugs. No one can blame them for wanting that. But wanting that does not mean that the desire can be met, or that there is an entitlement to such drugs, or that the pharmaceutical companies for some reason have an obligation to satisfy that want.

Ian Maitland argues that "because life-saving and life-enhancing medicines are priceless … it is especially urgent to leave companies free to charge market prices for them."[24] He assumes the market is operating fairly. If it did, and if the system produced more and better drugs than would otherwise be available, it would clearly be morally justified. My complaint is that the market is not allowed to operate freely, and I am also less trusting of the pharmaceutical industry's claim that any change in the system will lead to fewer breakthrough drugs being developed, since it is those drugs that have been the lifeblood of the industry. Even Daniel Vasella, the CEO of Novartis, acknowledges that the Japanese system of allowing prices for new drugs to be set high and then lowering them over time provides an incentive for drug companies to keep innovating.[25]

8.6 SHORTCOMINGS OF INTERNATIONAL POLICY

The failures of the market are not only duplicated but the difficulties of finding a remedy are multiplied in less developed countries, especially those of sub-Saharan Africa.

I have argued that the responsibility for providing drugs to all who need them varies depending on where the pharmaceutical companies operate and what products they make. I have argued that in the United States the responsibility is divided in one way. In countries with socialized medicine, the government bears the total responsibility for the cost of pharmaceutical drugs, while the drug industry retains the production and part of the access responsibility. In less developed countries the market fails to provide access to many and governments are unable or unwilling to make up for market failures because the governments often lack funding, are ineffective, or are corrupt. But those failures do not justify placing the responsibility for their resolution on pharmaceutical companies. The problem of how to provide access to needed drugs to all requires international action, with appropriate responsibility shared among drug companies, governments, international bodies such as the UN, and NGOs.

As in the case of the United States, there are two different areas in which the market fails. The first is with respect to those whom the market does not serve, namely those who cannot afford needed drugs that have already been developed, such as the AIDS drugs. The second is the lack of market incentive to develop new drugs for tropical diseases for which no drugs have been developed or for diseases for which older drugs are inadequate. The lack of market incentive is a result of the fact that those who suffer from the diseases cannot pay for any drugs that might be developed.

The access to some AIDS drugs has been partially alleviated by donation programs of some drug companies under their social responsibility programs. We have seen that these programs are subsidized by those in the developed countries, especially by the prices paid by those in the United States. We have also seen that such donation programs are rightly considered charity, and neither address nor claim to address the obligations that are imposed by people having a right to healthcare, and so to the basic available medicines they need. That such charity is praiseworthy is undeniable; nonetheless charity is clearly inadequate to solve the problem of lack of access. The obligation to ensure healthcare for all, we have seen, falls primarily on governments, and in the first instance on the governments of each individual country. I have argued that the obligation to rescue should not be construed to place the obligation to make up for government failure on pharmaceutical companies. They, like any other multinational that operates within a country, may rightly be taxed by the government for needed revenue to cover the government's obligation to satisfy the human rights of its people. But this is often insufficient, whether due to governmental corruption, inefficiency, or lack of sufficient sources of revenue due to lack of an adequate economic base. In such cases the obligation falls on the broader international community.

The second problem, the lack of adequate drug development for tropical diseases faces similar difficulties. No particular company can be faulted for not developing a drug for a particular disease. The production obligation in this case, I suggest, falls on the industry as a whole, on governments, and on NGOs.

What is needed is not only individual action but collective action. The pharmaceutical industry as a whole is the only agent that can develop and produce the needed drugs. Such drugs are not profitable to produce, and producing them all might well bankrupt many individual companies. So the burden of cost cannot fall entirely on them. Since the obligation is at least in part an industry obligation, then it is up to the industry to determine how to meet it. The pharmaceutical industry already acts industry-wide through such groups as the Pharmaceutical Research and Manufacturers of America (PhRMA) and the European Federation of Pharmaceutical Industries and Associations (EFPIA). It would be up to the industry to decide which companies could most efficiently attack which diseases and how the cost of development and delivery would be fairly shared by all. Consortia of companies might also be considered, with perhaps sharing of research. This approach would have a chance of addressing the global pharmaceutical needs that clearly are not met by the current practice of relying on individual pharmaceutical companies, their perception of their imperfect obligations, and their individual approaches to their social responsibility via give-away drugs-to-the poor programs. The next step is to see that the obligation for funding should be shared by governments and possibly others. The third is to make the burden fair for the pharmaceutical industries in comparison to all industries and develop some sort of fair redistribution mechanism.

The Orphan Drug Act provides one model for how to attack the problem. But this approach works in the United States because the US government provides tax incentives and guarantees seven years of exclusivity, among other incentives. It could do so for drugs needed for tropical diseases, but without the needed buyers these incentives are insufficient. Nor is the problem one that the United States, as opposed to other countries, has the obligation to solve. Once again the solution calls for joint action by many governments in conjunction with charitable foundations, the UN and other non-governmental organizations, research institutes and universities, and individual and corporate contributions, whether through taxation or donation or both.

In 2003 the Drugs for Neglected Diseases Initiative was started.[26] This is another model of global cooperation and it has resulted in 19 projects, of which 10 are in the discovery phase, 4 in preclinical development and 5 in the clinical phase. The problem is complex. While the burden for a solution does not fall only or even primarily on pharmaceutical companies, they are clearly part of the solution. Yet, they are not the primary bearers of the obligation to provide healthcare. As I have argued, governments are.

8.7 CONCLUSION

The failure of the system in the United States to provide all with adequate healthcare, including access to needed drugs, is not primarily the fault of the pharmaceutical industry, but the failure of the United States government both to let the market operate where it should and to make up for market failures when it should. Although I have not detailed the abuses of the system by some pharmaceutical companies,[27] I do not claim that no pharmaceutical companies are guilty of abusing the system. I do not justify such abuses and I have argued elsewhere that such abuses should be reined in by the industry or restricted by legislation.[28] Rather I have attempted to clarify where responsibility lies and to get some balanced perspective to offset what are often, it appears to me, misplaced criticisms. The pharmaceutical industry as a whole has done a great deal to extend longevity, shorten or make hospital stays unnecessary, and meet the expectations of people for new drugs. While far from perfect, the industry deserves some recognition for its accomplishments towards helping meet the human rights of people to healthcare. It deserves two cheers![29]

NOTES

1. From chart reproduced in Pfizer, *Economic Realities in Health Care Policy* 2, no. 2, "Pharmaceutical Innovation: Lowering the Price of Good Health," online at www.pfizer.com/pfizer/download/about_er22.pdf (accessed January 26, 2006).
2. National Center for Health Statistics, *National Vital Statistics Reports* 52, no. 3, September 18, 2003, as reported in *Infoplease*, "Life Expectancy at Birth by Race and Sex, 1930–2002," *Infoplease* online at www.infoplease.com/ipa/A0005148.html, (accessed January 26, 2006).
3. US Census Bureau Data, *Infoplease*, "Infant Mortality and Life Expectancy for Selected Countries, 2005" online at www.infoplease.com/ipa/A0004393.html (accessed January 26, 2006).

4. Neal A. Masia, "Pharmaceutical Innovation: Lowering the Price of Good Health," *Economic Realities in Health Care Policy* 2, no. 2 (2001), 11.

5. Frank R. Lichtenberg, "The Economic Benefits of New Drugs," *Economic Realities in Health Care Policy* 2, no. 2 (2001): 14–19.

6. One sustained critique of the industry is Marcia Angell, M. D., *The Truth About the Drug Companies: How They Deceive Us and What to Do About It* (New York: Random House, 2004).

7. For a fuller development of the details see, Richard T. De George, "Intellectual Property and Pharmaceutical Drugs: An Ethical Analysis," *Business Ethics Quarterly* 15, no. 4 (October, 2005): 549–575.

8. This is the effective period of patent protection. It typically takes at least ten years from the time a patent is granted to a drug's appearance on the market.

9. Clifford Krauss, "Ruling Has Canada Planting Seeds of Private Health Care," *The New York Times*, February 20, 2006, A4.

10. In the United States the recently passed Massachusetts healthcare bill comes closest to fulfilling this governmental obligation using free market means. It may be a model that other states and eventually the federal government could adopt. See, Pam Belluck, "Masscahusetts Sets Health Plan for Nearly All," *The New York Times*, April 5, 2006, A1, A12.

11. Sarah Lyall, "British Clinic Is Allowed to Deny Medicine," *The New York Times*, February 16, 2006, A6. See also Jeanne Whalen, "Britain Stirs Outcry by Weighing Benefits of Drugs Versus Price," *The Wall Street Journal*, November 22, 2005.

12. Krauss, "Ruling Has Canada Planting Seeds of Private Health Care," A4.

13. Geeta Anand, "As Biotech Drug Prices Surge, U.S. Is Hunting for a Solution," *The Wall Street Journal*, December 28, 2005, A1, A6.

14. Ibid.

15. Ian Urbina, "In Treatment of Diabetes, Success Often Does Not Pay," *The New York Times*, January 11, 2006, A1, A26.

16. Norman Daniels and J. Russell Teagarden, James E. Sabin, "An Ethical Template for Pharmacy Benefits," *Health Affairs* 22, no. 1 (Jan/Feb 2003): 125–137.

17. Anand, "As Biotech Drug Prices Surge, U.S. Is Hunting for a Solution."

18. Scott Hensley and Bernard Wysocki Jr., "As Industry Profits Elsewhere, U.S. Lacks Vaccines, Antibiotics," *The Wall Street Journal*, November 8, 2005, A1, A9.

19. Perhaps the best known statement and application of the principle with respect to alleviating hunger in the world is Peter Singer, "Famine, Affluence, and Morality," *Philosophy and Public Affairs*, I, no. 3 (Spring 1972): 229–243. Raziel Abelson, "Moral Distance: What Do We Owe to Unknown Strangers?" *The Philosophical Forum*, XXXVI, no. 1 (Spring 2005): 31–39 presents an argument against Singer's position.

20. There are many views on this topic. See, among others, Milton Zall, "The Pricing Puzzle," *mdd*, 4, no. 3, (March 2001): 36–38, 41, 42, available online at http://pubs.acs.org/subscribe/journals/mdd/v04/i03/html/03zaLL.HTML

(accessed March 6, 2006); Ross Brennan and Paul Baines, "Is There a Morally Right Price for Anti-retroviral Drugs in the Developing World?" *Business Ethics: A European Review* 15, no. 1 (January 2006): 29–43; and Ian Maitland, "Priceless Goods: How Should Life-Saving Drugs Be Priced?" *Business Ethics Quarterly* 12, no. 4 (2002): 451–480.

21. "Prescription Drug Prices in Canada, Europe and Japan," prepared by Minority Staff Special Investigations Division Committee on Government Reform US House of Representatives, April 11, 2001, available online at www.democrats.reform.house.gov/Documents/20040629103247-74022.pdf (accessed March 6, 2006). The same Committee in a June 2003 report, "Drug Pricing Analysis: Prescription Drug Prices for Uninsured Seniors in the U.S. Are Higher than Prices in Canada, Europe, and Japan" (available online at www.democrats.reform.house.gov/Documents/20040628104816-38372..pdf [accessed March 6, 2006]) states the average price of 5 popular drugs are 72% higher in the US.

22. Fortune 500 (2006), "Most Profitable Industries [2005]," *Fortune*, April 17, 2006, F-26. The most profitable industry was mining (including oil), followed by Internet services, commercial banks, and Network and communications equipment.

23. Masia, "Pharmaceutical Innovation: Lowering the Price of Good Health," 10.

24. Maitland, "Priceless Goods," 471.

25. Anand, "As Biotech Drug Prices Surge, U.S. Is Hunting for a Solution," A6.

26. For details on this initiative, see the DNDi website at www.dndi.org/.

27. For some representative criticisms of the industry, see (in addition to the book by Marcia Angell mentioned above), Suzanne Sataline, "Medical Journal: Drug Studies Hide Key Data," *The Wall Street Journal*, December 29, 2005, B1; "Consumer Beware: Are Medical Ads Good For Your Health?" *Focus on Healthy Aging*, September 2005, 4–5; Geeta Anand, "How Drugs for Rare Diseases Became Lifeline for Companies," *The Wall Street Journal*, A1, A18; and Sarah Joseph, "Pharmaceutical Corporations and Access to Drugs," *Human Rights Quarterly* 25, no. 2 (2003), 425–452.

28. De George, "Intellectual Property and Pharmaceutical Drugs."

29. Submitted May 15, 2006.

CHAPTER 9

The third face of medicine: ethics, business and challenges to professionalism

Mary Rorty, Patricia Werhane, and Ann Mills

Changes in how healthcare is delivered have brought into salience in the twenty-first century a new rhetoric for the art and science of medicine: medicine as business. But those changes – the move of medicine into organizations, the separation of payers from patients, and the strengthening of the interactions between business, medical research and physician care – need not mean the end of medical professionalism as expressed in the Hippocratic Oath. Nor need the new rhetoric herald the abandonment of research and patient care to commercialism.

We ask how medicine is addressing the changes in the ways in which healthcare is delivered, and recommend a re-examination of the traditional ethics of medicine in light of the contemporary challenge of this third face of medicine. We argue that the prioritizing of stakeholders can ameliorate the worry about business in medicine, because that analysis reminds us that the business and profession of healthcare holds as primary the value of patient care, regardless of who is paying. We recommend a systems-based approach to the reconciliation of potentially conflicting values, and organization ethics programs to keep the priorities in line.

9.1 THE CHANGING RHETORIC OF MEDICINE

For most of its history medicine was an art, a craft or trade like stained glass or carpentry, practiced by members of an often-hereditary guild and operating within a tradition of ethics, the Hippocratic tradition.[1] As advances in science and in technology combined to make it possible for the practitioners of this art to gradually address widening areas of the human condition, it became more popular, in the beginning of the last century, to start speaking of the science of medicine. The "art" aspect did not disappear, but medicine began to be considered both an art and a science.

At the beginning of the last century the Carnegie Foundation undertook an examination of the adequacy of the scientific foundations of the art of

198

medicine, and published the influential Flexner report.[2] Essentially a peda-gogical reform, it introduced both the scientization of medicine and its professionalization as well, as the "guild" and "craft" aspects of medicine were replaced by demands for licensure, credentialing, barriers to access and special privileges, consistent medical education and many of the professio-nal trappings of medicine as we know it today.

We can think of the transformation of emphasis that took place at the beginning of the last century in terms of an image drawn from Roman coinage: the god Janus, guardian of doorways. To the art of medicine was added another face, the science of medicine. The two faces of this Roman deity look to the past and to the future. For the physician of the twentieth century, the two faces represent two values or objectives for which the physician is responsible: the traditional value of the well-being of the present individual patient, and the forward looking value of the advance-ment of medical science, for the sake of the future patients. The professional ethics of medicine is clear about the priority of the two values, of course, and most physicians manage to construct lives of professional integrity that balance these two faces of medicine – but the Janus image, with its bifurcation of values, reminds us of the potential conflict of commitment between these two values.

In the mid twentieth century Henry Beecher called the attention of the wider public to research abuses by his professional colleagues that resulted from the drive to advance medical science over and above patient welfare.[3] Beecher's bombshell, his 1966 article in the *New England Journal of Medicine* calling attention to research abuses in 22 contemporary articles in medical journals, contributed to the so-called "birth of bioethics" in the 1960s and '70s. The imbalance between the two faces of the profession had both legal and social consequences. It led to increased attention to the ethical conduct of research, including the institution of Institutional Review Boards for medical research, and additional regulation on federally funded research.

By the end of the last century another association with medicine was becoming obvious – in the literature and in the lives of practicing physi-cians. Medicine is adding a third face: medicine as business. To add a third face to our image of medicine is to add another possible area for conflicts of interest and commitment. The rhetorical third face of medicine as business includes an explicit responsibility for the cost of medicine, an obligation to be responsible custodians of the resources of society.

It does not seem unreasonable to expect medicine to deliver care of high quality for a reasonable cost. But when financial considerations are incorporated into our understanding of the ethical obligations of the profession, it raises the possibility of ethical dislocations comparable to those that led to the research scandals toward the end of the last century, when prioritizing the advance of medical science through research led to abuses of the well-being of the research subjects. To what extent does a tighter relationship between medicine and business pose a threat to the prioritization of patient care in traditional ethics of medicine, as research and patient care become more tightly intertwined with commercialism? If cost control becomes a professional responsibility, will it take primacy over the obligation to deliver care of high quality? Does the acknowledgement of business as one face of medical practice condone the increasingly strong links of research and clinical practice to commercial considerations?

9.2   THE CHANGING CONDITIONS OF HEALTHCARE DELIVERY

The increasing demands for technological expertise and scientific advances in areas of biology, chemistry and engineering that were directly related to healthcare led to Flexner's requirement for scientific education, and the eventual incorporation of medical schools within universities and colleges.[4] The growth of research into the functions and disfunctions of the human body often requires a medical degree as a prerequisite. It was these changes in the knowledge base required for healthcare that led to the changes in the rhetoric of medicine, accentuating the science as well as the art of caring for patients.

The changes in healthcare delivery most visible at the beginning of this century raise into salience a different rhetoric, metaphors of business, reflecting the extent to which financial incentives and economic values permeate contemporary healthcare delivery – on the individual, organizational and wider social level. The opening of medicine to the pressures of the larger society – the mainstreaming of parochial and physician-dominated medicine – has shown some of its vulnerabilities, called attention to some of the failings of organized medicine, and made available for its analysis some useful ethical tools and mental models[5] for analysis developed in other areas. Because of its prominent place in the business section of the daily news pages, healthcare is receiving unprecedented scrutiny from investigative reporters, financial analysts, science reporters and pundits. It is the changes in healthcare delivery that have contributed to the changing rhetoric of medicine, accentuating the business, as well as the art and science, of the profession.

Connections between business and medicine in the US have been well chronicled, but we consider three.

A. *The Corporatization of Medicine*

The context in which healthcare is delivered in the United States is changing, and the direction is toward greater integration. The number of physicians practicing alone or with one partner has declined from 89% in 1965 to 66% in 1995, with increasing numbers in either larger practices or practicing within larger organizations.[6] Although for most of the last century solo practice as a fee-for-service small businessman was the norm, the physician of the twenty-first century will be more likely to practice in a group of more than four physicians, or in a clinic or hospital.[7]

The number of medical interventions available to physicians that require expensive technologies, institutional resources or in-patient care rises with innovations and advances in medical science and technology. Professional activity, especially in a medical specialty, requires coordination with other physicians, may take place in a clinic or hospital with shared access to up-to-date technology, which enables interventions of greater complexity (and at best, with greatly improved results) than were possible at the beginning of the twentieth century. To practice in a hospital means "team" medicine: working with the nurses, consultants from other specialties, chaplains, social workers, therapeutic specialists and unit directors, to coordinate care.

Many of the contemporary physician's relations are mediated, rather than direct. The agents of mediation are various. Insurers or the government are co-determinants of reimbursement. The healthcare organization may limit through its formulary what pharmaceuticals are available for in-patient treatment. A physician in a large practice or in a clinic may have less individual discretion about his panel of patients or use of his time. For those physicians who are involved with managed care organizations, a large and growing number, there are more limitations on the range of decisions for which any given physician has sole authority.

In his introduction to his 1999 book, *The Corporate Practice of Medicine*, Berkeley health economist James Robinson remarks that "in the waning decades of the twentieth century ... the basic structures of the healthcare system began to lose their uniqueness and came to resemble those in the mainstream of the economy."[8] Referring to the acceleration of some of the differences between the "old" and the "new" medicine, he comments "... [S]uddenly in the 1990s the storm of change broke upon the profession, sweeping away the illusion of continuity [with solo practice and fee-for-service payment] along with unquestioned clinical autonomy, unconstrained practice income, and unparalleled cultural authority."[9]

B. Change in the Mechanisms of Reimbursement for Care

With the failure of President Bill Clinton's attempt to institute a centrally administered national health plan (the fourth such attempt in the last century), both the individual providers and the institutions in which they practiced lost control over their fiscal resources as the mechanisms of reimbursement for healthcare began to undergo rapid change. The so-called "managed care revolution" of the end of the last century represented the entry into healthcare of organizations explicitly designated by the society to control healthcare costs – intermediaries between payer and provider that operated as if the quality of care was completely unrelated to its costs. The absence of a national health plan has left the US health system uniquely subject to "market" model approaches to healthcare delivery, and in recent decades many for-profit enterprises have become major players in the healthcare arena. Since 13–15% of national Gross Domestic Product is devoted to healthcare,[10] purported to be the seventh largest economic sector, it represents "big business" in terms of costs, investments – and in some cases, profits, as well.

Payment for healthcare services in the US has typically been through insurance programs offered through and subsidized by employers, but also through government via Medicare and Medicaid coverage for some segments of the population – complicated by the intervention of various managed care organizations toward the end of the century. The interests and priorities of the payers for care and patients, the recipients of care, potentially diverged, while developing mechanisms of adjudication between those competing interests flagged, overwhelmed by the pace of change.[11]

Medicine as a business of healthcare delivery faces anomalies that most businesses do not. Most businesses can set prices for their services, adjusting them as markets change. In healthcare, prices associated with Medicare and Medicaid are set by governmental agencies. In most businesses, the payer of a good or service is also the consumer of that service. The typical market model decrees that the informed customer can freely choose whether to purchase an excellent product at an appropriately high price, or a less expensive product for a lower cost, with the desired balance between cost and quality to be freely determined by that customer. But the separation of payers from patients in healthcare represents a structural incongruity that thwarts normal market mechanisms. There is no single "customer" who can balance cost and quality, and can take responsibility for that choice. The buyer is the payer, the employer or government agency, who contracts with the healthcare organization or managed care organization to deliver care to enrollees, and thus is the customer of the managed care organization. But it is the patient, the enrollee (or that subset of the enrollees who actually gets sick) who is the consumer. The market model is structurally inadequate to accommodate this bifurcation of the healthcare "customer."[12] Further, the information that is a precondition for informed free choice between options is hard to come by in evaluating competing health services.

Current reimbursement mechanisms seem divorced not only from patient interests, but from general medical interests as well. Health promotion and preventative care feature large in any discussion of the health of a population, but current reimbursement mechanisms favor interventions more than prevention, emergency care more than chronic care, and technological medicine more than public health, leading to a unique combination of high cost and mediocre health results.[13]

Healthcare is expensive to deliver, and the rapid changes in reimbursement policy over the last quarter century constantly threaten the financial viability of the healthcare organizations. There has been rapid expansion of hospital systems through mergers and consolidations (sometimes followed by catastrophic failures, as in the well-publicized case of Pennsylvania's Allegheny Health Education and Research Foundation[14]) and a massive conversion of charitable organizations to for-profit corporations. These trends have changed the conditions under which hospitals are expected to operate. Since access to care at a reasonable cost continues to be an expectation of citizens of their society, the level of trust and approval of the healthcare system continues to decline.

C. Interactions Between Business, Medical Research, and Patient Care

The individual physician cannot patent a surgical procedure, but he can have a financial interest in a lab or other supporting institution, hold stock in a pharmaceutical company, and have a financial as well as a professional interest in the devices that improve his surgical results, as can the institution with which he is affiliated.[15]

The availability of a drug or device for use is impacted not only by the formulary available in a given institution, but intertwined with Food and Drug Adminstration approval – and the people sitting on the panels that approve those drugs may have financial ties to the pharmaceutical company promoting them,[16] as may the authors of articles in the medical literature reporting on results of their use.[17]

Since physicians are the sole route of access to prescription drugs, the producers of those pharmaceuticals commit considerable resources to making them available and visible. The influence of company reps on medical education and continuing medical education has recently been publicized by the "no free lunch" movement among medical students, who are beginning to pressure their academic medical centers to exclude sponsored events like meals for exhausted residents and logo bearing pens, ID hangers or bookbags.[18] Physicians deny that their prescribing patterns are inappropriately affected by marketing strategies, but some empirical research suggests the efforts are not entirely without effect.[19] Patients, too, in some practices, are inundated with product promotions in waiting rooms, even at the most prestigious medical centers.

Sponsored research, whether from public or private sources, can be an important source of financial support to an academic institution, and private sponsorship can supplement shrinking public support. Twenty years of legislation encouraging technology transfer encourages the application and wider dissemination of research originating in public institutions, quietly blurring the lines between "pure" research publicly available for replication and application, and proprietary information associated with commercialization.

9.3 DEALING WITH THE RHETORIC OF MEDICINE AS BUSINESS

"From antiquity; medicine has been and continues to be both a business and a profession," proclaims one prominent commentator.[20] One does not need to deny the financial aspect of any service in order to make clear that some businesses are different than others. One of the differences between the old medicine and the new is the change of model of what kind of business it is, from that of the small businessman or craftsman to a more corporate model, and a more mediated, less direct one – where the physician has less control over all aspects of care delivery.

The term "business" does have a neutral, descriptive sense: A business is a *system of production that satisfies needs*. My business is my specific occupation or pursuit, the occupation, work or trade in which I am engaged. Medicine is not just any business, but a business that is a profession. A profession is one subset of businesses, an occupation with specific requirements, including an internal code of ethics, and members are almost universally required to swear some form of oath to uphold those ethics, therefore "professing" to a higher standard of accountability. Societies assume some responsibility for the health of their members, and the profession of medicine has traditionally served as the designated agent of that responsibility. In international documents, access to a basic level of healthcare is often included as a human right. To ignore the Hippocratic tradition in medicine and consider it only a business would be inadequate to some of the central elements and values of medicine, both as an individual enterprise (where the physician–patient relationship has a special status) and as a socially supported activity in the public interest.

Of course there is a pejorative sense of the term "business" as well. Those pejorative associations are most vividly illustrated by the character of Smallweed in the film version of Charles Dickens' *Bleak House*. Phil Davis did a superb job of creating a truly appalling character – "an old evil money-lender, entirely consumed by selfishness and greed," as he is described on the BBC website – whose most frequently repeated line is "I'm a businessman!"[21] The various associations and connotations of the language of business are confusing. Sometimes medicine is identified as a business, and acknowledged to be one, and sometimes it is contrasted with a business when the object is to make clear that it does not share some of the pejorative associations of that term. The major danger in the new rhetoric of medicine as business is the easy availability of the pejorative associations, and a tendency to refer to medicine as a business only when discussing the dangers of commercial associations, while ignoring that language when viewing it positively.

Nevertheless, thinking about medicine as a business does not and should not mean excluding or compartmentalizing ethics. Businesses have ethical responsibilities as well, as the growth and phenomenal success of our sister applied-ethics, business ethics, shows. To assume that businesses have only financial responsibilities distorts the social role of business and does an injustice to many visionary business leaders. We can acknowledge our compunctions about some of the "business practices" associated with recent changes in reimbursement for healthcare in the US today, and be alert to the possibility of conflicts of interests in both medical research and patient care – and still accept that medicine is a business: (1) that it costs money; that it is (2) a process of production (3) that provides a (sometimes costly) service (4) that fills an important social need, and (5) that must be financially sustainable.

9.4 DEALING WITH THE ETHICS OF PATIENT CARE AND RESEARCH UNDER HEALTHCARE'S CHANGING CONDITIONS

The opening of healthcare to the pressures of the larger society – the mainstreaming of parochial physician-dominated medicine – has shown

up some of the vulnerabilities of organized medicine, including an inability
to resist financial pressures, and collusion with special interests in blocking
government attempts to institute a single-payer health plan in the US. The
American Medical Association has been a notorious defender of the economic interests of the profession's members, while not entirely scrupulous
in its own financial dealings.[22] The media and governmental regulators have
been the primary source of intervention on behalf of the interests of
patients, although as is the nature of such interventions, they have often
been piecemeal stopgap measures, responses to particular incidents rather
than systemic, addressing structural incompatibilities. Healthcare reform
via investigative reporting may prove no more satisfactory in the long run
than medical care by MBAs proved to be during the early years of the
managed care movement.

Social attention to the cost of healthcare in the US has prompted debate
in the profession about whether a "new ethics" for the "new medicine" is
necessary or desirable. Should a physician offer all possible care to each
patient, regardless of the economic feasibility of that care? Given his social
role, is it appropriate for a physician to be the financial gatekeeper for the
society, or should those decisions be made by others – and if so, by whom?
There is an assumption in the current healthcare system that professional
responsibility and fiscal responsibility are and ought to be delegated to
different components of the healthcare system: administration and clini-
cian. Half of the literature on a "new ethics for medicine" recommends
incorporating cost control into an expanded notion of physician responsibility, and the other half recommends incorporating quality consciousness
into administrative responsibility. What direction should that move past
conflict and division of labor take? If a "new ethic" can be found, it will be
one that posits "high-quality care for a reasonable cost" as the common
objective for physicians and hospitals, for clinicians and managers – for the
sake of the patients. There are some resources and strategies available for
working toward this common ethical vision.

A. Systems-Based Ethical Thinking

It has been suggested that a systems perspective is needed to think about
important issues in healthcare. "A truly systemic view ... considers how
[this set of individuals, institutions and processes] operates in a system with
certain characteristics. The system involves interactions extending over
time, a complex set of interrelated decision points, an array of [individual,
institutional and governmental] actors with conflicting interests ... and a

number of feedback loops. Progress in analyzing [ethical issues] ... can only be made with a full understanding of the systemic issues."[23] An ethical analysis that takes into consideration a variety of agents and goals enables decision-making that best accommodates the complexity of many ethically troubling situations. "Systems thinking" or a "systems approach" has been discussed in the science and engineering literature for several decades, and one proponent suggests that any phenomenon, organization or subsystem should be dealt with from at least three perspectives: a technical, or fact-finding point of view; a social relationships, or organizational, perspective; and from an individual perspective, ranking problems, perspectives and alternate solutions, and evaluating the problem and its possible resolutions from those multiple perspectives.[24]

Organized medicine is adapting to the altered situation of the twenty-first century by adopting new mental models – new ways of talking about, and sometimes, new techniques for dealing with, healthcare delivery. Recent publications from the Institute of Medicine acknowledge the mutual implication and interpenetration of cost and quality, and the interdependence of the various levels of the healthcare system. The individual encounter of patient and physician affects, and is affected by, the structure of the organization within which that encounter occurs (be it a hospital, a private practice or a clinic), and the expectations that society has of its healthcare system determine, and are determined by, how healthcare is delivered on the individual and organizational level. Problems in that system cannot be solved on only one level without acknowledging the effects of any change on all the other levels. In particular, the Institute of Medicine's report on quality improvement introduces a useful model of complexity theory and suggests we think of the healthcare system as a complex adaptive system – that changes or interventions at any level resonate throughout the system, often in unpredictable ways. It recommends organic mental models, rather than mechanical ones, in helping to understand and improve healthcare delivery.[25]

Another area in which adaptation is taking place is in medical education. In many academic medical centers medical students are encouraged to sit in on courses in the sociology of organizations, business school courses, engineering school courses on systems analysis – as well as medical economics and policy and medical humanities. The profession is realizing the value of a broad education to deal with the changing social context of medicine. An interesting recent phenomenon in medical education is found in the Outcomes project of the American Council on Graduate Medical Education. The fifth Competency on professionalism states that

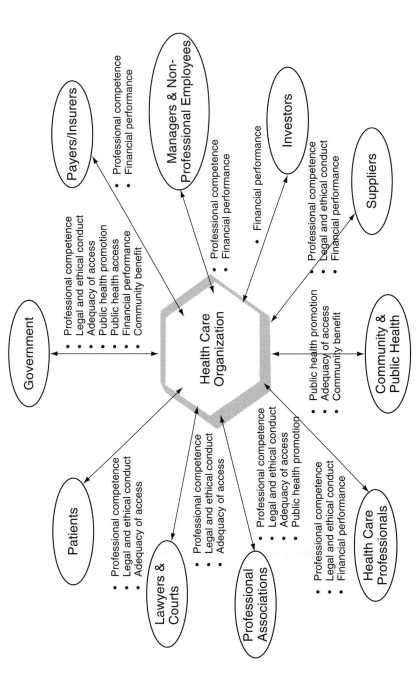

Figure 9.1 Standard stakeholder map

residents are expected to "demonstrate a commitment to ethical principles pertaining to provision or withholding of clinical care, confidentiality of patient information, informed consent, and *business practices* [our emphasis]." The sixth Competency addresses *systems-based* practice, calling explicit attention to the "larger context and system of healthcare," and requires residents to demonstrate an ability to effectively call on system resources to provide care of optimal value. They are called upon to "practice cost-effective healthcare and resource allocation" that does not compromise quality of care.[26]

These two accommodations have some things in common: an organic, rather than a mechanical, approach; emphasis on interrelations, not isolation; an expansive and inclusive approach, expanding, rather than narrowing, the range of focus; an approach that is adaptive and flexible, acknowledging mutual interactions between the profession and the environment of practice and working against compartmentalization. They encourage medical professionals to carefully observe the changing conditions of medical practice, and to be alert to threats they might pose to excellent professional practice. So how should we think about the interface of medicine, business, and the professions? We suggest that a values-based stakeholder approach is useful in thinking about the professional, clinical and economic dimensions of healthcare without sacrificing the primary value of quality patient care to demands for profitability or economic sustainability. Organization ethics and organization ethics committees, we will conclude, are mechanisms to address these problems in the actual delivery of healthcare.

B. *A Values-Based Stakeholder Approach*

Although often not explicitly characterized as such, healthcare ethics has become more systems-oriented. While professional ethics traditionally focuses on the patient/physician (or patient/nurse) dyad, ethical deliberation in healthcare has long since expanded, first to acknowledge the ethical value of the commitments of all the stakeholders in a given case, in clinical ethics,[27] and later through the encouragement of "organization ethics."

A standard stakeholder approach in healthcare might start with a provider organization and outline the various people and groups of people directly affected by or affecting the organization. So in a healthcare organization the primary stakeholders might include patients, medical professionals, payers, suppliers, government and public health professionals, and the community. A standard wheel-and-spoke stakeholder map illustrates this in a very simplistic way (Figure 9.1).

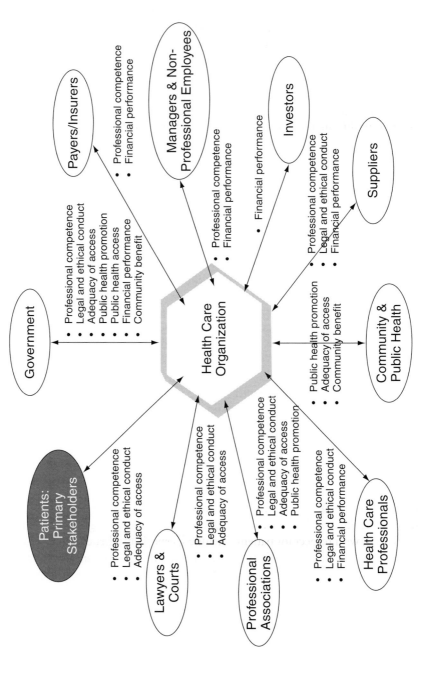

Figure 9.2 Prioritized stakeholder map

However, a stakeholder approach should prioritize the most important stakeholders in each scenario and also the values embedded in the wheel- and spoke relationships. Given the tight interconnections between business, the healthcare professions, and medicine, one might at first question whether those in the *business* of healthcare, e.g., pharmaceuticals, suppliers, for-profit providers, insurers, researchers, and others, value patient care as their first priority. This may or may not in fact be the case, and one of the challenges today for healthcare providers, for example, is how to provide the best error-free care at a decent cost.[28] Nevertheless, it seems obvious that any individual or organization claiming to be in *health*care, whether as payers, providers, manufacturers, or supplies of drugs, by definition, has as its first priority *health*. Otherwise one is not in healthcare. So our second iteration of the wheel-and-spoke stakeholder map would be Figure 9.2, placing patients as the primary stakeholder, and thus patient care as the first value priority. We would also include in that value patient autonomy and respect.

Healthcare professionals have the expertise and are the primary agents of the care that brings patients to the healthcare system. They are the second most valued stakeholder, since one cannot provide care without trained healthcare professionals. Prioritizing the rest of the stakeholders is often more controversial, but we would prioritize them as: third, researchers, who make improved healthcare possible, fourth, the community and public health, and fifth, payers (both governmental and private insurers). Linking that list to the values at stake, we have the following list:

1. patient care: the values of ameliorating disease and safeguarding health
   1a. patient autonomy and respect
2. healthcare professional expertise
3. research expertise and discovery
4. public health
5. economic sustainability

While this prioritization is somewhat controversial, it is our conviction that those in healthcare, in whatever role, must prioritize curing disease and health first, with respect for patients included, especially whenever a patient can self-manage the illness. Without healthcare professionals and researchers the whole sector cannot function, so the values of expertise and new knowledge are essential. Public health has to be critical for the prevention of disease and the health of the community, and unless a healthcare organization of any sort is not fiscally sustainable it will have to close. This does not preclude donor support for healthcare, and although charitable foundations have been converted to for-profit hospitals at an unprecedented rate in the last few decades, philanthropic and research foundations continue to be an important source of support, particularly in university medical centers. So we are not arguing that every healthcare center, delivery system or company has to be a profit center. But we do contend that no organization can function long without financial resources, from some source.

From a systems point of view, a stakeholder approach to ethical analysis makes clear the competing pressures to which both professional agents and healthcare organizations are subject, while emphasizing the importance of properly prioritizing the values constitutive to healthcare as a social institution – the best interests of the individual patients and high-quality patient care. To get to the system ethics we need, it will be necessary to align business practices with the values that justify our traditional and continuing social support of the healthcare system. That means aligning values throughout the system. Until we have a system-wide consensus on values, and appropriately allocate responsibility for implementing those values, we will not be able to progress. The threat to professional ethics is not because healthcare is a business, but because of business practices in healthcare based on values that are inappropriate for responsible medical care, practices that do not prioritize patient care as the first value priority. Of the ethical models available in the current system, we thus return to the old Hippocratic model as the proper approach to granting recipients of care their appropriate respect. But it is not just the physician's responsibility to reconcile ethics and business, it is an obligation of the whole system.

C. Organization Ethics

Mission statements and ethical guidelines of institutions acknowledge the appropriate prioritization of the values of healthcare. But implementing those ethical principles in the daily activity of a complex and busy institution is an ongoing challenge requiring constant balancing. Most individuals in healthcare organizations have an assigned role and the demands of that specific responsibility can lead conscientious professionals to lose sight of the other obligations of the organization. On the level of the health system as a whole, we do not have a shared ethic nor do we have a mechanism for allocating responsibility for implementing values. But some progress can be made on the organizational level in prioritizing values and aligning them with business practices. In 1995 the Joint Commission for Accreditation of Health Care Organizations added a requirement that each organization they accredit have an "organization ethics process," charged to scrutinize the effects of business processes and operational decisions on the quality of

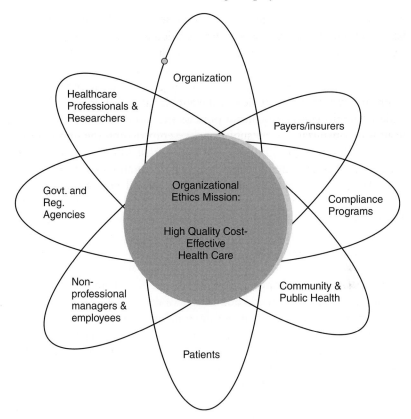

Figure 9.3 Organizational ethics model

patient care.[29] Additionally, an important Standard in the JCAHO manual requires that healthcare organizations address conflicts of interest.[30] A broader more process-oriented definition of healthcare organization ethics has since been advanced by the Virginia Healthcare Ethics Network:

Organization ethics consists of [a set of] processes to address ethical issues associated with the business, financial, and management areas of healthcare organizations, as well as with professional, educational, and contractual relationships affecting the operation of the healthcare organization.[31]

This definition includes the articulation, application, and evaluation of the organization's mission and values statements and encompasses all aspects of the operation of the healthcare organization including its business practices. Both approaches acknowledge that the quality of care experienced by patients depends in part on the relationships the healthcare organization has with its stakeholders. Both approaches insist that healthcare organizations pay attention to these relationships by creating a positive ethical climate throughout the healthcare organization.

A positive ethical climate has at least two important characteristics. First, it is an organizational culture in which the mission and vision of the organization inform the expectations for professional and managerial performance and are implemented in the actual practices of the organization. Second, a positive ethical climate embodies a set of values that reflect societal norms for what the organization should value, how they should prioritize their mission, vision and goals, and how the organization and the individuals associated with it should behave. Healthcare organization ethics directs attention to how the mission of the organization to provide excellent care at reasonable cost is carried out throughout the organization in its business, clinical, and professional practices, and works to bring its activities at all levels of function in line with its mission of excellent patient care.[32] Unlike alternative approaches to ethics in healthcare, this approach focuses on the ethical climate of the entire organization, and encompasses and integrates the resources and activities of clinical ethics, business ethics, and professional ethics within the organization. This approach requires an inclusive perspective that recognizes that the quality of care received by patients is the result of its business practices as well as its clinical and professional practices.

The requirement that healthcare organizations have an "organization ethics process" has been interpreted differently in various hospitals. Some institutions have a specifically designated committee or individual, others have distributed the various tasks associated with organization ethics. Some have integrated the requirement in its compliance activities which often functions as a combination of legal and financial oversight, to avoid fines under the Federal Sentencing Guidelines for billing fraud. Some institutions have Conflict of Interest committees. Since conflicts of interest may affect patient care and are often embedded in the business practices of various stakeholders, this perspective addresses conflicts of interest as well. In our view, however, any organizational initiative that focuses on the ethical climate of the healthcare organization will need to meet several conditions. It will need to develop strong reciprocal relations among its internal stakeholders. It must retain traditional values associated with healthcare delivery, despite changing conditions. It should be able to put the healthcare organization in a position to maintain its ethical and quality standards in its relationships with external stakeholders – payers, suppliers and other contractual partners.

To meet these conditions, an organization ethics program must have several characteristics. It must integrate clinical, professional, and business ethics in a way that aligns the interests of the organization with its major objectives. It must be structured in a way that presupposes shared responsibility and authority, as for instance in our stakeholder model. It must require and support regular and open communication between the individuals responsible for different organizational functions, seek procedural consensus within agreed-upon parameters, and support mechanisms for communication, negotiation, and recourse. We recommend integrating professional ethical standards, including the priority of patient care and the importance of excellent professionally based standards of care, into the mission and values statements, which direct institutional function. An organization ethics program which has these characteristics is in a position to help the organization align values across its relationships and business practices. Moreover, it may provide a model for the rest of the healthcare system.

9.5 CONCLUSION

At the beginning of the last century the Carnegie Foundation undertook an examination of the scientific foundations of the art of medicine. The context of healthcare delivery at that moment in history clearly signaled the need for reform in terms of better preparing doctors for the scientific and technical demands of their practice. The context of healthcare delivery at the beginning of this century is equally threatening, but in a different area. If the Flexner report defined and defended the parameters of the science of medicine, the next reform must define and defend the ethically appropriate boundaries of medicine in its relation to business. The call to the next generation of healthcare professionals to scrutinize the "business practices" associated with clinical care is a clear attempt to meet this demand, as is JCAHO's demand for organizations to scrutinize more carefully potential conflicts of interest in organization-level decision-making.

Flexner said of his subject, "The overwhelming importance of preventive medicine, sanitation, and public health indicates that in modern life the medical profession is an organ differentiated by society for its highest purposes, not a business to be exploited."[33] But the consensus at the beginning of this century is that indeed, if not merely a business, medicine is also a business. Medicine for money alone, not for its professional purposes, is exploitative; it is business in a pejorative sense. Practicing physicians, medical scientists and healthcare organizations of all types are involved in activities that require economic support, are subject to possible conflicts of interest, and are vulnerable to exploitation. Acknowledging this third face of medicine is the first step toward disciplining it and bringing it into balance with the art and science of the medical profession. Determining the ethical parameters for this third face of medicine is the challenge facing professional medicine in the coming century. If organized medicine as a profession should undertake to define what counts as fiscal responsibility in order for members of the profession to consider themselves ethically responsible, a new discussion might begin – one that would revitalize the Hippocratic tradition in the light of changing practice conditions.

NOTES

1. One of the histories – Douglas Guthrie's *Janus in the Doorway* (Springfield, IL: Charles Thomas, 1963) – traced it back to magicians, then to priests, and eventually to philosophers – a pleasing conceit. Hippocrates and Galen are counted among the philosophers. Steven H. Miles' *The Hippocratic Oath and the Ethics of Medicine* (New York: Oxford University Press, 2005), is the most recent in a series of thoughtful evaluations of the Hippocratic tradition.
2. Abraham Flexner, *Medical Education in the United States* (New York: Carnegie Foundation, 1910).
3. Henry Beecher, "Ethics and Clinical Research," *New England Journal of Medicine* 274, no. 24 (1966): 1354–1360.
4. Flexner, *Medical Education in the United States.*
5. In his *Tractatus Logico-Philosophicus* (New York: Routledge, 2001), Ludwig Wittgenstein hypothesized as an explanation of language use that true sentences have the same logical form as the facts that they picture (the "picture" theory of meaning). Although Wittgenstein abandoned this analysis of language in his later work, other thinkers have formulated similar suggestions. The term "mental model" was introduced by the Scottish philosopher and psychologist Kenneth Craik in *The Nature of Explanation* (New York: The Macmillan Company, 1943) for a kind of internal symbol or representation of reality that people use to understand specific phenomena. Neglected for 50 years, the term came back into usage in the 1990s in two applied disciplines – human–computer interface usability design and organizational analysis. Organizational theorist Peter Senge made great use of mental models in his introduction of systems thinking as a tool of strategic management in *The Fifth Discipline* (New York: Doubleday, 1990). In his work a mental model is extremely general – a way of looking at the world – but at the same time very powerful, determining, he suggests, how we think and act. We use the term in our work to call attention to the need to examine and sometimes alter entrenched ways of thinking in order to adequately meet changing conditions.
6. The statistics cited are from P. L. Havlicek, *Medical Groups in the US: A Survey of Practice Characteristics.* (Chicago, IL: American Medical Association, 1996): pp. 7–13.

7. The changes cited are instances of trends well chronicled by several authors, including Paul Starr, *The Social Transformation of American Medicine* (New York: Basic Books, 1982), Rosemary Stevens, *In Sickness and in Wealth: American Hospitals in the Twentieth Century* (New York: Basic Books, 1989) and James C. Robinson, *The Corporate Practice of Medicine* (Berkeley: University of California Press, 1999).

8. Robinson, *The Corporate Practice of Medicine*, p. 1.

9. Ibid., p. 2.

10. The percentage of GDP that goes to healthcare is higher in the US than in any other developed country, but the health of the population by standard international measures is mediocre in some measures and appalling in others.

11. Economist J. D. Kleinke offers an interesting case study for healthcare watchers. He wrote two books, separated by three years. In the first *Bleeding Edge: The Business of Health Care in the New Century* (Gaithersburg, MD: Aspen Publishers, 1998) he deplores the absence of economic rationality in healthcare system; in the second *Oxymorons: The Myth of a U.S. Health Care System* (San Francisco, CA: Jossey-Bass, 2001) he throws up his hands and proclaims that in the absence of some integration of the components of our non-system, no economic rationality is possible.

12. We were pleased with ourselves for seeing this problem with the market model. But it turns out the same point was made more elegantly and clearly by Haavi Morreim, *Balancing Act: The New Medical Ethics of Medicine's New Economics* (Washington, DC: Georgetown University Press, 1995), p. 22. She uses the term "purchaser" instead of "customer" to make the same point.

13. A 2006 *New York Times* series by N. R. Kleinfield on diabetes, described as "epidemic" in parts of New York City, pointed to the irrationality of a health service that funds amputations but does not provide the funding for adequate primary care that would prevent them. N. R. Kleinfield, *New York Times*, January 9–12, 2006.

14. Lawton R. Burns, John Cacciamani, James Clement, and Welman Aquino, "The Fall of the House of AHERF: The Allegheny Bankruptcy," *Health Affairs* 19, no. 1 (2000): 7–41. The history of the corporation is briefly chronicled by Lawton R. Burns in *LDI Issue Brief* 5(5) (February 2000), published by the Leonard Davis Institute of Health Economics, Philadelphia PA.

15. David Armstrong, "Delicate Operation: How a Famed Hospital Invests in Devices It Uses and Promotes." *Wall Street Journal*, December 12, 2005.

16. P. Lurie, M. Almeida, N. Stine, A. R. Stine, and S. Wolfe, "Financial Conflict of Interest Disclosure and Voting Patterns at Food and Drug Administration Drug Advisory Committee Meetings," *Journal of the American Medical Association* 295 (2006): 1921–1928.

17. M. K. Cho and L. A. Bero, "The Quality of Drug Studies Published in Symposium Proceedings," *Annals of Internal Medicine* 124, no. 5 (1996): 485–489.

18. See http://nofreelunch.org. The website includes selected references and a link to a more comprehensive database sponsored by the WHO, www.drugpromo.org.

19. Cf. R. F. Adair and L. R. Holmgren: "Do Drug Samples Influence Resident Prescribing Behavior?" *American Journal of Medicine* 118, no. 8 (2005): 881–884 and J. P. Orlowski and L. Wateska "The Effects of Pharmaceutical Firm Enticements on Physician Prescribing Patterns," *Chest* 102, no. 1 (1992): 260–273.

20. G. D. Lundberg, "The Business and Professionalism of Medicine," *Journal of the American Medical Association* 278, no. 20 (1997): 1704. One has only to read the sentence to realize that of course that is true. But at the same time its obviousness only became clear in a certain historical moment, when professionals had to distinguish between the honorific, pejorative and descriptive senses of that term. He continues, "Physicians are by definition both entrepreneurs and professionals." The suggestion that physicians have always been entrepreneurs is less obvious, especially considering medicine internationally, although some of the examples above confirm the entrepreneurial spirit of many US physicians.

21. This description of Smallweed is taken directly from the PBS website advertising the series. The site is illustrated with a snarling snapshot of Phil Davis' Smallweed. BBC Press Office, *Bleak House*. Available at www.bbc.co.uk/pressoffice/pressreleases/stories/2005/10_october/04/bleak_who.shtml.

22. The American Medical Association has consistently resisted governmental attempts to institute a national health system and in the early part of the last century refused membership to physicians who were employees. For a critical treatment of the history of the organization see James Rorty, *American Medicine Mobilized* (New York: W. W. Norton, 1939). For a case study of the AMA's deal with Sunbeam to endorse products in the 1990s see A. Nanda and K. Haddad, "The AMA-Sunbeam Deal: Serpent on the Staff Meets Chainsaw Al." Case # 9–801–326, Harvard Business on Line, January 2001, October 2002, and F. B. Charatan, "American Medical Association Apologizes for Commercial Deal," *British Medical Journal* 315 (1997) 501–504.

23. Susan Wolf, "Toward a Systemic Theory of Informed Consent in Managed Care." *Houston Law Review* 35 (1998), 1631–1681, 1675. For further development of a systems-approach to healthcare see P. Werhane, *Moral Imagination and Management Decision-Making* (New York: Oxford, 1999).

24. Ian Mitroff and Harold Linstone, *The Unbounded Mind* (New York: Oxford University Press, 1993), esp. Chapter 6. For an extended discussion of systems thinking, see Patricia Werhane, "Moral Imagination and Systems Thinking," *Journal of Business Ethics* 38 (2002): 33–42.

25. Institute of Medicine Committee on Quality and Health Care in America, *Crossing the Quality Chasm: A New Health Care System for the 21st Century* (Washington DC: Institute of Medicine, 2001), especially the appendix by Plsik. For a discussion of the usefulness of complexity theory for analyzing ethical issues in healthcare, see Mills, Rorty and Werhane (2003), "Complexity and the Role of Ethics in Health Care," *Emergence* 5, no. 3 (2003): 6–21.

26. Cf. Mills and Rorty, "Business Practices, Ethical Principles and Professionalism" *Organizational Ethics* 2, no. 1 (2005): 30–43, reprinted in

Professionalism in Tomorrow's Healthcare System, ed. Mills, Chen, Werhane, and Wynia (Hagerstown, MD: University Publishing Group, 2005), 101–124.

27. Fletcher, Spencer and Lombardo, *Fletcher's Introduction to Clinical Ethics.* (Hagerstown, MD: University Publishing Group, 2005), Chapter 1 and Appendix 2.

28. Computerized systems revealing drug interactions, for instance, have been shown to be very useful for avoiding one common kind of medical error, but changing the computer system throughout a healthcare system represents a considerable initial investment.

29. The beginning of the century saw a number of publications defining organization ethics, including Spencer, Mills, Rorty and Werhane, *Organization Ethics in Health Care* (New York: Oxford University Press, 2000).

30. Joint Commission Resources: *2005 Comprehensive Accreditation Manual for Hospitals*, RI Chapter, Patient Rights and Organizational Ethics Standards (Oakbrook Terrace, IL: JCAHO 2005) Standard RI.1.20: The hospital addresses conflicts of interest.

31. Spencer *et al.*, *Organization Ethics in Health Care* p. 212.

32. Ibid.

33. Flexner, *Medical Education in the United States.*

CHAPTER 10

Theoretical foundations for organizational ethics: developing norms for a new kind of healthcare

George Khushf

Current efforts to advance an organizational ethic for healthcare are motivated by problematic developments that are both pervasive and deep. Many sense that something radical is happening to healthcare. Representative changes include deskilling, where services once performed by specialists are being performed by generalists, and those performed by professional nurses are now performed by nurse technicians. They include the horizontal and vertical integration of services, with an attendant blurring of the distinction between insurer and provider. Health services researchers are now hired by hospitals to provide profiling and develop guidelines and clinical pathways. "Case managers" are in some contexts replacing physicians as coordinators of care. Perhaps most significantly, institutions are emerging as active agents of healthcare, with administrators playing a role in configuring clinical practice. These and many other similar developments seem to be but expressions of a fundamental transformation. How are we to make sense of these changes, and how should we respond? For some, the answer seems closely linked to an ethic that is attentive to the middle level organizations that now configure care.

THE NATURE OF CURRENT TRANSFORMATIONS IN HEALTHCARE: TWO INTERPRETATIONS

The form that an organizational ethic will take depends on how the above-mentioned developments are interpreted. We generally find two fundamentally different interpretations. The first kind is well represented by Edmund Pellegrino, the current chair of the President's Council on Bioethics. He sees the problematic changes as an assault by market forces on the scientific and ethical integrity of medical practice. For him, there is a logic of medicine and a different logic of economics and the market. Driven by an interest in controlling runaway costs in the healthcare sector, we have unleashed market forces that now threaten sound medical practice. The changes we are witnessing thus involve a threat in which an alien, economic logic works like a virus to disrupt the integrity of healthcare.[1] In response, he highlights what he regards as the scientific and ethical core of medicine; namely, a physician–patient encounter, understood in fiduciary terms, where a scientifically trained physician draws on the knowledge base of the profession to address the assault on personal identity posed by illness. Since institutions and economic incentives now encroach, distorting this core clinical interaction, the key task is one of limiting their role and power. The appropriate response to current transformations thus involves fighting the market forces, regulating managed care (and other intrusions of institutional and administrative oversight), and fostering the virtues of the profession. Here "virtue" is closely associated with a character and habit of mind that upholds the classical fiduciary obligations, and thus advances the best interests of the patient. The basic orientation is thus one of recovery: reasserting the classical ideals in the face of distorting influences. This is the dominant view.[2] It assumes that the radical changes involve a threat, at best motivated by the constraints of finite resources, but more often the outgrowth of greed.

I will argue for an alternative interpretation, one that provides a more positive account of the transformations that are currently taking place. On this alternative account, perhaps best represented by a series of influential Institutes of Medicine (IOM) reports such as *To Err is Human: Building a Safer Health System* (2000) and *Crossing the Quality Chasm: A New Health System for the 21st Century* (2001), current changes do not involve the imposition of an alien logic, but rather emerge from the way modern medicine and technology have themselves evolved. The problematic features we now see are then not simply the result of recent market developments, but are rather long-term problems arising from the biomedical model itself, exacerbated when older mechanisms of shifting costs are eliminated. New structural changes can then be seen as deeply challenging the older model. At the heart of these developments is a shift from an individually oriented, individually practiced medicine to a systems-based, community-oriented form of healthcare, where organizations emerge as agents of healthcare practice. Within this systems-based approach we then find resources for addressing deficiencies in the biomedical model that could not otherwise be addressed. The task is then to develop the norms for responsible agency, so that the promise is realized, and so pathological forms are prevented.

The negative and positive interpretations of this change reflect two stances toward the emerging paradigm, each with its own vision of the science, ethics, and socioeconomic configurations appropriate to healthcare practice. Each stance involves a different approach to organizational ethics. Those who advocate the dominant view, who see the Vandals at the gate threatening decay and loss, want to uphold the long-held medical ideals. Organizational ethics, on this model, presupposes a distinction between administrative and clinical jurisdictions, and it mobilizes diverse stakeholders to check the intrusion of business and commercial interests. The alternative, more positive account of current changes, does not yet have the benefit of a fully articulated and broadly accepted scientific and ethical ideal. Instead, it struggles to grasp and bring to language the fundamental structure of that constellation that is only now taking form. Here a central task of organizational ethics involves the interpretive work of facilitating the development of a vision and values that can inform ongoing efforts to appropriately implement a systems-based form of healthcare.

I think the importance of the interpretive work for an organizational ethic that takes a systems-based approach has not been sufficiently appreciated, and my goal in this chapter is to flesh out this task in a preliminary way. To accomplish this, I am going to follow a strategy that is clearly manifest in the IOM reports on error and quality, and which was earlier seen in the work of George Engel, when he advanced his biopsychosocial model of medicine.[3] They first sketch what they see as the deficient, traditional account, outline its problems, and then advance an alternative vision. Following this pattern, I will sketch core features of the traditional biomedical model, and consider some of the ethical problems integral to that model. I will then consider how bioethicists have attempted to respond to these deficiencies in medicine, and argue that the reigning bioethical orthodoxy is inadequate, because it does not sufficiently challenge the assumptions integral to the biomedical model. I take The Study to Understand Prognoses and Preferences for Outcomes and Risks of Treatments (the SUPPORT study) as representative of this failure.[4] Finally, I show how a systems perspective offers opportunities to address concerns that have been important in bioethics. The task is then to carry forward the transformation that has already been initiated, and I close by highlighting the interpretive work that lies ahead if we are to realize this promise.

THE BIOMEDICAL PARADIGM: THE PHYSICIAN AS LOCUS OF KNOWLEDGE AND PRACTICE

Many see in the structural transformations taking place, the emergence of a more impersonal, bureaucratic kind of healthcare. This "market-based healthcare" is then contrasted with the good old days of a caring, more humane medicine. However, such arguments forget that the good old days were not always so great, and that the problems of reductionism and impersonal care have been endemic to biomedicine. Here I wish to show how these problems are not first introduced as a result of market pressures; rather they arise from the inner logic of the biomedical model itself, and they have resisted the best efforts of previous reform.

In order to articulate the basic elements of the traditional biomedical model, I'll draw on Abraham Flexner's *Medical Education in the United States and Canada.*[5] The pattern of education advanced therein still governs the way medicine is understood, taught, and practiced. While there is some debate about whether the *Flexner Report* actually brought about the changes in American medical education, or whether it simply anticipated and articulated changes that were already well under way in the early part of the twentieth century, there is a broad recognition that the *Report* does capture the core concerns associated with the establishment of medicine as a science.[6] It is thus a representative document for articulating the most important features of the reigning biomedical paradigm.

Here I highlight five important elements of that paradigm.

1. Medicine must be grounded in the basic sciences and follow the scientific method

Flexner evaluated the state of American medical education against a blue-print that was largely derived from the newly formed Johns Hopkins School of Medicine. His report introduced the basic requirements in the sciences for premedical education, and the distinction between the basic science and clinical years of medical school. At the heart of his proposed blueprint was the assumption that medical knowledge should be provided with a scientific basis. This meant that knowledge of a patient's illness should be configured in terms of a disease that was accessible to the laboratory sciences. According to Flexner, it was a waste of time to even put students in a clinical setting until they had sufficient knowledge of pathological anatomy and physiology. Only then could they properly understand what they saw manifest in an actual patient.[7]

To say that medicine must be a science meant much more than it must be based on the laboratory sciences, and thus rooted in the results of scientific research. For Flexner, it also meant that medicine in its practice must follow the same method that directs research; there is no distinction in kind between the medical researcher and clinical practitioner.[8] The scientific method is seen in the way a researcher formulates a preliminary hypothesis from the data that is at hand, and then seeks to test that hypothesis. In the same way, a physician obtains data by taking a patient's history and from the physical exam. From this a preliminary hypothesis, called a diagnosis, is formulated. It is then tested in three ways. Ideally, a laboratory test is available, which can conclusively confirm or disconfirm the initial hypothesis. When this is not available, the physician must manage uncertainty. "The fact that disease is only in part accurately known does not invalidate the scientific method in practice. In the twilight region probabilities are substituted for certainties."[9] A successful management of a patient's disease can be viewed as a probabilistic confirmation of the initial disease hypothesis. However, when success does not come and the patient dies, the third and most effective means for testing the hypothesis becomes available, the autopsy. The task of pathology is to appreciate the full scope of disease in its nature and effects, and "only the autopsy can disclose these."[10]

Modern medicine is thus "scientific" in a double sense. First, it is rooted in the basic or laboratory sciences. Second, its approach to diagnosis and treatment is directed by the scientific method. For Flexner, these are the key marks that distinguish modern "scientific" medicine, from its previous "empiric" and "dogmatic" forms. Current efforts at realizing an evidence-based medicine are in clear continuity with this Flexnerian ideal.

2. Health is defined as absence of disease

With the emergence of the clinico-pathological method of the Paris school, there was a fundamental reconceptualization of the nature of disease.[11] The patient's illness was no longer configured in terms of dis-ease; namely, that absence of ease that characterizes the experience of the patient. "Pain," which previously was itself a disease category, now became a mere symptom.[12] The category of disease was reserved for disruptions of normal anatomy or physiology. It became a defect in the body machine.[13] The anatomist (who alone can give the "total picture of disease") "views the body ... as a machine to be taken to pieces, the more perfectly to comprehend how it works."[14] Health is present as long as there is no such defect.[15]

Integral to this disease concept is the assumption of a value-free, theoretical core, which configures the line between normal and pathological as a function of science, not individual or socioeconomic values. Today, this standard is perhaps best reflected in a Boorsian disease concept, where disease is taken as a species atypical diminishment of species typical function or functional ability. By working with such an account, advocates of a Flexnerian ideal seek an objective basis for grounding the work of medicine, and distinguishing it from nonmedical goods. Such assumptions are integral to recent attempts to restrict health coverage to "medical necessity," with the implied claim that such necessity is a function of scientific standards, which provide a value-free basis for adjudicating among claims on resources.

3. Ethical norms and economic structures serve to establish conditions of scientific practice

There is a close link between medical scientific ideals, ethical norms, and economic structures that is rarely appreciated, but has important implications for bioethical reflection. The link can be seen in the Flexner Report, where arguments for the reform of medicine and medical education follow three steps. First, Flexner articulates the scientific ideal.[16] Second, he shows how social and economic realities of early twentieth-century medicine often undermine that ideal.[17] Third, ethical norms and socioeconomic reform are proposed to eliminate factors that distort scientific practice and thus establish the conditions for a modern medicine (this is developed throughout the Report). This pattern of argument is also found in many other medical professional settings; for example, in the ethical reflection of the American Medical Association (AMA) or American College of Surgeons (ACS) on "fee splitting."[18]

Since one of the functions of ethical norms is to sustain the conditions of scientific practice, one cannot fully understand the ethical norms without appreciating the scientific ideals. The Flexnerian model assumes that science has its own norms and logic, which can be clearly articulated independent of ethics and economics. Science is a value-free endeavor, directed by the canons of knowing truly and intervening effectively. There is thus no place for any sectarianism or dogma.[19] "All physicians, summoned to see the sick, are confronted with precisely the same crisis: a body out of order."[20] The physician is a scientist who uses the scientific method to fix defects in the body machine. Since ethics and economics involve values, and science is objective and value free, there is an important asymmetry between the ethics and science of medicine: Science can be understood and developed independent of an account of ethical norms, while ethics is dependent upon the science, coming in as a second step and addressing the use and abuse of the independently formulated, foundational science.

While a central concern of ethical reflection, according to this traditional paradigm, is to exclude social and economic factors that may distort and hinder the scientific ideal, that was not its only function. Obviously, beyond this, a medical ethic seeks to assure that the vulnerable patient is not exploited, and that the patient's best interest is served (a concern that can be traced all the way back to the Hippocratic oath). However, it was generally assumed that the patient's best interest is automatically served when good scientific practice is realized, because that is the context most conducive to fixing the body machine. The patient's good was equated with medical good. The fiduciary ideals associated with the physician–patient relation were thus regarded as complementary to the ideals of scientific practice.

4. The physician is captain of the ship

Modern medicine embodies assumptions of meritocracy. Power should be vested in the one who has knowledge; in other words, the person who is an authority should also be in authority to direct action. Practically, this has meant that the physician, as the master of medical science, should direct the activities of healthcare.[21] Nurses and other healthcare professionals were legitimate authorities to the degree that they were initiated into the knowledge possessed by the physician, but their status was always subservient.[22] There were, of course, additional tasks of personal care or counseling, for example, but these were often regarded as if they were outside the core concern of medicine, which was to fix the body machine. Other healthcare workers such as nurses were free to address those additional concerns as long as they gave priority to the proper medical ones.

5. Institutions serve as locus of practice or as payer, but should not interfere with clinical practice

This element of the traditional paradigm was rarely stated, but it follows directly from the other characteristics of medicine. Institutions such as hospitals or insurance companies (a later development) were to play no role in influencing clinical practice. As Haavi Morreim has so nicely argued, these institutions were "silent partners," providing the locus and conditions for practice (the hospital) or paying for services (insurer).[23] Payment was supposed to follow as a separable second step, following an intervention that was based on scientific standards alone.

While many features of our healthcare landscape have changed, these five elements of the Flexnerian model of medicine still are implicit assumptions of the dominant interpretation of current transformations in healthcare. It is assumed that healthcare is practiced by individuals trained in a value-free science of medicine. Organizations are concerned with resources, either as coordinators of space, technology, and nonmedical labor (hospitals) or as payers for services (insurance). Organizational ethics is thus an aspect of business ethics. For advocates of the traditional paradigm, the task of such an ethic is to provide norms for institutions that enable medical practitioners to realize their scientific ideals. That means protecting a domain for clinical discretion and thus excluding social and economic factors from playing a role in configuring the norms of practice. The reason "organizational ethics" has recently become such an important topic is thus tied to the perceived need to limit their role and prevent administrators from compromising medical professional ideals. Clinical ethics, on this model, is neatly separated from organizational ethics. The former is concerned with the medical aspects of care, while the latter is concerned with the business aspects. Business (with its economic logic) and clinical practice (with its medical logic) are to remain separate. If any balancing of resources is needed (and many still are unclear about the need for this), then it should take place at macro-ethical levels (social policy) and not impinge on the dynamic of clinical reasoning and practice.

PROBLEMS WITH THE BIOMEDICAL PARADIGM

I will, following Engel, call the cluster of assumptions integral to Flexner's medicine the "biomedical model." The benefits of this model are obvious: the transformation they initiated provided effective means for overcoming diseases that previously would have been debilitating or fatal. However, there was also a dark side, which has been extensively discussed in the bioethics literature. Put simply, medicine has been reductionistic. It has advanced narrow, medical ends, and has often been inattentive to the broader personal and communal ends that are important to patients and the larger population. Many of the central developments of medical ethics involve an attempt to overcome this medical reductionism. When we consider these old complaints, it becomes clear that many of the troubling features of recent note are actually expressions of these long-standing problems, and not new developments caused by structural changes in healthcare.

For the sake of our discussion, I will consider just three representatives of the many problematic areas, and briefly consider how bioethicists have attempted to respond:

1. Medicine is depersonalizing

There is a fundamental distinction between persons or subjects and objects. Subjects reside in a world of meaning, specify their own ends, have values, and serve as partners in collaborative actions. Objects, by contrast, are fixed; they have a determinate structure and patterns of response, which can be predicted. Objects reside in a realm of brute fact. Although this simple dichotomy is, of course, highly problematic from a philosophical perspective, it still captures an important moral insight. Patients are both subjects and objects; both agents and "broken bodies." The dynamic of the physician–patient encounter is thus a complex one, involving a subtle balance between subject–subject and subject–object aspects of the encounter.

In the Flexnerian model, the subject–object aspects of the encounter became overly dominant, and the voice of the patient was muted. There were, in fact, two problematic assumptions. First, within medicine, the patient's good was narrowly understood; problems were seen as defects in the body-machine, and patient good was understood in terms of fixing this defect. Second, such medicine was paternalistic: physicians assumed that patients yielded up their bodies to a physician's agency, and that their task was to advance the good as they understood it, whether or not patients properly appreciated or valued this good. On the basis of these assumptions, medicine was doubly depersonalizing: it regarded patients as objects, as defective machines; and it discounted the patient's own experience and ends, silencing the agent, and transforming her into a passive recipient of medical actions.

Such a stance began with the first encounter between physician and patient. Through the process of history taking, the physician was not really interested in the historical narrative of the patient, but rather used the patient's voice as the point of departure for getting at a disease entity that is independent of that voice and narrative.[24] The patient's complaint and experience is regarded as epiphenomenal, and the task was to translate the patient's expression of "dis-ease" (the illness experience) into a scientifically specifiable deviation from species norms of functional ability (disease). Many have noted how this process – integral to the method of scientific medicine – can exacerbate the patient's suffering. Their status as subject is discounted, exacerbating the patterns of alienation integral to the illness experience. Another way of framing this is to say that such a medicine was insufficiently attentive to the "wounded humanity" of the patient, and that it needed to reorient its focus to the body as lived, rather than just the object-body.[25]

The problems of medicine's depersonalizing, objectivizing, technologically driven orientation were vividly captured in the image of a dying patient, attached to a respirator and receiving aggressive medical interventions well after the patient could reasonably benefit from these. This image provided a symbolic articulation of the way medicine at every level is seduced by high tech gadgetry, and how patients and family are lost from view.

Modern bioethics arose partly as a response to these deficiencies in medicine; to give voice to patients, and thus overcome the silence that characterized medicine (the "silent world of doctor and patient"[26]). Personal interaction involves modes of communication and reflection that allow patients to articulate their values and the character of their own identity. Since medicine did not provide this space for self-expression, ethical ideals were advanced, which would supplement the object–object features of the clinical encounter. These ideals are perhaps best expressed in ethical standards of informed consent; they were also integral to the development and use of advance directives, and they motivated many of the norms that are now integral to human subjects research.

2. *Care is fragmented*

Another, commonly addressed problem in medicine concerns its atomism. There is a pervasive assumption that problems can be divided into subunits without loss. As Flexner says of the body – it is a machine to be broken into parts, the more perfectly to understand it – so too for all things. Wholes are divisible. Patient problems are divisible. They can be parsed into discrete units, and addressed visit by visit. Each intervention addresses a component of the broader task. Thus arises the acute care, intervention orientation, which so pervasively characterizes modern medicine, and which makes it unresponsive to the problems of chronic disease and prevention.

The problems of fragmentation go far beyond the atomizing approach to patient problems, and they are intertwined with the problems of depersonalization. Because a patient's good is narrowly defined in terms of medical ends, there is insufficient appreciation of the tasks performed by other healthcare professionals. Nurses, for example, have an ethic that emphasizes a response to the patient's illness experience.[27] Pastoral care workers address spiritual concerns. Social workers consider broader psychosocial factors integral to well-being. Family members and friends provide community. Administrators assist in coordinating the care for all patients or, in the case of an insurer, assure that the broader economic interests of a patient population are sufficiently addressed. There may be a trade-off, for example, between the most effective medical solution (focused on the disease) and the most appropriate nursing solution (focused on the patient's experienced well-being). In some cases, the patient's own account of "best interest" might require that a physician serve as a nurse's assistant. However, as long as the medical aspects of healthcare are given lexical priority and problems parsed to various health workers and over discrete episodes of care, such cooperative, coordinated care does not emerge.

While the problems associated with fragmented, acute, intervention-oriented care have been oft recognized, bioethicists have not been effective at conceptually or practically addressing the issues. For the most part, people have assumed that these problems of fragmentation are a function of macro-ethical issues related to health systems and policy; they are thus separated from the problems of depersonalization that are "solved" by doctrines of informed consent or advance directives. I'll consider this shift to a macro-ethical arena in greater detail, but at this stage simply want to note how many of these problems of fragmentation reside very close to the arena of clinical care, and they are functions of relatively local features of health systems. Why shift so readily to the macro-level?

3. The cost crisis

Many people attribute the high costs and fragmented, intervention-oriented form of US medical care to the indemnity-based, fee-for-service systems of reimbursement that characterized the periods of runaway health inflation (1960s–1980s); further, they see the continued prevalence of these problems as the outgrowth of new economic structures (like those associated with DRGs or managed care) designed to mitigate the problems raised by those earlier market structures. These explanations are problematic, because they do not sufficiently consider the deep resonance between core assumptions integral to the biomedical model and the incentives and logic of the indemnity-based systems of healthcare.

The fee-for-service, indemnity-based systems arose naturally from Flexner's core assumptions. While Flexner himself considered medicine as a social good, and he sought public support for institutions of healthcare, he also regarded the method and content of medicine in atomistic terms. He sought to design economic structures of medical practice, so that the clinical encounter would be completely insulated. Later, as insurance schemes emerged, Flexner's core ideal meant that financial matters had to enter at a secondary stage, after the physician had determined what was medically indicated. It was thus natural to divide up care into their discrete bits, and to bill for them post hoc. (The core features of "cost plus" medicine.)

When bioethicists consider these problems of cost, they shift to a macro-ethic. Advancing some account of justice, and motivated by efficiency and

effectiveness considerations, they seek to advance mechanisms for prioritizing health services that integrate "evidence-based standards" (largely
regarded as functions of the science) with broadly accepted social values.
However, the influential work in these areas rarely involves a deep challenge
to the core assumptions of Flexner's medicine. As with the micro-ethical
solutions (e.g., informed consent), we find an attempt to supplement the
scientific core, and thus integrate features of the biomedical model with
broader social values that address questions of prioritization and resource
utilizations. Problems of health systems are seen to reside within the social
and economic configurations of healthcare. The "science" of medicine –
and with it the core features of the medical model itself – are seen as
something different, and separate from those health systems, and thus as
having an integrity that lies outside of social dispute regarding the design of
these health systems.

THE COMPLICITY OF BIOETHICS

While there is, of course, considerable diversity in the bioethics literature, I
think a crude distinction can be drawn between what I'll call "orthodox
bioethics" and other variants. In the early days of modern bioethics, there
were many influential critics of medicine, who deeply questioned fundamental assumptions integral to the Flexnerian model. Here I'd include
figures like Paul Ramsey, Hans Jonas, Richard Zaner, Drew Leder, Leon
Kass, Stanley Hauerwas, and James Gustafson, just to mention a few.
Gerald McKenny has provided a nice review of their contributions along
with many other such critics in his book, *To Relieve the Human Condition*.
These deep criticisms have been increasingly marginalized in favor of
bioethical reflection which takes for granted what McKenny calls the
Baconian features of medicine: exactly those features I have highlighted in
my discussion of the Flexnerian model.[28] The current reaction among
mainstream bioethicists to Leon Kass's work with the President's Council
of Bioethics is representative of how such deep critical reflection is today
regarded: it is seen as unscientific, and any attempt to make explicit and
engage core assumptions of biomedical research or practice is seen as an
intrusion and distortion of the science.

In place of such deep criticism, "bioethical orthodoxy" takes for granted
the biomedical model, and provides an *ethical supplement*; as, for example,
we saw in ethical doctrines of informed consent. Following the assumptions
integral to Flexner's medicine, the world is parsed into a micro- and macro-
ethic. The micro-ethics concerns the interpersonal aspects of clinical care.

At its heart is an ideal of a collaborative physician–patient interaction, where competent patients are provided with the information they need to understand care options, so their own values might direct a holistic care they directly authorize. Macro-ethics concerns the social systems and health policies which are designed to provide cost-effective, integrated care in an equitable manner. In both cases, we have assumed two strands, one of fact and hard science, and another of values, and the work of ethics has involved integrating the supervening values strand. The collusion of bioethical orthodoxy with the assumptions of biomedicine is especially apparent in the literature on the structural transformations that are currently taking place in healthcare, and in the recommendations for organizational ethics and managed care. The physician–patient relation is made central, and it is assumed that ethical and economic domains are neatly separable from those of medical science, each involving its own logic. When economic values play a role in configuring clinical practice, as they do with many of the incentives introduced by managed care, then it is simply assumed that there is a violation and distortion of the integrity of medicine, or, in the more nuanced approaches, there is some attempt to "balance" the diverse interests. The function of ethics, on this model, is to identify and exclude or mitigate the encroachment of the alien logic. Traditional ideals of informed consent are put forth as the solution, and one works with an individually oriented, individually practiced healthcare, which abstracts discussion of ethics from any considerations of the institutionally based, communally oriented character of current healthcare practice.

Despite unquestionable gains, the solutions that constitute the "orthodoxy" of the bioethics community have proven inadequate. The ethical ideals of informed consent are rarely even approximated. Instead, we have a legal doctrine, which in practice is satisfied by a laundry list of risks and the signing of a form. Advance directives are too often a sham, only respected when physicians independently decide that it is time to forego treatment. Researchers see Institutional Review Boards as obstacles, asking about the tricks for "getting something through the IRB." While all these developments provide important protections, we need to recognize how high-sounding ideals are not even approximated in practice. Bioethical orthodoxy is a largely ineffective overlay on top of an unresponsive, unrepentant medical reductionism. The core ethical commitments mentioned – those of informed consent, advance directives, etc. – address the everyday practice of medicine. But the field's influence is only at the margins, when some dilemma or crisis emerges. The tools that have influenced practice – for example, those associated with ethics committees or the theories of principlism and casuistry – work to resolve problems that threaten the complacency of the healthcare arena. Bioethics becomes a means for managing those crises that resist resolution in medical terms, and that have the risk of moving into the legal arena. As Jonathan Imber argues, "[b]ioethics is the public relations division of modern medicine."[29] It functions like the "patient advocate" in a hospital setting; namely, as a tool by which the medical establishment can manage and thus dissipate a more radical challenge to the status quo.

As long as the core commitments of the Flexnerian paradigm remain unchallenged, bioethics will be unable to respond to the problems that arise from that model. As Drew Leder notes:

If we wish to reform medical practice in fundamental ways it is not sufficient to propose piecemeal changes in medical education, financing, and the like, while leaving unchallenged the conceptual structure upon which modern medicine rests.[30]

The inability of "orthodox bioethics" to address the problems associated with biomedicine is well documented in the Study to Understand Prognoses and Preferences for Outcomes and Risks of Treatments.[31] SUPPORT can be viewed as a test of the effectiveness of the orthodox bioethical response to the problems inherent in modern medicine. The study had two parts. Phase I involved an observation of end of life care at several institutions. It was found that patients often did not have advance directives respected and that they were not provided with good pain management. Generally, there was poor communication between physicians and patients. In order to overcome these problems, a phase II intervention was initiated. This intervention presupposed the centrality of the physician–patient relation, and advocated the traditional bioethical solutions. Respect for advance directives (the ethical response) came in as a second step. Rather than provide a more radical challenge to traditional modes of practice, the intervention assumed that problems could be solved by a supplement. Nurses were hired to mediate information between physicians and patients, with the assumption that when physicians had the relevant information they would account for it in their clinical decision-making. In all areas, however, the intervention failed to alter any of the outcomes.

The investigators of SUPPORT thus did not provide reasons for being optimistic about the capacity of the standard bioethical means for overcoming the problems inherent in the traditional model of medicine.

In conclusion, we are left with a troubling situation. The picture we describe of the care of seriously ill or dying persons is not attractive. One would certainly prefer to envision that, when confronted with life-threatening illness, the patient and family would be included in discussions, realistic estimates of outcome would be valued, pain would be treated, and dying would not be prolonged. That is still a worthy vision. However, it is not likely to be achieved through an intervention such as that implemented by SUPPORT. Success will require reexamination of our individual and collective commitments to these goals, more creative efforts at shaping the treatment process, and, perhaps, more proactive and forceful attempts at change.[32]

THE SYSTEMS TURN: GEORGE ENGEL AND THE IOM REPORTS ON ERROR AND QUALITY

Two influential proposals have deeply questioned the assumptions integral to current biomedicine and its bioethical orthodoxy, although I will argue they both have not questioned deeply enough. The first proposal, that of George Engel, is more theoretical, and it was primarily associated with developments in medical education. The second proposal, advanced recently by the Institutes of Medicine (IOM) in a series of reports on error and quality, focuses on the structuring of health systems. I see in these the appropriate basis for an organizational ethic, and will suggest that our task is to try to carry these projects forward; to re-form them so they best realize the deepest ideals of healthcare.

In a series of influential essays, and through his work with the University of Rochester School of Medicine, George Engel advanced a foundational criticism of what he called the "biomedical model of medicine."[33] He argued that biomedicine involved an outmoded, positivistic notion of science, which assumed that the world can be broken into bits and pieces, and which configured the human problems of illness in terms of an underlying disease mechanism.[34] While Engel was motivated by many of the core problems addressed by orthodox bioethics – for example, by the need to more appropriately understand the patient's good, and respond in a personal way – he did not think these ends were best addressed by "ethics" or "art."[35] Instead, he advanced a new science. To integrate the diverse sciences, he advanced a systems-theoretic framework, which could account for the multiple hierarchical levels of patient care, ranging from the low-level molecular interactions, through cells, tissues, organs and organ systems, and up to the individual patient. Past this, patients are nested within two-person relations, families, communities, societies, all the way up to ecosystems.[36]

Engel's proposal was insightful, but in two important ways it fell short. First, like Flexner, he presumed that the needed change involved realizing a more appropriate scientific ideal.[37] This, by itself, was unproblematic. However, he strongly distinguished his psychosocial "science" from medical "art," and downplayed the degree to which any "art" or "science" of humans would be informed by variable cultural, philosophical, and religious traditions.[38] By insisting so strongly on the scientific character of his proposals, he lost the opportunity for more constructive dialogue and collaboration with alternative, ethics and humanities-based approaches, such as those advanced by medical phenomenologists like Pellegrino and Thomasma.[39] Because he did not make explicit how values should play their role, he was unable to clarify how his systems science unavoidably depended on evaluations that were variable and contingent on socioeconomic context. He also was insufficiently attentive to the hermeneutical aspects of his systems model, and thus to the degree that his science was "soft," and thus subject to criticisms of bias.

The second problem with Engel's work concerns his traditional emphasis upon the physician as agent, with an individual patient as subject.[40] Through his systems theory, he brought into view the multiple ways patients are nested within familial, institutional, and social contexts. But his examples and emphasis always assumed an individual physician, who was providing care for an individual patient. For this reason, he only tangentially considered how systems might configure care, and how quality and even the agency of healthcare might be nested within these systems.

While influential in its day – nearly all physicians or medical schools are "biopsychosocial" in name – medicine was not fundamentally changed by his proposals. Hardly anyone is aware of the systems theoretic tools that were integral to his alternative, and the "psychosocial" aspects are now seen as mere supplements; to this extent, Engel's proposal has had the same impact as that of bioethical orthodoxies. Engel knew too well that such a supplement was not enough; that a far deeper rethinking of medicine was needed, if there were to be any difference in practice.

The second proposal, advanced in the 1990s and early 2000s by the IOM, is in many ways more practical, and is already deeply changing the landscape of healthcare practice. Initially focusing on error, the IOM committee challenged the fragmented, piecemeal manner in which error and quality were advanced in medicine. Most significantly, they argued that the very structure and organization of healthcare had now evolved in such a way that care could no longer be seen as a simple function of individual professionals. To address medical errors and advance quality, healthcare had to be viewed in systems terms. A series of proposals were advanced to facilitate the needed systems transformations.[41]

For our purposes, one of the important features of the IOM proposals involves the altered climate in which their proposed shift from individual professionals to systems is received. When Engel advanced his systems shift, he did it in an ideal way: it was a proposal for changing the mental landscape of medicine, with the hope that practice would follow. However, the IOM proposals have a largely descriptive tone. They seek to systematically express changes that have already taken place, and thus provide a more appropriate model for the current realities of healthcare. This altered material reality is a key feature of our current context, and one of the motivating factors behind an organizational ethic.

There is also one problem with the IOM reports. They start by highlighting the gap between the results of medical research and the realities of medical practice. The systems transformations are then motivated by the need to bring these into accord; to overcome the "quality chasm." However, they never deeply question whether the gap may be a function of the atomistic way this medical research is conducted and reported. They simply presuppose the biomedical ideals of science and research, even as they deeply challenge other aspects of that medicine by their systems shift. To this extent, they fall short of Engel's critical insights.

The next step should thus involve a deeper integration of Engel's biopsychosocial alternative with the IOM's reflection on the systems that now configure care.

THE ALTERNATIVE PARADIGM: ORGANIZATIONS AS AGENTS OF HEALTHCARE PRACTICE

This brings us to the cusp of our current task. We are faced with structural transformations that are motivated by considerations of both cost and quality. Most react to these developments as a threat. They just highlight the economic developments, and emphasize how a bureaucratic, administrative logic intrudes upon the clinic. Like class-warfare politics, this pits "labor" against "management." The world then bifurcates into individuals and social institutions – the micro and macro – and the middle level institutions are lost from view. However, when we see how the more problematic features – e.g., the impersonal, fragmented, acute-oriented focus – are long-standing, pervasive features of a biomedical model that has resisted previous reform efforts, then we can take an alternate strategy. Instead of criticism, our task should involve an attempt to rightly appreciate the underlying promise inherent in these emergent structures, and make this explicit, so we might work together to realize a richer vision of what healthcare can and should be like. Here there is an attempt to open a middle space: to bring into view the domains where people can collaborate to realize a more appropriate vision. While recent developments do involve significant challenges and often take pathological form, they also offer opportunities; in fact, they offer the means to address many of the problems that have remained unresolvable in the older paradigm.

The work of transforming this middle level space is, first of all, an interpretive work, and I'll close by considering five areas where I think this work needs to be done. Before I do this, however, I wish to highlight an important implication of the systems perspective, one that deeply challenges traditional ways of framing normative reflection. In the work of Engel and the IOM reports, we cannot separate the descriptive project (i.e., sketch the new form of medicine, with its new science) and the normative project (sketch how medicine should be reconfigured). At the heart of my argument has been the claim that current ways of framing normative issues in medicine depend on assumptions that are themselves intertwined with models we have had of science and medicine. The altered material conditions of medicine problematize not just medicine, but these dominant traditions of ethics. As a result, we will not be able to neatly distinguish organizational ethics from descriptive accounts that seek to highlight the features of the emerging systems of healthcare practice. The normative, descriptive, and constructive work are deeply intertwined. Similarly, we cannot neatly disentangle the business aspects of medicine (and an associated business ethic) from those aspects concerned with quality. As Haavi Morreim has shown, every clinical decision is also a resource allocation decision. The balance between individual and population good is unavoidably operationalized in the way resources are utilized. Under Flexnerian assumptions, we can neatly disentangle the domains of science, ethics, and economics. But the systems turn brings us to the place where these issues must be addressed together. An appreciation of the entanglement of these problem sets is central to the gain a systems perspective provides. However, at the same time, this entanglement also provides the primary challenge: namely, how can we constructively address the issues of quality, access, and efficiency in a systematic, coherent manner? The first task of an organizational ethic must thus involve an appreciation of the needed systems stance.[42]

Integral to the normative project of such an organizational ethic is an interpretive project. The task here is to bring into view the core features of the emergent patterns of healthcare; to advance these as alternatives to the biomedical model. In this interpretive work, we identify and provide a preliminary clarification of the features that should be central in an emerging model of healthcare. I'll now put these descriptively – as an account of what healthcare is becoming – but I want to emphasize that these are anticipatory. The work of interpretation is to see things as they can and should be, but to do this faithfully, as a response to current material realities. If the work of interpretation is done well, then others will be able to glimpse that form of life that emerges. Once glimpsed, they too can collaborate to bring to completion what has begun. To this end, I close by sketching what might be regarded as the chapter headings in this project.

These are the features integral to the emerging model of healthcare.

1. Healthcare is now practiced by institutions; it is no longer just practiced by individuals

Consider the following citation from the Institutes of Medicine Report, *To Err is Human*:

The common initial reaction when an error occurs is to find and blame someone. However, even apparently single events or errors are due most often to the convergence of multiple contributing factors. Blaming an individual does not change those factors and the same error is likely to recur. Preventing errors and improving safety for patients require a systems approach in order to modify the conditions that contribute to errors. People working in health care are among the most educated and dedicated workforce in any industry. The problem is not bad people; the problem is that the system needs to be made safer.[43]

We see here a shift that goes far beyond their discussion of error. Originally, we blamed individuals when an error occurred because we saw individuals as the primary agents of care. The IOMs shift in accountability simultaneously presupposes a shift in agency. The emergence of organizations as agents in healthcare is perhaps one of the most significant aspects of the current paradigm shift, underlying many of the other developments. One often hears as an accusation that "administrators are practicing medicine." It is assumed that this is self-evidently wrong. Thus when administrators influence the drug formulary at a hospital or alter clinical pathways or use health services research to make a policy, then this is generally taken as an example of the way medicine is now distorted by external factors, primarily economic ones. However, these developments are not just motivated by cost considerations. As David Eddy notes, an interest in quality alone justifies many of the encroachments on physician authority.[44] Healthcare now requires a team, its technology involves massive administrative coordination, and the diversity of services involved is beyond the skills and knowledge of any single individual or profession.[45] Administrators are trained in new forms of coordination, and they are learning to incorporate

the health services research capacities needed for utilizing outcomes information, providing profiling, and developing guidelines and clinical pathways. One cannot point to any individual as the locus of these healthcare
services. Rather, one must point to the healthcare institution, or, even
beyond that, the network of institutions.[46] A similar case could be made
by considering a particular disease, rather than focusing on the array of
services; for example, by highlighting the public health, behavioral, nurse
and physician components of the prevention and treatment of diabetes or
syphilis.[47] Although this complex, multi-professional, institutionally based
practice is the current reality of healthcare, ethical reflection still speaks as if
healthcare is primarily practiced by individuals. An organizational ethic
should descriptively characterize this new role, explore diverse forms of
organizational and team agency, and help clarify norms that can govern the
institutions and professionals that practice in these new settings.

2. Holistic health concepts

It is not coincidental that George Engel first worked out elements of his
biopsychosocial model by attempting to provide an alternative to the
biomedical health concept.[48] In a later essay, he considers "frequently
voiced complaints by patients that physicians are insensitive, callous,
neglectful, arrogant and mechanical in their approaches," and observes
that while "[t]here are undoubtedly many reasons for this situation, ...
the most important is the pervasive influence of the biomedical model of
disease."[49] To address the deficiencies, we need to shift away from the
biomedical conceptualization, which regards health as the absence of disease, toward a more comprehensive health concept, in which psychosocial
and spiritual factors are included and positive notions of human well-being
guide action.[50] We already see such a shift taking place. It is most con-
spicuous in areas where patient assessment of quality of care and quality of
life are included in outcome assessment.[51] Such "subjective" elements of
well-being were systemically discounted in the traditional biomedical
model. When broader psychosocial and spiritual factors are incorporated,
however, there may be a tension between courses of action motivated by
broader health concepts and those motivated by narrower ones. In the
context of the traditional paradigm, any constraint on the biomedical
configuration of reality is simply regarded as an unwarranted limit on
medicine. However, from a broader perspective, it is not simply a question
of limits; it is rather a question of the most appropriate response to a human
need. Behind many of the tensions that emerge with current

transformations, one thus finds alternative accounts of the outcome that should be promoted, namely, the health of the patient and community. An organizational ethic should clarify these broader concepts of well-being, show how they might inform health practices, and provide norms for integrating traditional biomedically oriented standards with broader psychosocial accounts. Here Engel's earlier work might provide valuable guidance.

3. Healthcare is broader than medicine

In the traditional paradigm, healthcare was equated with medicine, and the core ethical relation was between physician and patient. Other healthcare workers were regarded as poorly trained and inferior relative to physicians. Today this is changing. Knowledge is broadly spread between administrators, nurses, social workers, psychologists, pastoral care workers, public health workers, and physicians. Each has extensive training in one area, but not in all. One can no longer assume that a physician is best situated to exercise authority and coordinate the different elements of care. In some cases, physicians are still best trained to captain the ship. But in other areas, administrators, nurses, or another professional makes the best captain. In either case, medicine becomes but one aspect of a more encompassing form of healthcare, and physicians move from the central healer to an equal member of a broader, interprofessional team.[52] An organizational ethic should consider how such teams best function, and how the most appropriate interprofessional collaborations might be advanced so the goals of healthcare might be realized. In doing this, it can provide a clearer picture of how diverse professionals can most effectively coordinate their activities so the important goals of health systems are best realized.

4. Healthcare is oriented toward the health of individuals and the community

In presenting his general systems theory, Engel notes how there are nested hierarchies, and each level of that hierarchy has its own integrity and dynamic.

Each system implies qualities and relationships distinctive for that level of organization, and each requires criteria for study and explanation unique for that level. In no way can the methods and rules appropriate for the study and understanding of the cell as cell be applied to the study of the person as person or the family as family. Similarly, the methods needed to identify and characterize the components of the cell have to be different from those required to establish what makes for the wholeness of the cell.[53]

Traditionally, medicine has focused on just one level of that hierarchy: that of the individual patient. Now, with the shift to health systems, we also see an increased emphasis upon addressing the health of the community or populations more generally. We are thus witnessing a shift from an individualism, which ignores the social context of health and healing, toward a broader communal orientation, which accounts for the interrelation between individuals and community, and which appreciates the psychosocial dimensions of well-being.[54] Often this is put as a move from individually oriented to population-based healthcare.[55] Administrative and organizational responsibilities – financial as well as health responsibilities – are often for a specified population. This requires decisions that balance individual and communal interests, and that give priority to the health of a specified population (e.g., those insured by a network) at the expense of others in society.[56] Such balance has been doubly criticized, first because it insufficiently accounts for the vulnerable individual, second because it focuses on a particular population, rather than the whole population. These two criticisms are in tension, and they both miss their mark.

The traditional criticism, raised often in the medical journals, that the population focus works against the fiduciary ideal, misses the weakness in the traditional focus of medicine.[57] Yes, there was an orientation toward the individual patient. But physicians largely ignored the fact that the patient was part of a family and community, and they did not incorporate these facts into the care of the patient. The community-focused care that is emerging integrates the traditionally individualized care with a practice that is responsive to the person as a social creature. Psychosocial care does not just mean accounting for social and psychological factors in caring for individuals, as it has traditionally meant under the influence of medicine. It should also involve an appreciation of the broader cultural and moral ways that an individual is knit together with others in community, and account for the responsibilities of that individual to the community. This is a part of what is involved in respecting that individual as a moral agent.[58]

Another, less often heard criticism of organizationally based healthcare is that it is oriented toward a particular population, rather than to all people. Such focus toward a particular community is contrasted with the comprehensive focus of a national health plan. However, there are underappreciated opportunities associated with this middle ground between individual and universal healthcare. The United States is a multicultural society, and these diverse values lead to alternative rankings of various goods. When healthcare focused narrowly on a biomedically defined disease, then the impact of values pluralism on the initial construction of medical reality was relatively small, since there was a broad consensus on the biomedical health concepts. However, as one moves toward more comprehensive health concepts, the impact of alternative values on the construction of healthcare reality becomes more pronounced. Various organizational configurations of healthcare can be aligned with particular communities. The value of an organizationally based system is that it allows for alternative health systems, which map on to diverse communities. Individuals can then opt into those systems that best reflect their own values.[59] This provides a third way between individualism, on one side, and governmentally based systems, on the other.[60]

Of all the elements of the new paradigm that are here discussed, this communal middle ground where individuals opt into organizations that reflect their values is the furthest from being realized. Employers still control much of the access, and healthcare institutions have not closely aligned themselves with the values of a particular community. However, I am considering these elements in terms of their promise, not what is already realized. And of all the elements here considered, the community-oriented aspect has the most promise for providing a genuine alternative to the classical opposition between individual and government, or between liberal vs. communitarian polities. It is responsive to concerns associated with values pluralism, addresses the importance of the individual, and simultaneously appreciates the communal character of human being. An organizational ethic should explore the rich potential of this "middle place" between the micro- and macro-, and make clear how such an inter-ethic can address challenges that have resisted our previous efforts.

5. There is a new dialectic between normative and scientific aspects of healthcare

Normative considerations are increasingly playing a role in the configuration of what has traditionally been regarded as a purely scientific or clinical domain. Political considerations influence recommendations about breast cancer screening mammography, and economic ones influence the determination of what is "medically necessary." Physicians find themselves subject to guidelines, clinical pathways, and profiling, which are at least partly influenced by cost–benefit assessments and by outcomes information that incorporates "subjective" assessments of well-being. For the person initiated into Flexnerian ideals, all of this involves a corruption of the scientific basis of medicine. No longer can one work with a two step process, in which medicine is first configured by science, and then, as a second step, the ethical use and abuse of this independently formulated, scientifically grounded practice is addressed. The two parts merge, and there is a dialectic between ethical and scientific domains of reflection.

The type of reconfiguration taking place is similar to what attended the rise of the Paris school of medicine. At that time, the clinical medicine of the nosographist was separate from the science of the anatomist. Through the pathological anatomy of Morgagni, the foundation was provided for a reconfiguration, in which these previously independent domains were restructured so that each was an essential component of the other. With this paradigm shift, the basic clinic–laboratory dialectic of modern medicine emerged. It is this structure that was at the heart of Flexnerian ideals. Now we find a similar kind of reconfiguration, but the clinic–laboratory structure, which is the "science," is now essentially related with domains of normative reflection, which includes ethical, sociological, and economic factors that explicitly influence even the most basic scientific distinctions; for example, the line between the normal and the pathological. An organizational ethic should provide guidance for thinking through and constructively addressing this deep integration of the descriptive/scientific and normative/ethical.

With these reconfigurations, bioethics is fundamentally altered. As Pellegrino and Thomasma have argued, ethical reflection must be more intimately integrated into medicine and tied to foundational, critical reflection on the nature of the healthcare enterprise itself.[61] They also correctly note that "[t]he philosophy of medicine must be based on a choice that is guided by an initial hunch about what is important in medicine."[62] The task is not simply to create an ethical overlay, but to more radically probe the potential of healthcare, in order to articulate its telos and work toward realizing latent opportunities for addressing the health needs of individuals and communities. However, Pellegrino and Thomasma are wrong when they assume that the core is associated with the physician–patient relation, and that what is important about that relation is "cure." In this initial stipulation at the heart of their philosophical endeavor, they opt into exactly those motifs that are called into question by the emerging paradigm, where the core relation shifts to that between institution and patient population, and the focus of healthcare shifts from cure to a broader account of care. An organizational ethic for the new paradigm must configure the conditions of the possibility of this organizationally based, community-oriented care. How one conceives such an ethic thus depends upon one's stance toward the emerging paradigm. To view organizational ethics as simply a form of business ethics involves a stance within the Flexnerian model, where the physician–patient relation is central, and organizational interests are external and alien. I have tried to sketch the basic tenets of the alternative, and thus move one step toward the realization of the opportunities afforded by the current transformations in healthcare.

NOTES

1. The theme pervades much of Pellegrino's writings. Representative arguments can be found in Edmund Pellegrino, "Medical Economics and Medical Ethics: Points of Conflict and Reconciliation," *Journal of the Medical Association of Georgia* 69 (1980): 175–183; Edmund Pellegrino, "Interests, Obligations, and Justice: Some Notes Toward an Ethic of Managed Care," *Journal of Clinical Ethics* 6, no. 4 (1995): 312–317; Edmund Pellegrino, "Rationing Health Care: Inherent Conflicts with the Concept of Justice," in *The Ethics of Managed Care: Professional Integrity and Patient Rights*, ed. W. B. Bondeson and J. Jones, (Dordrecht: Kluwer Academic Publishers, 2002), pp. 1–18; Edmund Pellegrino and David Thomasma, *A Philosophical Basis of Medical Practice: Toward a Philosophy and Ethic of the Healing Professions* (Oxford: Oxford University Press, 1981), Chapter 12. A more detailed assessment of Pellegrino's claims is found in George Khushf, "Organizational Ethics and the Medical Professional: Reappraising Roles and Responsibilities," in *The Health Professional as Friend and Healer*, ed. Judith Kissell and David Thomasma (Washington, DC: Georgetown University Press, 2000), pp. 148–162.

2. Jerome Kassirer provides an older review of the public perception (and reinforces it). This view has not significantly changed. Jerome Kassirer, "Managing Managed Care's Tarnished Image," *New England Journal of Medicine* 337, no. 5 (1997): 338–339.

3. George Engel, "The Clinical Application of the Biopsychosocial Model," *The American Journal of Psychiatry* 137, no. 5 (1980): 535–544 and George Engel, "How Much Longer Must Medicine's Science Be Bound By A Seventeenth Century World View?" in *The Task of Medicine: Dialogue at Wickenburg*, ed. Kerr L. White (Menlo Park, CA: The Henry J. Kaiser Family Foundation, 1988), pp. 113–136.

4. SUPPORT Principal Investigators, "A Controlled Trial to Improve Care for Seriously Ill Hospital Patients," *Journal of the American Medical Association* 272 (1996): 1591–1598.

5. Flexner, Abraham, *Medical Education in the United States and Canada: A Report to the Carnegie Foundation for the Advancement of Teaching* (New York: The Carnegie Foundation for the Advancement of Teaching, 1910).

6. Lester King argues that "The so-called Flexner report … is probably the most grossly overrated document in American medical history." Lester King, "The Flexner Report of 1910," *Journal of the American Medical Association* 251, no. 8

(1984): 1079–1086. David Banta more modestly argues that the developments in medical education were only partly a result of the Report. David H. Banta, "Medical Education: Abraham Flexner – A Reappraisal," *Social Science and Medicine* 5 (1971): 655–661. However, these authors simply dispute the role of the Flexner Report in bringing about the changes that it advocates, arguing that Flexner articulated ideas for which there was already a broad consensus. All writers agree that the Report represents the paradigm of twentieth-century American medicine. For a good review of its ongoing influence, see Barbara Barzansky and Norman Gevitz, eds., *Beyond Flexner: Medical Education in the Twentieth Century* (New York: Greenwood Press, 1992).

7. Flexner, *Medical Education*, 91, note 1, cites von Struempell: "We ought first to procure for the student clear pathological conceptions; only then will it be easy for him to follow the clinical instruction intelligently and profitably. I consider it absolutely necessary that the instruction in general pathology and pathological anatomy should precede the clinic."

8. Ibid., p. 22.

9. Ibid., p. 55.

10. Ibid., p. 67.

11. Good reviews of the paradigm shift that took place with the emergence of the Paris School can be found in Michel Foucault, *The Birth of the Clinic: An Archaeology of Medical Perception* (New York: Vintage Books Edition, 1994) and Georges Canguilhem, *The Normal and the Pathological*, translated by Carolyn R. Fawcett (New York: Zone Books, 1991). The shift in disease concepts is outlined in George Khushf, "What is at Issue in the Debate about Concepts of Health and Disease? Framing the Problem of Demarcation for a Post-Positivist Era of Medicine," in *Health, Science, and Ordinary Language*, ed. L. Nordenfelt (New York: Rodopi Press, 2001), pp. 123–169; 215–225.

12. H. Tristam Engelhardt, *Foundations of Bioethics* (Oxford: Oxford University Press, 1996), pp. 208–217.

13. A good discussion of the mechanical model of the human body and disease is found in Drew Leder, "A Tale of Two Bodies: The Cartesian Corpse and the Lived Body," in *The Body in Medical Thought and Practice*, ed. Drew Leder (Dordrecht: Kluwer Academic Publishers, 1992), pp. 17–35.

14. Flexner, *Medical Education*, p. 58

15. A prominent defense of this view of disease, with an explicit claim to have made explicit the implicit notion found in medical disease classifications, can be found in Christopher Boorse, "A Rebuttal on Health," in *What is Disease?*, ed. James Humber and Robert Almeder (Totowa, NJ: Humana Press, 1997), pp. 1–134.

16. Flexner, *Medical Education*, Chapters 2, 4, 6.

17. Ibid., Chapters 3, 5, 7, 8.

18. A review of these developments is provided by Mark Rodwin, *Medicine, Money and Morals: Physicians' Conflicts of Interest* (New York and Oxford: Oxford University Press, 1993).

19. Flexner, *Medical Education*, Chapter 10.

20. Ibid., p. 164.

21. Nancy King, Larry Churchill, and Alan Cross, eds., *The Physician as Captain of the Ship: A Critical Reappraisal* (Dordrecht: D. Reidel Publishing Company, 1988).

22. A review of this approach to nursing can be found in Patricia M. Donahue, *Nursing: the Finest Art* (St. Louis: The C.V. Mosby Company, 1985).

23. E. Haavi Morreim, *Balancing Act: The New Medical Ethics of Medicine's New Economics* (Washington, DC: Georgetown University Press, 1995).

24. Stanley Reiser, *Medicine and the Reign of Technology* (Cambridge: Cambridge University Press, 1978), p. 196.

25. Arthur Frank, *The Wounded Storyteller: Body, Illness, and Ethics* (Chicago, IL: The University of Chicago Press, 1995) and Leder, "A Tale of Two Bodies."

26. Jay Katz, *The Silent World of Doctor and Patient* (Baltimore, MD: The Johns Hopkins University Press, 2002).

27. American Nurses' Association, *Nursing: A Social Policy Statement* (Kansas City: American Nurses' Association, 1995) and American Nurses' Association, *Nursing's Social Policy Statement* (Kansas City: American Nurses' Association, 1980).

28. Gerald McKenny, *To Relieve the Human Condition: Bioethics, Technology, and the Body* (New York: State University of New York Press, 1997).

29. Jonathan Imber, "Medical Publicity before Bioethics: Nineteenth-Century Illustrations of Twentieth-Century Dilemmas," in *Bioethics and Society: Constructing the Ethical Enterprise*, ed. Raymond DeVries and Jonardan Subedi, (New Jersey: Prentice Hall, 1998), pp. 16–37, at 30.

30. Leder, "A Tale of Two Bodies," 24.

31. SUPPORT, "A Controlled Trial."

32. Ibid., 1597.

33. George Engel, "How Much Longer Must Medicine's Science Be Bound By A Seventeenth Century World View?" in *The Task of Medicine: Dialogue at Wickenburg*, ed. Kerr L. White (Menlo Park, CA: The Henry J. Kaiser Family Foundation, 1988), pp. 113–136; George Engel, "The Clinical Application of the Biopsychosocial Model," *The American Journal of Psychiatry* 137, no. 5 (1980): 535–544; George Engel, "Biomedicine's Failure to Achieve Flexnerian Standards of Education," *Journal of Medical Education* 53 (1978): 387–392; George Engel, "The Biopsychosocial Model and the Education of Health Professionals," *Annals of the New York Academy of Sciences* 310 (1978): 169–181; George Engel, "The Care of the Patient: Art or Science?" *The Johns Hopkins Medical Journal* 140 (1977): 222–232; George Engel, "A Unified Concept of Health and Disease," *Perspectives in Biology and Medicine* (summer 1960): 459–485.

34. Engel, "How Much Longer."

35. Engel, "The Care of the Patient."

36. Engel, "The Clinical Application."

37. Engel, "Biomedicine's Failure."

38. Engel, "The Care of the Patient."

39. Pellegrino and Thomasma, *A Philosophical Basis of Medical Practice*.

40. Engel, "The Clinical Application."

41. Institute of Medicine, *Crossing the Quality Chasm: A New Health System for the 21st Century* (Washington, DC: National Academies Press, 2001) and Institute of Medicine, *To Err is Human: Building a Safer Health System* (Washington, DC: National Academies Press, 2000).

42. E. Haavi Morreim, *Balancing Act: The New Medical Ethics of Medicine's New Economics* (Washington, DC: Georgetown University Press, 1995).

43. IOM, *To Err is Human*, 49.

44. David Eddy, *Clinical Decision Making: From Theory to Practice* (Sudbury: Jones and Bartlett Publishers, 1996), p. 2.

45. Pellegrino and Thomasma, *A Philosophical Basis of Medical Practice*, Chapter 11.

46. Stephen Shortell, "The Evolution of Hospital Systems: Unfulfilled Promises and Self-Fulfilling Prophesies," *Medical Care Review* 45, no. 2 (1998): 177–214. A comparison of Shortell's account of "systemness" and Engel's discussion of systems theory reveals how institutions now serve as integrated agents of practice. Engel, "The Clinical Application."

47. This integrated, multi-disciplinary approach to disease is best seen in community-oriented primary care. For a good review of the initial work done in this area (focusing on syphilis) see M. Susser, "Pioneering Community-Oriented Primary Care," *Bulletin of the World Health Organization* 77, no. 5 (1999): 436–438 and Sidney Kark, "The Pholela Health Centre," *Bulletin of the World Health Organization* 77, no. 5 (1999 [1952]): 439–447. Kark outlines the basic elements of his health centre: "The essential features which have developed include care of the sick and prevention of illness by the doctor and nurse, associated with a programme of health education carried out by specially trained "health assistants" acting under the direction of the doctor. The result has been a very closely integrated curative, preventive and promotive health service in which there is an ever increasing appreciation of the community's health needs and an understanding of the various families served." Today these coordinated activities are increasingly associated with institutions, especially community hospitals and managed care organizations.

48. Engel, "A Unified Concept of Health and Disease."

49. Engel, "The Biopsychosocial Model," 169.

50. The need for a broader concept of health was explicit in an early essay by George Engel, "A Unified Concept of Health and Disease." Many of the concerns addressed in this essay were later expanded, as Engel developed his prominent "biopsychosocial model of medicine." Today there is a large literature on health concepts. The public health and nursing literature strongly emphasizes the need for broader health concepts, while a narrower biomedical concept is implicit in most of the medical literature.

51. A good review of the debates surrounding the quality of life and its assessment in medicine can be found in Lennart Nordenfelt, *Concepts and Measurement of Quality of Life in Health Care* (Dordrecht: Kluwer Academic Publishers, 1994).

52. The need for a more cooperative, interprofessional model is well captured in the title of an essay by Michael Stoto (ed.), "Sharing Responsibility for the Public's Health: A New Perspective from the Institute of Medicine," *Public*

Health Management Practice 3, no. 5 (1997): 22–34. Stoto outlines the linkage between broader health concepts and systems such as those of managed care, which prominently feature the organization as an agent of healthcare practice. This work has been updated in Committee on Assuring the Health of the People, Institute of Medicine, *The Future of the Public's Health in the 21st Century* (Washington, DC: National Academies Press, 2003) and Lawrence Gostin, Jo Ivey Boufford, and Martinez Rose Marie, "The Future of the Public's Health: Vision, Values, Strategies," *Health Affairs* 23, no. 4 (2004): 96–107.

53. "The Clinical Application," 536

54. Committee for the Study of the Future of Public Health, *The Future of Public Health*. (Washington, DC: National Academy Press, 1988).

55. Steven Miles and Robert Koepp, "Comments on the AMA Report 'Ethical Issues in Managed Care,'" *Journal of Clinical Ethics* 6 (1995): 306–311.

56. Mark Hall, "Physician Rationing and Agency Cost Theory," in *Conflicts of Interest in Clinical Practice and Research* ed. Roy Spece, David Shimm, and Allen Buchanan (Oxford: Oxford University Press, 1996), pp. 228–250.

57. The approach generally found in medical journals is well represented by the editors of the *New England Journal of Medicine*. Classic statements are provided by Jerome Kassirer, "Managing Care – Should We Adopt a New Ethic?" *New England Journal of Medicine* 339, no 6 (1998): 397–398 and Marcia Angell, "Medicine: the Endangered Patient-Centered Ethic," *Hastings Center Report* 17, no. 1 (1987): 12–13.

58. Morreim, *Balancing Act*, Chapter 7

59. Robert Veatch addresses these issues in terms of "pairing based on 'deep values'" in Robert Veatch, "Who Should Manage Care? The Case for Patients," *Kennedy Institute of Ethics Journal* 7, no. 4 (1997): 391–402 and Robert Veatch, "Abandoning Informed Consent," *Hastings Center Report* 25, no. 2 (1995): 5–12.

60. A general, theoretical account of this "third way" is discussed in George Khushf, "Solidarity as a Moral and Political Concept: Beyond the Liberal/Communitarian Impasse," in *Solidarity*, ed. Kurt Bayertz (Dordrecht: Kluwer Academic Publishers, 1999), pp. 57–79. The issue is addressed in the context of healthcare in Khushf, George, "A Radical Challenge to the Traditional Conception of Medicine: On the Need to Move Beyond Economic Factors When Considering the Ethics of Managed Care," in *The Ethics of Managed Care: Professional Integrity and Patient Rights*, ed. W. B. Bondeson and J. Jones (Dordrecht: Kluwer Academic Publishers, 2002), pp. 75–91.

61. Pellegrino and Thomasma, *A Philosophical Basis of Medical Practice*, p. 224: "It is now essential that ethics as a formal discipline be recognized to be as integral to the practice of responsible medicine as the basic and clinical sciences."

62. Ibid., 49.

CHAPTER II

A crisis in medical professionalism: time for Flexner II

Daniel Wikler

Abraham Flexner's *Medical Education in the United States and Canada*,[1] published in 1910 for the Carnegie Foundation for the Advancement of Teaching, is widely credited with giving American and Canadian medicine its good name. Research for the report was undertaken at a time when the status of medicine as a learned profession in the United States and Canada was in real jeopardy due, in large part, to the very uneven level of scientific training and sophistication of medical graduates and practitioners. Flexner traveled the length and breath of both countries, visiting every medical school, documenting lapses, praising successes where he found them, and recommending sweeping reforms. Astonishingly, they were enacted. Half of the medical schools closed their doors. The Report transformed American and Canadian medicine, bonding the profession to university science and propelling American and Canadian medicine toward its science-based destiny.[2]

Weak science is not a problem in American medicine today – thanks, in large part, to the upgrading of standards, nearly a century ago, that we associate with Flexner's name. Nevertheless, the Flexner report is still worth studying – and, I believe, also worth emulating. Just as in Flexner's time a century ago, deep structural faults within the foundations of the nation's system for delivering healthcare have the potential to undermine medicine's claim to the status of a profession. The nature of the threat, however, has changed. The integrity of American medicine – its practitioners, its educators, its scientists, and even its public regulators – is seriously threatened by an epidemic of conflict of interest whose symptoms signal the corruption of the medical mission and the profession's ideals. If the medical system is not yet in crisis over these practices, this is because they are overshadowed, at present, by other failings of our system of healthcare, including cost and lack of access – both of which are exacerbated by the pervasive integrity problems stemming from conflict of interest. Moreover, the threat to medical professionalism is more difficult to perceive and understand. The cash flows are largely masked, and their import is not always immediately obvious. For these and other reasons, the public – unlike many insiders – is not yet aware of the scope and the seriousness of the threat to medical professionalism. When the public does find out, the consequent loss of trust could adversely affect not only physicians but, more importantly, the public's health. Effective medical treatment can be difficult to achieve in the absence of the therapeutic alliance that emerges within a healthy doctor–patient relationship.

Physicians and medical scientists who benefit from these arrangements may enjoy the money, prestige, and other advantages that they bring without requirement of actual work, but this is a short-term and short-sighted strategy. All could lose once the story is out, and the stakes are high. As Flexner understood a century ago, what is at risk when the integrity of medicine is threatened is not only the prestige and autonomy of doctors, but the health of the public. For Flexner, the latter was the single appropriate standard for gauging the adequacy of medical education. Poorly trained doctors were less likely to be able to help their patients to become and stay healthy. Similarly, the public's health – and to an appreciable extent also, its wealth – should be our central concern in evaluating the looming crisis in professionalism today in the field of health. If the problems are as serious as they now seem to be, we must be prepared to emulate Flexner also in insisting on sweeping reforms.

MEDICAL PROFESSIONALISM AND CORRUPTION

During the past few years, a remarkable number of well-researched, articulated, and passionate books have been published on the serious moral compromises that have been made by doctors, medical scientists, and medical institutions in the pursuit of money. These include Jerome Kassirer's *On the Take*,[3] Marcia Angell's *The Truth About the Drug Companies*,[4] John Abramson's *Overdosed America*,[5] and Jerry Avorn's *Powerful Medicines: The Benefits, Costs, and Risks of Prescription Drugs*.[6] Though they vary in focus, all four of these excellent books document, both in aggregate data and in instructive case studies, the extent to which the profession of medicine has been colonized, seduced, compromised, and undermined by the drug industry and other commercial interests (and by revenue-enhancing initiatives on the doctors' part). Though the books vary in emphasis and tone, the authors' indignation is evident on the written page. And this sense of moral outrage is all the more impressive in light of the professional standing of their authors, all of them former editors-in-chief of *The New England Journal of Medicine*, or faculty at Harvard Medical

School, or both. Any one of these volumes ought to occasion a searching examination of the structural faults in the foundations of America's medical profession; together, they and many of the preceding chapters in this book, demand Flexner-level, root-and-branch reforms.

Unless they are very naïve, individuals familiar with today's health system are aware of the great success of pharmaceutical firms and other commercial interests in their costly campaign to influence what doctors learn, believe, think, and do. Though their stated mission – the development, manufacture, and distribution of products that reduce the burden of disease and disability – would serve the public interest, these entities must also earn profits, and it is sometimes more rewarding to seek to influence those who recommend products to their patients than by creating products worthy of being recommended. Conflicts between what is good for the industry and what protects patients' health are detailed extensively in these books, and have been the subject of a stream of television and newspaper exposés. Selective reporting of data from clinical trials of proprietary drugs, distorting physicians' perceptions of the benefits and risks of products, is published in the very best journals.[7] Companies conspire with doctors in promoting off-label uses for which drugs have not been shown safe or effective. Doctors are given large sums of money by drug companies and device manufacturers to give talks to peers, acting in effect as surrogate sales staff. So-called "Key Opinion Leaders" – practitioners and scientists of sufficient reputation to add luster to a product – are added to the payroll; and to enhance that investment, their careers are promoted at company expense.[8] Medical journals, according to Richard Smith, long-time editor of *BMJ*, "... are an extension of the marketing arm of pharmaceutical companies."[9] His colleague Richard Horton, editor of *The Lancet*, states that "Journals have devolved into information laundering operations for the pharmaceutical industry."[10] Medical schools and professional societies have come to rely upon industry money for educating doctors throughout their training and subsequent careers, yielding a measure of control over its content. Entire academic departments develop reputations within the trade as "owned" by particular drug companies. Medical schools face increasing pressure to loosen restrictions on financial relationships with companies active in their fields; faculty gain leverage through opportunities to migrate to the least restrictive schools.

With some exceptions, the nation's doctors, medical educators, health officials and leaders play along. Do they not know (or should they not know) that these common practices may be undermining the moral ideals of the profession of medicine? One possible response is that they remain

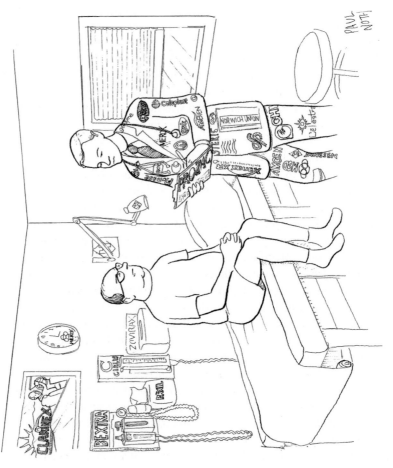

Figure 11.1 *The New Yorker*, July 7 and 14, 2008, p. 64

confident that they can accept the money and other benefits from industry without surrendering their independence; indeed, without their beliefs and practices being affected at all. A growing body of research[11] strongly suggests that these are illusions. Others may be unaware of the pervasiveness of the problem.[12] Some may be convinced that the advantages to the public, such as the incentives to bring laboratory discoveries quickly to the bedside, outweigh any possible drawbacks – and that curbs on conflict of interest have drawbacks as well.[13] But the most straightforward explanation for the acquiescence and collaboration of physicians and medical sciences in these problematic practices is, of course, money: extra wealth for themselves, or for institutions or projects that they support. Weak laws, regulations, and academic rules, inconsistently enforced, open the door to profit-seeking behavior that leaves the "purists" who act as doctors and scientists have traditionally been expected to act questioning their attachment to seemingly antiquated scruples and acutely aware of the foregone income.

From the industry's point of view, these substantial sums are a sound investment, at least in the short term. The cost of influencing doctors and medical scientists is often much less than the potential rewards. The reasons are perfectly obvious. We trust doctors to act in our interests, and we assume that scientists pursue the truth. Paying doctors and scientists to betray this trust can bring rewards to investors – at least, until the public finds out. Erosion of medical integrity is not a mere detail, but rather strikes at the heart of what it is to practice medicine. The basis for medicine's claim to be a profession rather than a trade, exchanging a degree of self-governance and autonomy to trusted experts, is the assurance that this trust will not be misplaced. The hallmarks of professional status address this basis for trust. They include a long period of education that not only imparts technical skills but also inculcates a professional identity based on the values of service. And after training is completed, professional healers submit to peer review, licensing, regulation, and discipline. Much the same is true of medical scientists, whether or not they are physicians. This capsule account of professionalism is, to be sure, an ideal rather than an actual description of how medicine is or ever has been practiced. But it is a regulative ideal, the standard by which actual practice is judged. These ideals remain in force even when doctors and scientists cut corners, make compromises, and occasionally cheat. But they cannot survive when it becomes normal and ordinary to rely on – or to seek out – under-the-table payment for flouting these values. That day may be close at hand.

To many practicing physicians, this talk of an impending crisis will sound like hyperbole. Doctors, understandably, benchmark their dedication to

professional goals and standards by observing their peers. When conflict of
interest is pervasive, those who accept relatively small benefits from companies may take pride in their refusal to take (or seek) much more; and even
those who do can always identify others whose entanglements are still more
extensive. For all the dissatisfaction and grumbling among American doctors today, few refuse every opportunity to play ball according to the new
rules and only a handful feel the kind of indignation that results in a book
like Kassirer's *On the Take*.

For most practicing physicians and medical scientists, the impending
crisis in professionalism looks and feels very different to doctors and to other
citizens, respectively. That is unavoidable and understandable, given the
differences in their preoccupations and concerns. The integrity issue is
simultaneously a question of medical ethics and public health risk.

For physicians and medical scientists, the threat to the integrity of the
profession is also a question of personal integrity. When the bait is offered,
the doctor or scientist must decide whether to reach for it or to decline.
Some may embrace the short-term advantage with nary a qualm. But even
those who are troubled must perform some moral calculations. Physicians
and scientists who insist on resisting all temptations may place their most
cherished projects at risk. Funding can dry up; colleagues may back off;
prominent billing at meetings may be hard to come by. If one's highest
priority is relieving the burdens of the sick, trade-offs must be made that can
make industry sponsorship and (therefore) control a cost worth paying –
especially when other sources of support are becoming scarcer.

From a public and public health perspectives, however, the problems and
the choices look different. While the moral fiber of physicians and scientists
who rigorously refrain from the conflicted practices that collectively
threaten the professionalism of American medicine is worthy of praise,
what matters most is that these practices are permitted and tolerated, with
only the most egregious offenses brought to the public's attention. While it
would be laudatory if physicians and scientists could elude the control and
influence that have resulted from industry expenditures,[14] it comes as no
surprise that most have not. What is important for the country as a whole is
what incentives lie in wait for those doctors who are inclined to respond.
This will largely be determined by changes in laws and regulations and in
their enforcement both by government and in academia.

That is a political question, not one of personal morality, and barring a
miraculous stiffening of physician's moral backbones, it will require a
political answer. What sort of answer this will be, should it come to pass,
will depend on how deeply the public is disillusioned and on the political

alignment of the moment (which depends in part on the political strength of the drug, medical device, and healthcare industries). The practices documented in the works cited here include both lawful actions (e.g. signing on as expert speaker for a company that expects one's talks to increase sales) and violations of laws and regulations. The boundary between what is legal and what may be "merely" unethical, however, is of limited significance. It may, for example, simply reflect the current strength of the interested parties in their efforts to remove penalties from the kinds of promotional activities they would like to conduct. If these activities are properly judged corrupt while illegal, they remain corrupt after being legalized – perhaps more so, since their legalization is further evidence of corruption. If the routine practices of industry, physicians, their scientists, and medical institutions come to be viewed as corrupt, they could be made illegal once again. But even that might not be sufficient to restore the trust essential to the effective practice of medicine.

THE NEED FOR FLEXNER II

These issues can also be addressed in less moralistic terms. Gregg Bloch points out[15] that Kenneth Arrow's classic 1963 paper, "Uncertainty and the Welfare Economics of Medical Care,"[16] viewed physician adherence to the norms of professionalism as self-serving, over the long term: "… implicit in Arrow's account is a short-term/long-term trade-off: physicians resist bed-side financial temptation case-by-case in order to reap reputational (and financial) rewards from the profession's perceived adherence to this ethic. The norm of fidelity is, by this account, a product of the marketplace." Seen in this light, the Flexner report is even more apropos. It, too, has been interpreted as serving the interests of the medical elite of the time,[17] who sought to differentiate themselves from their poor relations, the poorly trained purveyors of patent medicine who could not be trusted to avoid exploitation of the patient's vulnerability, due to illness and relative lack of expert knowledge.

Why not, then, convene a "Flexner II" commission to assess the magnitude of the current threat to medical professionalism and to recommend any needed reforms? The approaching centenary of the original provides a suitable occasion to honor it – not only by praise, but by emulation. A Flexner II would go beyond the 1910 document, which was limited to addressing the threat to medical professionalism posed by inadequate medical education, to identify threats to the integrity of the profession that arise throughout a physician's career. This detail aside, the new inquiry would, like its predecessor, propose reforms designed to shore up those aspects of medical professionalism that best protect the public's health. A Flexner II initiative could seek first to assess the magnitude of the current threat, taking into account (as I have not done here) the positive impact of financial entanglements between industry and physician and medical scientists. Perhaps its investigations would support a much more complacent view of these matters, reassuring the public that no crisis looms, that abuses can be curbed without draconian reforms, and that the benefits of these financial ties do indeed outweigh their drawbacks. If, on the other hand, the thesis of an impending crisis in pubic confidence of medical science and practice is sustained, a Flexner II commission could emulate its namesake in promulgating sweeping proposals for change. Its charge would be to state the least-disruptive measures that could be counted on to shore up the claims of American medical care to be a profession, a practice governed in fact and not merely in theory by the ideals and norms that justify the public's trust and serve the public's health. These reforms could scarcely be less thorough than those urged by the Flexner report of 1910; and these, as we have seen, were largely carried out.

This chapter has addressed only American issues. Perhaps this is too parochial. Global health issues have become matters of great public interest; they are also an outlet for youthful idealism, akin to the Civil Rights movement of decades long past. After many years of neglect, interest in corruption in global health is growing among researchers, donors, and governments.[18] Problems of medical professionalism are even more acute in countries such as India and China than in the United States. Though both of those countries are served by a growing and well-trained medical elite, most of their citizens receive medical care from private practitioners whose claims to professionalism are marginal at best. In China, officials complain that doctors moved directly from the status of *state employees* in the socialist era to *entrepreneurs* in the current market-oriented economy. They did not pause to consider an intermediate or alternative status of *professional*, and a highly dissatisfied public is now paying the price. If a Flexner II commission were created in the United States, similar initiatives in India, China, and other countries might take up the same tasks. Though these might best be largely independent – the nature of the problems and the range of possible solutions differ from one country to the next – a simultaneous effort might bolster each nation's resolve, and periodic sharing of interim results could enhance the analysis of data and add to the impact of novel suggestions for reform.

Would a Flexner II initiative make any difference? Surely some optimism is warranted. Properly financed, it could carry out just the research needed to inform the commission's eventual recommendations; and if done well these findings might offer facts that speak for themselves. Since the focus would be on the public health impact of financial entanglements among scientists, medical practitioners, and industry, everyone has a stake in the outcome. If the thesis of impending crisis is sustained, one of the goals of such a commission would be to increase the number of people in the country who understand this. At the same time, it would be unrealistic to expect that the industry would refrain from seeking to influence or capture such a potentially influential body – not only after its work began, but in its initial design and choice of membership and staff. A Flexner II commission would have to earn its credibility even before it came to exist, by insulating itself from the very influences over medical research and decision-making that it would seek to investigate.

A Flexner II commission could be undertaken as a private venture, as the original was. Perhaps some of the same foundations would be willing to offer support. But it would have maximum impact if carried out by a United States governmental agency with sufficient funding and authority. In recent years, most new federal administrations have created limited-term bioethics commissions. The President's Council on Bioethics that served 2001–2008 was primarily concerned with biomedical technology. The agenda for a bioethics commission – whether it continues as the President's Council or is replaced by a new agency – could usefully address ethical issues of grave importance to the nation whose effect on the health and well-being of Americans is tangible and immediate. If the nation is in fact on the verge of a crisis in medical professionalism, the current administration's ethicists could find no better undertaking than a Flexner II study of the current status of medical integrity and the measures needed to protect the public's health in the years to come.[19]

NOTES

1. The Carnegie Foundation, Bulletin Number Four: *Medical Education in the United States and Canada: A Report to the Carnegie Foundation for the Advancement of Teaching* ("The Flexner Report") (New York: The Carnegie Foundation, 1910).
2. This capsule history of the Flexner Report and its impact omits nearly every bone of contention among historians: its origins, the intentions of those who instigated and funded Flexner's report (and who selected Abraham Flexner, whose field was education rather than medicine), whether the report was in itself an agent of change, whose interests it served, and how to weigh its virtues against its less benign effects, including the sharp reduction in the diversity of the

medical workforce. The account given here, which simply summarizes conventional wisdom, is adequate for present purposes. For the real story, see Paul Starr, *The Social Transformation of American Medicine* (New York: Basic Books, 1982); Gerald Markowitz and David Rosner, "Doctors in Crisis: A Study of the Use of Medical Education Reform to Establish Modern Professional Elitism in Medicine," *American Quarterly* 25, no. 1 (March 1973): 83–107; Rosemary Stevens, *American Medicine and the Public Interest* (Berkeley, CA: University of California Press, 1998); and other standard histories of medical care in the United States.

3. Jerome P. Kassirer, *On the Take: How Medicine's Complicity with Big Business can Endanger Your Health* (Oxford: Oxford University Press, 2005).

4. Marcia Angell, *The Truth About Drug Companies: How They Deceive Us and What to Do About It* (New York: Random House, 2004).

5. John Abramson, *Overdosed America: The Broken Promise of American Medicine* (New York: HarperCollins, 2004).

6. Jerry Avorn, *Powerful Medicines: The Benefits, Risks, and Costs of Prescription Drugs* (New York: Alfred A. Knopf, 2004).

7. See especially Abramson, *Overdosed America*, documenting the publication – in such journals as *The New England Journal of Medicine* – of selective results of series of trials; the full set of data, though located by Abramson in the web pages of the Food and Drug Administration, were not submitted to *The New England Journal of Medicine*'s referees and were not taken into account in the editorial decision to accept the reports for publication.

8. Ray Moynihan, "Key opinion leaders: independent experts or Drug Reps in Disguise?" *British Medical Journal* 336 (2008): 1402–1403; Giovanni Fava, "Should the drug industry work with key opinion leaders? No," *British Medical Journal* 336 (June 21, 2008): 1405.

9. Richard Smith, "Medical Journals Are an Extension of the Marketing Arm of Pharmaceutical Companies," *PLoS Med* 2, no. 5 (2005): e138.

10. Richard Horton, "The Dawn of McScience," *New York Review of Books* 51, no. 4 (2004): 7–9.

11. See e.g. Sheldon Krimsky, *Science in the Private Interest: Has the Lure of Profits Corrupted Medical Research?* (Lanham, MD: Rowman and Littlefield, 2003); and Eric Campbell, "Doctors and drug companies – scrutinizing influential relationships," *The New England Journal of Medicine* 357, no. 18 (November 1, 2007): 1796–1797.

12. Eric G. Campbell, Joel S. Weissman, Susan Ehringhaus, Sowmya, *et al.*, "Institutional Academic Industry Relationships," *The Journal of the American Medical Association* 298, no. 15 (October 17, 2007): 1779–1786.

13. Thomas Stossel, "Regulating Academic–Industrial Research Relationships – Solving Problems or Stifling Progress?" *The New England Journal of Medicine* 353, no. 10 (September 8, 2005): 1060–1065.

14. Some organized efforts to provide counter-influences on physicians show promise. *No Free Lunch* is an organization of "health care providers who believe that pharmaceutical promotion should not guide clinical practice. Our mission

is to encourage health care providers to practice medicine on the basis of scientific evidence rather than on the basis of pharmaceutical promotion. We discourage the acceptance of *all* gifts from industry by health care providers, trainees, and students." (quoted from www.nofreelunch.org, accessed June 23, 2008). Other initiatives seek to weaken the industry's ability to influence physicians' understanding of the relative merits of drugs through "counter-detailing", a labor-intensive effort to field knowledgeable counterparts to industry "detail men" (and women) who offer unbiased evaluations to individual physicians. The State of Pennsylvania has contracted with Harvard's Dr. Jerry Avorn to set up a statewide program, the Independent Drug Information Service. See Emily Singer, "Aggressive drug marketing tactics trigger backlash," *Nature Medicine* 13, no. 4 (April 2007): 393.

15. Gregg Bloche, "The Market for Medical Ethics," *Journal of Health Politics, Policy, and Law* 26, no. 5 (2001): 1099–1112; see also Gregg Bloche, "Trust and Betrayal in the Medical Marketplace," *Stanford Law Review* 55 (2002): 919–954.
16. Kenneth Arrow, "Uncertainty and the Welfare Economics of Medical Care," *American Economics Review* 53, no. 5 (1963): 941–973.
17. Gerald E. Markowitz and David Karl Rosner, "Doctors in Crisis: A Study of the Use of Medical Education Reform to Establish Modern Professional Elitism in Medicine," *American Quarterly* 25, no. 1, (March 1973): 83–107
18. Transparency International, *Global Corruption Report 2006: Corruption and Health*, (London: Pluto Press, 2006).
19. The author thanks John Abramson, Leon Eisenberg, and Tara Vian for valuable suggestions and comments.

Bibliography

Aaron, Henry J. and William B. Schwartz, "Managed Competition: Little Cost Containment Without Budget Limits," *Health Affairs* 12 (1993): 204–215.

Abelson, Raziel, "Moral Distance: What Do We Owe to Unknown Strangers?" *The Philosophical Forum* XXXVI, no. 1 (Spring 2005): 31–39.

Abrams, Thomas, "The Regulation of Prescription Drug Promotion," in *Ethics and the Pharmaceutical Industry*, ed. Michael A. Santoro and Thomas M. Gorrie (New York: Cambridge University Press, 2005), pp. 153–169.

Abramson, John, *Overdosed America: The Broken Promise of American Medicine* (New York: HarperCollins, 2004).

Adair, R. F. and L. R. Holmgren, "Do Drug Samples Influence Resident Prescribing Behavior?" *American Journal of Medicine* 118, no. 8 (2005): 881–884.

Aikin, Kathryn J., John L. Swasy, and Amie C. Braman, "Patient and Physician Attitudes and Behaviors Associated With DTC Promotion of Prescription Drugs: Summary of FDA Survey Research Results, Final Report," November 19, 2004. Available at www.fda.gov/cder/ddmac/researchka.htm (accessed July 1, 2008).

Akin, J., N. Birdsall, and D. Ferranti, *Financing Health Services in Developing Countries: An Agenda for Reform*, (Washington, DC: World Bank, 1987).

Allman, Richard L., M.D., "The Relationships Between Physicians and the Pharmaceutical Industry: Ethical Problems with the Every-Day Conflict of Interest," *Healthcare Ethics Committee Forum* 15, no. 2 (2003): 155–170.

American Medical Association, *American Medical Association Code of Medical Ethics*, 2006–7 edition (Chicago, IL: American Medical Association, 2006).

American Nurses' Association, *Nursing: A Social Policy Statement* (Kansas City: American Nurses' Association, 1995).

American Nurses' Association, *Nursing's Social Policy Statement* (Kansas City: American Nurses' Association, 1980).

Anderson, Gerard F., Peter S. Hussey, Bianca K. Frogner, and Hugh R. Waters, "Health Spending in the United States and the Rest of the Industrialized World," *Health Affairs* 24, no. 4 (July/August 2005): 903–914.

Anderson G. M., Beers M. H., Kerluke K., "Auditing Prescription Practice Using Explicit Criteria and Computerized Drug Benefit Claims Data," *Journal of Evaluation in Clinical Practice* 3 (1998): 283–294.

Angell, Marcia, "Medicine: the Endangered Patient-Centered Ethic," *Hastings Center Report* 17, no. 1 (1987): 12–13.
The Truth About the Drug Companies: How They Deceive Us and What To Do About It (New York: Random House, 2004).
Arneson, Richard, "The Principle of Fairness and Free-Rider Problems," *Ethics* 92 (1982): 616–633.
Arnold, Denis G., "Coercion and Moral Responsibility," *American Philosophical Quarterly*, 38, no. 1 (January 2001): 53–67.
"Merck & Riverblindness," in *Ethical Theory and Business*, 8th edn., ed. Tom L. Beauchamp, Norman E. Bowie, and Denis G. Arnold (Englewood Cliffs, NJ: Pearson-Prentice Hall, 2009), pp. 101–102.
Arnold, Denis G. and Norman E. Bowie, "Sweatshops and Respect for Persons," *Business Ethics Quarterly* 8, no. 2 (2003): 221–242.
Arnold, J. D., "Incidence of Injury During Clinical Pharmacology Research and Indemnification of Injured Research Subjects at the Quincy Research Center," in President's Commission for the Study of Ethical Problems in Medicine and Biomedical and Behavioral Research, *Compensating for Research Injuries: The Ethical and Legal Implications of Programs to Redress Injured Subjects* (Washington, DC: US Government Printing Office, Stock No. 040-000-00455-6, 1982; the Appendix to this Report is Stock No. 040-000-00456-4), Appendix pp. 275–302.
Arrow, Kenneth, "Uncertainty and the Welfare Economics of Medical Care," *American Economics Review* 53, no. 5 (1963): 941–973.
The Association of the British Pharmaceutical Industry, "Code of Practice for the Pharmaceutical Industry," 2006. Available at www.pmcpa.org.uk (accessed June 12, 2007).
Avorn, Jerry, *Powerful Medicines: The Benefits, Risks, and Costs of Prescription Drugs* (New York: Vintage Books, 2005).
Avorn, Jerry, M. Chen, and R. Hartley, "Scientific versus Commercial Sources of Influence on the Prescribing Behavior of Physicians," *American Journal of Medicine* 73 (1982): 4–8.
Avorn, Jerry and Stephen B. Soumerai, "Improving Drug-Therapy Decisions through Educational Outreach: A Randomized Controlled Trial of Academically Based Detailing," *The New England Journal of Medicine* 308 (1983): 1457–1463.
Banta, David H., "Medical Education: Abraham Flexner – A Reappraisal," *Social Science and Medicine* 5 (1971): 655–661.
Baron, Richard, "An Introduction to Medical Phenomenology: I Can't Hear You While I'm Listening," *Annals of Internal Medicine* 103 (1985): 606–611.
Barzansky, Barbara and Norman Gevitz, eds., *Beyond Flexner: Medical Education in the Twentieth Century* (New York: Greenwood Press, 1992).
Beauchamp, Tom L., "Who Deserves Autonomy, and Whose Autonomy Deserves Respect," in *Personal Autonomy*, ed. James Stacey Taylor (Cambridge: Cambridge University Press, 2005), pp. 310–330.

Beauchamp, Tom L., Bruce Jennings, Eleanor D. Kinney, and Robert J. Levine, "Pharmaceutical Research Involving the Homeless," *Journal of Medicine & Philosophy* 27, no. 5 (2002): 547–564.

Beck, R. G., "The Effects of Co-Payment on the Poor," *Journal of Human Resources* 9 (1974): 129–142.

Beecher, Henry, "Ethics and Clinical Research," *New England Journal of Medicine* 274, no. 24 (1966): 13154.

Behrman, Rachel E., Deputy Director, Food and Drug Administration, "The Impact of Direct-to-Consumer Advertising on Seniors' Health and Health Care Costs." Testimony before the Special Committee on Aging, United States Senate, September 22, 2005, 3. Available at www.hhs.gov/asl/testify/t050929.html.

Berliner, Howard, "The Larger Perspective on the Flexner Report," *International Journal of Health Services* 5, no. 4 (1975): 573–592.

Bloche, Gregg, "The Market for Medical Ethics," *Journal of Health Politics, Policy, and Law* 26, no. 5 (2001): 1099–1112.

"Trust and Betrayal in the Medical Marketplace," *Stanford Law Review* 55 (2002): 919–954.

Bodenheimer, Thomas, "Rising Health Care Costs. Part 2: Technological Innovation," *Annals of Internal Medicine* 142:11 (2005): 932–937.

Boorse, Christopher, "Health as a Theoretical Concept," *Philosophy of Science* 44 (1977): 542–573.

"A Rebuttal on Health," in *What is Disease?*, ed. James Humber and Robert Almeder (Totowa, NJ: Humana Press, 1997), pp. 1–134.

Borger, Christine, Sheila Smith, Christopher Truffer, *et al.*, "Health Spending Projections Through 2015: Changes on the Horizon," *Health Affairs Web Exclusive*, February 22, 2006, W61.

Boström, H., "On the Compensation for Injured Research Subjects in Sweden," in President's Commission for the Study of Ethical Problems in Medicine and Biomedical and Behavioral Research, *Compensating for Research Injuries: The Ethical and Legal Implications of Programs to Redress Injured Subjects* (Washington, DC: US Government Printing Office, Stock No. 040-000-00455-6, 1982; the Appendix to this Report is Stock No. 040-000-00456-4), Appendix, pp. 309–322.

Bowie, Norman E., *Business Ethics: A Kantian Perspective* (Malden: Blackwell Publishers, 1999).

Boyce, Nell, "Code of conduct for bioethics branded 'soft' on corporate ties," *Nature* 417, no. 6892 (2002): 885.

"A View from the Fourth Estate," *Hastings Center Report* 32, no. 3 (2002): 16–17.

Brass, Eric P, "Changing the Status of Drugs from Prescription to Over-the-Counter Availability," *The New England Journal of Medicine* 345, 11 (2001): 810–816.

Brenkert, George G, "Marketing and the Vulnerable," *Business Ethics Quarterly* Special Issue 1 (1998): 7–20.

Brennan, Ross and Paul Baines, "Is There a Morally Right Price for Anti-retroviral Drugs in the Developing World?" *Business Ethics: A European Review* 15, no. 1 (January 2006): 29–43.

Brody, Baruch, *Ethical Issues in Drug Testing, Approval, and Pricing* (New York: Oxford University Press, 1995).

"Intellectual Property and Biotechnology: The U.S. Internal Experience – Part I" and "… Part II." *Kennedy Institute of Ethics Journal* 16 no. 1 (2006): 1–38 and 16, no. 2 (2006): 105–128.

Brody, Baruch, Nancy Dubler, Jeff Blustein, *et al.*, "Bioethics Consultation in the Private Sector," *Hastings Center Report* 32, no. 3 (2002): 14–20.

Brody, Howard, *Hooked: Ethics, the Medical Profession, and the Pharmaceutical Industry* (Lanham, MD: Rowman & Littlefield Publishers, 2007).

Brook, R. H., J. E. Ware, Jr., W. H. Rogers, *et al.*, "Does Free Care Improve Adults' Health?" *New England Journal of Medicine* 309, no. 23 (1983): 1426–1434.

Brown, Hannah, "Sweetening the Pill," *British Medical Journal* 334 (2007): 664–666.

Buchanan, A., D. Brock, N. Daniels, and D. Wikler, *From Chance to Choice: Genetics and Justice* (New York: Cambridge University Press, 2000).

Burns, Lawton R., John Cacciamani, James Clement, and Welman Aquino, "The Fall of the House of AHERF: The Allegheny Bankruptcy," *Health Affairs* 19, no. 1 (2000): 7–41.

Busse, Reinhard, Jonas Schreyogg, and Klaus-Dirk Henke, "Regulation of Pharmaceutical Markets in Germany: Improving Efficiency and Controlling Expenditures," *International Journal of Health Planning and Management* 20, no. 4 (2005): 329–349.

Cain, D., G. Loewenstein, and D. Moore, "The Dirt on Coming Clean," *Journal of Legal Studies* 34, no. 1 (2005): 1–25.

Calfee, John E., "Public Policy Issues in Direct-to-Consumer Advertising of Prescription Drugs?" July 8, 2002. Available at www.fda.gov/ohrms/dockets/dailys/02/Sep02/092302/02N-0209_emc-000183–01.pdf (accessed July 1, 2008).

Callahan, Daniel, *False Hopes: Overcoming the Obstacles to a Sustainable, Affordable Medicine* (New Brunswick, NJ: Rutgers University Press, 1999).

Callahan, Daniel and Angela A. Wasunna, *Medicine and the Market: Equity v. Choice* (Baltimore, MD: Johns Hopkins Press, 2006).

Campbell, Eric, "Doctors and drug companies – scrutinizing influential relationships," *New England Journal of Medicine* 357, no. 18 (2007): 1796–1797.

Campbell, Eric G., Joel S. Weissman, Susan Ehringhaus, *et al.*, "Institutional academic industry relationships," *Journal of the American Medical Association* 298, no. 15 (2007): 1779–1786.

Canguilhem, Georges, *The Normal and the Pathological*, translated by Carolyn R. Fawcett (New York: Zone Books, 1991).

Cardon P. V., F. W. Dommel, and R. R. Trumble, "Injuries to Research Subjects: A Survey of Investigators," *New England Journal of Medicine* 295 (1976): 650–654.

2

64

264 *Bibliography*

The Carnegie Foundation, *Bulletin Number Four: Medical Education in the United States, and Canada: A Report to the Carnegie Foundation for the Advancement of Teaching ("The Flexner Report")* (New York: The Carnegie Foundation, 1910).

Carpenter, William T, "How the Doctor can Counter Commercial Bias in the Dissemination of Pharmacotherapeutic Knowledge," *The Journal of Nervous and Mental Disease* 190, no. 9 (2002): 593–596.

Casarett, David, Jason Karlawish, and David A. Asch, "Paying Hypertension Research Subjects: Fair Compensation or Undue Inducement," *Journal of General Internal Medicine* 17 (2002): 651–653.

Castro, Leonardo D. de, "Exploitation in the Use of Human Subject for Medical Experimentation: A Re-Examination of Basic Issues," *Bioethics* 9 (1995): 259–268.

Center for Global Development, *Making Markets for Vaccines: Ideas into Action (a report)* (Washington, DC: Center for Global Development, 2005).

Charatan, F. B., "American Medical Association Apologizes for Commercial Deal," *British Medical Journal* 315 (1997): 501–504.

Cho, M. K. and L. A. Bero, "The Quality of Drug Studies Published in Symposium Proceedings," *Annals of Internal Medicine* 124, 5 (1996): 485–489.

Cialdini, R. B., *Influence: The Psychology of Persuasion* (New York: Quill William Morrow, 1993).

Committee for the Study of the Future of Public Health, *The Future of Public Health* (Washington, DC: National Academies Press, 1988).

Committee on Quality of Health Care in America, Institute of Medicine, *Crossing the Quality Chasm: A New Health System for the 21st Century* (Washington, DC: National Academies Press, 2001).

Committee on Quality of Health Care in America, Institute of Medicine, *To Err Is Human: Building a Safer Health System* (Washington, DC: National Academies Press, 2000).

Committee on Assuring the Health of the People, Institute of Medicine, *The Future of the Public's Health in the 21st Century* (Washington, DC: National Academies Press, 2003).

Commission on Health Research for Development, *Health Research: Essential Link to Equity in Development* (New York: Oxford University Press, 1990).

Common Rule for the Protection of Human Subjects, "U. S. Code of Federal Regulation?" 45 CFR 46.116 (as revised October 1, 2003).

Council for International Organization of Medical Societies, *International Ethical Guidelines for Biomedical Research Involving Human Subjects.* Available at www.cioms.ch/frame_guidelines_nov_2002.htm

Craik, Kenneth, *The Nature of Explanation* (New York: The Macmillan Company, 1943).

Creese, A., "User Charges for Health Care: A Review of Recent Experience," *Health Policy and Planning.* 6, no. 4 (1991): 309–319.

Dana, Jason and George Loewenstein, "A Social Science Perspective on Gifts to Physicians from Industry." *Journal of the American Medical Association* 290 (2003): 252–255.

Daniels, Norman, "Fair Process in Patient Selection for Antiretroviral Treatment for HIV/AIDS in WHO's 3 by 5 Program." *The Lancet*, 366 (2005): 169–171.

Just Health Care (New York: Oxford University Press, 1985).

"Justice, Health and Health Care," *American Journal of Bioethics* 1, no. 2 (2001): 3–15.

"Rationing Medical Care: A Philosopher's Perspective on Outcomes and Process," *Economics and Philosophy* 14 (1998): 27–50.

"The Profit Motive and the Moral Assessment of Health Care Institutions," *Business and Professional Ethics Journal* 10, no. 2 (1991): 3–30.

"Toward Ethical Review of Health System Transformations," *American Journal of Public Health* 96, no. 3 (2006): 447–451.

Daniels, Norman, J. Bryant, R. A. Castano, *et al.*, "Benchmarks of Fairness for Health Care Reform: A Policy Tool for Developing Countries," *Bulletin of the World Health Organization* 78 (2000): 740–750.

Daniels, Norman, W. Flores, and J. Gomez-Juaregui, "Benchmarking Fairness in Reproductive Health. Consultation on Health Sector Reform, Equity and Reproductive Health," Geneva, December 1, 2004. Available at: www.who.int/reproductive-health/tcc/meeting_documents/daniels_et_al.pdf

Daniels, Norman, Walter Flores, Supasit Pannarunothai, *et al.*, "An Evidence-Based Approach to Benchmarking the Fairness of Health Sector Reform in Developing Countries," *Bulletin of World Health Organization* 83 (2005): 534–540.

Daniels Norman, Bruce P. Kennedy, and Ichiro Kawachi, *Is Inequality Bad for Our Health?* (Boston, MA: Beacon Press, 2000).

"Why Justice Is Good for Your Health: Social Determinants of Health Inequalities," *Daedalus* 128, no. 4 (1999): 215–251.

Daniels, Norman, Donald Light, and Ronald Caplan, *Benchmarks of Fairness for Health Care Reform.* (New York: Oxford University Press, 1996).

Daniels, Norman and James E. Sabin, *Setting Limits Fairly: Can We Learn to Share Medical Resources?* (New York: Oxford University Press, 2002).

Daniels, Norman, Russell J. Teagarden, and James E. Sabin, "An Ethical Template for Pharmacy Benefits," *Health Affairs* 22, no. 1 (Jan/Feb 2003): 125–137.

Danzon, Patricia M. and Jonathan D. Ketcham, "Reference Pricing of Pharmaceuticals for Medicare: Evidence from Germany, the Netherlands, and New Zealand," *Frontiers in Health Policy Research* (National Bureau of Economic Research) 7 (2004): 1–54.

Daugherty, Christopher K., Donald M. Banik, Linda Janish, and Mark J. Ratain, "Quantitative Analysis of Ethical Issues in Phase I Trials," *IRB* 22 (May/June 2000): 6–14.

Davis, K., "Consumer-Directed Health Care: Will It Improve Health System Performance?" *Health Services Research.* 39, no. 4 (part 2) (2004): 1219–1234.

De George, Richard T., "Intellectual Property and Pharmaceutical Drugs: An Ethical Analysis," *Business Ethics Quarterly* 15, no. 4 (October 2005): 549–575.

DeBruin, Debra A., "Looking Beyond the Limitations of 'Vulnerability': Reforming Safeguards in Research," *The American Journal of Bioethics* 4 (2004): 76–78.

"Reflections on Vulnerability," *Bioethics Examiner* 5 (2001): 1, 4, 7.

Department of Health and Human Services National Institutes of Health, *NIH Response to the Conference Report Request for a Plan to Ensure Taxpayers' Interests are Protected: A Plan to Ensure Taxpayers' Interests are Protected,* July 2001. Available at www.nih.gov/news/070101wyden.htm (accessed March 22, 2007).

Department of Health and Human Services, "Pharmaceutical Company Gifts and Payments to Providers," in *Work Plan for Fiscal Plan 2002* (Washington, DC: DHHS, 2001).

Department of Health and Human Services, Office of the Inspector General, *Prescription Drug Promotion Involving Payments and Gifts: Physicians' Perspectives.* OEI-01-90-00481 (Washington, DC: DHHS, 1991).

Dickert, Neal and Christine Grady, "What's the Price of a Research Subject?: Approaches to Payment for Research Participation," *New England Journal of Medicine* 341 (1999): 198–203.

Donahue, Patricia M., *Nursing: the Finest Art* (St. Louis, MO: The C.V. Mosby Company, 1985).

Donohue, Julie M., Marisa Cevasco, and Meredith B. Rosenthal, "A Decade of Direct-to-Consumer Advertising of Prescription Drugs," *New England Journal of Medicine* 357 (2007): 673–681.

Eddy, David, *Clinical Decision Making: From Theory to Practice.* (Sudbury: Jones and Bartlett Publishers, 1996).

Elliot, Carl, "The Drug Pushers," *The Atlantic Monthly* (April 2006): 2–13.

Emanuel, Ezekiel, "Ending Concerns about Undue Inducement," *Journal of Law, Medicine, & Ethics* 32 (2004): 100–105.

Engel, George, "A Unified Concept of Health and Disease," *Perspectives in Biology and Medicine* (summer 1960): 459–485.

"Biomedicine's Failure to Achieve Flexnerian Standards of Education," *Journal of Medical Education* 53 (1978): 387–392.

"How Much Longer Must Medicine's Science Be Bound By A Seventeenth Century World View?" in *The Task of Medicine: Dialogue at Wickenburg,* ed. Kerr L. White (Menlo Park, CA: The Henry J. Kaiser Family Foundation, 1988).

"The Biopsychosocial Model and the Education of Health Professionals," *Annals of the New York Academy of Sciences* 310 (1978): 169–181.

"The Care of the Patient: Art or Science?" *The Johns Hopkins Medical Journal* 140 (1977): 222–232.

"The Clinical Application of the Biopsychosocial Model," *The American Journal of Psychiatry* 137, no. 5 (1980): 535–544.

Engelhardt, H. Tristram, *Foundations of Bioethics* (Oxford: Oxford University Press, 1996).

Evans, R. G., M. L. Barer, and T. R. Marmor, *Why Are Some People Healthy and Others Not?* (New York: Aldine de Gruyter, 1994).

Faber, Knud, *Nosograpy in Modern Internal Medicine* (New York: Paul B. Hoeber, 1922).

Faden, Ruth R. and Tom L. Beauchamp, *A History and Theory of Informed Consent* (New York: Oxford University Press, 1986).

Families USA, "Enough to Make You Sick: Prescription Drug Prices for the Elderly?" June 2001. Available at www.familiesusa.org/assets/pdfs/Enough-to-Make-You-Sick.pdf (accessed June 14, 2006).

Families USA, "Health Care for People or Drug Industry Profits?" 2005. Available at www.familiesusa.org/assets/pdfs/The-Choice.pdf (accessed March 22, 2007).

Families USA, "Sticker Shock: Rising Prescription Drug Prices for Seniors?" June 2004. Available at www.familiesusa.org/assets/pdfs/Sticker_Shock5942.pdf (accessed June 14, 2006).

Faunce, T. S. and G. F. Tomossy, "The UK House of Commons Report on the Influence of the Pharmaceutical Industry: Lessons for Equitable Access to Medicines in Australia," *Monash Bioethics Review* 23, no. 4 (2005): 38–42.

Fava, Giovanni, "Should the drug industry work with key opinion leaders? No," *British Medical Journal* 336 (2008): 1405.

Feinberg, Joel, *Harm to Others, vol. 1 of The Moral Limits of the Criminal Law* (New York: Oxford University Press, 1984), pp. 32–36.

Feldman, Roger and Michael Morrissey, "Health Economics: A Report on the Field," *Journal of Health Politics, Policy and Law* 15, no. 3 (1990): 627–646.

Fleck, Ludwik, *Genesis and Development of a Scientific Fact* (Chicago, IL: University of Chicago Press, 1981).

Fletcher, J. C., E. M. Spencer, and P. A. Lombardo, *Fletcher's Introduction to Clinical Ethics* (Hagerstown, MD: University Publishing Group, 2005).

Flexner, Abraham, *Medical Education in the United States and Canada: A Report to the Carnegie Foundation for the Advancement of Teaching.* (New York: The Carnegie Foundation for the Advancement of Teaching, 1910).

Flory, James H. and Philip Kitcher, "Global Health and the Scientific Research Agenda," *Philosophy and Public Affairs* 32, no. 1 (2004): 36–65.

Foucault, Michel, *The Birth of the Clinic: An Archaeology of Medical Perception* (New York: Vintage Books, 1994).

Frank, Arthur, *The Wounded Storyteller: Body, Illness, and Ethics* (Chicago, IL: The University of Chicago Press, 1995).

Freeman, Jerome W. and Brian Kaatz, "The Physician and the Pharmaceutical Detail Man: An Ethical Analysis," *The Journal of Medical Humanities and Bioethics* 8, no. 1 (1987): 34–39.

Friedman, Hershey H. and Paul J. Herskovitz, "The Effect of a Gift-Upon-Entry on Sales: Reciprocity in a Retailing Context," *Mid-American Journal of Business* 5, (1990): 49–50.

Fuchs, Victor, "Economics, Values, and Health Care Reform," *Journal of Health Politics, Policy and Law* 15, no. 3 (1996): 1–29.

Fuchs, Victor R. and J. S. Hahn, "How Does Canada Do It? A Comparison of Expenditures for Physicians' Services in the United States and Canada," *New England Journal of Medicine* 27:323:13 (1990): 884–890.

Galvin, Robert S., Suzanne Delbanco, Arnold Milstein, and Greg Belden, "Has the Leapfrog Group Had an Impact on the Health Care Market?" *Health Affairs* 24, no. 1 (2005): 228–233.

Gathei, James T., "Third World Perspectives on Global Pharmaceutical Access," in *Ethics and the Pharmaceutical Industry*, ed. Michael A. Santoro and Thomas M. Gorrie (New York: Oxford University Press, 2005), pp. 336–351.

Gert, Bernard, "Coercion and Freedom," in *Coercion: Nomos XIV*, ed. J. Roland Pennock and John W. Chapman (Chicago, IL: Aldine, Atherton Inc., 1972), pp. 36–37.

Global Forum for Health Research, *The 10/90 Report of Health Research 2003–2004* (Geneva: Global Forum for Health Research, 2004).

Goozner, Merrill, *The $800 Million Pill: The Truth Behind the Cost of New Drugs* (Berkeley, CA: University of California Press, 2004).

Gostin, Lawrence, Jo Ivey Boufford, and Martinez Rose Marie, "The Future of the Public's Health: Vision, Values, Strategies." *Health Affairs* 23, no. 4 (2004): 96–107.

Gouldner, Alvin W., "The Norm of Reciprocity: A Preliminary Statement," *American Sociological Review* 25, (1960): 161–178.

Grady, Christine, "Money for Research Participation: Does It Jeopardize Informed Consent?" *American Journal of Bioethics* 1 (2001): 40–44.

Greenspan, Patricia, "The Problem with Manipulation," *American Philosophical Quarterly* 40 (2003): 155–164.

Griffith, David, "Reasons for Not Seeing Drug Representatives," *British Medical Journal* 319, no. 10 (1999): 69–70.

Grodin, Michael A. and Leonard H. Glantz, eds., *Children as Research Subjects: Science, Ethics, and Law* (New York: Oxford University Press, 1994).

Guthrie, Douglas, *Janus in the Doorway* (Springfield, IL: Charles Thomas, 1963).

Haddad, S. and P. Fournier, "Quality, Cost and Utilisation of Health Services in Developing Countries. A Longitudinal Study in Zaire," *Social Science and Medicine*, 40, no. 6 (1995): 743–753.

Hall, Mark, "Physician Rationing and Agency Cost Theory," in *Conflicts of Interest in Clinical Practice and Research*, ed. Roy Spece, David Shimm, and Allen Buchanan (Oxford: Oxford University Press, 1996), pp. 228–250.

Halpern, Scott, Jason Karlawish, David Casarett, Jesse Berlin, and David A. Asch, "Empirical Assessment of Whether Moderate Payments are Undue or Unjust Inducements for Participation in Clinical Trials," *Archives of Internal Medicine* 164 (2004): 801–803.

Hart, H. L. A., "Are There Any Natural Rights?" *Philosophical Review* 64 (1955): 175–191.

Havlicek, P. L. *Medical Groups in the US: A Survey of Practice Characteristics* (Chicago, IL: American Medical Association, 1996).

Hawthorne, Fran, *Inside the FDA: The Business and Politics Behind the Drugs We Take and the Food We Eat* (Hoboken, NJ: John Wiley & Sons, 2005).

Hemminki, Elina, "Commercial Information on Drugs: Confusing the Physician?" *Journal of Drug Issues* 18, (1988): 245–257.

"Content Analysis of Drug-Detailing by Pharmaceutical Representatives," *Medical Education* 11, (1977): 210–215.

Hemminki, Elina and Terttu Pesonen, "The Function of Drug Company Representatives," *Scandinavian Journal of Social Medicine* 5, (1977): 105–114.

Henderson, Gail E., Arlene M. Davis, and Nancy M. P. King, "Vulnerability to Influence: A Two-Way Street," *American Journal of Bioethics* 4 (2004): 50–53.

Herman, Barbara, "Leaving Deontology Behind," in *The Practice of Moral Judgment* (Cambridge, MA: Harvard University Press, 1993).

Herzlinger, Regina E., "Let's Put Consumers in Charge of Health Care," *Harvard Business Review* 80, no. 7 (2002): 44–50, 52–55, 123.

Hewlett, Sarah E., "Consent to Clinical Research – Adequately Voluntary Or Substantially Influenced?" *Journal of Medical Ethics* 22 (1996): 232–236.

"Is Consent to Participate in Research Voluntary," *Arthritis Care and Research* 9 (1996): 400–404.

Hill, Thomas E. Jr., *Dignity and Practical Reason in Kant's Moral Theory* (Ithaca, NY: Cornell University Press, 1992).

Hodges, Brian, "Interactions with the Pharmaceutical Industry," *Canadian Medical Association Journal* 153 (1995): 553–559.

Hoey, J., "Ads and prescription pads?" *Canadian Medical Association Journal* 169, no. 5 (September 2, 2003): 381.

Hollon, Matthew F., "Direct-to-Consumer Advertising: A Haphazard Approach to Health Promotion," *Journal of the American Medical Association* 293, no. 16 (April 2005): 2030–2033.

"Direct-to-Consumer Marketing of Prescription Drugs: Creating Consumer Demand," *Journal of the American Medical Association* 281, no. 4 (January 1999): 382–384.

Hollon, Tom, "FDA Uneasy About Placebo Revision," *Nature Medicine* 7, no. 1 (2001): 7.

Hopper, J., M. Speece, and J. Musial, "Effects of an Educational Intervention on Residents' Knowledge and Attitudes Toward Interactions with Pharmaceutical Representatives," *Journal of General Internal Medicine* 12 (1997): 639–642.

Horton, Richard, "The Dawn of McScience," *New York Review of Books* 51, no. 4 (2004): 7–9.

House of Commons Health Committee, *The Influence of the Pharmaceutical Industry*, Fourth Report of Session 2004–05. London: Stationery Office, 22 March 2005. Available at www.parliament.the-stationery-office.co.uk/pa/cm200405/cmselect/cmhealth/42/42.pdf (accessed June 12, 2007).

Hubbard, Tim and James Love, "A New Trade Framework for Global Healthcare R&D," *PloS Biology* 2, no. 2 (2004): 0147–0150. Available at http://biology.

plosjournals.org/archive/1545–7885/2/2/pdf/10.1371_journal.pbio.0020052-L. pdf (accessed June 23, 2008).

Human, Delon, "Conflicts of Interest in Science and Medicine: The Physician's Perspective," *Science and Engineering Ethics* 8, no. 3 (2002): 273–276.

Institute of Medicine, *Crossing the Quality Chasm: A New Health System for the 21st Century* (Washington, DC: National Academies Press, 2001).

Institute of Medicine, *To Err is Human: Building a Safer Health System* (Washington, DC: National Academies Press, 2000).

Janis, Irving L., Donald Kay, and Paul Kirshner, "Facilitating Effects of Eating-While-Reading on Responsiveness to Persuasive Communications," *Journal of Personality and Social Psychology* 1 (1965): 181–186.

Jansen, L. A. and D. P. Sulmasy, "Bioethics, Conflicts of Interest and the Limits of Transparency," *Hastings Center Report* 33, no. 4 (2003): 40–43.

Jefferson, Thomas, "Letter to Isaac McPherson?" August 13, 1813. Reprinted in *Life and Selected Writings of Thomas Jefferson*, ed. A. Koch and W. Peden (New York: Modern Library, 1972), pp. 276–277.

Joint Commission Resources, *2005 Comprehensive Accreditation Manual for Hospitals*, RI Chapter, Patient Rights and Organizational Ethics Standards (Oakbrook Terrace, IL: JCAHO, 2005).

Joseph, Sarah, "Pharmaceutical Corporations and Access to Drugs," *Human Rights Quarterly* 25, no. 2 (2003): 425–452.

Kaiser Family Foundation, "Trends and Indicators in the Changing Health Care Marketplace?" 2006, www.kff.org/insurance/7031/ti2004–1-21.cfm (accessed August 12, 2007).

Kant, Immanuel, *Groundwork for the Metaphysics of Morals*. Translated by Arnulf Zweig (Oxford: Oxford University Press, 2002).

Kaphingst, Kimberly A., Rima E. Rudd, William DeJong, and Lawren H. Daltroy, "Literacy Demands of Product Information Intended to Supplement Television Direct-to-Consumer Prescription Drug Advertisements," *Patient Education and Counseling* 55 (2004): 293–300.

Kark, Sidney, "The Pholela Health Centre," *Bulletin of the World Health Organization* 77, no. 5 (1999 [1952]): 439–447.

Kass, Nancy E., Jeremy Sugarman, Ruth Faden, and Monica Schoch-Spana, "Trust: The Fragile Foundation of Contemporary Biomedical Research," *Hastings Center Report* 25 (September/October 1996): 25–29.

Kassirer, Jerome, "Managing Care – Should We Adopt a New Ethic?" *New England Journal of Medicine* 339, no.6 (1998): 397–398.

"Managing Managed Care's Tarnished Image," *New England Journal of Medicine* 337, no. 5 (1997): 338–339.

Kassirer, Jerome P., *On the Take: How Medicine's Complicity with Big Business Can Endanger Your Health* (Oxford/New York: Oxford University Press, 2005).

Katz, Dana, Arthur L. Caplan, and Jon F. Merz, "All Gifts Large and Small: Toward an Understanding of the Ethics of Pharmaceutical Industry Gift-Giving," *The American Journal of Bioethics* 3, no. 3 (2003): 39–46.

Katz, Russell, "FDA: Evidentiary Standards for Drug Development and Approval," *NeuroRx: The Journal of the American Society for Experimental NeuroTherapeutics* 1 no. 3 (2004): 307–316.

Kawachi, Ichiro and Bruce P. Kennedy, *The Health of Nations: Why Inequality is Harmful to Your Health* (New York: New Press, 2002).

Keeler, E. B. and J. E. Rolph, "The Demand for Episodes of Treatment in the Health Insurance Experience," *Journal of Health Economics*. 7, no. 4 (1988): 337–367.

Keith, Alison, "Information Matters: The Consumer as the Integrated Health Care System," in *Prescription Drug Advertising: Empowering Consumers Through Information. Published by Pfizer as part of the series Economic Realities in Health Care Policy*, 2, 1. (East Brunswick, NJ: Pfizer, 2001). Available at www.pfizer.com/about/public_policy/resources.jsp (accessed July 1, 2008).

Khushf, George, "A Radical Challenge to the Traditional Conception of Medicine: On the Need to Move Beyond Economic Factors When Considering the Ethics of Managed Care," in *The Ethics of Managed Care: Professional Integrity and Patient Rights*, ed. W. B. Bondeson and J. Jones (Dordrecht: Kluwer Academic Publishers, 2002), pp. 75–91.

"A Radical Rupture in the Paradigm of Modern Medicine: Conflicts of Interest, Fiduciary Obligations, and the Scientific Ideal," *Journal of Medicine and Philosophy* 23, no. 1 (1998): 98–122.

"Organizational Ethics and the Medical Professional: Reappraising Roles and Responsibilities," in *The Health Professional as Friend and Healer*, ed. Judith Kissell and David Thomasma (Washington, DC: Georgetown University Press, 2000), pp. 148–162.

"Reconceptualizing Health and Disease," *Journal of Medicine and Philosophy* 20, no.5 (1995): 461–473.

"The Scope of Organizational Ethics," *HEC Forum* 10, no.2 (1998): 127–135.

"What Is At Issue in the Debate About Concepts of Health and Disease? Framing the Problem of Demarcation for a Post-positivist Era of Medicine," in *Health, Science, and Ordinary Language*, ed. L. Nordenfelt (New York: Rodopi Press, 2001), pp. 123–169; 215–225.

"Why Bioethics Needs the Philosophy of Medicine: Some Implications of Reflection on Concepts of Health and Disease," *Theoretical Medicine* 18, no. 4 (1993): 145–163.

King, Lester, "The Flexner Report of 1910," *Journal of the American Medical Association* 251, no. 8 (1984): 1079–1086.

King, Nancy, Larry Churchill, and Alan Cross, eds., *The Physician as Captain of the Ship: A Critical Reappraisal* (Dordrecht: D. Reidel Publishing Company, 1988).

Kipnis, Kenneth, "Vulnerability in Research Subjects: A Bioethical Taxonomy," National Bioethics Advisory Commission. *Ethical and Policy Issues in Research Involving Human Participants*, vol. 2. (Bethesda, MD: Government Printing Office, 2002), G1–13.

Kleinke, J. D., *Bleeding Edge: The Business of Health Care in the New Century* (Gaithersburg, MD: Aspen Publishers, 1998).
Oxymorons: The Myth of a U.S. Health Care System (San Francisco, CA: Jossey-Bass, 2001).
Kligman, Michael and Charles Culver, "An Analysis of Interpersonal Manipulation," *The Journal of Medicine and Philosophy* 17 (1992): 186–187.
Kligman, Michael and Charles M. Culver, "Interpersonal Manipulation," *Journal of Medicine and Philosophy* 17 (1992): 173–197.
Klosko, George, "Presumptive Benefit, Fairness, and Political Obligation," *Philosophy and Public Affairs* 16 (1987): 241–259.
Kottow, M. H., "The Vulnerable and the Susceptible," *Bioethics* 17 (2003): 460–471.
Kravitz, Richard L., Ronald M. Epstein, Mitchell D. Feldman, *et al.*, "Influence of Patients' Requests for Direct-to-Consumer Advertised Antidepressants: A Randomized Controlled Trial," *Journal of the American Medical Association* 293, 16 (April 2005): 1995–2002.
Krimsky, Sheldon, *Science in the Private Interest: Has the Lure of Profits Corrupted Medical Research?* (Lanham, MD: Rowman and Littlefield, 2003).
Kuhn, Thomas, *Structure of Scientific Revolutions, 3rd edn.* (Chicago, IL: University of Chicago Press, 1996).
The Lancet Editorial, "Structural Adjustment Too Painful," *The Lancet* 344 (November 19, 1994): 1377–1378.
Lanjouw, Jean Olson, "Beyond TRIPS: A New Global Patent Regime," *CGD Brief* 1, no. 3 (2002). Available at www.iprsonline.org/ictsd/docs/cgdbrief003.pdf (accessed June 14, 2006).
Lanjouw, Jean Olsen and William Jack, "Trading Up: How Much Should Poor Countries Pay to Support Pharmaceutical Innovation?" *CGD Brief* 4, no. 3 (2004). Available at www.cgdev.org/content/publications/detail/2842/ (accessed June 14, 2006).
Law, Jacky, *Big Pharma: How Modern Medicine is Damaging Your Health and What You Can Do About It* (New York: Carroll & Graf, 2006).
Leakey, Richard E. and Roger Lewin, *People of the Lake* (New York: Anchor Press, 1978).
Leder, Drew, "A Tale of Two Bodies: The Cartesian Corpse and the Lived Body," in *The Body in Medical Thought and Practice*, ed. Drew Leder (Dordrecht: Kluwer Academic Publishers, 1992), pp. 17–35.
Lemmens, Trudo and Benjamin Freedman, "Ethics Review for Sale? Conflict of Interest and Commercial Research Review Boards," *Milbank* Quarterly 78, no. 4 (2000): 547–584.
Lesar, T. S., Briceland L. L., Delcoure K., *et al.*, "Medication-Prescribing Errors in a Teaching Hospital: A Nine-Year Experience," *Archives of International Medicine* 28 (1997): 1569–1576.

Levi-Strauss, Claude, *The Elementary Structures of Kinship* (Boston, MA: Beacon Press, 1969).

Levine, Carol, Ruth Faden, Christine Grady, Dale Hammerschmidt, Lisa Eckenwiler, and Jeremy Sugarman (for the Consortium to Examine Clinical Research Ethics), "The Limitations of 'Vulnerabililty' as a Protection for Human Research Participants," *American Journal of Bioethics* 4 (2004): 44–49.

Lexchin, Joel, "Doctors and Detailers: Therapeutic Education or Pharmaceutical Promotion?" *International Journal of Health Services* 19, no. 4 (1989): 663–679.

"What Information Do Physicians Receive from Pharmaceutical Representatives?" *Canadian Family Physician* 43, (1997): 941–945.

Lichtenberg, Frank R., "The Economic Benefits of New Drugs," *Economic Realities in Health Care Policy* 2, no. 2 (2001): 14–19.

Light, Donald W., "Basic Research Funds to Discover Important New Drugs: Reframing the 10/90 Report on Research for Neglected Diseases," in *Monitoring Financial Flows for Health Research 2005: Behind the Global Numbers*, ed. M. A. Burke and A. de Francisco (Geneva: The Global Forum for Health Research, 2006), pp. 17–35.

"Making Practical Markets for Vaccines," *PloS Medicine* 2: 10: e271 (2005): 101–105. Available at www.plosmedicine.org (accessed June 23, 2008).

Light, Donald W. and Joel Lexchin, "Foreign Free Riders and the High Price of U.S. Medicines," *British Medical Journal* 331 (2005): 958–960.

Lohr, K. N., R. H. Brook, C. J. Kamberg, *et al.*, "Use of Medical Care in the Rand Health Insurance Experiment. Diagnosis- and Service-Specific Analyses in a Randomized Controlled Trial," *Medical Care* 24, no. 9 (Suppl) (1986): S1–87.

Love, James, "CPTech Comments on U.S. Department of Commerce Study of International Drug Pricing," Consumer Project on Technology, July 1, 2004. Available at www.cptech.org/ip/health/rndtf/drugpricestudy.html (accessed June 14, 2006).

Love, James and Sean Flynn, "Legal and Policy Issues Concerning Parallel Trade (aka Re-Importation) of Pharmaceutical Drugs in the United States," March 31, 2004. Available at www.cptech.org/ip/fsd/love03312004.pdf (accessed June 14, 2006).

Love, James and Tim Hubbard, "Make Drugs Affordable: Replace TRIPs-Plus by R&D-Plus," 2004. Available at www.cptech.org/ip/health/rndtf/bridges042004.pdf (accessed June 14, 2006).

Lundberg, G. D., "The Business and Professionalism of Medicine," *Journal of the American Medical Association* 278, no. 20 (1997): 1704.

Lurie, N., N. B. Ward, *et al.*, "Termination of Medi-Cal Benefits: A Follow-up Study One Year Later," *New England Journal of Medicine.* 314, no. 19: 1266–1268.

Lurie, P., M. Almeida, N. Stine, A. R. Stine, and S. Wolfe, "Financial Conflict of Interest Disclosure and Voting Patterns at Food and Drug Administration Drug Advisory Committee Meetings," *Journal of the American Medical Association* 295 (2006): 1921–1928.

Macklin, Ruth, "Bioethics, Vulnerability, and Protection," *Bioethics* 17 (2003): 472–486.
"'Due' and 'Undue' Inducements: On Paying Money to Research Subjects," *IRB* 3 (1981): 1–6.
"Response: Beyond Paternalism," *IRB: A Review of Human Subjects Research* 4 (March 1982): 6–7.
Maitland, Ian, "Priceless Goods: How Should Life-Saving Drugs Be Priced?" *Business Ethics Quarterly* 12, no. 4 (2002): 451–480.
Markowitz, Gerald E. and David Karl Rosner, "Doctors in Crisis: A Study of the Use of Medical Education Reform to Establish Modern Professional Elitism in Medicine," *American Quarterly* 25, no. 1 (March 1973): 83–107.
Marmot, Michael and Richard G. Wilkinson, *Social Determinants of Health* (Oxford: Oxford University Press, 1999).
Masia, Neal A., "Pharmaceutical Innovation: Lowering the Price of Good Health," *Economic Realities in Health Care Policy* 2, no. 2 (2001): 11.
Mauss, Marcel, *The Gift* (London: Routledge & Kegan Paul, 1954).
McGee, Glenn, "Subject to Payment?" *Journal of the American Medical Association* 278 (July 16, 1997): 199–200.
McKenny, Gerald, *To Relieve the Human Condition: Bioethics, Technology, and the Body* (New York: State University of New York Press, 1997).
McKinnell, Hank, *A Call to Action: Taking Back Health Care for Future Generations* (New York: McGraw-Hill, 2005).
McNeill, Paul, "Paying People to Participate in Research: Why Not?" *Bioethics* 11 (1997): 390–396.
Melander, Hans, Jane Ahlqvist-Rastad, Gertie Meijer, and Björn Beermann, "Evidence B(i)ased Medicine – Selective Reporting of Studies Sponsored by Pharmaceutical Industry: Review of Studies in New Drug Applications," *British Medical Journal* 326 (2003): 1171–1173.
Menzel, Paul T., "Justice and the Basic Structure of Health Care Systems," in *Medicine and Social Justice: Essays on the Distribution of Health Care*, ed. R. Rhodes, M. Battin, and A. Silvers. (New York: Oxford University Press, 2002), pp. 24–37.
Strong Medicine: The Ethical Rationing of Health Care (New York: Oxford University Press, 1990).
Merleau-Ponty, *Phenomenology of Perception*. Translated by C. Smith (London: Routledge and Kegan Paul, 1962).
Merz, Jon F., Glenn E. McGee, and Pamela Sankar, "'Iceland Inc.'?: On the Ethics of Commercial Population Genomics," *Social Science & Medicine* 58, no. 6 (2004) 1201–1209.
Meulen, Ruud ter, Wil Arts, and Ruud Muffels, eds., *Solidarity in Health and Social Welfare in Europe* (Dordrecht: Kluwer Academic, 2001).
Miles, Steven H., *The Hippocratic Oath and the Ethics of Medicine* (New York: Oxford University Press, 2005).
Miles, Steven and Robert Koepp, "Comments on the AMA Report 'Ethical Issues in Managed Care,'" *Journal of Clinical Ethics* 6 (1995): 306–311.

Mills, Ann E. and Mary V. Rorty, "Business Practices, Ethical Principles and Professionalism," *Organizational Ethics* 2, no. 1 (2005): 30–43. Reprinted in *Professionalism in Tomorrow's Healthcare System*, ed. Mills, Chen, Werhane and Wynia, (Hagerstown, MD: University Publishing Group, 2005), pp. 101–124.

Mills, Ann E., Mary V. Rorty and Patricia H. Werhane, "Complexity and the Role of Ethics in Health Care," *Emergence* 5, no. 3 (2003): 6–21.

Mintzes, Barbara, "Direct to Consumer Advertising is Medicalising Normal Human Experience," *British Medical Journal* 324 (April 13, 2002): 908.

Mintzes, Barbara, Morris L. Barer, Richard L Kravitz, *et al.*, "Influence of Direct to Consumer Pharmaceutical Advertising and Patients' Requests on Prescribing Decisions: Two Site Cross Sectional Survey," *British Medical Journal* 324 (February 2, 2002): 278–279.

Mitroff, Ian and Harold Linstone, *The Unbounded Mind* (New York: Oxford University Press, 1993).

Morelli, John, "The Fairness Principle," *Philosophy and Law Newsletter* (American Philosophical Association) Spring (1985): 2–4.

Morreim, Haavi E., *Balancing Act: The New Medical Ethics of Medicine's New Economics* (Washington, DC: Georgetown University Press, 1995).

Morselli, P. L., "Are Phase I Studies without Drug Level Determination Acceptable?" *Fundamental and Clinical Pharmacology* 4 Suppl. 2 (1990): 125s–133s.

Moses, S., F. Manji, J. E. Bradley, *et al.*, "Impact of User Fees on Attendance at a Referral Centre for Sexually Transmitted Diseases in Kenya," *The Lancet* 340 (1992): 463–466.

Moynihan, Ray, "Key Opinion Leaders: Independent Experts or Drug Reps in Disguise?" *British Medical Journal* 336 (2008): 1402–1403.

Nagel, Thomas, "Justice and Nature," *Oxford Journal of Legal Studies* 17, no. 2 (1997): 303–321.

Nanda A. and K. Haddad, "The AMA-Sunbeam Deal: Serpent on the Staff Meets Chainsaw Al," *Harvard Business on Line* Case # 9–801–326, January 2001.

National Bioethics Advisory Commission, *Ethical and Policy Issues in Research Involving Human Participants*, vol. 1. (Bethesda, MD: Government Printing Office, 2001).

National Center for Health Statistics, *National Vital Statistics Reports*, vol. 52, no. 3, September 18, 2003. As reported in *Infoplease*, "Life Expectancy at Birth by Race and Sex, 1930–2002." Available at www.infoplease.com/ipa/A0005148.html (accessed January 26, 2006).

National Commission for the Protection of Human Subjects of Biomedical and Behavioral Research, *The Belmont Report: Ethical Guidelines for the Protection of Human Subjects* (Washington, DC: DHEW Publication (OS) 78–0012, 1978).

Nelson, Robert M. and Jon F. Merz, "Voluntariness of Consent for Research: An Empirical and Conceptual Review," *Medical Care* 40 (2002): Suppl., V69–80.

Newcomer, Lee N.,"Medicare Pharmacy Coverage: Ensuring Safety Before Funding," *Health Affairs* (March/April 2000): 59–62.

Newhouse, Joseph P., "Consumer-Directed Health Plans and the RAND Health Insurance Experiment," *Health Affairs* 23 (2004): 107–113.

Newton, Lisa H., "Inducement, Due and Otherwise," *IRB: A Review of Human Subjects Research* 4 (March 1982): 4–6.

NIHCM (National Institute for Health Care Management Research and Education Foundation), *Changing Patterns of Pharmaceutical Innovation* (Washington, DC: NIHCM, 2002).

Nordenfelt, Lennart, *Concepts and Measurement of Quality of Life in Health Care* (Dordrecht: Kluwer Academic Publishers, 1994).

Nozick, Robert, *Anarchy, State, and Utopia* (New York: Basic Books, 1974).

"Coercion," in *Philosophy, Science and Method: Essays in Honor of Ernest Nagel*, ed. Sidney Morgenbesser, Patrick Suppes, and Morton White (New York: St. Martin's Press, 1969), pp. 440–472.

Nuremburg Code *Trials of War Criminals before the Nuremberg Military Tribunals under Control Council Law No. 10, Vol. 2* (Washington, DC: US Government Printing Office, 1949), pp. 181–182.

Orlowski, James P. and Leon Wateska, "The Effects of Pharmaceutical Firm Enticements on Physician Prescribing Patterns: There's No Such Thing as a Free Lunch," *Chest* 102, no. 1 (1992): 270–273.

Orme, M., J. Harry, P. Routledge, and S. Hobson, "Healthy Volunteer Studies in Great Britain: The Results of a Survey into 12 Months Activity in this Field." *British Journal of Clinical Pharmacology* 27 (February 1989): 125–133.

Palmer, Tom G., "Are Patents and Copyrights Morally Justified? The Philosophy of Property Rights and Ideal Objects," *Harvard Journal of Law & Public Policy* 13, no. 3 (1990): 817–865.

"Intellectual Property: A Non-Posnerian Law and Economics Approach," *Hamline Law Review* 12, no. 2 (1989): 261–303.

Palmisano, P. and J. Edelstein, "Teaching Drug Promotion Abuses to Health Profession Students," *Journal of Medical Education* 55 (1980): 453–455.

Parente, Stephen T., Roger Feldman, and Jon B. Christianson, "Evaluation of the Effect of a Consumer-Driven Health Plan on Medical Care Expenditures and Utilization," *Health Services Research* 39, no. 4, part 2 (2004): 1189–1210.

Pellegrino, Edmund, "Interests, Obligations, and Justice: Some Notes Toward an Ethic of Managed Care," *Journal of Clinical Ethics* 6, no. 4 (1995): 312–317.

"Medical Economics and Medical Ethics: Points of Conflict and Reconciliation," *Journal of the Medical Association of Georgia* 69 (1980): 175–183.

"Rationing health care: Inherent conflicts with the concept of justice," in *The Ethics of Managed Care: Professional Integrity and Patient Rights*, ed. W. B. Bondeson and J. Jones (Dordrecht: Kluwer Academic Publishers, 2002), pp. 1–18.

"The Ethics of Medicine: the Challenges of Reconstruction," *Transactions and Studies of the College of Physicians of Philadelphia*, ser 5, 9, no. 3 (1987): 179–191.

"The Metamorphosis of Medical Ethics: A 30-Year Retrospective," *Journal of the American Medical Association* 269, no. 9 (1993): 1158–1162.

Pellegrino, Edmund and David Thomasma, *A Philosophical Basis of Medical Practice: Toward a Philosophy and Ethic of the Healing Professions* (Oxford: Oxford University Press, 1981).

Peppin, John F., "An Engelhardtian Analysis of Interactions Between Pharmaceutical Representatives and Physicians," *The Journal of Medicine and Philosophy* 22 (1997): 623–641.

"Pharmaceutical Sales Representatives and Physicians: Ethical Considerations of a Relationship," *The Journal of Medicine and Philosophy* 21 (1996): 83–99.

Petersson, Bo, "Health, Doctors and the Good Life," in *Dimensions of Health and Health Promotion*, ed. Lennart Nordenfeldt and Per-Erik Liss (Amsterdam: Editions Rodop, 2003).

Petty, R. E. and D. T. Wegener, "The Elaboration Likelihood Model: Current Status and Controversy," in *Dual Process Theories in Social Psychology*, ed. S. Chaiken and Y. Trope. (London: Guilford, 1999).

Pfizer, "Pharmaceutical Innovation: Lowering the Price of Good Health," *Economic Realities in Health Care Policy* 2, no. 2. Available at www.pfizer.com/pfizer/download/about_er22.pdf (accessed January 26, 2006).

PhRMA, "Code of Interactions with Health care Professionals," 2004. Available at www.phrma.org/files/PhRMA%20Code.pdf (accessed March 22, 2007).

PhRMA, "Pharmaceutical Marketing & Promotion Q&A: Tough Questions, Straight Answers." Available at www.phrma.org/files/Tough_Questions.pdf (accessed July 1, 2008).

PhRMA Office of Accountability, "Report of Second Survey of Signatory Companies," 2006. Available at: www.phrma.org/office_of_accountability/ (accessed July 1, 2008).

Pogge, Thomas W., "Human Rights and Global Health," *Metaphilosophy* 36 (2005): 182–209.

Prosser, Helen and Tom Walley, "Understanding why GPs see Pharmaceutical Representatives: A Qualitative Interview Study," *British Journal of General Practice* 53, (2003): 305–311.

Rawls, John, *A Theory of Justice* (Cambridge, MA: Harvard University Press, 1971).

Raz, Joseph, *Value, Respect, and Attachment* (Cambridge: Cambridge University Press, 2001).

Reiser, Stanley, *Medicine and the Reign of Technology* (Cambridge: Cambridge University Press, 1978).

Relman, Arnold S., "Defending Professional Independence: ACCME's Proposed New Guidelines for Commercial Support of CME," *Journal of the American Medical Association* 289, no. 18 (2003): 2418–2420.

"Separating Continuing Medical Education from Pharmaceutical Marketing," *Journal of the American Medical Association* 285 (2001): 2009–2012.

Resnick, David, "Research Participation and Financial Inducements," *American Journal of Bioethics* 1 (2001): 54–56.

Reuter, Lars, "The Ethics of Advertising Strategies in the Pharmaceutical Industry," *Ethics & Medicine; A Christian Perspective on Issues in Bioethics* 19, no. 3 (2003): 171–175.

Rice, Thomas and Kathleen R. Morrison, "Patient Cost Sharing for Medical Services: A Review of the Literature and Implications for Health Care Reform," *Medical Care Review* 51, no. 3 (1994): 235–287.

Robinson, James C., *The Corporate Practice of Medicine* (Berkeley, CA: University of California Press, 1999).

"Health Savings Accounts – the Ownership Society in Health Care," *New England Journal of Medicine* 353 (2005): 1199–1202.

"Reinvention of Health Insurance in the Consumer Era," *Journal of the American Medical Association* 291, no. 15 (2004): 1880–1886.

Rodwin, Marc A., *Medicine, Money, and Morals: Physicians' Conflicts of Interest* (New York: Oxford University Press, 1993).

Rorty, James, *American Medicine Mobilized* (New York: W. W. Norton, 1939).

Rosenthal, Meredith and Norman Daniels, "Beyond Competition: The Normative Implications of Consumer Driven Health Plans," *Journal of Health Politics, Policy, and Law* 31, no. 3 (2006): 671–685.

Rosenthal, Meredith and Julie M. Donohue, "Direct-to-Consumer Advertising of Prescription Drugs," in *Ethics and the Pharmaceutical Industry*, ed. Michael A. Santoro and Thomas M. Gorrie (New York: Cambridge University Press, 2005), pp. 169–184.

Rosenthal, Meredith, Charleen Hsuan, and Arnold Milstein, "A Report Card on the Freshman Class of Consumer-Directed Health Plans," *Health Affairs* 24, no. 6 (2005): 1592–1600.

Rosenthal, Meredith and Arnold Milstein, "Awakening Consumer Stewardship of Health Benefits: Prevalence and Differentiation of New Plan Models," *Health Services Research* 39 (part 2) (2004): 1055–1070.

Rudinow, Joel, "Manipulation," *Ethics* 88 (1978): 338–347, 339.

Russell, S. and L. Gilson, "User Fee Policies to Promote Health Service Access for the Poor: A Wolf in Sheep's Clothing?" *International Journal of Health Services* 27 (1997): 359–379.

Safer, Daniel J., "Design and Reporting Modifications in Industry-Sponsored Comparative Psychopharmacology Trials," *The Journal of Nervous and Mental Disease* 190, no. 9 (2002): 583–592.

Saltman, Richard B. and Hans F. W. Dubois, "The Historical and Social Base of Social Health Insurance Systems," in *Social Health Insurance Systems in Western Europe*, ed. Richard B. Saltman, Richard Busse, and Josep Figueras (Maidenhead: Open University Press, 2004), pp. 21–32.

Sandel, Michael, "What Money Can't Buy: The Moral Limits of Markets," The Tanner Lectures in Human Values. Available at www.tannerlectures.utah.edu/lectures/sandeloo.pdf.

Schmidtz, David, *The Limits of Government: An Essay on the Public Goods Argument* (Boulder, CO: Westview Press, 1991).

Schonfeld, Toby L., Joseph S. Brown, Meaghann Weniger, and Bruce Gordon, "Research Involving the Homeless," *IRB* 25 (September/October 2003): 17–20.

Scitovsky, A. A. and N. M. Snyder, "Effect of Coinsurance on Use of Physician Services," *Social Security Bulletin* 35, no. 6 (1972): 3–19.

Secretary of State for Health, *Government Response to the Health Committee's Report on the Influence of the Pharmaceutical Industry*, 2005. Available at www.official-documents.gov.uk/document/cm66/6655/6655.pdf (accessed June 12, 2007).

Sen, Amartya, *Inequality Reexamined* (Cambridge, MA: Harvard University Press, 1992).

Senge, Peter, *The Fifth Discipline* (New York: Doubleday, 1990).

Shaughnessy, Allen F., David C. Slawson, and Joshua H Bennett, "Separating the Wheat from the Chaff: Identifying Fallacies in Pharmaceutical Promotion," *Journal of General Internal Medicine* 9, no 10 (1994): 563–568.

"Teaching Information Mastery: Evaluating Information Provided by Pharmaceutical Representatives," *Family Medicine* 28, no 3, (1996): 166–167.

Shortell, Stephen, "The Evolution of Hospital Systems: Unfulfilled Promises and Self-Fulfilling Prophesies," *Medical Care Review* 45, no. 2 (1998): 177–214.

Sibille, M., N. Deigat, V. Olagnier, D. Vital Durand, and R. Levrat, "Adverse Events in Phase one Studies: A Study in 430 Healthy Volunteers," *European Journal of Clinical Pharmacology* 42 (1992): 389–393.

Silvers, Anita, "Historical Vulnerabililty and Special Scrutiny: Precautions against Discrimination in Medical Research," *American Journal of Bioethics* 4 (2004): 56–57.

Simmons, John A., "The Principle of Fair Play," *Philosophy and Public Affairs* 8 (1979): 307–337.

Singer, Emily, "Aggressive Drug Marketing Tactics Trigger Backlash," *Nature Medicine* 13, no. 4 (April 2007): 393.

Singer, Peter, "Famine, Affluence, and Morality," *Philosophy and Public Affairs* I, no. 3 (Spring 1972): 229–243.

Smith, Adam, *An Inquiry in the Nature and Causes of the Wealth of Nations*, ed. R. H. Campbell and A. S. Skinner, 2 vols. (Oxford: Oxford University Press, 1976), pp. i, ii, 27.

Smith, Richard, "Medical Journals Are an Extension of the Marketing Arm of Pharmaceutical Companies," *PLoS Medicine* 2, no. 5 (2005): e138.

Soumerai, Stephen B. and Jerry Avorn, "Predictors of Physician Prescribing Change in an Educational Experiment to Improve Medication Use," *Medical Care* 25, no. 3 (1987): 210–221.

"Principles of Educational Outreach ('Academic Detailing') to Improve Clinical Decision Making," *Journal of the American Medical Association* 263, no. 4 (1990): 549–556.

Spencer, Edward M., Ann E. Mills, Mary V. Rorty, and Patricia H. Werhane, *Organization Ethics in Health Care* (New York: Oxford University Press, 2000).

Stange, Kurt C., "Time to Ban Direct-to-Consumer Prescription Drug Marketing," *Annals of Family Medicine* 5 (2007): 101–104.

Starr, Paul, *The Social Transformation of American Medicine* (New York: Basic Books, 1982).

Steinbrook Robert, "Gag Clauses in Clinical Trial Agreements," *The New England Journal of Medicine* 352 (2005): 2160–2162.

Stevens, Rosemary, *American Medicine and the Public Interest* (Berkeley, CA: University of California Press, 1998).

  In Sickness and in Wealth: American Hospitals in the Twentieth Century (New York: Basic Books, 1989).

Stoops, Nicole, US Census Bureau, *Educational Attainment in the United States: 2003* (Washington DC: June 2004). Available at www.census.gov/prod/2004pubs/p20-550.pdf (accessed July 1, 2008).

Stossel, Thomas, "Regulating Academic–Industrial Research Relationships – Solving Problems or Stifling Progress?" *The New England Journal of Medicine* 353, no. 10 (September 8, 2005): 1060–1065.

Stoto, Michael, ed., "Sharing Responsibility for the Public's Health: A New Perspective from the Institute of Medicine," *Public Health Management Practice* 3, no. 5 (1997): 22–34.

Strang, David, Micheline Gagnon, William Molloy, *et al.*, "National Survey on the Attitudes of Canadian Physicians Towards Drug-Detailing by Pharmaceutical Representatives," *Annals of the Royal College of Physicians and Surgeons of Canada* 29, no 8, (1996): 474–478.

SUPPORT Principal Investigators, "A Controlled Trial to Improve Care for Seriously Ill Hospital Patients," *Journal of the American Medical Association* 272 (1996): 1591–1598.

Susser, M., "Pioneering Community-Oriented Primary Care," *Bulletin of the World Health Organization* 77, no. 5 (1999): 436–438.

Sutton, Laura B., J. A. Erlen, J. A. M. Glad, and L. A. Siminoff, "Recruiting Vulnerable Populations for Research: Revisiting the Ethical Issues," *Journal of Professional Nursing* 19 (2003): 106–112.

Tishler, Carl and Suzanne Bartholomae, "The Recruitment of Normal Healthy Volunteers," *Journal of Clinical Pharmacology* 42 (2002): 365–375.

Toombs, S. Kay. *The Meaning of Illness: A Phenomenological Account of the Different Perspectives of Physician and Patient* (Norwell: Kluwer Academic Publishers, 1993).

Toop, Les and Dee Mangin, "Industry Funded Patient Information and the Slippery Slope to New Zealand," *British Medical Journal* 335 (October 2007): 694–695.

Transparency International, *Global Corruption Report 2006: Corruption and Health* (London: Pluto Press, 2006).

Tsai, Alexander C., "Policies to Regulate Gifts to Physicians From Industry," *Journal of the American Medical Association* 290, no. 13 (2003): 1776.

USPTO. www.uspto.gov (accessed June 23, 2008).

United States National Commission for the Protection of Human Subjects of Biomedical and Behavioral Research, *The Belmont Report: Ethical Principles and Guidelines for the Protection of Human Subjects of Research* April 18, 1979 (Bethesda, MD: United States Government Printing Office, 1979).

US Census Bureau Data, "Infant Mortality and Life Expectancy for Selected Countries, 2005," *Infoplease.* Available at www.infoplease.com/ipa/ A0004393.html (accessed January 26, 2006).

US Federal Trade Commission, *Generic Drug Entry Prior to Patent Expiration: An FTC Study* (Washington, DC: US Government Printing Office, July 2002).

US Federal Trade Commission and Department of Justice, *Improving Health Care: A Dose of Competition* (Washington, DC: US Government Printing Office, 2004).

US Food and Drug Administration, "CDER NDAs Approved in Calendar Years 1990–2004 by Therapeutic Potential and Chemical Type," 2005. Available at www.fda.gov/cder/rdmt/pstable.htm (accessed October 17, 2007).

US Food and Drug Administration, Division of Drug Marketing, Advertising, and Communications, "Prescription Drug Advertising and Promotional Labeling," *Center for Drug Evaluation and Research Handbook*, p. 8. Created April 16, 1998; revised November 7, 2006. Available at www.fda.gov/cder/ddmac/FAQS.HTM#reminder (accessed July 1, 2008).

US General Accounting Office, *Technology Transfer: NIH-Private Sector Partnership in the Development of Taxol*, Report GAO-03–829 (June 2003) (Washington, DC: US General Accounting Office, 2003).

Valuenza, Abel Jr., Nik Theodore, Edwin Melendez, and Ana Luz Gonzalez, "On the Corner: Day Labor in the United States" (2006): Available at www.sscnet.ucla.edu/issr/csup/uploaded_files/Natl_DayLabor-On_the_Corner1.pdf (accessed July 1, 2008).

Van Gelderen C. E., T. J. Savelkoul, W. van Dokkum, and J. Meulenbelt, "Motives and Perceptions of Healthy Volunteers Who Participate in Experiments," *European Journal of Clinical Pharmacology* 45 (1993): 15–21.

Veatch, Robert, "Abandoning Informed Consent," *Hastings Center Report* 25, no. 2 (1995): 5–12.

"Who Should Manage Care? The Case for Patients," *Kennedy Institute of Ethics Journal* 7, no. 4 (1997): 391–402.

Waddington C. J. and K. A. Enyimayew, "A Price to Pay: The Impact of User Charges in Ashanti-Akim District, Ghana," *International Journal of Health Planning and Management*, 5 (1989):17–47.

Wager, Elizabeth, "How to Dance with Porcupines: Rules and Guidelines on Doctors' Relations with Drug Companies," *British Medical Journal* 326, (2003): 1196–1198.

Washburn, Jennifer, *University Inc.: The Corporate Corruption of Higher Education* (New York: Basic Books, 2005).

Wazana, Ashley, M.D., "Physicians and the Pharmaceutical Industry: Is a Gift Ever Just a Gift?" *Journal of the American Medical Association* 283, no. 3 (2000): 373–380.

Weber, Leonard J., *Profits Before People?: Ethical Standards and the Marketing of Prescription Drugs* (Bloomington, IN: University of Indiana Press, 2006).

Business Ethics in Healthcare: Beyond Compliance (Bloomington, IN: University of Indiana Press, 2006).

Werhane, Patricia, *Moral Imagination and Management Decision-Making* (New York: Oxford, 1999).

"Moral Imagination and Systems Thinking," *Journal of Business Ethics* 38 (2002): 33–42.

Wilkinson, Martin and Andrew Moore, "Inducement in Research," *Bioethics* 11 (1997): 373–389.

"Inducements Revisited," *Bioethics* 13 (1999): 114–130.

Wittgenstein, Ludwig, *Tractatus Logico-Philosophicus* (New York: Routledge, 2001).

Wolf, Susan, "Toward a Systemic Theory of Informed Consent in Managed Care," *Houston Law Review* 35 (1998): 1631–1681.

Woolhandler, S., T. Campbell, and D. U. Himmelstein, "Costs of Health Care Administration in the United States and Canada," *New England Journal of Medicine* 21:349(8) (2003): 768–775.

World Medical Association, "Ethical Principles for Medical Research Involving Human Subjects," adopted by the 18th WMA General Assembly Helsinki, Finland, June 1964 and amended by the 29th WMA General Assembly, Tokyo, Japan, October 1975, 35th WMA General Assembly, Venice, Italy, October 1983, 41st WMA General Assembly, Hong Kong, September 1989, 48th WMA General Assembly, Somerset West, Republic of South Africa, October 1996, and 52nd WMA General Assembly, Edinburgh, Scotland, October 2000. Available at: www.wma.net/e/policy/b3.htm.

Youngner, Stuart J. and Robert Arnold, "Who Will Watch the Watchers?" *Hastings Center Report* 32, no. 3 (2002): 21–22.

Zall, Milton, "The Pricing Puzzle," *Modern Drug Discovery* 4, no. 3 (March 2001): 36–38, 41, 42. Available at http://pubs.acs.org/subscribe/journals/mdd/v04/i03/html/03zaLL. HTML (accessed March 6, 2006).

Zarafonetis, C. J. D., P. A. Riley Jr., P. W. Willis III, *et al.*, "Clinically Significant Adverse Effects in a Phase I Testing Program," *Clinical Pharmacology and Therapeutics* 24 (1978): 127–132.

Ziegler, Michael G. M.D., Pauline Lew, Pharm.D., Brian C. Singer, Pharm.D., "The Accuracy of Drug Information From Pharmaceutical Sales Representatives," *Journal of the American Medical Association* 273, no. 16 (1995): 1296–1298.

Zweifel, Peter and Willard G. Manning, "Moral Hazard and Consumer Incentives in Health Care," in *Handbook of Health Economics*, ed. A. J. Culyer and J. P. Newhouse (Amsterdam: Elsevier Science BV, 2000).

Index

Abramson, John 250
academic detailing 118–121
accountability
    justice and 39, 55
    market-friendly systems 54, 55
    organizational ethics 238
Actimmune 8
administration costs 42
adoption 158
advance directives 232
Advanced Cell Technologies 152
advanced market commitments 75–76
advertising. See DTC advertising; marketing
Affymetrix 151
agency 104, 113
aging population 42
AIDS 5, 52, 103, 121, 170, 187–189, 193–194
Allegheny Health Education and Research
    Foundation 203
American Association of Retired Persons 142
American College of Surgeons 225
American Council on Graduate Medical
    Education 207
American Enterprise Institute 23
American Medical Association 22, 113, 114, 117,
    152, 206, 225
American Society of Bioethics and
    Humanities 156
Amgen 10
Angell, Marcia 21, 63, 72–73, 77, 119, 120, 250
anti-free-riding principle 69
anti-retroviral therapies 52
antidepressants 11
Aquinas, Thomas 185
Arizona State University 151
Arnold, Denis 10, 131
Arrow, Kenneth 255
Arthritis Foundation 159
Association of the British Pharmaceutical
    Industry (ABPI) 104, 106, 114
Astra Zeneca 151

atomism 229–230
Australia 171
autonomy 104–109, 113, 148
Avastin 176
Aventis 4
avian flu 173
Avorn, Jerry 250
AZT 121

Bayer 9, 136
BBC 205
Beauchamp, Tom 7, 83–97
Beecher, Henry 199
Belgium 27
Belsito, Marybeth 160
Bernays, Edward 159
bias
    disclosure worsening bias 162–165
    DTP marketing and 104–109
    medical journals 111
    self-serving bias 164
bioethicists, power 155
bioethics
    industry funding. See industry-funded
        bioethics
    models. See healthcare models
biomedical model
    alternative paradigm 236–244
    characteristics 222–227
    complicity of bioethics 231–234
    cost crisis 230–231
    critics 234–236
    depersonalizing medicine 227–229
    ethical norms and economic structures 225–226
    fragmentation of care 229–230
    grounding in sciences 223
    health as absence of disease 224–225
    orthodoxy 231–234
    paternalism 228
    physician-centered 226, 232
    problems 227–231

insurance
  biomedical model 230
  private health insurance 28–29
  uninsurance 2, 52, 181
  US premiums 2
intellectual property rights 4, 63–65
  See also drug patents; patents
InterMune 8
Internet 159
Israel 27
Italy 27, 70, 190

Jack, William 82
Japan 171, 192
Johns Hopkins School of Medicine 223
Johnson & Johnson 11, 13
Joint Commission for Accreditation of
    Health Care Organizations (JCAHO)
    212–213, 215
Jonas, Hans 231
journals. *See* medical journals
justice
  ability to pay 40
  access to drugs 49–50, 69–70, 75
  benchmarks 40–41, 55–57
  CDHPs and 48
  clinical trials and 95–97
  free-riding on research and 68–69
  healthcare markets 1–3, 23, 24, 36–41
  lobbying and 190
  market mechanism 170
  Les Misérables 185–186
  Rawls 37, 38–39

Kaiser Family Foundation 143
Kant, Immanuel 104, 140
Kark, Sidney 247
Kass, Leon 231
Kassirer, Jerome 22, 117, 250, 254
Key Opinion Leaders 153, 251
Khushf, George 14, 220–244
Kleinfield, N. R. 217
Kleinke, J. D. 217
Krimsky, Sheldon 156
Kryzewski, Mike 158

Lanjouw, Jean Olson 63, 72, 77, 82
lectures 153–154
Leder, Drew 231, 233
Levitra 9, 136
Lexchin, Joel 71
life, right to 172, 176
life expectancy 169
Light, Donald 71, 75, 76
Lipitor 8, 9

lobbying 190
Locke, John 64, 185
Love, James 82
Lunesta 137, 140

McKenny, Gerald 231
McKinnell, Hank 133–134
Maitland, Ian 129, 192
malaria 4, 74
malpractice costs 42
manipulation 88–89, 90, 94, 112–113, 143
marginal social costs 82
market fallacy 33
market strategies
  accountability 54, 55
  broken promises 35–36, 41–52
  competition. *See* competition
  developing countries and 50
  effectiveness 170
  ethical and scientific review 52–57
  evaluation of market practices 28–30
  health costs promise 36
  healthcare models 30
  market-friendly solutions 35–36
  United States 3, 35–57
    advertising control 179–181
    drug pricing 178–179
    market failures 181–182
marketing
  direct to consumers. *See* DTC advertising
  direct to physicians. *See* detailing
  disguised 159–160
  drug patent system and 67
  illegal marketing 7–8, 251
  regulation v. innovation 118–121
  spending 191–192
  US drug advertising control 179–181
Martin, Mark 136
medical education 14–15, 207–209, 223–227
medical journals
  bias 111
  fiduciary ideal 241
  ties with industry 11, 15, 111, 152, 156, 251
Medicare, competitive plans and 44, 49–50
Melander, Hans 111
Melarsoprol 4
Menzel, Paul 6, 62–77
Merck 5, 8, 10, 11, 108, 139, 140, 151, 152, 159, 191
Merck Company Foundation 151
Merctizan 5
mergers 203
Millennium Pharmaceuticals 151
Mills, Ann 13, 198–216
Les Misérables 185–186
monopolies 43–44, 50